# ADVERTISING TODAY

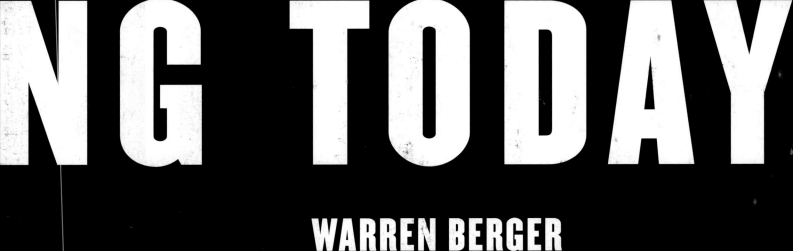

NG TODAY

WARREN BERGER

Think different.

# CONTENTS

# 1. INTROI

# WHY ADV

# MATTERS.

ODUCTION:
ERTISING
HONESTLY.

ARTIST: EVGENY MITTA, RUSSIAN, BORN 1962 (MOSCOW)

STOLICHNAYA

Stolichnaya
Ohranj

ORANGE FLAVORED
RUSSIAN VODKA

internet: http://www.stoli.com

FOR GIFT DELIVERY OF STOLICHNAYA® OHRANJ VODKA (EXCEPT WHERE PROHIBITED BY LAW) CALL 1-800-243-3787. OHRANJ PRODUCT OF RUSSIA, ORANGE FLAVORED VODKA, 35% ALC./VOL., 100% GRAIN NEUTRAL SPIRITS. ©1996 CARILLON IMPORTERS LTD., TEANECK, NJ.

strategies ("One-on-One with One-to-One's
Rogers," *Wired* 4.03, page 152).

These principles have been working just
more than 100 years under the more prosaic
direct marketing, though only in the last seve
have software and other high-tech marketer
ered the cost-effective benefits that direct-r
media and lead-generation strategies offer.

In 1886 Richard Sears, a railroad telegraph
tor, found himself with a supply of undelivera
pocket watches. He also had a list of 20,000 sta
masters, each of whom, he reasoned, would be
logical prospect for an accurate watch. He mai
the watches "one-to-one" to his fellow railroad

As direct marketing has blown the doors off
marketing, a parade of individuals and compan
have attempted to divert the stream through
own little marketing mill by renaming it. We
had relationship marketing, target marketing,
marketing, customer bonding, and, yes, one-to-
marketing, long before Rogers came along.

And before Weinberger becomes too frighte
by Rogers's so-called learning brokers, he ought
to check out the activities of major list brokers
as Worldata Inc. with its WebConnect link broke
service and Direct Media's CatalogLink, both of
which are designed to facilitate the kind of one-
one communications Rogers seems to think she
discovered.

As for the issue of privacy, the Direct Marketi
Association has been addressing that prickly pro
lem, with increasingly better results, for many y
"Junk mail," I often say, "is an offer sent to the w
person." The DMA and most everyone else in the
industry is working hard to make sure we get the
right person, the first time.
**George Duncan**
duncdirect@aol.com

**Barksdale's Barking**
To quote Jim Barksdale ("Netscape's Secret Wea
*Wired* 4.03, page 154): "I don't know of a compa
that's created a brand quicker than we have. An
the way, over a period of a year and a half we
never run an ad."

Now, I can truly admire the pride he has in N
scape's accomplishments, but he must not have
surfing the Web during that year and a half. If I
that "Download Netscape Now" banner on one m
site's ad space I think I'll go looney. Oh, and if he
means print ads, please ask him to turn to page
of *Wired Scenarios* 1.01.
**Art Thompson**
art@sensenet.com

**Our Hubble Apologies**
Tired: *Wired* magazine. For not publishing the UR
the Hubble Space Telescope Eagle Nebula pictu

Perhaps the first question to be asked of a book about advertising is: *Why?*

Why create an enduring document for something as ephemeral and disposable as advertising? Why take the time to analyze a form of communication that often consists of not much more than a cheery jingle and a simplistic slogan? And above all, why charge good money for a book stocked with imagery that is, each day, foisted upon all of us free of charge and against our will?

Here are two answers. One, because advertising matters. Two, because some advertising matters more than the rest.

The second statement is easier to defend, so let's start there: Almost everyone, including advertising's most dedicated practitioners, freely acknowledges that the vast majority of it is banal, unimaginative, mind-numbing. We've all winced at those hyperactive car commercials heralding a "sale-a-bration!" at the local dealership . . . and

the detergent ads in which stains on shirts magically disappear for the hundredth time (though no one cared or believed it the first time). We've flipped through endless fashion-magazine ads so posed and lifeless they seem to bore even the models appearing in them. And we've all seen quite enough of Snuggles, the Fabric Softener Bear. We encounter these all-too-familiar images hundreds of times daily—mere static that we ignore or tune out.

But then along comes something that reminds us how powerful advertising can be: A swing-dancing Gap clothing commercial that manages to be visually arresting and exhilarating, even upon the tenth viewing; a sobering anti-drunk-driving ad that brings home, just for a moment, the specific horror of a traffic accident; an elegant Nike print campaign that somehow expresses our own unspoken feelings about personal achievement (and maybe inspires us to actually take that jog we've

been meaning to take). This rare strain of advertising—it probably amounts to no more than 5 percent of all ads, if that much—is the kind that breaks through the clutter by virtue of its style, cleverness, and originality. That 5 percent is the focus of this book. The other 95 percent shall be left on the cultural scrap heap, where it belongs.

As to the first point, that advertising matters, a more detailed case can and should be made. Because even with the acknowledgment that some ads are better than others, there is still a prevailing sense that advertising, as a whole, adds little of value or substance to the culture— and that it is therefore not worthy of the kind of thoughtful appreciation or analysis one might devote to, say, architecture. But this view seems out of step with the reality of today, wherein advertising is even more pervasive than the architecture that surrounds us (and sometimes, the commercials are also better

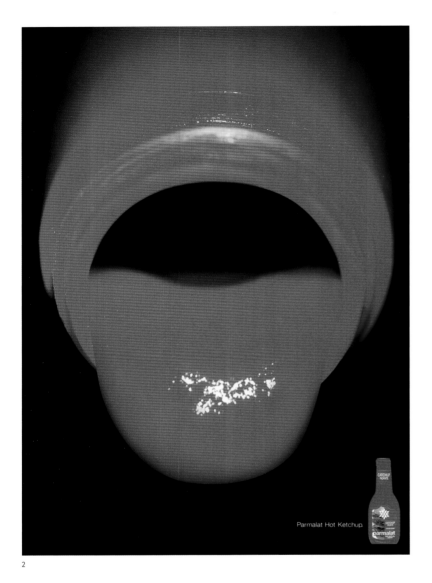

2

Parmalat Hot Ketchup.

designed than the buildings). Advertising almost certainly has a greater influence on our lives. The typical television viewer watches more than 40,000 commercials a year, and—contrary to popular belief—usually pays attention. A recent survey by the Starch Roper research firm found that people today actually like watching commercials more than ever before, no doubt because ads have evolved to become far more watchable in recent years. But entertainment value aside, today's ads also inform and guide many of the important decisions we make— not just the cars we drive but whether we take entrepreneurial risks or choose to lead a healthy lifestyle or plan ahead for retirement or donate to charity. The ways in which ads are affecting and shaping our attitudes, lifestyles, and culture are too numerous to tally.

But let's count off a few anyway. What follows is a list of nine reasons advertising truly matters, and why, therefore, the very best of it is worthy of further examination.

### 1. ADVERTISING IS ONE OF THE PISTONS THAT DRIVE THE GLOBAL ECONOMY.
More than $400 billion a year is spent on advertising worldwide; beyond that, the economic impact of advertising touches just about every consumer-product industry, from cars to candy bars. There is much more to be said about this, but since this book is about the aesthetic and cultural aspects of advertising, we'll leave further financial analysis to the economists and the bean counters.

### 2. "IT MAY BE THE MOST POWERFUL ART FORM ON EARTH."
So says Mark Fenske, a highly regarded American copywriter known for his groundbreaking advertising for Nike and other brands. While Fenske is clearly a biased source, he makes a point that is contentious but worth

considering. "Art is something that reinterprets for people the life they're leading; it allows you to experience what you know about life," Fenske says. "And because advertising deals with the minutiae of everyday life, any art that comes out of it is going to be particularly relevant and powerful." While some fine arts have become increasingly esoteric and removed from people's everyday experience, Fenske argues, advertising can—in rare instances— make a revealing statement "about something that happened to you that very day." Perhaps that morning, you were distraught to discover there was no milk in the refrigerator. Subsequently, you saw a "Got Milk?" commercial vignette that captured and crystallized the feelings of that experience; you found yourself empathizing with the poor fellow who can't enunciate the words "Aaron Burr" because there's no milk to wash the cookies from his

©1998 Callard & Bowser-Suchard Inc.

http://www.altoids.com

4

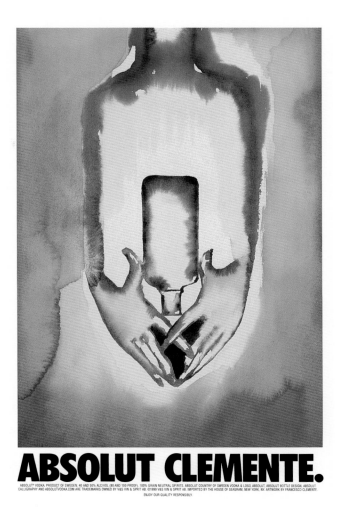

## ABSOLUT CLEMENTE.

ABSOLUT® VODKA. PRODUCT OF SWEDEN. 40 AND 50% ALC/VOL (80 AND 100 PROOF). 100% GRAIN NEUTRAL SPIRITS. ABSOLUT COUNTRY OF SWEDEN VODKA & LOGO, ABSOLUT, ABSOLUT BOTTLE DESIGN, ABSOLUT CALLIGRAPHY AND ABSOLUTVODKA.COM ARE TRADEMARKS OWNED BY V&S VIN & SPRIT AB. ©1999 V&S VIN & SPRIT AB. IMPORTED BY THE HOUSE OF SEAGRAM, NEW YORK, NY. ARTWORK BY FRANCESCO CLEMENTE.
ENJOY OUR QUALITY RESPONSIBLY.

5

mouth. At that moment, Fenske and others maintain, the ad becomes a form of popular art.

It is still controversial to call advertising art—though less and less so, now that major museums around the world house permanent collections of ads, and Absolut vodka posters are framed and hung on walls like paintings. But there remains a large contingent that insists advertising cannot be art for the simple reason that it is conceived for commercial purposes, and controlled and financed by corporations. Of course, many artists through the years have been commercially motivated, and Renaissance painters were financed and controlled by patrons like the Medicis—who were apt to demand that certain details be inserted into the artwork, much the way a business client often insists that the logo be made more prominent in an ad. And all of that was happening long before the lines between art and commerce really started to blur.

Today, artful filmmakers like Woody Allen and Spike Lee shoot ads in their spare time, top photographers are sponsored by camera companies, and serious novelists sometimes negotiate the Hollywood film rights to their work before the ink is dry on the page. In the current environment, is there any point in trying to ferret out the commercial intentions or ambitions that may lurk in the heart of someone embarking on the creative process?

Within the ad industry itself, the question of whether advertising is, or ever can be, an art form is a highly divisive issue. Many advertising professionals think it's dangerous for ad creators to begin to think of themselves as artists— because it may lead them to forget that their primary purpose, always, is to sell the product. "Advertising can be a popular art form—but that should happen by coincidence, not design," says the American ad executive Andy Berlin. Greg DiNoto, who runs the New York ad agency

DiNoto Lee, says, "Persuasion—advertising—can be art, but ultimately that's for the consumer and the world at large to decide. Advertisers get into trouble when they attempt to make art that persuades, instead of persuasion that might be art."

Indeed, the challenge for advertising creators is always to maintain a delicate balance—producing something pleasing to the audience that also serves the business purpose of the client. It is one of the trickiest tightropes in all the creative world. Sometimes ads lean too much in the direction of art or entertainment, and stray too far from the original selling purpose and the product. When that happens, the viewer is likely to love the commercial—but will have no idea, afterward, whose commercial it was. At that point an ad can still be artful but must nevertheless be judged a failure. "When the art becomes an end in itself, the advertising becomes pointless," says the Singapore-based ad creator Neil French. "It's still art, but it ain't advertising."

# Yo Quiero Taco Bell.

6. **TACO BELL**
TBWA/CHIAT/DAY,
LOS ANGELES, 1997
The Chihuahua became a pop-
culture phenomenon in this
campaign for a Mexican-food
chain (though not everyone
approved of the dog's Spanish
accent).

**WHY ADVERTISING MATTERS. HONESTLY.**

7

7. **LEVI STRAUSS EUROPE –
STA-PREST**
BARTLE BOGLE HEGARTY,
LONDON, 1999
The British equivalent of the
Taco Bell Chihuahua, "Flat Eric"
was a mysterious orange
puppet that had Europe talking
in 1999 (though the puppet and
his partner never spoke a word).

8. **LITTLE CAESARS PIZZA**
CLIFF FREEMAN & PARTNERS,
NEW YORK, 1995
The campaign presented absurd
scenarios such as the "Training
Camp" commercial, in which
pizza deliverymen were sent to
boot camp.

There are many people, both inside and outside the ad industry, who view advertising as much more of a science, grounded in sophisticated research, focus-group studies, and formulaic selling approaches. And, certainly, all of those elements do figure prominently in the creation of ads. But the real mystery of advertising is that it so often defies science and measurement. With all the vast amounts of money and effort devoted to research, analysis, and testing (in the U.S. last year, companies spent more than $100 million researching and testing their own ads), often the most powerful advertising springs from pure intuition—from one person or perhaps two, sitting quietly in a room somewhere and dreaming up off-the-wall ideas. "Just do it," the Nike tag line that is one of the most powerful single lines of ad copy produced in advertising in the past twenty years, was penned by a soft-spoken writer in Oregon named Dan Wieden—with no help

from studies or research committees. Wieden sat down at his desk one day, and, in a matter of minutes, just did it.

Most of the advertising in this book was created that way—by one or two people relying on gut feelings while endeavoring to say something original and insightful about a product (and sometimes a very mundane product, at that). Copywriters and art directors usually fail at this task, and produce the expected—the messages that are obvious and don't stand out from the clutter (ad people call this nondescript advertising "wallpaper"). But the best ad creators seem to know instinctively what will resonate. "They have a talent they're born with, and they happen to wander into advertising, where that particular talent begins to grow and flower," says the celebrated British advertising writer Tim Delaney. "It isn't easy to measure this intuitive talent, or even to explain how it works. At the root of it is the ability to somehow fathom and

piece together all sorts of disparate information about people and products, and then come up with an idea that captures the imagination of the public or the individual. It's more magic than anything else."

However, even Delaney is not sure it should be called art. "Persuasion can certainly be thought of as an art form—particularly when it brings together a combination of creative elements that are not entirely logical," he says. "But I think an art form should be an altogether pure thing that tries to illuminate what's really important, like the meaning of life. Advertising does sometimes shine a torch on certain truths, but they're usually more mundane truths—for example, the way you feel deep down about your car." But that's good enough for the American art director George Lois, who believes Pablo Picasso's observation that "art is the lie that tells the truth" can be applied to great advertising. "Almost all

8

products are comparable in quality," Lois has noted, "but when advertising is great advertising—when it's inventive, irreverent, audacious, and loaded with chutzpah—it literally becomes a benefit for the product, and Picasso's 'lie' becomes the truth. Food tastes better, clothes feel better, cars drive better."

Given its utilitarian nature, perhaps the best way to think of advertising is as a kind of folk art, rather than a fine art. "There used to be a lot of pride taken in the creation of very utilitarian things," observes Dan Wieden of Wieden + Kennedy. "In fact, we dig them up all over the world now; we look at vases and bowls and forks and spoons from different eras and cultures. At the time, they were basically commodities—but the person making them cared enough about them to put something special into them, and that made them art. I think the same thing, perhaps, could be true for this slimy business."

### 3. IT IS SHAPING THE POPULAR CULTURE.

In the late 1990s, the aforementioned Gap "Khakis Swing" commercial seized on a burgeoning trend, swing dancing, and turned it into a raging phenomenon in America. Around the same time, a series of commercials created by the Los Angeles agency TBWA/Chiat/Day for Taco Bell restaurants managed to turn a Chihuahua into a media star that was soon appearing on talk shows, T-shirts, and magazine covers, while also stirring political protest (Hispanic groups thought the talking dog's Spanish accent was offensive). Meanwhile, the catchphrases that had seemed to be on everyone's lips around that time—"Just do it," "Think different," "I've Fallen and I Can't Get Up"—were far more likely to have come from ads than from books or even movies.

This is not just an American phenomenon. In Germany, a series of British-made Levi's ads featuring a mysterious, lifelike puppet called

Flat Eric became so wildly popular that Levi's stopped running the ads (because the brand, seeking "hipness," wanted to be talked about by some people but not everybody). In England, commercials for a soft drink called Tango featured an orange-painted man who slapped everyone's ears; so naturally, people on the streets of London started slapping one another's ears, like the orange Tango man. In Australia and New Zealand, a recent Toyota commercial had one word of dialogue repeated over and over—the profane term *bugger*. Subsequently, "the swear word became something of a national obsession," says local journalist Paul Panckhurst, and it started showing up in newspaper headlines on a regular basis. Meanwhile, in Brazil these days, advertising jingles are sung in pubs. "Advertising has become so entrenched in the Brazilian culture that it is one of the preferred topics of conversation in bars, along with soccer and politics,"

# Finally something to get up for.

Sweetened crunchy flakes. Honey oat clusters and raisins.

Kellogg's Raisin Bran Crunch

**Breakfast is back**™

9

10

says Sergio Caruso of the Brazilian agency Carillo Pastore Euro RSCG. Caruso adds that "the names of some of Brazil's advertising people have become part of the layman's repertoire," and "more Brazilians now want to become advertising people than doctors, engineers, or journalists."

All of this is not necessarily an encouraging sign for civilization. Brazil undoubtedly needs good doctors a lot more than it needs clever ad-makers. And this would probably be a better world if all of us were more apt to quote Shakespeare than Chiat/Day. On the other hand, ads are providing at least *some* piece of common culture in a media world that is becoming increasingly fragmented. Popular commercials may be among the last pieces of shared communication, which is perhaps why people talk about them so much. The latest car ads are the bridge that crosses over from the Lifetime women's cable channel to the ESPN

sports channel to the business magazines, connecting all of those disparate audiences.

More and more, advertisers aren't just a central part of the cultural mix, they're a determinant. Once upon a time, television shows and magazines tried to appeal to the public first—then sold that popularity to advertisers. In recent years, that priority has changed somewhat. Today, the TV programs we see and the publications we read are more likely to be conceived and engineered with specific advertising demographics in mind. And so, when television seems to be overtaken by programming geared to teenagers, or when every new magazine seems to be targeting young "lads" with raging hormones, blame it on advertising. These days, a show or a magazine is deemed a hit not so much because the public says so as because advertisers say so—and are willing to pay a higher rate to sponsor it, which begets more shows and

magazines that are similar. In effect, advertising today isn't just influencing the culture—it is programming it.

## 4. IT IS ENDLESSLY ENTERTAINING. (SOMETIMES.)

Beginning with the Creative Revolution that swept through advertising in the 1960s, many of the creators of ads have made a conscious effort to imbue their work with cleverness, humor, emotion, and style. Commercials also began to take on a more cinematic flavor, telling stories that could be powerful. As more than one media critic has observed, the ads were sometimes better than the shows they interrupted. Why wouldn't they be? Each small story had a point and a message. And with each ad, the creators could start with a clean slate—they didn't have to beat the same old sitcom story line to death again every week.

The rise of entertainment-driven advertising in recent years may have provided countless

WHY ADVERTISING MATTERS. HONESTLY.

*Fiery Fries.*

amusing moments for the audience, but it has been a source of constant controversy within the industry itself, owing to the schizophrenic nature of advertising. Should the ad's primary purpose be to entertain or to tout the product? Is it possible to do one without compromising the other? These questions have divided the ad business into two rival camps, the hard-sellers against the "creatives." The former tends to believe that ads should always focus on providing compelling reasons to buy, and should hammer that sales pitch home through volume and repetition. But the creatives believe this is pointless because today's media-savvy audience tunes out such overt sales pitches; the only way to engage such an audience, they contend, is by offering them a laugh or a moving moment—in hopes that the audience will come away feeling good about the brand that brought them that good feeling. Lately, the creative camp has been winning the advertising war—or, as one industry

pundit commented recently, "The creatives have taken over the asylum."

Is this a good thing? For the business itself and the brands that subsidize it, it's anybody's guess whether entertaining soft sell works better than old-fashioned hard sell; there are studies that can prove either side of the argument. (In fact, there are studies in advertising that can prove anything; as one might imagine, advertisers are masterly at constructing an argument to promote any viewpoint.) Interestingly, when it comes to measuring most commercials' direct impact on actual sales results—which can be influenced by an almost infinite number of factors aside from ads—advertisers don't seem to know much more than they did a century ago, when the businessman John Wanamaker famously commented, "I know half of my advertising is wasted—I just don't know which half."

However, a case can be made that we, the audience, are better off when creative advertising

prevails. Today's more entertainment-driven soft-sell ads—even the ones that end up being a bit oblique or bizarre—are probably the least offensive form of advertising. They recognize that they are intruding in our homes and offer something in return: a joke, a story, a pretty picture. And in so doing, they tend to avoid some of the more negative aspects of advertising, such as battering us with silly slogans or denigrating the competition (political ads, which generally are not produced by ad agencies, demonstrate how bad advertising can be when it is devoid of all creativity—all that's left is the lies, the slander, and the pandering).

But as shoppers and consumers, wouldn't we be better off if ads dispensed with the distracting stories and eye-catching designs, and simply provided us with the straight facts about products—the features, benefits, and reasons to buy? Probably not. Conventional ads that rattle on about features and benefits and

12

11. **BURGER KING**
SAATCHI & SAATCHI,
SINGAPORE, 1997
This ad turns a mere french fry
into something incendiary.

12. **ABC TELEVISION**
TBWA/CHIAT/DAY,
LOS ANGELES, 1997
The campaign argued that it was
acceptable to watch TV, even if it
meant neglecting other domestic
or more cerebral duties.

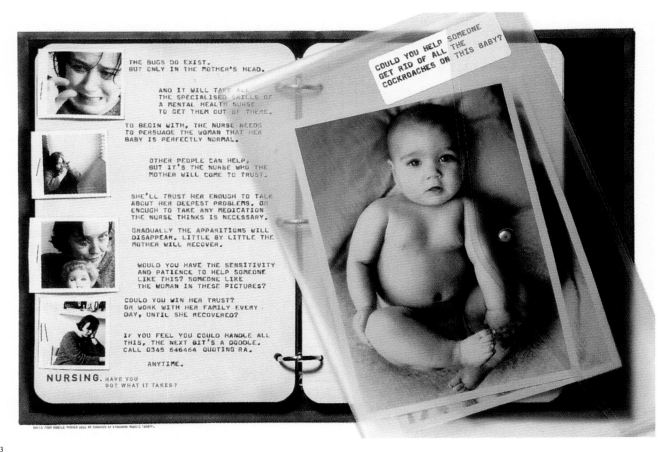

13

13. **BRITISH DEPARTMENT OF HEALTH**
SAATCHI & SAATCHI,
LONDON, 1997
Tackling the tough issue of mental illness, the campaign challenged people to empathize and to devote their lives to helping.

14. **PARTNERSHIP FOR A DRUG-FREE AMERICA**
DDB NEEDHAM,
CHICAGO, 1988
The gun-up-the-nose imagery in this ad shocked some, but cocaine usage dropped sharply following the appearance of this campaign.

15. **NIKE**
WIEDEN + KENNEDY,
PORTLAND, 1992
This campaign, written by women for women, touched on deep feelings and became a source of inspiration.

14

15

"rack-and-pinion steering" often must resort to exaggeration and hyperbole. Worse than that, they're boring. Advertisers can't help it: In today's parity marketplace, most products are comparable in quality. But you can't say that in an ad without riling the client (who, like a proud parent, frequently harbors the illusion that his baby really is better than everyone else's). For a shopper seeking hard, reliable facts on a product, advertising will never be a good resource; better to read articles in *Consumer Reports* or other unbiased sources. Look to the ads for humor and style—those are about the only worthwhile things they can provide.

Some cultural watchdogs have a problem with ads that try to entertain or be stylish and artful; they see this kind of advertising as the wolf in sheep's clothing, distracting us with humor or beauty, while actually manipulating us to buy, buy, buy. But that suggests a somewhat condescending view of the savvy media citizens of the twenty-first century. It's a viewpoint that would have us believe that only the tweedy academics and cynical journalists have figured out what's really going on—while the rest of us poor sheep are still being herded around by devious advertisers. The reality is that today even the average couch potato has an advanced degree when it comes to decoding media images and messages, with an understanding of satire, irreverence, hyperbole. We all have built-in "rubbish detectors" that are as sensitive as that of any media-studies professor (if not more so; after all, academics don't watch much TV except when they're stooping to analyze it). As Fenske notes, today's viewers watch daily reruns of sophisticated TV programs like "Seinfeld" and "Monty Python's Flying Circus," and they get the inside references, the jokes within the jokes. And so they probably also can grasp that, for example, an advertiser that mocks its own ad is doing so to try to gain our trust. Yes, we get it—we know there's a sell in there somewhere. But we'll play along. We want that little surprise, the tiny chuckle, the sappy greeting-card-induced tear—that moment of fun that a truly entertaining ad provides.

## 5. IT CAN ENLIGHTEN AND INSPIRE.

Someone once said that "Nike killed the three-martini lunch." That may be an overstatement of the transformative power of Nike ads. But maybe not. There can be no doubt that the athletic-shoe company's stirring campaigns, urging people to become more active, live healthier, go the extra mile, put in maximum effort, and overcome personal obstacles, have had a tangible impact on the lives of people around the world. In particular, Nike's ads directed toward women, with headlines like "You are not a goddess," "Ever wish you were

AVOIDING DISASTER IS NOT SOMETHING WE CARE TO THINK ABOUT. WE NEED TO BE PREPARED FOR CATASTROPHES THAT CAN SUDDENLY HAPPEN ANYWHERE AT ANY TIME, BE IT A WAR IN RWANDA OR A PLANE GOING DOWN IN THE RUAHINES. FOR MILLIONS THE RED CROSS EMBLEM HAS BECOME

A FAMILIAR AND REASSURING SIGHT IN THE AFTERMATH OF A DISASTER. WE PREPARE OURSELVES FOR AN INSTANT RESPONSE, AND THROUGH OUR FIRST AID AND RESCUE COURSES, WE ALSO PREPARE YOU. ALTHOUGH WE MAY ASK FOR YOUR HELP NOW AND THEN, ONE DAY YOU MIGHT NEED OURS.

16. **NEW ZEALAND RED CROSS**
SAATCHI & SAATCHI
NEW ZEALAND, WELLINGTON, 1995
An artful, dramatic visual campaign that reminded New Zealanders why the Red Cross still matters.

17

THE REPUBLICANS MET IN SAN DIEGO. AND FOR FOUR DAYS THEY PROCLAIMED HOW THEY REPRESENT EVERYTHING TRULY "AMERICAN." THEN THE DEMOCRATS GATHERED IN CHICAGO AND TALKED ABOUT HOW THEY'RE INFINITELY MORE "AMERICAN" THAN THEIR RIVALS. YET OF ALL THE PATRIOTIC ISSUES BOTH PARTIES DISCUSSED, ONE SUBJECT WAS SORELY MISSING: BASEBALL. AFTER ALL, HOW CAN YOU DISCUSS HOW "AMERICAN" YOU ARE WITHOUT EVEN BRIEFLY COVERING THE NATIONAL PASTIME? CONSIDER THIS, WHAT IF A KEYNOTE SPEAKER HAD BEGUN THEIR RHETORIC-FILLED SPEECH BY SAYING: "BEFORE I START, I'M JUST WONDERING WHAT EVERYONE THINKS ABOUT THE YANKS ACQUIRING CECIL? AND WHAT'S UP WITH MADDUX AND ALEX RODRIGUEZ THIS SEASON?" THAT ODD LITTLE COMMENT WOULD'VE SAID EVERYTHING ABOUT A POLITICAL PARTY'S "AMERICAN-NESS." BUT IT DIDN'T HAPPEN. AND FURTHERMORE, THE REPUBLICANS DIDN'T SPEND ANY TIME AT NEARBY JACK MURPHY STADIUM, THOUGH THE PADRES WERE BATTLING FOR A PLAYOFF BERTH, AND THE DEMOCRATS DIDN'T VISIT EITHER COMISKEY OR WRIGLEY. AND WHEN YOU START THINKING ABOUT THE BIGGER ISSUES – THE DEMOCRATS HOLDING THEIR CONVENTION IN A BASKETBALL STADIUM (THE UNITED CENTER) AND THE REPUBLICANS SELECTING AN EX-QUARTERBACK FOR THEIR VICE PRESIDENTIAL CANDIDATE – YOU HAVE TO THINK THAT A THIRD POLITICAL PARTY IS DESPERATELY NEEDED. AFTER ALL, IT'S BASEBALL. AND YOU'RE AN AMERICAN.

FUNDING FOR THIS MESSAGE PROVIDED BY ESPN, A PATRIOTIC NETWORK DEVOTED TO BRINGING HARD-WORKING AMERICANS THE 1996 DIVISION PLAYOFFS, BEGINNING OCTOBER 1. ESPN

18

17. **NIKE**
WIEDEN + KENNEDY,
PORTLAND, 1990
An early ad in the "Just do it"
campaign captured the
loneliness and exhilaration of
the long-distance runner.

18. **ESPN SPORTS NETWORK**
WIEDEN + KENNEDY,
PORTLAND, 1996
The cable channel and its ad
agency recognized that sports
fans are a nation unto
themselves.

19

19. **PARTNERSHIP FOR A DRUG-FREE AMERICA**
GOODBY SILVERSTEIN & PARTNERS, SAN FRANCISCO, 1992
Proving it isn't easy to "just say no," the boy in this commercial was shown traveling a circuitous route, the "Long Way Home," to avoid streetcorner drug dealers.

20. **VISA**
BATEY ADS, SINGAPORE, 1996
The campaign mirrored a changing culture in Asia, with the arrival of credit cards and self-indulgence .

a boy?" and "If you let me play sports . . .," caused the company to be flooded with letters from women and girls across America, who confessed that the ads had been taped to their walls for daily inspiration.

It's not just Nike that has had this kind of effect. Over the past thirty years, public-service advertising has reminded a generation of kids that drugs cook your brain, doing so with simple indelible frying-pan imagery that packed a thousand times the power and authenticity of, say, former First Lady Nancy Reagan imploring people to "just say no." Ads have helped persuade people to buckle up, to clean up (who can forget the Native American driven to tears by litter?), to pay more attention to the kids, to consider the plight of the homeless, to drive more responsibly, to practice contraception in India, to abolish apartheid in South Africa, to support medical research, to quit smoking. (On the flip side, advertising

also has had a long history of persuading us to start smoking; and even though cigarette ads have been greatly diminished and restricted, in this particular area the industry still has much penance to do.) For those who suspect that advertising can't really influence intractable social problems, there is evidence to suggest otherwise. One particularly moving commercial from the American ad agency Goodby Silverstein & Partners, titled "The Long Way Home," showed the plight of an inner-city child forced to take a circuitous route to and from school in order to avoid having to pass by local drug dealers. The commercial had only a limited run, but follow-up studies in the markets where it aired revealed surprising shifts in the attitudes and behavior of young people exposed to the ad; it actually seemed to break through the wall. Not all "good cause" advertising is this effective, and some of it is created for self-serving reasons (see Chapter 9). But

the best of it has almost certainly changed minds and lives.

## 6. IT IS A MIRROR THAT REFLECTS OUR VALUES, HOPES, DREAMS, AND FEARS.
The author Marshall McLuhan called advertisements "the richest and most faithful daily reflections that any society ever made of its entire range of activities," which means we can learn a lot about our society by studying it. Advertising is often accused of telling us what to think, of manipulating attitudes and behavior—which it sometimes does. (A quick aside: Ads directed at young children and political ads have long been considered the most coldly manipulative and least artful kinds of advertising; that's why both categories have been largely omitted from this book.) But more often, advertising tries to reflect and reinforce attitudes and behavioral trends that have already begun to take hold. Ads didn't create the self-indulgent, status-obsessed spirit of the

VISA GOLD. He who has the gold makes the rules.

JUST T

JUST TO THE SIGNPOST.

JUST TO THE SIGNPOST...

JUST TO THE TRUCK.

JUST TO THE KERB.

JUST TO THE CROSSROADS.

THE CAR.

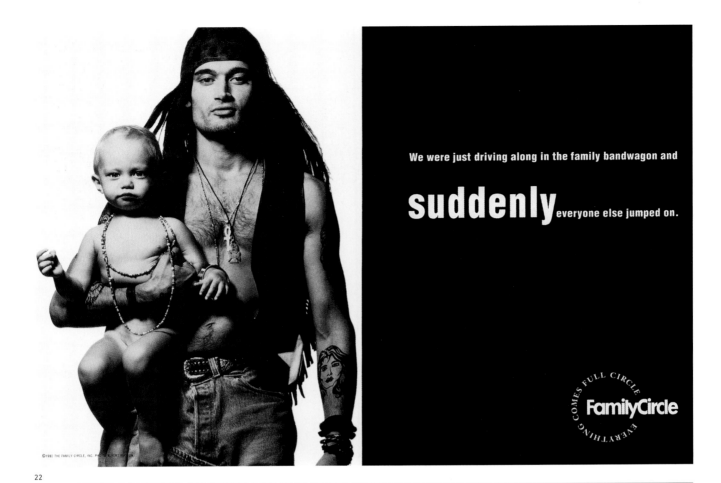

We were just driving along in the family bandwagon and

**suddenly** everyone else jumped on.

EVERYTHING COMES FULL CIRCLE
**FamilyCircle**

©1990 THE FAMILY CIRCLE, INC. PHOTO: ALBERT WATSON

22

# Would you like to sit next to you at dinner?

The Economist

23

21. (PREVIOUS SPREAD)
**ADIDAS**
LEAGAS DELANEY, LONDON,
1995
Like Nike, Adidas used its ads to
urge people to go the extra mile
(and to associate this achievement with Adidas shoes).

22. **FAMILY CIRCLE MAGAZINE**
KIRSHENBAUM BOND &
PARTNERS, NEW YORK, 1992
Ads occasionally lead, but more
often mirror, social trends and
changing demographics—
though advertisers, like this
one, often claim to be ahead of
the pack.

23. **THE ECONOMIST**
ABBOTT MEAD VICKERS,
LONDON, 1998
This campaign asked pointed
questions, emphasizing the
point that reading *The
Economist* could make you a
more interesting person.

24. **BERNIE'S TATTOOING**
THE MARTIN AGENCY,
RICHMOND, VIRGINIA, 1990
A little ad, for a local tattoo
parlor, that ultimately became
a part of advertising lore and a
regional movement.

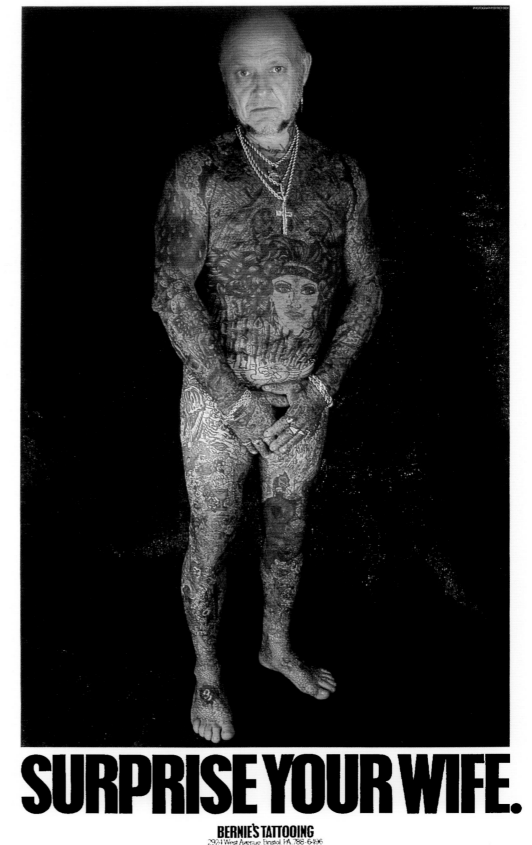

24

**WHY ADVERTISING MATTERS. HONESTLY.**

25

L'original

America in the 1980s—but the ads of that period, taken as a whole, do form a rich and revealing portrait of that species known as the "Yuppie." Similarly, ads didn't create the renewed emphasis, a few years later, on family values—but advertising indisputably picked up that ball and ran with it.

Advertising's mirror is sometimes of the fun-house variety, distorting reality to have us believe that the life going on around us is something different from what it actually is. The clichéd Norman Rockwell approach to ads—projecting wholesome happy families, or hardworking, good-natured farmers amid lush fields, played to the sound track of "The Heartbeat of America"—still is in use in the U.S., particularly by more conventional and conservative marketers.

But if you look closely at today's ads, there is less and less of the old-fashioned imagery that tended to idealize and sanitize. Many ads

now are more realistic snapshots of the culture, not all of them pretty or comforting. A gritty series of Miller High Life ads rhapsodizing about all things macho undoubtedly reflects longings by conflicted modern men to rediscover their "inner guy." Meanwhile, the increasingly aggressive behavior depicted in ads lately— deranged stalkers, people physically attacking one another, the sorts of images that would have been unthinkable in advertising a few years back—clearly represents one more warning bell about the violence that has overtaken the culture. And as irony becomes inescapable in today's ads, one must wonder whether some pundits are right in suggesting that current society seems to be losing its capacity for smirk-free, earnest discussion. Conversely, amid all the cynicism, the reemergence of the old American ad character Mr. Whipple seems to speak to our desire to return to a more innocent past. And finally, there are

all those get-rich-quick Internet stock-trading ads that have flooded the airwaves the past couple of years (what would the famous Smith Barney pitchman John Houseman, whose ads used to sing the praises of making money "the old-fashioned way," have made of all this?). One thing is certain: Years from now, when historians want to know what it was like to live at the dawn of the new millennium, ads like these will all be precious artifacts.

### 7. IT KNOWS OUR SECRETS.

Decades ago, when American books like *The Hidden Persuaders* and *Subliminal Seduction* were popular, the air was rife with conspiracy theories about advertising: that it was engaging in mind-control tactics or planting concealed messages. For the most part, these were paranoid fantasies, but advertisers do have a few tricks up their sleeves. In recent years, they've become highly adept at getting inside our

26

The creators of Apriori clothing were pleasantly surprised to discover other companies using their designs in a similar fashion.

*apriori*

Available at Saks Fifth Avenue.

**25. EVIAN**
EURO RSCG, NEW YORK
AND PARIS, 1999
This campaign encouraged con-
sumption of Evian bottled water,
*"L'original,"* in unexpected ways.

**26. APRIORI ESCADA**
WEISS WHITTEN STAGLIANO,
NEW YORK, 1992
Showing the playful side of
fashion, this ad campaign drew
parallels between stylish clothes
and simple objects.

# Get paid to think up stuff like this.

Some ad agency actually paid a writer and an art director to think up this crazy visual idea for an ad. But coming up with wildly creative solutions to real marketing problems is what advertising is all about. And, after 8 semesters at Art Center, you'll have a good portfolio and a good shot at landing a job in a field that's financially as well as creatively rewarding. Call us at 818-584-5035. Or write to Admissions, Art Center College of Design, 1700 Lida St., Pasadena, CA, 91103.

**ArtCenter**

28

**27. ART CENTER COLLEGE OF DESIGN, PASADENA, CALIFORNIA**
FALLON McELLIGOTT, MINNEAPOLIS, MINNESOTA, 1992
This design school promoted the lure of advertising in a nutshell: people are encouraged to think of crazy ideas, which sometimes defy logic and succeed wildly.

**28. BUDWEISER**
GOODBY SILVERSTEIN & PARTNERS, SAN FRANCISCO, 1997
Frogs and lizards became characters in this memorable ongoing series of TV commercials; the brand name was briefly flashed on screen, lest we forgot who was telling the tale.

Wilt Chamberlain.    Cardmember since 1976.
Willie Shoemaker.    Cardmember since 1966.

It's not just what you say.

It's how you say it.

30

**29. AMERICAN EXPRESS**
OGILVY & MATHER,
NEW YORK, 1987
A classic portrait by photographer
Annie Leibovitz, one of the ads
in a campaign that conveyed the
image of American Express as
an exclusive club.

**30. AAA SCHOOL OF
ADVERTISING**
THE JUPITER DRAWING
ROOM, JOHANNESBURG, 1997
This ad made the point that
advertising works best when it
doesn't state the obvious.

heads. This may conjure up images of hypnosis and high-tech mind-reading gadgetry—and, in very rare instances, advertisers may use these tools (including skin sensors that measure a subject's response to an ad) as part of research. But most of the time, advertisers study us the old-fashioned way—just by watching. In the past fifteen years ad agencies have refined the science of cultural anthropology, largely via a process developed in the UK known as "planning." What planners do, simply, is observe people as they eat, shop, converse, and putter about the house (it's not uncommon for a planner to live with willing research subjects for extended periods of time). Planners then hand these observations over to the people who create ads—which is why you may find yourself, upon watching an ad, wondering, "How did they know I felt that way about bananas?"

On the other hand, sometimes ad creators are able to connect with our deepest feelings simply because they have an instinctive, God-given understanding of human nature. The Salk Institute in La Jolla, California, in honoring the legendary American adman Bill Bernbach, once said of him, "He could explain us to ourselves." That's reason enough to take a closer look at Bernbach's ads: not to understand him but to understand yourself. Besides, if advertising is going to study you and figure out all your secrets, shouldn't you do the same thing to it in return?

## 8. IT GAINFULLY EMPLOYS SOME OF OUR MOST TALENTED ACTORS, DESIGNERS, WRITERS, FILMMAK-ERS, WORLD LEADERS, AND PERFORMING ANIMALS.

Maybe it all started when the American ad executive Jerry Della Femina announced, "Advertising is the most fun you can have with your clothes on." In recent years, the ad business has been a magnet for young talent. More and more advertising schools have popped up all over the world, attracting the best art directors and writers. Talented filmmakers—who years ago wouldn't have touched ads for fear of sullying their reputations—now jump at the chance to make "thirty-second movies." No one—not Jerry Seinfeld, not Madonna, not the Dalai Lama, not the hottest new hip-hop star of the moment—is too cool or too important to appear in an ad these days. And never, ever before have there been so many ripe career opportunities for talking dogs and loquacious lizards.

## 9. IT IS INESCAPABLE AND CANNOT BE KILLED.

Recently, Pizza Hut stamped its logo on a rocket to the moon. This is understandable—on this planet, it seems there is no place left in which to squeeze an ad. There are ads in bathroom stalls, ads stamped on fruit, ads in the bottom of your cocktail glass, ads under your feet as you amble down the street (a favorite: the Kirshenbaum & Bond lingerie ad

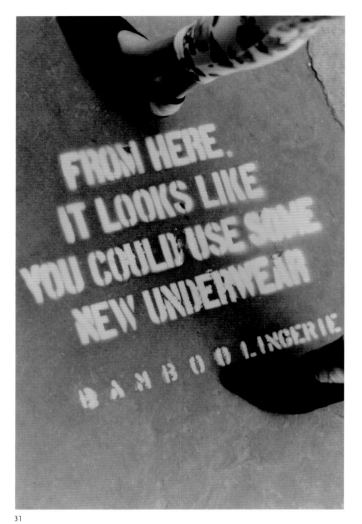

31

31. **BAMBOO LINGERIE**
KIRSHENBAUM BOND &
PARTNERS, 1992
Advertising in unexpected
places, like this ad printed on
a sidewalk, has the power to
startle—though it can also
feel invasive.

32. **KAIZEN**
PALMER JARVIS DDB,
VANCOUVER, 1995
According to this Canadian
campaign for a media-placement
company, it's all about getting
your ad in the right place at the
right time.

stenciled on New York sidewalks that read, "From here, it looks like you could use some new underwear"). Ogilvy & Mather now practices what it calls "360-degree branding"—the idea that you, the consumer, shall encounter the brand everywhere you turn in the course of your day. That is the new mission of advertising. The proliferation of ads used to be a Western phenomenon, but now ads are ubiquitous in China; they are planted in all kinds of unexpected places throughout South Africa (big practitioners of "guerrilla advertising"); and they're running wild throughout Tahiti.

For a while, in the mid-1990s, a rumor began to spread that advertising was an endangered species. The Internet was surely going to kill it (*Wired* magazine, to make this point, featured a cover with the New York ad creators Richard Kirshenbaum and George Lois blindfolded before a firing squad). But by the late 1990s, it became clear that the Silicon Valley whiz-kids

were as hooked on advertising as everybody else; they quickly poured huge sums of their newfound money into the coffers of conventional ad agencies, to make old-fashioned TV commercials about their Web sites. The ad executives laughed all the way to the bank, just as they had when doomsayers predicted that the VCR or the remote control or the expansion of cable would spell the end of advertising. One can state this loud and clear: Advertising will change, will mutate, will reinvent itself. But for the foreseeable future, it isn't going away. (Except for the occasional little jaunt to the moon and back.)

The prospect of being more and more enveloped by 360-degree advertising, with no escape hatch in sight, is hardly cause for a "sale-a-bration." But it only reaffirms the point that quality and good taste in advertising really *do* matter, and they matter more and more as ads continue to proliferate. Cognizant of this,

the American ad executive Jeff Goodby believes that advertisers have an environmental obligation. "If people are going to have to encounter this every day," he says, "then I think we have a responsibility to produce something that has a certain amount of style or wit. I don't want to add to the cultural pollution that's out there." As evidenced by Goodby's work throughout this book, he has done more than his share to improve the advertising landscape, as have Bernbach, Wieden, Delaney, Lee Clow, John Hegarty, Oliviero Toscani, Bob Barrie, Nizan Guanaes, and others. This book celebrates their work and supports the hope that many others, who continue to weave the cocoon that surrounds us, will follow their good examples.

DR. MILLER
PSYCHIATRIST
640-4336

Creative media solutions.

KAIZEN

BRITISH COLUMBIA (604) 640-4336
ALBERTA (403) 421-1010
SASKATCHEWAN (306) 757-1044
MANITOBA (204) 925-8525

32

# 2. WHE
# GOT S

N ADS
MART.

# Think small.

Our little car isn't so much of a novelty any more.

A couple of dozen college kids don't try to squeeze inside it.

The guy at the gas station doesn't ask where the gas goes.

Nobody even stares at our shape.

In fact, some people who drive our little flivver don't even think 32 miles to the gallon is going any great guns.

Or using five pints of oil instead of five quarts.

Or never needing anti-freeze.

Or racking up 40,000 miles on a set of tires.

That's because once you get used to some of our economies, you don't even think about them any more.

Except when you squeeze into a small parking spot. Or renew your small insurance. Or pay a small repair bill. Or trade in your old VW for a new one.

Think it over.

1

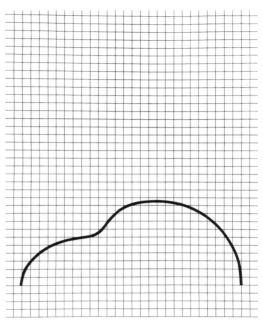

Is the economy trying to tell you something?

2

1. **VOLKSWAGEN**
DOYLE DANE BERNBACH,
NEW YORK, 1960
"Think small." This ad from
1960 launched advertising's
Creative Revolution.

2. **VOLKSWAGEN**
DOYLE DANE BERNBACH,
NEW YORK, EARLY 1970s
First, DDB had the nerve to
shrink the car in the ads; in this
one, they didn't show it at all.

Imagine that the year is 1960, and you are reading the February 22 issue of *Life* magazine. Toward the front of the publication, amid colorful advertising images of Chevrolets and soft drinks, you come upon a stark, black-and-white full-page advertisement for the Volkswagen Beetle automobile. Something about this ad catches your eye and stops you from turning the page. Maybe it's because the picture of the car is so tiny; cars in ads are not supposed to be minimized this way. You read the headline: "Think small." Again, something seems amiss: This is a time in America when "bigger is better" is the credo, when Cadillacs rule the road and a prosperous population is living large. Why think small? You seek an explanation in the copy at the bottom of the page, which tells you, in effect, that this car is not for everyone. Other ads in this magazine are urging you to keep up with the Joneses, but this one is issuing a challenge: Go against the flow. Forget about appearances. Use

your head. It's a message that seems almost insurrectionist in these Eisenhower times (John F. Kennedy had not yet been nominated for president of the U.S. as you were reading this), but it's couched in language that is understated, self-deprecating, with a wry sense of humor. One ad winkingly refers to the German car being "as American as Apple Strudel." You savor the last line, squint at the small picture of the Beetle one more time. Only then do you finally turn the page, unaware that you've just absorbed the advertising equivalent of "the shot heard round the world."

The Volkswagen campaign of the 1960s, created by the New York ad agency Doyle Dane Bernbach, was the launching point of a revolution in advertising. If you were one of the magazine or newspaper readers who happened upon that infamous "Think small." ad, and the equally stirring ads in the series that followed, it may not have persuaded you to run out and buy a Beetle—even the most compelling advertising

rarely sends people scampering to the store (though Volkswagen's sales did increase substantially that year). However, the ad may well have caused you to adjust your thinking about a funny-looking foreign car, and maybe about cars in general, and social conformity, and heaven knows what else. And maybe it changed the way you would approach some ads from now on: No longer could you assume that an ad was obvious and one-dimensional, a mere sales pitch. Now, suddenly, there were ads with an unspoken message and a complex personality; ads that were capable of engaging you in a dialogue, and that challenged you to keep up with their level of wit and intelligence.

Advertising wasn't supposed to be this complicated. Before Doyle Dane Bernbach and others ignited what would be called the Creative Revolution, ads were primarily populated by cute characters and icons—the Jolly Green Giant; Snap, Crackle & Pop; Speedy, the Alka-Seltzer

3

3. **VOLKSWAGEN**
DOYLE DANE BERNBACH,
NEW YORK, 1963
"Snow Plow," one of the first
cinematic, storytelling
commercials, revealed how the
man who drives the snow plow
manages to get to the snow
plow: in a VW Beetle, of course.

4. **EL AL AIRLINES**
DOYLE DANE BERNBACH,
NEW YORK, 1957
Tearing up the page: DDB's art
directors broke the established
rules of layout and design.

mascot; and dancing cigarettes—accompanied by cheery jingles and slogans ("You'll wonder where / the yellow went / when you brush your teeth / with Pepsodent"). And to drive these messages home, the advertiser's hammer was simple repetition; the advertising of old wasn't trying to engage you so much as beat you into submission with a smile and a song that just kept coming back.

To be sure, there were some advertising mavericks who tried to buck this simplistic approach and imbue their work with more style and subtlety. David Ogilvy, for example, founder of New York–based Ogilvy & Mather, introduced the world to more intriguing, enigmatic advertising characters, like the eye-patched Hathaway man in the 1950s. Still, the prevailing force in the ad industry pre-1960 was Rosser Reeves, head of Madison Avenue's Ted Bates Agency, who believed that advertisers should follow simple formulas that were foolproof in manipulating consumers. The idea was to identify a compelling

reason people should buy a product—Reeves called this the "Unique Selling Proposition"—and then harp on that point, over and over. Reeves's mission, and that of advertising as a whole, was simply to "get a message into the heads of as many people as possible at the lowest possible cost." Was there any style or substance to the message? That hardly seemed to matter at the time; to the disciples of the Reeves approach, advertising was, beneath the warm and fuzzy images and slogans, a cold and efficient science of the business world.

Bill Bernbach, on the other hand, had a different take. A writer from the Bronx who worked at several Madison Avenue agencies before opening his own in 1949, Bernbach believed that advertising was "fundamentally persuasion," and that persuasion was more art than science. While many advertisers swore by the power of redundancy, Bernbach felt that consumers would be more apt to respond to

novelty. The impact of an ad, he reasoned, "is a direct result of how fresh and original it is, because you react strongly to something you've never seen or heard before." To come up with those fresh ideas, Bernbach felt that ad creators had to approach their task in the manner of artists—trusting their intuition, rather than relying on formulas and research.

Bernbach had another insight that would fundamentally change advertising in years ahead. In his early days, at the William Weintraub agency, he worked alongside the great graphic designer Paul Rand. In developing ideas with Rand, Bernbach became convinced that writers and art directors should brainstorm while working on an ad campaign (previously, most ads were created in more of an assembly-line fashion: "A copywriter would write a headline and then slip it under the art director's door, expecting a layout in return," recalls DDB veteran Bob Levenson). Bernbach felt that "if two good people

On
Dec. 23
the
Atlantic
Ocean
became
20%
smaller

The first jet-prop
in transatlantic service,
El Al's new Bristol Britannia,
flies you to
London 2¼ hours faster
than ever before.

EL AL
ISRAEL AIRLINES

See your travel agent or El Al Israel Airlines, 610 5th Ave., N. Y. 20, PL 1-3400. Also Philadelphia, Chicago, Los Angeles, Montreal

4

## It lets me be me:

In hair color, as in make-up, clothes, love, work…a woman wants to be herself. Not somebody else's idea of what she is, or should be. That's what women like about Nice'n Easy.® Whether you want to color or conceal, to change a little or a lot, Nice'n Easy assures you of beautiful coverage, healthy-looking hair and honest color that becomes part of you.

No wonder, now more than ever, it sells the most. Nice'n Easy. From Clairol.

*Nice'n Easy*

5

*Hathaway's batiste broadcloth shirt is 100 per cent lightweight cotton. It weighs a third less than ordinary broadcloth.*

## Hathaway announces the first <u>summer-weight</u> <u>broadcloth</u>

THIS NEW HATHAWAY shirt is the world's first *batiste broadcloth*. It is the best news in lightweight shirts since Hathaway brought out batiste Oxford fifteen summers ago.

Until now, nobody has been able to reduce the weight of broadcloth without sacrificing some of its luster and softness. The secret of how this has at last been done remains overseas with our weavers. And they have a right to it. They spent ten years of trial and error perfecting this revolutionary broadcloth.

More news. Hathaway has put a *two-button cuff* on the batiste broadcloth shirt. If you are now wearing an ordinary single-button cuff, notice how the corners tend to cross at an angle. A *pair* of buttons keeps the corners squared —so that your cuff forms a perfect circle around your wrist. Very neat-looking—particularly under a jacket.

About $9. White, blue, Scotch Dawn, Cactus or Sahara. Solid or stripes.

For names of stores, and a free copy of Hathaway's informative little *Dictionary of Shirts and Shirtings*, write C. F. Hathaway, Waterville, Maine. Call OXford 7-5566 in New York.

6

**5. CLAIROL NICE 'N EASY**
DOYLE DANE BERNBACH, NEW YORK, 1971
Written by DDB's Phyllis Robinson, this campaign was a breakthrough in terms of preaching individualism to women.

**6. HATHAWAY**
OGILVY & MATHER, NEW YORK, 1960
David Ogilvy put an eye patch on "the man in the Hathaway shirt," suggesting to readers that there was an untold story behind the ad.

**7. LEVY'S RYE BREAD**
DOYLE DANE BERNBACH, NEW YORK, 1967
DDB's campaign featuring ethnic faces "helped people feel comfortable with America's diversity," noted the journalist Michael Kinsley.

**8. OHRBACH'S**
DOYLE DANE BERNBACH, NEW YORK, 1959
Early DDB print ads, like this one for a New York clothing retailer, showed the clean and spare design that would later distinguish the Volkswagen campaign.

## You don't have to be Jewish

## to love Levy's
### real Jewish Rye

7

8

get together, an art director and a copywriter, sometimes you don't know who's writing the copy and who's doing the art because you get excited about the thought—which is the important thing."

This simple notion of doubling up writers and art directors—which is status quo today—had a groundbreaking, profound effect on the creative process of advertising: It served to knock down the wall between copy and art, and between the literal and the visceral aspects of advertising. In this new unified approach, creative teams sought out not just the clever line or the pretty picture but a seamless union of the two in the form of the big idea or "concept" that would resonate.

Bernbach's New York agency, formed with business partners Ned Doyle and Maxwell Dane, was stocked with creative people who had artistic sensibilities. The copywriter Phyllis Robinson idolized author Dorothy Parker; the art director Bob Gage had studied under renowned designer

Alexey Brodovitch of *Harper's Bazaar;* Helmut Krone, meanwhile, was a designer's designer, with a unique vision of how an advertising page might look. Still, Doyle Dane Bernbach was not a place to indulge artistic whims; Bernbach believed that selling the product was the first order of business. And the doctrine at the agency was that there was no room for cleverness or ornamentation that was not directly tied to selling the product (Bernbach once remarked that if you're going to show a man upside down in an ad, it should be for a reason—such as to show that the pockets in his pants keep his money from falling out). Research certainly played a role at the agency; Bernbach's teams immersed themselves in the cultures of the companies they worked for, and also studied the products closely. But as they sought to forge an emotional connection between those products and the people who might use them, DDB's creative teams were encouraged to trust their own intuition and instincts. "Listen to

the ideas percolating up from your unconscious," Bernbach advised his creative troops.

They did, and the results were astounding. Prior to the VW campaign, the agency had made a name for itself with playfully designed ads for Ohrbach's department store, and with its campaign for Levy's bread, which would eventually proclaim that "you don't have to be Jewish to love Levy's" (featuring the faces of Native Americans, Asians, and African-Americans, this advertising was years ahead of its time, and "helped people feel comfortable with America's ethnic diversity in a way that any number of human relations commissions could not," wrote the journalist Michael Kinsley). The agency's ads for El Al Airlines broke all the rules of airline advertising—they didn't show planes, stewardesses, or flight schedules. One ad, making the point that El Al's flights were 20 percent less expensive, showed a picture of the ocean, with part of the image ripped away. The headline read, "On Dec. 23, the Atlantic Ocean

**Lemon.**

This Volkswagen missed the boat.
The chrome strip on the glove compartment is blemished and must be replaced. Chances are you wouldn't have noticed it; Inspector Kurt Kroner did.
There are 3,389 men at our Wolfsburg factory with only one job: to inspect Volkswagens at each stage of production. (3000 Volkswagens are produced daily; there are more inspectors

than cars.)
Every shock absorber is tested (spot checking won't do), every windshield is scanned. VWs have been rejected for surface scratches barely visible to the eye.
Final inspection is really something! VW inspectors run each car off the line onto the Funktionsprüfstand (car test stand), tote up 189 check points, gun ahead to the automatic

brake stand, and say "no" to one VW out of fifty.
This preoccupation with detail means the VW lasts longer and requires less maintenance, by and large, than other cars. (It also means a used VW depreciates less than any other car.)
We pluck the lemons; you get the plums.

9

9. **VOLKSWAGEN**
DOYLE DANE BERNBACH,
NEW YORK, 1960
The famous "Lemon" ad: Copy that seems at first glance like criticism actually praises the German carmaker for its high standards.

10. **VOLKSWAGEN**
DOYLE DANE BERNBACH,
NEW YORK, 1964
A typical example of the wry, self-deprecating humor that distinguished the early VW series from other ads.

became 20% smaller." (Bob Levenson recalls that when he first saw that ad as a young man riding the Manhattan subway, it struck him that "it was the perfect blend of words and pictures, and I hadn't seen anything like it." Shortly thereafter, he applied for a job at DDB). These early campaigns "lit the fire of the Creative Revolution," says Robinson. "Clients and creative people started coming to the agency, saying, 'Whatever you're doing, I want to get in on this.'"

But the Volkswagen campaign was the real breakthrough for DDB—and for advertising as a whole. Initially, there were reservations among Bernbach's employees (a significant number of whom were Jewish) about even working on the German account, recalls Robinson. "Some people at the agency didn't want to have anything to do with it," she says. But Bernbach maintained that Hitler and the old Germany were history, and it was time to move on. George Lois, then a young art director at the agency and part of the

anti-Volkswagen faction, recalls that Bernbach at one point showed him a newspaper article about Israel buying military parts from Germany— the point being, if Israel could now do business with the Germans, so could DDB. Lois, along with writer Julian Koenig and art director Helmut Krone, was part of the agency team that traveled to Germany to visit the Volkswagen factories, prior to beginning work on the ads. "You have to remember this wasn't that long after World War II, and I felt almost embarrassed to be walking around in that place," Lois says. But at the same time, the visitors couldn't help noticing the obvious dedication and passion of the car's German engineers—who seemed to take pride in the smallest details of their work. The result of their labor was a car that was unorthodox in its look and design, highly efficient and practical, small but indomitable.

Sometime during the factory visit it began to occur to Koenig that the car's perceived

drawbacks—the things that made it different from the more bloated American cars—were in fact its strengths. All that was required was the boldness to state that without apology, which Koenig did with his "Think small." headline. His partner Krone, a noted perfectionist, initially had trouble figuring out how to visually maximize the impact of this idea. He eventually produced a layout in which the tiny car seemed almost adrift in a sea of white space—a total departure from the cluttered ads of the day. The two-word headline was punctuated with a period (Krone's idea), and even that little period was, itself, a statement— a kind of anti-shout. "Bernbach took the exclamation point out of advertising," Krone would later remark, "and I put in the period." The "Think small." ad seemed to violate every advertising dictum of the day, and in doing so had a profoundly liberating effect within the advertising creative community. The ad would subsequently be held up as a banner for the new advertising, a

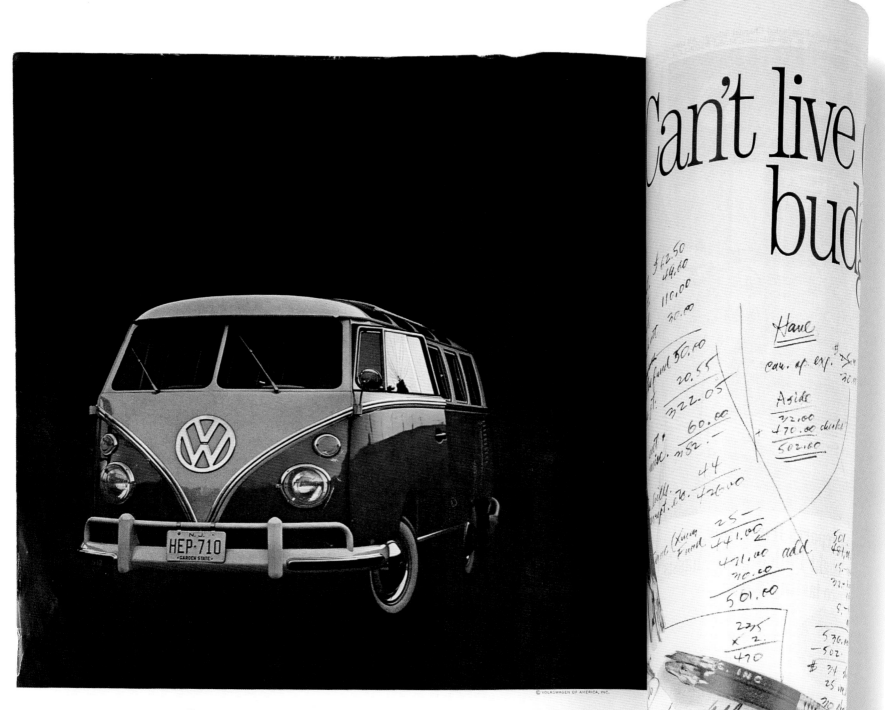

## Somebody actually stole one.

We were tickled pink to hear that somebody wanted a Volkswagen Station Wagon badly enough to go out and steal one.

It wasn't so long ago that we practically couldn't give them away.

So when Martin Carlson reported his loss to the police, we took it as a triumph.

In its own way, the VW Station Wagon is one of the world's best getaway cars.

You can escape north or south of the border. (The VW engine can't freeze up or boil over because it's cooled by air.)

You can go farther in a VW than in any police car (24 mpg is our average).

You have 21 windows to spot anyone who's tailing you.

And it carries more loot (170 cu. ft.) than the biggest regular wagon you can steal.

Sadly, the whole theory blew apart when Mr. Carlson found his VW abandoned in the very spot he had left it.

Maybe everyone isn't ready for it, after all.

Not even crooks.

# Nine Ways to Improve an Ad

**Rule: Show the product.**
Don't turn it into a postage stamp or a test of failing eyesight. Show it. Boldly. Dramatically. Excitingly. Like this:

There. See the difference already? Now, I'll admit the headline no longer makes complete sense—but that brings us to another obvious improvement.

**Rule: Don't use negative headlines.**
"Think Small" may be very clever, very witty...but what an idea to leave in the minds of everyday readers.

"Think BIG!" Now I ask you—isn't that better? Isn't it more positive, more direct? And note, too, the interesting use of type to punch home the excitement of the idea.

Well that brings us to still another improvement—and one of the most important rules in advertising.

**Rule: Whenever possible, mention your product name in the headline.**
Which the people who thought up this ad could have done so very, very easily.

See how the ad is beginning to jell? How it's really starting to come alive.

Let's see another way we can breathe some life into it—with a warming touch of humanity.

**Rule: Whenever possible, show people enjoying your product.**

That's more like it. A gracious mansion. A carefree band of dancers. And best of all, a proud pair of thoroughbreds.

Now for an improvement to correct a fault in the product itself. You'll note that the VW, unfortunately, is totally lacking in news. From year to year, while other cars bring out a host of exciting changes—it stays its own dowdy self.

**Rule: Always feature news in your advertisement.** And if you have no news, invent it. Like this:

How's that for news?

**Rule:** (One of the most obvious of the bunch) **Always give prominent display to your product logo.**
And I don't mean an arty jumble of initials no one can read; I mean a proud unashamed logo like this:

There. Now they know who's paying for the ad!

**Rule: Avoid all unpleasant connotation about your product.**

Which brings us to a somewhat delicate area: the country of origin of the Volkswagen car. Now I don't have to dwell on the subject of World War II and its attendant unpleasantness for you to grasp my meaning. Let's simply say that it might be wise to "domesticate" the car, so to speak.

VOLKSWAGEN—THE ALL-AMERICAN CAR!

And in a flash, apple strudel turns into good old apple pie!

**Rule: Always tell the reader where he can buy your product.**

Where can you buy a Volkswagen?

"At your friendly authorized Volkswagen dealer." Note the warmth of words like "friendly." And the use of "Authorized" to make sure that prospects don't stumble into places that are unauthorized.

One rule to go. The most important rule of all.

**Rule: Always localize your ads.**

And mind the way you spell the dealer's names.

There you have it. No clever, precious, self-conscious waste of space like the ad we started with; but an honest hard-hitting, two-fisted ad like this that really sells.

I said "sells." ■

12

11. (PREVIOUS SPREAD)
**"NINE WAYS TO IMPROVE
AN AD"**
FRED MANLEY, 1963
Manley, an American ad
executive, created a facetious
presentation showing how the
"Think small." ad could be
ruined by applying conventional
rules of advertising. (The
piece originally appeared in
*Communication Arts* magazine.)

12. **EASTERN AIRLINES**
YOUNG & RUBICAM,
NEW YORK, EARLY 1970s
This TV commercial, "Diver,"
featured inviting scenes from an
Acapulco vacation, imbuing
Eastern with a soaring spirit.

13. **BETTER VISION INSTITUTE**
DOYLE DANE BERNBACH,
NEW YORK, MID-1960s
Using Braille to draw the
attention of the sighted.

compelling argument against following the established rules. (One creative director at the time, Fred Manley, developed a visual presentation with the sarcastic title "Nine Ways to Improve an Ad" (see page 52–53). Manley began by showing his audience the simple, powerful "Think small." ad, and then methodically weakened and destroyed it by cluttering it with all of the standard elements used in more conventional advertising.)

Koenig and Krone followed up "Think small." with a series of equally striking print ads, including the famous "Lemon" ad—whose one-word headline, placed under an image of the car, seemed to be insulting the product. Who could resist reading the copy to find out why? It explained that the particular car pictured had been rejected by a VW inspector because of a minor blemish on the chrome strip in the glove compartment. "We pluck the lemons, you get the plums," the ad concluded. In effect, the ad played "Gotcha!" with the reader, but it didn't come off as

an advertising trick; instead, the modest tone of the ads—indeed, the willingness to acknowledge flaws to begin with—made "Lemon," and the whole VW campaign, seem like the first "honest" advertising ever produced. As longtime DDB veteran Roy Grace acknowledges, it wasn't any high-minded moral imperative that drove the agency to try to be more honest in its ads; "it was more a case of feeling the ads would work better because people would find that honesty refreshing," he says. "Lemon" became the model for a more candid approach to advertising that is followed by top creative agencies to this day. "DDB taught us all to celebrate the truth about the brand, even if that truth is a potential liability," says Greg DiNoto, creative director at the New York agency DiNoto Lee. "The idea is, don't divert the consumer's attention away from the funny shape of the little German car—instead, lead with the funny shape. Diffuse the issue and let people embrace the car's otherness." The result, DiNoto

concludes, is that "potential liability becomes a mark of individuality and charm." (The "Think small." sensibility can be seen in modern ad campaigns such as Apple's "Think different"—which not only recalls the famous VW headline but also celebrates "otherness"; the campaign converts Apple's small, low-market-share niche into a badge of honor, making Apple ownership seem like an exclusive club for freethinkers.)

Just as DDB turned "lemons" into assets for VW, the agency performed similar feats of marketing jujitsu for other clients. The rental-car company Avis had come to DDB as a perennial runner-up to market leader Hertz. Rather than trying to work around that drawback, DDB embraced it as a strength. The concept was that "number two tries harder," and that it sometimes pays to go with the less popular choice; for example, one tongue-in-cheek ad pointed out, "the line at our counters is shorter." It wasn't easy to convince the client that it made sense to brag

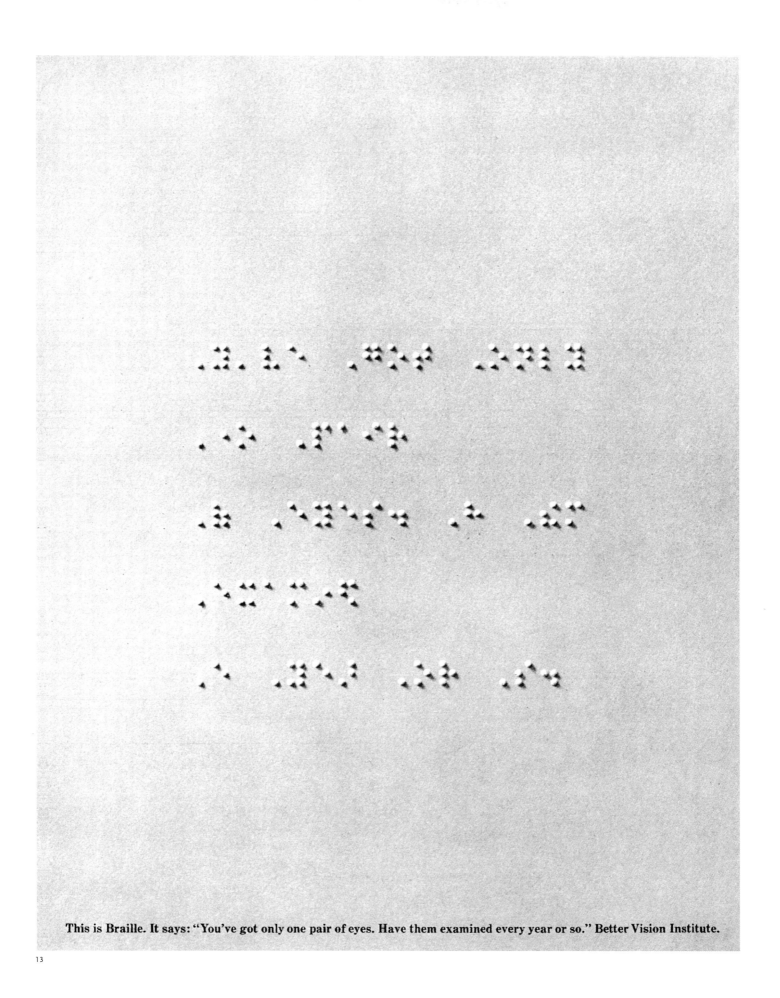

This is Braille. It says: "You've got only one pair of eyes. Have them examined every year or so." Better Vision Institute.

The dandelion is one of nature's prettiest villains. It's not only good to eat, there was a time when people took it as medicine.

But here in Marysville, Ohio, where we have our main grass research farms, it's just another weed.

In fact, it's a bully. It pushes the good grass out of the way and takes the food in the soil for itself. This is one weed that doesn't die every year. It's a tough perennial with roots that go down as far as 2 feet.

And that pretty yellow blossom turns into a white puffball full of seeds that the wind carries all over your lawn.

You can't stop dandelions from coming in, the way you can with crabgrass.

You have to get this pest to get rid of it. But it's easy to lick.

Leave one bit of its root and the dandelion will be back.

# We'll get these dandelions out of your lawn and that's a promise.

And don't make it hard on yourself by trying to dig it out. Leave one bit of that root and back she'll come.

But just spend 30 minutes with your spreader and our *Turf Builder* Plus-2*. Your dandelion population (and a lot of other weeds) will be on the way out in a matter of days. That's our promise.

And the *Turf Builder* in this is our own slow-release fertilizer. It will also feed your lawn for up to 2 months.

In fact, if you also spend 30 minutes with our straight Turf Builder*—say once in July and once again in September—

your grass will be so thick there won't even be room for weeds to come in. Good thick turf helps crowd weeds out.

Your Scotts retailer can tell you all about weeds. (We've probably even had him out here to see how we do it.) But you can call us toll-free if you like: (800) 543-1415. From Ohio: (800) 762-4010, from the Dakotas and Nebraska West call: (800) 543-0091.

You might also like to get our quarterly, Lawn Care*. It's free and it's filled with good things to know about grass.

Just write us here in Marysville, Ohio. You don't need a street address. We've been here since just after the Civil War.

14

## Avis is only No.2 in rent a cars. So why go with us?

We try damned hard.

(When you're not the biggest, you have to.)

We just can't afford dirty ash-trays. Or half-empty gas tanks. Or worn wipers. Or unwashed cars. Or low tires. Or anything less than seat-adjusters that adjust. Heaters that heat. Defrosters that defrost.

Obviously, the thing we try hardest for is just to be nice. To start you out right with a new car, like a lively, super-torque Ford, and a pleasant smile. To know, say, where you get a good pastrami sandwich in Duluth.

Why?

Because we can't afford to take you for granted.

Go with us next time.

The line at our counter is shorter.

TIME, FEBRUARY 1, 1963

15

## Who do you think of first when you think of rent a cars? Certainly not Avis.

How one of our customers made out his check.

It must be nice to be a household word. Like Jell-O, Coke or Kodak.

But we're not. Avis is only No. 2 in rent a cars, and it's always the big fellow you think of first.

So we have to try harder. Hoping the people who stumble on us will come back for more.

(We probably have the world's most fussed-over Fords. Spick and span and nicely in tune.)

And when someone calls us by the wrong name, we turn the other cheek.

After all, it doesn't matter what you call us.

Just so you call.

16

**14. SCOTTS LAWN PRODUCTS**
DOYLE DANE BERNBACH,
NEW YORK, MID-1960s
The designer Helmut Krone
constantly experimented with
"the new page." Here he
surrounded the text with a
grass border.

**15 AND 16. AVIS**
DOYLE DANE BERNBACH,
NEW YORK, 1963
In a bit of marketing jujitsu,
DDB turned a problem (the fact
that Avis lagged behind Hertz in
the rental car market) into an
asset by arguing that "No. 2
tries harder."

# Give dad an expensive belt.

12 YEARS OLD WORLDWIDE •
BLENDED SCOTCH WHISKY 86 PROOF •
GENERAL WINE & SPIRITS CO., NEW YORK, N.Y.

**FIRST SHOWING OF A NEW POLAROID LAND FILM.** This is an enlargement of an actual 60-second picture of Louis Armstrong. It was taken with a new film, just introduced, which is twice as sharp as the previous film. With this latest development, the Polaroid Land Camera not only gives you pictures in 60 seconds, but pictures of exceptional clarity and brilliance. Polaroid Land Cameras start at $72.75. The new film can be identified by a star on the box.

18

about being a runner-up, and the task was made more difficult when Bernbach prescreened the "We're No. 2 idea" with a panel of consumers and found that it did not score well. "But he stuck with the idea anyway," Levenson recalls. When it ran, it was a hit with the public and became one of the most famous ad campaigns in history.

The campaigns for Volkswagen, Avis, and other clients were popular and effective for years—because the agency's creative teams found ways to freshen them, to add new twists and surprises. DDB's art directors constantly experimented with new designs. Bob Gage was the first to try to "explode the page," says Robinson, referring to his bold use of white space, photography, and type treatments; "You would have to look to Toulouse-Lautrec's posters to find another artist with as wide an influence on the printed advertising message," she says. Gage's disciple, Krone, was forever trying to create "the new page," in which he would violate any rules he seemed to have estab-

lished in previous ads—replacing large pictures with small ones; moving the headline from top of page to the bottom. Krone used design elements to suggest a feeling about a brand (something that is quite common in ads now but was not at the time). He created a grass border around ads for Scotts lawn products; for Porsche he made some of his ads resemble pages from a technical engineering report. Krone understood that an ad's design didn't just dress up the concept—it could be the concept. The agency's writers, meanwhile, continually used language or scenarios that hadn't been seen in advertising before. One memorable VW commercial was set in a funeral procession and involved the reading of a will (in it, the deceased has decided to leave his wealth to the only relative who is fiscally responsible—the one who drives a VW, of course). At the time, says Roy Grace, "a funeral was the worst thing you could have in a commercial—and that's why it was so right." Similarly, for Chivas Regal, simply using a

line like "Give Dad a little belt for Christmas" was a risqué use of vernacular in advertising. Not everyone approved of what the agency was doing at the time, recalls Grace. "A lot of mainstream advertisers didn't understand it, couldn't do it themselves, and became very vocal about saying that we were wasting clients' money by using humor that supposedly wasn't appropriate for ads," he says. "Even David Ogilvy was still saying at the time that ads shouldn't be using humor."

But the the mid-1960s, DDB was not the only agency producing this new style of more candid and provocative advertising. In effect, Bernbach helped trigger a new wave of "advertisers with attitude," who took a more hard-hitting approach in their ads. Lois and Koenig had left DDB to form Papert Koenig Lois, which took the wry wit of DDB and infused it with more of a street-smart edge; the same could be said of one of PKL's own young hires, Carl Ally, who soon left and formed Carl Ally Inc., which emerged as a third leader in

# INTERVIEW: GEORGE LOIS

George Lois burst onto the advertising scene in the early 1960s, at the dawn of advertising's Creative Revolution, as a feisty art director at Doyle Dane Bernbach. He went on to start his own competing agency, Papert Koenig Lois, nearly as influential as DDB in those days. Lois is associated with some of advertising's most famous campaigns—from "I want my Maypo" to "I want my MTV"—but his contributions didn't end there. As the designer of some of *Esquire* magazine's unforgettable covers—artist Andy Warhol drowning in a soup can, boxer Muhammad Ali posed as Saint Sebastian, and others—Lois showed that his ability to convey powerful messages was not limited to pitching products.

## YOU'VE CALLED DDB "THE FIRST CREATIVE AGENCY." WHAT MADE THAT SO?

To preface, there was a lot of great advertising before Bernbach, mostly in the form of great copy lines—"They laughed when I sat down at the piano" or "I'd walk a mile for a Camel." But almost never was there a marriage of real visual design that worked with the copy. Bernbach had an epiphany. It came out of his early work with the great designer Paul Rand. He saw Rand create advertising that had modern, humanistic imagery. He couldn't hire Rand, but he brought in Bob Gage and other great art directors, then put them in the same room with great writers—which had never been done—and they worked toward a common cause. And somehow, one plus one equaled three, and it changed everything. It created a new kind of advertising, with a new attitude, a new power, a new simplicity.

## WHAT WAS THE ATMOSPHERE LIKE AT DDB?

When I first got there I knew I was in Nirvana. I loved knowing there was great talent around me. You could stick your head in almost any door and you knew the guy was doing great work. But the best thing about it was Bernbach—he truly understood what a great idea was, and he could sell that idea to a client. I have to say, there was a kind of arrogance that developed at DBB because they knew how good they were, and there was a lot of competitiveness. But there wasn't one day that I didn't love it there.

## ANY MEMORIES OF THE VOLKSWAGEN CAMPAIGN "THINK SMALL."?

I remember that when we came back from visiting Germany, [DDB copywriter] Julian Koenig was going crazy. He had this headline, "Think small.," but he told me Helmut [Krone] didn't want to do a layout for it. Meanwhile Bernbach had some other idea; he was trying to get Helmut to do a close-up of a wheel with a reflection of a family in it—which would have been just terrible. And that went on for a week, and then finally Helmut did a "Think small." layout. And the advertising came out and everyone went crazy.

## HOW DID YOU GO FROM DESIGNING ADS TO *ESQUIRE* COVERS, AND HOW WAS THAT DIFFERENT?

I was running my agency PKL, and the publicity we got back then was unbelievable. I got a call one day from [*Esquire* editor] Harold Hayes, asking me to help with covers. I did one cover on a weekend, it was a hit, and I did another. And I did that for the next ten years, on weekends, while running my ad agency. It was a different process, because when I do advertising, I always think in words, like "I want my MTV." What I want is a mnemonic slogan, a great copy line, that is impossible to ignore—and then I marry that with a great visual. With the *Esquire* covers the thinking was all visual—you just have a theme, like avant-garde in pop art, and the visual idea of Warhol in the soup can comes out of that.

## SOME PEOPLE MIGHT BE WILLING TO CONSIDER THOSE MAGAZINE COVERS ART, BUT PERHAPS NOT YOUR ADS. WHY IS THAT?

Oh, yes, that's true. In fact, I was at a memorial service for the designer Saul Bass and I met Steven Spielberg and Martin Scorsese, who were big fans of the old *Esquire* covers. They asked what I've been doing since then, and I told them I'm an advertising man. And I could see they thought, "Advertising?" Like I sold out or something.

When I wrote a book years ago and called it *The Art of Advertising*, a lot of art directors were really disturbed that I would use that word. And I said, "F—- you, I'm an artist; I don't care what you think you are." The major thing in advertising is that it's got be cause and effect; the idea must work on people. But I do it my way, and I try to make it bright, inventive, surprising

thinking, and do it in a way that architecturally looks the way I want it to look. To me, that's an art. Maybe it's not art with a capital *A*, but it's some kind of art.

## WHAT HAS SURVIVED FROM THE CREATIVE REVOLUTION, AND WHAT HAS BEEN LOST?

It's all been lost. With the influx of communications schools, everybody in America has been through marketing courses that teach advertising as a science, not an art—that you can construct an ad in a scientific way and test it to make sure it works. And if you try to tell these people advertising is an art, they look at you askance. So we've lost the great clients who instinctively reacted to things as human beings.

Also, now it's considered uncool to do advertising to younger people that actually sells. Because they know so much about marketing, and know you're trying to sell them, so advertisers now think, "We better not ask them for the sale." What you get is hip, ambiguous advertising. Witness all this dot-com crap—95 percent of it, you don't understand what the company even does. If you actually try to sell something, a dot-com client will say to you, "No, young people don't want to be sold to." Are you kidding me? A great idea is a great idea. And people do want to be sold to. Great advertising in and of itself becomes a benefit of the product. You have to use ideas and imagery to bring a vitality to a brand, an attitude that makes people fall in love with the product because they love the advertising. And you must do that unabashedly.

## Drive it like you hate it.

### You can hurt a Volvo,
### but you can't hurt it much.

This Volvo was bought new in Ann Arbor, Michigan, in 1956. Its owner paid $2345 for it, complete. He has raced it, pulled a camp-ing trailer halfway across the country with it, his kids climb all over it, and it's seldom under cover. It has 80,261 miles on it. The head has never been off, the brakes have never been relined, the original tires lasted 55,000 miles, the clutch hasn't been touched, the valves have never been adjusted (much less ground), and it will still top 95 mph. Total cost of repairs exclusive of nor-mal maintenance: One hood latch, $4.50. One suspension rod, $40.00. Not all Volvos will do this. But Volvos have a pretty good average. One enthusiastic owner in Wyoming wrote us that he has driven his Volvo over 300,000 miles without major repair. We think he's exaggerating. It's probably closer to 200,000 miles.

Volvo 122S compact. Like the Volvo above, it runs away from other popular-priced compacts in every speed range, gets over 25 miles to the gallon like the little economy imports, is virtually indestructible.

20

19.AND 20. **VOLVO**
CARL ALLY INC., NEW YORK,
MID-1960s
Ally became Bernbach's rival,
and his Volvo campaign
challenged VW. According to
Ally's ads, the little German car
might be smart and cute, but the
Swedish car was a lot tougher.

*vol. 9, no. 8 — august, 1962*

# PLAYBOY.

Rome — P. 54

Red Line — P. 38

Party — P. 46

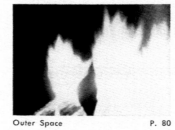

Outer Space — P. 80

## CONTENTS FOR THE MEN'S ENTERTAINMENT MAGAZINE

HUGH M. HEFNER *editor and publisher*

A. C. SPECTORSKY *associate publisher and editorial director*

ARTHUR PAUL *art director*

JACK J. KESSIE *managing editor*     VINCENT T. TAJIRI *picture editor*

FRANK DE BLOIS, JEREMY DOLE, MURRAY FISHER, TOM LOWNES, SHELDON WAX *associate editors;* ROBERT L. GREEN *fashion director;* DAVID TAYLOR *associate fashion editor;* THOMAS MARIO *food & drink editor;* PATRICK CHASE *travel editor;* J. PAUL GETTY *consulting editor, business and finance;* CHARLES BEAUMONT, RICHARD GEHMAN, WALTER GOODMAN, PAUL KRASSNER, KEN W. PURDY *contributing editors;* ARLENE BOURAS *copy editor;* RAY WILLIAMS *editorial assistant;* BEV CHAMBERLAIN *associate picture editor;* DON BRONSTEIN, MARIO CASILLI, POMPEO POSAR, JERRY YULSMAN *staff photographers;* REID AUSTIN *associate art director;* PHILIP KAPLAN, JOSEPH H. PACZEK *assistant art directors;* WALTER KRADENYCH, ELLEN PACZEK *art assistants;* JOHN MASTRO *production manager;* FERN HEARTEL *assistant production manager •* HOWARD W. LEDERER *advertising director;* JULES KASE *eastern advertising manager;* JOSEPH FALL *midwestern advertising manager;* VICTOR LOWNES III *promotion director;* NELSON FUTCH *promotion manager;* DAN CZUBAK *promotion art director;* HELMUT LORSCH *publicity manager;* BENNY DUNN *public relations manager;* ANSON MOUNT *college bureau;* THEO FREDERICK *personnel director;* JANET PILGRIM *reader service;* WALTER J. HOWARTH *subscription fulfillment manager;* ELDON SELLERS *special projects;* ROBERT S. PREUSS *business manager and circulation director.*

"Pssst, Wolfschmidt."

"What's this, a talking soda?"

"Let's get together, Wolfschmidt."

"I'll bet you say that to all the vodkas."

"Only you, Wolfschmidt. You've got taste."

"Can you squeeze me in?"

### Pssst: Want to try something delicious this summer?

Try the Wolfschmidt Pssst! (Wolfschmidt vodka, soda, ice and lemon squeezed in.) Soda has never tasted this good before. Wolfschmidt makes it possible. It has the touch of taste that marks genuine old world vodka. More?
GENERAL WINE AND SPIRITS COMPANY, NEW YORK 22, N.Y., MADE FROM GRAIN, 80 OR 100 PROOF. PRODUCT OF U.S.A.

21. **WOLFSCHMIDT VODKA**
PAPERT KOENIG LOIS,
NEW YORK, 1962
In the early 1960s, the sassy art director George Lois believed ads should have an attitude; this series featured sexy banter between vodka and mixers— perfect for placement in a "men's entertainment magazine."

"You're some tomato.
We could make beautiful Bloody Marys together.
I'm different from those other fellows."

"I like you, Wolfschmidt.
You've got taste."

Wolfschmidt Vodka has the touch of taste that marks genuine old world vodka. Wolfschmidt in a Bloody Mary is a tomato in triumph. Wolfschmidt brings out the best in every drink. General Wine and Spirits Company, N.Y. 22. Made from Grain, 80 or 100 Proof. Prod. of U.S.A.

22

A Coty Cremestick turned Alice Pearce…into Joey Heatherton.

And you thought lipsticks weren't important, eh? Another Cremestick trick: they're moisturizing, but they're never greasy. And zip! They're on in a stroke. Ask Alice Pearce.

Some luscious Cremestick colors:

23

**22. WOLFSCHMIDT VODKA**
PAPERT KOENIG LOIS,
NEW YORK, 1962
Another in the classic series of
George Lois ads in which the
vodka and a potential companion
engage in cocktail-party
seduction.

**23. COTY CREMESTICK**
PAPERT KOENIG LOIS,
NEW YORK, LATE 1960s
Mocking the conventional
"before and after" approach to
cosmetics advertising, PKL
transformed an ordinary woman
into actress Joey Heatherton,
one of the original Golddiggers
on the "Dean Martin Show."

the Creative Revolution. Marty Cooke, now a creative director with M&C Saatchi and a veteran of DDB, says the agencies PKL and Ally "were the Rolling Stones to DDB's Beatles . . . they were more aggressive, more cynical." That was perhaps a reflection of the personalities involved in these two spin-off agencies: Lois was known almost as much for his New York tough-guy manner as for his designer's eye; he referred to his advertising as "poison gas" and remarked that his mission was to "spray it and watch people fall." Once, when faced with a resistant client, Lois threw open the window in a skyscraper office and threatened to jump out if the client didn't approve his campaign. Carl Ally was just as volatile: A former fighter pilot, he lived by the slogan, posted in his office, "Comfort the afflicted, afflict the comfortable."

That toughness was evident in the ads created by both agencies, including PKL's saucy, sexy ads for Wolfschmidt vodka, in which the randy bottle propositioned tomatoes and oranges. (Lois would

also become famous for creating the line "I want my Maypo," which, a couple of decades later, he recycled for a new client, as "I want my MTV.") Ally, meanwhile, shot back at Bernbach on behalf of Hertz ("No. 2 says he tries harder. Than who?"). And like DDB, Ally sang the virtues of a small foreign car, the Volvo—but Ally made the little car seem not so much smart and cute as just plain tough. "Drive it like you hate it" was one Ally headline.

One of the key writers in Ally's stable was a former juvenile delinquent from Chicago named Ed McCabe, who'd worked his way up from a mailroom job and who wore bandages on his arms to conceal his tattoos. After writing a number of stellar campaigns for Ally, McCabe struck out on his own, starting Scali McCabe Sloves—where he continued to create groundbreaking ad campaigns for Perdue chicken (he introduced one of the least photogenic ad spokesmen ever seen in Frank Perdue, and turned him into a major celebrity),

Hebrew National ("We answer to a higher authority"), and Maxell tape. McCabe epitomized the Young Turk of advertising's creative world: He brought a Hemingwayesque quality to ad copywriting, punching out staccato copy that often seemed like an outright challenge ("My chickens eat better than you do," one Perdue ad barked). Appropriately, McCabe lived fast and hard, venturing out to bars to work on ad campaigns— and sometimes not returning for weeks. A typical tale had him walking down the street talking to a Ford executive when he noticed a beautiful woman in a car stopped at a traffic light; he draped himself on the hood of the car as the shocked client watched. "My attitude," he later explained to a journalist, "was that I could wait for Ford."

The macho culture that dominated the New York–based Creative Revolution would set the tone in advertising for years to come. Even thirty-odd years later, as the new millennium arrived, creative advertising remained primarily a man's world;

# No. 2 says he tries harder.

# Than who?

We wouldn't, for a minute, argue with No. 2. If he says he tries harder, we'll take him at his word.

The only thing is, a lot of people assume it's us he's trying harder than.

That's hardly the case. And we're sure that No. 2 would be the first to agree.

Especially in light of the following.

### A car where you need it.

The first step in renting a car is getting to the car. Hertz makes that easier for you to do than anybody else.

We're at every major airport in the United States. And at some airports that are not so major. Ever fly to Whitefish, Montana? Some people do. And have a Hertz car waiting.

No matter how small the airport you fly to, if it's served by a commercial airline, 97 chances out of 100 it's also served by Hertz or by a Hertz office within 20 minutes of it.

In all, Hertz has over 2,900 places throughout the world where you can pick up or leave a car. Nearly twice as many as No. 2.

### Can't come to us? We'll come to you.

We have a direct-line telephone in most major hotels and motels in the U.S. It's marked HERTZ and it's in the lobby. Pick it up, ask for a car, and we'll deliver one to the door. You often can't get a cab as easily.

### What kind of car would you like?

When you rent from Hertz, you're less likely to get stuck with a beige sedan when you want a red convertible. We have over twice as many cars as No. 2.

Not only is our fleet big, it's varied. We do our best to give you what you want. From Fords, to Mustangs, to Thunderbirds, to Lincolns and everything in between. Including the rather fantastic Shelby GT 350-H.

### Who's perfect?

When you rent a new car from us or anybody else, you expect it to be sitting there waiting, ready to go, looking like new.

On that score we claim no superiority over our competition. They goof once in awhile. We goof once in awhile.

Except when we goof it bothers us more because people don't expect the big one to goof. And to make up for it, if our service is not up to Hertz standards we give you $50 in free rentals.* Plus an apology.

No. 2 gives a quarter plus an apology. And advertises that he "can't afford" to do more.

We feel the other way about it. We can't afford to do less.

Besides, the $50 comes out of the station manager's local operating funds. This tends to keep him very alert...and our service very good.

### Hot line.

When you're in one city and you're flying to another city and you want to have a car waiting when you arrive and you want it confirmed before you leave, we can do it for you. Instantly. In any one of 1,038 U.S. cities. No other rent a car company can make that statement.

The major reason we can do it is because we recently installed one of the world's most advanced reservations systems.

After all, with the supersonic jets in sight and one hour coast to coast flights in prospect, you'll need some quick answers.

We can give them to you today.

### About credit.

If you've got a national credit card with most any major company, you've got credit with us.

### About rates.

You can rent a car from Hertz by the day and the mile, by the weekend, by the week, by the month, by gift certificate, by revolving credit, by sundry other ways in between.

We offer all these rates for two reasons. To stay ahead of competition. To get more people to rent cars.

When you go to rent a Hertz car just tell the Hertz girl how long you want the car and roughly how much driving you'll be doing. She'll figure out the rate that's cheapest for you.

### Speak up No. 3.

Is it you that No. 2 tries harder than?

*There's one thing you have to do for us: Fill out our Certified Service form and mail it to our main office in its self-addressed envelope. Upon verification we'll send you $50 in rental certificates by return mail.

©Hertz System, Inc., 1966

# Hertz

25

## 24. HERTZ
CARL ALLY INC., NEW YORK, 1966
Again, Ally fired back at Bill Bernbach, as the rental car company Hertz cleverly used Avis's own slogan as a reminder of who's best.

## 25. HEBREW NATIONAL
SCALI McCABE SLOVES, NEW YORK, 1974
The writer Ed McCabe belittled Uncle Sam in this classic TV commercial, which asserted that the kosher hot dog manufacturer Hebrew National had to "answer to a higher authority."

## 26. VOLVO
SCALI McCABE SLOVES, NEW YORK, 1970
McCabe took on the big American automobile, declaring that "Fat cars die young!"

## 27. PERDUE CHICKEN
SCALI McCABE SLOVES, NEW YORK, EARLY 1970s
McCabe pioneered the regular-guy-as-spokesman: Frank Perdue, founder of a family chicken empire, wasn't a pretty face, but he came across as tough and honest.

26

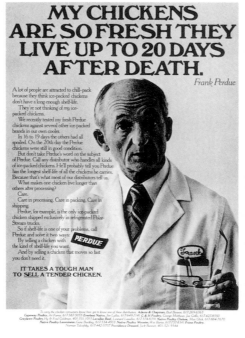

27

# NO OTHER AUDIO TAPE DI

# LIVERS HIGHER FIDELITY.

# maxell.

The Tape
That Delivers
Higher Performance.

Does she...or doesn't she?'

Hair color so natural only her hairdresser knows for sure!

MISS CLAIROL® HAIR COLOR BATH!

29

Does she...
or doesn't she?

Hair color so natural only her hairdresser knows for sure!

MISS CLAIROL® HAIR COLOR BATH®

30

28. (PREVIOUS SPREAD)
**MAXELL**
SCALI McCABE SLOVES,
NEW YORK, 1979
Despite the headline and copy,
this image said all there was to
know about Maxell cassette
tape's powerful sound. The
poster was found on college
dormitory walls around the U.S.
in the 1980s.

29 AND 30. **MISS CLAIROL**
**HAIR COLOR**
FOOTE CONE & BELDING,
NEW YORK, 1961
Copywriter Shirley Polykoff
posed an intriguing question in
a groundbreaking campaign that
launched in the late 1950s.
Some ads in the series balanced
the sexually suggestive headline
with wholesome imagery.

31. **HORN & HARDART**
SCALI McCABE SLOVES,
NEW YORK, 1970s
This ad for an Automat-style
restaurant chain featured
another tough, uncompromising
headline from Ed McCabe,
whose ads tried to cut through
the often misleading boasts of
advertising.

today, the vast majority of the industry's best-known creative directors, both in the U.S. and around the world, are men. Part of the reason for that may be attributable to the tone and style of advertising that was forged in the 1960s—rooted in aggressive, cocky, blunt, in-your-face humor. "If you looked at the work we produced," Lois says, "it was usually obvious from the attitude that a man had written it." The copywriters who broke through in the 1960s "were the guys who grew up on street corners in New York, cracking jokes and making everyone laugh," says Grace. As these hardscrabble entrepreneurs opened their agencies and began to chase new accounts, there was a spirit of fraternalism, of going off to war together, that undoubtedly led to discrimination (unconscious or otherwise) against women. Then, too, ad managers on the client side were usually men—and the agency executives believed that many of these male clients would tend to feel more comfortable entrusting the stewardship of their

brands to other men. On the other hand, Lois says, many women opted not to enlist in this particularly grueling war. "It was brutal; you had to work fourteen-hour days to make it in advertising then," he says. "A lot of women didn't want to give up their lives to it."

But a few women did, and they left their mark. Robinson, the pioneering copywriter at DDB who worked on Levy's, Ohrbach's, Polaroid, and other classic campaigns, was one of them. Another was Shirley Polykoff, a copywriter at Foote, Cone & Belding who sent Clairol hair-coloring sales through the roof with the line "Does she or doesn't she?," which suggested that women could reinvent themselves without apology, and without anyone else even knowing for sure. But the single most successful woman from that period—and perhaps to this day in advertising—was Mary Wells, who initially became a star at DDB and then went on to launch her own agency, Wells Rich Greene. Wells proved that her advertising

could be as mischievous as that of any of the men; with a Benson & Hedges campaign that focused on the disadvantages of B&H's longer cigarettes, she poked fun at her own product. For Alka-Seltzer, Wells introduced the memorable line "I can't believe I ate the whole thing." And she brought a sense of playful stylishness to companies like Braniff Airlines—which, under her guidance, painted its planes in bright colors and announced "the end of the plain plane."

Though their styles and approaches differed, the leaders of the American creative scene of the 1960s had certain common attributes. All were inveterate rule-breakers—in fact, that was perhaps the defining characteristic of all of them, and it separated them from creative predecessors like Ogilvy and Leo Burnett. Burnett had exerted a profound influence on advertising and on American culture with his agency's creation of advertising icons like the Marlboro Man, the Jolly Green Giant, and Tony the Tiger, but the reliance

## You can't eat atmosphere.

**Horn & Hardart. It's not fancy. But it's good.**

31

on such icons became, in itself, a formula that was followed faithfully by Burnett. Similarly, Ogilvy created brilliant soft-sell ads for clients like Rolls-Royce—one of his most memorable headlines was "At 60 miles an hour the loudest noise in this new Rolls-Royce comes from the electric clock"—but he, too, insisted that sensible ads must adhere to certain basic principles and guidelines; in fact, Ogilvy set down those rules in his best-selling handbooks on advertising. But the likes of Bernbach, Lois, Ally, McCabe, and Wells, along with a West Coast insurrectionist named Howard Gossage, had no use for such formulas. To some extent, they were products of their time: The author Thomas Frank has noted that the writers and artists driving the Creative Revolution were truly part of the 1960s spirit of the counterculture; they may have worked within the "establishment" of Madison Avenue, but they were also trying their best to overthrow that old bureaucracy and its conservative ways.

Moreover, the new advertisers—unlike many of their predecessors—had come into advertising not just to build a successful business but to make a statement. Whether or not they fancied themselves artists (some did, most didn't), they all wanted to have an impact on the culture, and all wanted to be respected for their creative abilities in the same way that, say, filmmakers were. According to McCabe, "We wanted to be able to tell our family and friends that we were in advertising and, when we told them [which ads] we were doing, watch the disdain on their faces melt into something almost like admiration."

Eventually, they succeeded. As the public gained a new appreciation of advertising, "the cocktail circuit buzz found television commercials, for the first time, more compelling than the programs," observed one publication, and advertising's creative stars "were favored guests of talk show hosts . . . and their entrances at the rococo photographers' parties of the 1960s set off

a stir the way hot young fashion designers do in trendy nightclubs today."

What grew out of this period was a cult of creativity in advertising, which became the magnet that would continue to draw young writers and artists to the business in years ahead—not just in America but around the world. The DDB revolution was, indeed, televised, and everyone was watching. One of the first places it migrated to was London, which, in the early 1960s, caught the Bernbach fever. Tim Delaney, now one of the UK's best-known creative directors, was a teenager when he first saw DDB's ads, at a gallery show in London; he became a fan for life. "The DDB approach to advertising particularly resonated in the UK for several reasons," says Delaney. "We were weaned on the BBC, which taught us to respect visual imagery, and we also had a very strong writing ethos in our national newspapers. And so we were nurtured with a certain appreciation for pictures and words, and when we saw

Oh, the disadvantages of our longer cigarette. Benson & Hedges 100's

Warning: The Surgeon General Has Determined That Cigarette Smoking Is Dangerous to Your Health.

17 mg. "tar," 1.1 mg. nicotine, av. per cigarette, FTC Report, Oct. '74.

Regular and Menthol

32. AND 33.
**BENSON & HEDGES**
WELLS, RICH, GREENE, NEW YORK, 1968–75
The agency headed by Mary Wells took a page out of DDB's book by playing up "the disadvantages" of B&H's longer cigarettes.

32

# The disadvantages of advertising Benson & Hedges 100's.

Oh, you've had your disadvantages with our longer cigarette... now we've come head on with ours. If you think we have a space problem here... imagine the disaster on match book covers.

Notwithstanding, Benson & Hedges 100's, regular and menthol, have become the most popular new cigarette, maybe of all time. Perhaps all those extra puffs had something to do with it.

BENSON & HEDGES

33

**MIDDLE TAR** As defined by H.M. Government
H.M. Government Health Departments' WARNING: CIGARETTES CAN SERIOUSLY DAMAGE YOUR HEALTH

34

MIDDLE TAR As defined by H.M. Government
DANGER: H.M. Government Health Departments' WARNING: THINK ABOUT THE HEALTH RISKS BEFORE SMOKING

35

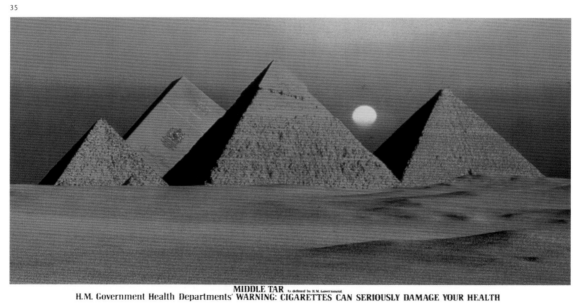

**MIDDLE TAR** As defined by H.M. Government
H.M. Government Health Departments' WARNING: CIGARETTES CAN SERIOUSLY DAMAGE YOUR HEALTH

36

The Rolls-Royce Silver Cloud II — $15,655 P.O.E. (Delivery costs slightly higher in Alaska and Hawaii.)

# "At 60 miles an hour the loudest noise in this new Rolls-Royce comes from the electric clock"

*What makes Rolls-Royce the best car in the world? "There is really no magic about it—it is merely patient attention to detail," says an eminent Rolls-Royce engineer.*

1. "At 60 miles an hour the loudest noise comes from the electric clock," reports the Technical Editor of THE MOTOR. The silence inside the car is uncanny. Three exhaust mufflers tune out sound frequencies—acoustically.

2. Every Rolls-Royce engine is run for four hours at full throttle before installation, and each car is extensively test-driven over varying road surfaces. Every Rolls-Royce has its "History Book"—an *eleven-page* signed record of all operations and inspections performed on the car. This goes into the Company's permanent files.

3. The Rolls-Royce Silver Cloud II is designed as an *owner-driven* car. It has power steering, power brakes and automatic gear-shift. It is very easy to drive and to park. Women handle the car with ease.

4. The finished car spends a week in the final test-shop, being fine-tuned. Here it is subjected to ninety-eight separate ordeals. For example, the engineers use a stethoscope to listen for axle-whine. Silent operation of *every* part is the standard for acceptance.

5. The new eight-cylinder aluminium engine is even more powerful than the previous six-cylinder unit, yet *it weighs ten pounds less*. It accelerates from zero to 60 miles an hour in 11.4 seconds. (ROAD AND TRACK test report.)

6. The coachwork is given as many as *nine* coats of finishing paint—*hand rubbed*.

7. Every Rolls-Royce takes the "Monsoon Test." Windows are rolled up and the car is pelted with water and air at gale force. *Not a drop may come through.*

8. By moving a switch on the steering column, you can adjust the shock-absorbers to suit road conditions. (The lack of fatigue in driving this car is remarkable.)

9. Another switch defrosts the rear window, by heating a network of 1360 almost invisible wires in the glass.

10. The seats are upholstered with eight hides of English leather—enough to make 128 pairs of soft shoes.

11. A picnic table, fashioned of inlaid French walnut, slides out from under the dash. Two more swing out behind the front seats.

12. The engine cooling fan is *lopsided*. Its five blades are unequally spaced and pitched to take thick and thin slices of air. Thus it does its work in a *whisper*. The company goes to fantastic lengths to ensure peace and quiet for the occupants of the car.

13. There are *three* independent brake linkages. The Rolls-Royce is a very *safe* car—and also a very responsive and *lively* car. It cruises serenely at eighty-five. Top speed is in excess of 100 m.p.h.

14. The gas tank cannot be opened without the driver's consent: you unlock it electrically from a button on the dash.

15. Automatic transmission, power brakes and power steering are *standard*. So are the radio, heating and ventilating equipment, walnut panelling, seats adjustable for tilt and rake, and white sidewall tires. The Rolls-Royce people do not designate essential equipment as "optional extras."

16. The Bentley is made by Rolls-Royce. Except for the radiator shells, they are identical motor cars, manufactured by the same engineers in the same works.

The Bentley costs $300 less, because its radiator is simpler to make. People who feel diffident about driving a Rolls-Royce can buy a Bentley.

**ROLLS-ROYCE AND BENTLEY**
PRICE. The car shown above costs $15,655 P.O.E. Delivery costs slightly higher in Alaska and Hawaii.

If you would like to try driving a Rolls-Royce or Bentley, write or telephone any dealer listed below. For further information or complete list of U. S. dealers, write Mr. Richard L. Yorke, Vice President, Rolls-Royce Inc., Room 465, 45 Rockefeller Plaza, New York, N. Y.

| | | | |
|---|---|---|---|
| NEW YORK, N. Y. J. S. INSKIP, INC.—DISTRIBUTOR | Detroit (Ferndale), Mich. Falvey Motor Sales Company | Miami, Fla. Waco International Salon | St. Louis, Mo. Gruet Motor Car Company |
| Atlanta, Ga. Import Motors Ltd., Inc. | Greenville, S. C. Judson T. Minyard, Inc. | Milwaukee (Thiensville), Wisc. Milrace Motors Ltd. | St. Paul, Minn. Schneider Motors Co. |
| Baltimore, Md. General Pontiac Corporation | Hartford, Conn. Russ Seeli, Inc. | Nashville, Tenn. E. Gray Smith | Schenectady, N. Y. Van Curler Motor Co., Inc. |
| Boston, Mass. Foreign Motors, Inc. | Indianapolis, Ind. Messrs. Schaler-Waters | Pittsburgh, Penna. Motorfair — Rolls-Royce — Pittsburgh | Washington, D. C. Flood Pontiac Company |
| Bryn Mawr, Penna. Warrington Motors Imports, Inc. | Kutztown, Penna. Nick Ciliberti Pontiac | Providence, R. I. J. S. Inskip, Inc. | West Palm Beach, Fla. Taylor Imported Motors |
| Chicago (Wilmette), Ill. Imperial Motors, Inc. | Louisville, Ky. Koster-Swope Imports | Richmond, Va. Mooers Motor Car Co. | Wilkes-Barre, Penna. Lewis Wolfe, Inc. |
| Cincinnati, O. Charles Raymond, Inc. | Memphis, Tenn. Pryor Oldsmobile Company | Shaker Heights, O. Salter Automotive Imports, Inc. | |

37

# All of us come from someplace else.

**Just once, you should walk down the same street your great-grandfather walked.**

Picture this if you will.

A man who's spent all his life in the United States gets on a plane, crosses a great ocean, lands.

He walks the same streets his family walked centuries ago.

He sees his name, which is rare in America, filling three pages in a phone book.

He speaks haltingly the language he wishes he had learned better as a child.

As America's airline to the world, Pan Am does a lot of things.

We help business travelers make meetings on the other side of the world. Our planes take goods to and from six continents. We take vacationers just about anywhere they want to go.

But nothing we do seems to have as much meaning as when we help somebody discover the second heritage that every American has.

**America's airline to the world.**

See your travel agent.

38

the work of DDB, something clicked. Particularly among a whole generation of working-class lads who gravitated toward advertising in the 1960s. They found that they could create street-smart, savvy ads just like Bill Bernbach." The British agency that emerged as the leader of the local movement, Collett Dickenson Pearce, had been greatly inspired by DDB, and hired a number of DDB's "missionaries" in England. CDP's ads for Hovis, Birds Eye, Heineken, Benson & Hedges, and Fiat Strada had all the freshness and originality of DDB's work, with perhaps even more distinctive style. And the agency didn't need to import much talent, because it was busy developing plenty of its own—including Charles Saatchi, who would go on to form the agency that bore his name, as well as the young commercial-makers Ridley Scott and Alan Parker, who eventually made their mark in the film world. In subsequent years, Delaney's own agency, Leagas Delaney, would, along with shops like Bartle Bogle Hegarty

and Abbott Mead Vickers, carry the creative flame forward in the 1980s as England became a new creative mecca. Gradually, the Creative Revolution began to spread to other parts of the world, including Australia, where agencies like Campaign Palace, with British expatriate Lionel Hunt at the creative helm, produced ads that bore the unmistakable stamp of DDB—the same look, the same wit, the same cheeky attitude. Eventually, the DDB influence even made its way to Asia, transported by expatriates from America, the UK, or Australia. One could walk into a creative agency in Singapore, says local ad man and author Jim Aitchison, and find people studying Bernbach.

Interestingly, while the fever was spreading around the world, it was beginning to subside in America. As the business recession of the 1970s squeezed advertising, and caused clients to tighten budgets and demand immediate results from the ads they did run, Mary Wells sounded what some would consider to be the death knell

for the Creative Revolution: "Hard times demand hard selling," she declared. What followed in the late 1970s and early 1980s was a period in which much of American advertising (with exceptions, of course) seemed to regress to formula and conservatism. And the mid-1980s brought a wave of mergermania to the ad industry that didn't help matters; by the late 1980s, there were few dynamic and independent creative agencies operating on Madison Avenue. Many agencies, including DDB itself, were swallowed by international conglomerates, and creativity was usually not the top priority in these business arrangements which tended to favor a more research- driven, risk-averse approach to advertising.

Still, Bernbach's conceptual, idea-driven approach to advertising couldn't be killed. It simply migrated to smaller regional American markets, where there was still room for experimentation. The rise of regional advertising in

39

40

41

41. **JOHN SMITHS YORKSHIRE BITTER**
BOASE MASSIMI POLLETT, LONDON, 1982
In this TV commercial, "Two Tricks," a fiesty dog amuses two chaps enjoying pints of beer in a British pub.

42. **ANSETT AIRLINES**
CAMPAIGN PALACE, MELBOURNE, 1981
Lionel Hunt brought an irreverent style to ads Down Under; this one, in particular, caused a stir when it first appeared.

43. **TALON ZIPPERS**
DELEHANTY KURNIT & GELLER, NEW YORK, EARLY 1970s
This long-running series found endless ways to play off the open-fly joke and the potential vulnerabilities caused by an inferior zipper.

## If the hostess was out of uniform would you know which airline you were flying with?

Until recently probably not.
But from next June you won't be in any doubt at all.
Ansett will be offering you a real choice of the planes you fly in, the times you depart, and the services you get both in the air and on the ground.
In June we start taking delivery of our new fleet of 12 Boeing 737's and new generation 727's and start pensioning off our DC9's.
This means we'll soon be offering you Boeing comfort and reliability on all our jet routes.
Just as important, more planes will mean far greater frequency. And no more identical schedules.

You'll be far more likely to find a departure time that suits you, rather than one that just suits the airline.
And you'll check-in faster, get on and off quicker, and get your baggage sooner.
We'll also be offering major service benefits that we can't reveal now for reasons that will be obvious to readers who are also in a highly competitive situation. But don't wait until next June to try the new Ansett. Our competitive philosophy is showing up right now in lots of little ways that already make flying with us just that much better.
But you ain't seen nothing yet. **ANSETT**

42

A prominent New York stockbroker just went public.

It's bad enough when the market takes a sudden plunge.
But when your trouser zipper goes down, you lose another kind of security.
So for your own good, look for the Talon Zephyr®nylon zipper next time you buy yourself a suit or a pair of slacks.
The Zephyr zipper is designed not to snag, or jam. And a little device called Memory Lock® will make sure your zipper stays up.
So all you'll have to worry about going down are your stocks.

43

America was made possible by a number of factors, including the spread of computers, fax machines, and other technology that enabled clients to work with agencies located anywhere. But what really drove the trend was the reluctance of talented writers and art directors from around the country to go to New York—where they knew they would have to toil in large, stifling corporate environments. Seeking a more creative alternative, many began to open their own small local shops, often starting with modest hometown accounts, then building a national reputation via award-winning creative work. In Minneapolis, Minnesota; Richmond, Virginia; Portland, Oregon; and San Francisco, agencies like Fallon McElligott, the Martin Agency, Wieden + Kennedy, and Goodby Silverstein all, to some extent, carried Bernbach's tradition forward to the present. "Bernbach was my Che Guevara," says the copywriter Ernie Schenck, whose Providence, Rhode Island, agency Pagano

Schenck & Kay was one of the small regional agencies leading the late-1980s wave of new creativity. "What we learned from Bernbach," says Schenck, "is that you could create great work by isolating a single, compelling point, and you could give it an emotional resonance by putting visuals and words together in unexpected ways. Conceptual advertising totally reshaped the way we think about advertising, both as creators and consumers." Schenck's sentiments are echoed in places like Amsterdam, where the creative director Johan Kramer of the agency KesselsKramer says, "Bernbach's work understood that consumers are intelligent and recognize manipulation. All his books are here on our tables—we see them as advertising bibles."

Bernbach himself didn't live to see the second coming of the revolution; he passed away in 1982, just as Fallon McElligott was making a name for itself, and as Wieden + Kennedy was opening its doors. At the time of his death, few outside the

ad world grasped the importance of what this advertising man had accomplished, and the dominant effect he'd had on a medium that would come to dominate the culture. *Harper's* magazine was one of the few to observe this at the time, noting in 1983 that Bernbach "probably had a greater impact on American culture than any of the distinguished writers and artists who have appeared in the pages of *Harper's* during the past 133 years." What *Harper's* failed to note was that the impact extended far beyond "American culture"; Bernbach, as would eventually become clear, changed not just America but the world. He helped to forge a style and an attitude that are now part of the ad/cultural vernacular in Bangkok, in Johannesburg, in Warsaw, as well as in Ernie Schenck's Providence. As the following pages demonstrate, it is a way of thinking and communicating that crosses borders and yet needs little or no translation. The advertising concept— Bernbach's baby—is now a universal language.

# 3. A NEW LANGUAGE

# VISUAL EMERGES.

W hen building a mousetrap," the San Francisco adman Howard Gossage once advised, "always leave room for the mouse."

Gossage's point was that when people interact with advertising, as with other forms of communication, they don't necessarily want everything spelled out for them; give them points A and B, but allow them to make the mental leap to C themselves. This is not an easy concept for a salesman to accept; it runs counter to the driving instinct to complete the sale, leaving nothing to chance. (As decreed by the *Über*salesman character in American playwright David Mamet's drama *Glengarry Glen Ross,* the first law of selling is "A-B-C: Always Be Closing.")

Bill Bernbach and other leaders of the 1960s Creative Revolution understood and accepted the "mouse" theory—indeed, they often used a "less is more" approach to selling, keeping ads simple, challenging readers to figure out the point of a headline like "Lemon." However, in many of the ads from this period, beneath the double-entendre headline and the intriguing photograph, way down at the base of the ad, you invariably found the anchor of logic. Why should car buyers "Think small."? Doyle Dane Bernbach clearly and persuasively articulated the answer to that by citing reasons—sometimes three or four of them—in the copy at the bottom.

Bernbach had sought to tear down the wall between art and copy in advertising and had, to a large extent, succeeded in doing that (in the post-DDB world, as writers and art directors brainstormed to try to find the "big idea" that would captivate hearts and minds, that idea could come from either party, or from both simultaneously). Nevertheless, the advertising produced by Bernbach, Ally, McCabe, and others of that period was still ruled by language and logic. With few exceptions (DDB's Helmut Krone, for example, had understood early on that design could drive the idea), a print ad's art elements—the layout, the photography, the typography—usually served to amplify or clarify the headline, while the body copy closed the sale.

All of this worked fine in the world of yesteryear, when one could reasonably assume that people might read an advertisement from beginning to end, provided it was clever enough. By the 1980s, that was beginning to seem like a quaint notion. The decade that ushered in MTV and computer games seemed to trigger a realization that perhaps the visual aspects of advertising mattered as much as—if not more than—the verbal. If, as the success of the newspaper *USA Today* suggested, people weren't willing to devote much time to reading news stories, why on earth would they spend time reading ads?

Moreover, there was a growing belief in advertising that logic might not be the best tool for persuading people anymore. Some considered this heresy, but it was catching on nonetheless. The classic way of approaching

**Nothing gets your attention like wallpaper.**

For simple ways to make your home more striking, see a local wallpaper dealer. © 1999 Wallpaper Council.

2

"I never read The Economist."

Management trainee. Aged 42.

3

The Economist

4

advertising—which had survived even Bernbach's revolution—was to find a product's point of difference, Rosser Reeves's so-called Unique Selling Proposition, and use that as the basis for making a case. Even Bernbach, who resisted Reeves's formulaic approach, still tended to build much of his advertising around the USP—by arguing, for example, that the Volkswagen was more efficient and better engineered than other cars (though Bernbach adorned the logic with wit and style, to make it more palatable).

But gradually, product parity in the marketplace—whether in the category of cars or ballpoint pens—made it increasingly difficult for an advertiser to issue a credible claim of superiority. As TBWA/Chiat/Day executive Bob Kuperman noted, "With more product parity, the differences and unique benefits became increasingly slight, and more easily copied by competitors that didn't have any of their own." So it became

necessary for advertisers to distinguish themselves by other means—one of which, Kuperman noted, was by developing a unique and powerful visual style in their ads.

Gradually, advertisers would begin to downplay persuasive copy and experiment more with innovative layout, minimalist design, unusual typography. In some cases, they would engage the audience in lively visual games and riddles that often required no words at all, and that played to emotion more than logic. In recent years, this has evolved as a modern form of communication—a visual shorthand—that can now be found posted on walls or in the pages of magazines around the world. It is expertly produced by agencies like DM9 DDB Publicidade in São Paulo, Brazil, or TBWA Hunt Lascaris, in South Africa, or Leo Burnett in Chicago. The Singapore-based advertising writer Jim Aitchison calls it "the international language of graphics." Relying on signs and

symbols, free association, and visceral reactions, it is an ideal form of communication for advertisers that are trying to cross all boundaries, and for consumers that no longer have time or patience for logical explanations.

The new visual style of print ads didn't arrive overnight. To a great extent, the 1960s sensibility in advertising lasted not only throughout the 1970s but well into the 1980s, with ads that continued to look similar to what DDB was producing earlier—the same head/photo/copy layout and the same wry sense of humor. The DDB model was so solid and so effective that advertisers were loath to meddle with it, other than to perhaps tinker with the typeface (for example, sans serif headlines gave way to Franklin Gothic in the early 1980s). Moreover, the DDB revolution had instilled in many creative people the belief that on any ad campaign, the concept reigned supreme—and that too much stylistic tinkering could undercut a great

A NEW VISUAL LANGUAGE EMERGES.

5

6

**5. ALBANY LIFE**
LOWE HOWARD SPINK,
LONDON, 1985
A classic juxtaposition with a
surprising headline; in UK print
ads, the 1960s style flourished
well into the 1980s.

**6. TIMBERLAND**
LEAGAS DELANEY,
LONDON, 1989
Early on, Tim Delaney's agency
relied on devastating headlines
like this one; gradually it moved
toward a more visual style.

**7. WINDSOR CANADIAN**
FALLON McELLIGOTT,
MINNEAPOLIS, MINNESOTA,
1990
A leader of the American regional
movement, Fallon understood
that sometimes less is more—
a strong image required
minimal copy.

idea or, worse still, might be used to mask the fact there was no idea in the ad at all. For these reasons, the now "classic" 1960s look became almost sacrosanct—and continued to yield some of the best advertising of the 1980s, even if the style was starting to seem a bit familiar. BMW's ads, created by the New York agency Ammirati & Puris, could have easily been done years earlier by DDB (except for the "It's good to be rich" 1980s mentality that pervades the campaign). Similarly, campaigns produced across the ocean by hot new 1980s British agencies like Leagas Delaney and Lowe Howard Spink, for clients like Timberland and Albany Life, bore a classic look—not that it made them any less striking. If anyone was beginning to suspect that headlines had lost their power by the 1980s, Tim Delaney could have silenced them with one of his audacious lines for Timberland; in an ad for moccasins, above a picture of a Native American, he wrote: "We stole their land, their buffalo and

their women. Then we went back for their shoes."

But even among creative purists, some quiet tinkering was happening, particularly off the beaten path in America. In cities like Minneapolis, Minnesota, and Richmond, Virginia, up-and-coming regional creative agencies like Fallon McElligott and the Martin Agency were beginning to cross the bridge from more verbal, logic-driven advertising to something more visual and emotional. The revitalization of simple print ads by these "boondock" agencies came out of necessity; if Madison Avenue of the 1980s was a place where big-budget, slickly produced, star-studded Pepsi commercials were the order of the day, Richmond and Minneapolis represented a whole different universe, where modest clients—businesses with names like Bernie's Tattooing and the 7th Street Barbershop—couldn't even dream of TV commercials but could afford to do print ads (indeed, print is the most democratic form of

advertising; even a local dog trainer can afford a print ad, particularly if he/she hires an attention-hungry agency that may create the ad for free, and might even help put up the posters).

Luckily for the barber shops and tattoo parlors in Minneapolis, Richmond, and Providence, the burgeoning ad agencies in those towns had become a haven for some of advertising's most talented craftsmen. The regional print world became advertising's equivalent of the independent-filmmaking segment of the movie business—a place where budgets and resources were limited but where original ideas were in great supply. To some ad creators, this represented the purest and most challenging form of advertising; its creators couldn't rely on celebrity endorsers or special-effect film techniques, as many commercials do. Nor could they bludgeon people with the redundancy made possible by big media budgets. They had to engage an audience that was rapidly turning

## Fortunately, every day comes with an evening.

# Whose birthday is it, anyway?

The Episcopal Church believes the important news at Christmas is not
who comes down the chimney, but who came down from heaven. We invite you to come and join
us as we celebrate the birth of Jesus Christ.
**The Episcopal Church**

9

v-neck sweater $19.99

chefmate™ waffle baker $24.99

fashion and housewares.

10

IF A TREE FALLS
IN THE FOREST AND
YOU'RE NOT THERE
TO HEAR IT, DOES IT
MAKE A SOUND?

YES, IT JUST MIGHT
TAKE 7 OR 8 YEARS.

11

**10. TARGET**
KIRSHENBAUM BOND &
PARTNERS, NEW YORK, 1996
In the late 1990s, Target stores
began to use a playful visual
approach to make the point
that it sells both fashion
and housewares.

**11. TAYLOR GUITARS**
VITRO ROBERTSON,
SAN DIEGO, CALIFORNIA,
1992
Instead of showing the product,
a fine guitar, the ad shows the
woods where the instrument's
natural material originated.

pages or walking down the street with print ads and posters that relied on the most basic elements—writing, photography, graphic design, and that most important element of all, intrigue.

The print craftsmen demonstrated that striking imagery could be the great equalizer, bringing attention to small, obscure clients. In Richmond, the Martin Agency promoted a local tattoo parlor with a poster of a man who was naked and covered with tattoos, his hands clasped over his private parts; the headline read, "Surprise your wife." It was a piece of advertising that was seen and discussed around the country. Similarly, the Minneapolis agency Fallon McElligott, while known for its clever copy, kept those words to a minimum—many ads had not much more than one line and a stirring image. For a local barbershop, the agency used an extreme close-up of Moe of the Three Stooges, with the headline "A bad haircut is no laughing matter." For the Episcopal Church, it juxtaposed

pictures of Santa Claus and Jesus Christ, and asked, "Whose birthday is it, anyway?" An ad for Purina made a point about chemical additives in dog food by simply showing a dog poised over his dish, wearing a gas mask. The agency understood, early on, that a picture could tell an entire story, as in a Windsor Canadian liquor ad showing a laborer face-to-face with a dog that had just trekked footprints across his freshly paved sidewalk; "Fortunately, every day comes with an evening" was the ad's only copy. Fallon McElligott's art directors, like the talented veteran Bob Barrie, took the view that as the media landscape grew more complex and noisy, ads should get quieter. "It only stands to reason that the simplest messages will cut through and be remembered," says Barrie. And it is the image, Barrie noted, that has the power to stop people in their tracks.

Perhaps the biggest breakthrough campaign of the 1980s, in terms of demonstrating visual

power, was the Absolut vodka campaign from the TBWA agency, based in New York. It debuted in 1980, with a picture of an Absolut bottle and a halo, headlined, "Absolut Perfection." The co-creator Geoff Hayes came up with the idea at home one evening while watching an episode of the television show *The Honeymooners,* demonstrating that the best advertising ideas aren't necessarily inspired by elaborate research, nor from gazing upon masterpieces at the museum. In one sense, the Absolut campaign was a throwback: It prominently featured the product in its bottle—not unlike the way soft-drink ads from the past once consisted of simple pictures of the bottle, or someone drinking from it. But there was an important difference: Those old-fashioned poster-style ads showing the product were doing only that, without conveying an idea. Then, after the pretty posters, came the next generation of ads that did convey ideas, but primarily through words. Now Absolut

# Perception.

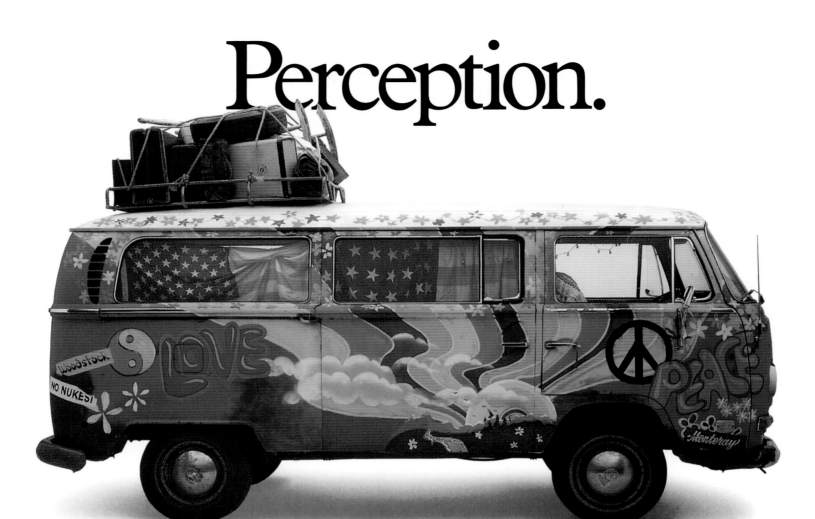

# Reality.

If you still think a Rolling Stone reader's idea of standard equipment is flowers on the door panels and incense in the ashtrays, consider this: Rolling Stone households own 5,199,000 automobiles. If you've got cars to sell, welcome to the fast lane. Source: Simmons 1984

Nothing like a delicious turkey for opening a bottle of rose wine **RENÉ BARBIER**

represented the next stage in the evolution—using the picture to convey the idea. It was also one of the first ad campaigns to create a visual riddle that invited the reader to play along. Particularly as the series evolved, often the image of the vodka bottle was not immediately discernible; one had to study the ad to find it, or to make the connection between image and headline. Absolut ads invited the audience to become part of the communication process, and readers eagerly joined in.

Another seminal campaign in developing advertising's visual language came a few years later, in the mid-1980s, from Fallon McElligott. The agency had taken on the account of *Rolling Stone* magazine, a publication dearly loved by its readers but underappreciated by advertisers—who seemed to think of those readers as pot-smoking hippies who were not apt to buy cars or expensive clothing. But in fact, *Rolling Stone* knew that its readers, particularly by the

mid-1980s, did not fit that easy stereotype; many were successful, affluent, and acquisitive. A conventional ad might have tried to explain this at great length, with demographic data and statistical charts. But the creative team on the campaign, Nancy Rice and Bill Miller, came up with an idea that put the whole argument into visual shorthand—a simple juxtaposition of the "Perception" of a *Rolling Stone* reader as compared to the "Reality." Miller jotted down the first juxtapositions on a napkin in a coffee shop; subsequently, Rice dressed them up into finished ads, but the truth is they never became much more elaborate than what Miller had put on the napkin—just white space, with the two pictures side by side. The power of the campaign lay in the images that were chosen and the way they related to each other (cigarette-rolling paper was juxtaposed with Post-it notes; Earth shoes were paired with Nike running shoes), and also in the way that his campaign, like Absolut, invited

readers to connect the dots—an interactive approach that would become a staple of print ads in years to come. (In fact, the "Perception/ Reality" campaign is undoubtedly one of the most widely imitated ad campaigns ever; more than fifteen years after it was created, and years after *Rolling Stone* stopped running it, other advertisers continued to juxtapose contrasting images to make the point their product is not what you think it is.)

The success of the Absolut and *Rolling Stone* campaigns made it abundantly clear that highly visual print ads, rooted in a strong idea, could have a resounding impact even in a world of television and other media clutter. By the 1990s, "with the expansion of electronic media, the public was growing less and less willing to submit to content, and advertisers were beginning to rely more on the power of imagery," observed the renowned art director John Doyle of the San Francisco agency Publicis/Hal Riney & Partners.

PURE JOY.
SMIRNOFF®

Printers, like all electronic equipment, keep getting cheaper and better, but Epson has set a new standard with its first inkjet color printer. The Stylus Color gives you near-photorealistic output at 720 dpi. I used to go to the local service bureau and shell out US$12 per page for Canon color copier prints. This printer is going to pay for itself in no time flat.
Stylus Color: US$699.
Epson America Inc.:
(800) 289 3776,
+1 (310) 782 0770.

Wire yourself to the WaveRider jr. – via electrodes and conductive jelly – and let your body make music. This small electronic device, in conjunction with a Mac or PC, converts your body's biosignals into musical notes, allowing you to play your heart like a drum, your brain like a piano, and your arm muscles like a trombone. You can designate notes, ranges, scales, and keys or create your own custom setups. The Pro, MAX, and MAX Pro versions of the WaveRider give you more channels and lots of extra goodies, allowing the ultra intense to write their own biosignal-to-MIDI output algorithms.
WaveRider jr.: US$750, MAX jr.: $1,250, Pro: $1,500, MAX Pro: $2,000. WaveAccess:
+1 (510) 526 5881.

A NEW VISUAL LANGUAGE EMERGES.

15. **ARMANI EXCHANGE**
WEISS WHITTEN STAGLIANO,
NEW YORK, 1990
This campaign used utilitarian
yet iconic images as stand-ins
for the product. A nut and bolt
tell us the fashion designer has
gone back to basics.

16. **EVERLAST CLOTHING**
GOLDSMITH/JEFFREY,
NEW YORK, 1993
Even a grimy sweatshirt can
be a thing of durable beauty,
particularly when photographed
dramatically and matched with
a clever headline.

## Armani. Store. Clothing. Basics. Period.

ARMANI EXCHANGE

*jeans, t-shirts, shirts, accessories, etc. $30 to $100*
*568 broadway at prince, new york city  opening in december.*

15

This is not one of those scented ads. Good thing.

16

Striking, artistic photography was increasingly central to great advertising, as demonstrated by Annie Leibovitz's stunning portraits campaign for American Express, featuring subjects like basketball giant Wilt Chamberlain standing with the diminutive jockey Willie Shoemaker. But elegant pictures alone were not the solution; the challenge facing advertising designers in the 1990s, according to Doyle, was "to find a visual execution that would tell a narrative, the way the copy once did," and thereby convey the essence of a brand through imagery.

To do that, some advertisers began to use easily recognizable symbols to convey some particular thought about a product or brand. The image appearing in the ad was not the product itself but a stand-in; the ad became a visual analogy. To promote the clothing of Giorgio Armani, the New York agency Weiss Whitten Stagliano showed not clothes but an image of a nut and bolt—to make the point

that the designer had gone "back to basics." Similarly, Gary Goldsmith, a highly regarded creative director first with his own New York agency, Goldsmith/Jeffrey, and later with Lowe & Partners, created ads that, for example, displayed a suit of armor to make a point about the lack of comfort of men's suits. To express the sense of fun involved in driving a Mercedes-Benz, Goldsmith's Lowe agency created an ad that was nothing more than a picture of a rubber duck. (No object was too mundane to become a centerpiece in a Goldsmith ad; one of his best-known ads, for Everlast, featured a tattered, sweat-stained sweatshirt, with the wonderful headline "Good thing this isn't one of those scented ads.") By focusing on and beautifying unusual objects, ad designers like Goldsmith and Marty Weiss of Weiss Whitten Stagliano could create an arresting visual that stopped readers, prompting them to ask, "What's *that* thing doing in this ad?" For those who might

also wonder, "Where is the product?," the German creative director Guido Heffels offered this response: "We're not paid to put the product in the ad, but rather in the consumer's mind."

Not surprisingly, the use of symbols and visual analogies has been embraced by international advertisers because such highly visual advertising "travels seamlessly from one culture to the next and loses nothing in translation," says Jeff Weiss, the creative director at Amster Yard, which produces advertising that runs throughout Europe as well as in America. At the Buenos Aires agency Agulla & Baccetti, creative director Sebastian Wilhelm says the preponderance of highly visual ads partly stems from the fact that "nobody likes to read long headlines, let alone body copy." But Wilhelm also notes that visual advertising coming from South America is "meant to be understood cross-culturally," which is why the ads are more apt to refer to universal images and icons, rather

A NEW VISUAL LANGUAGE EMERGES.

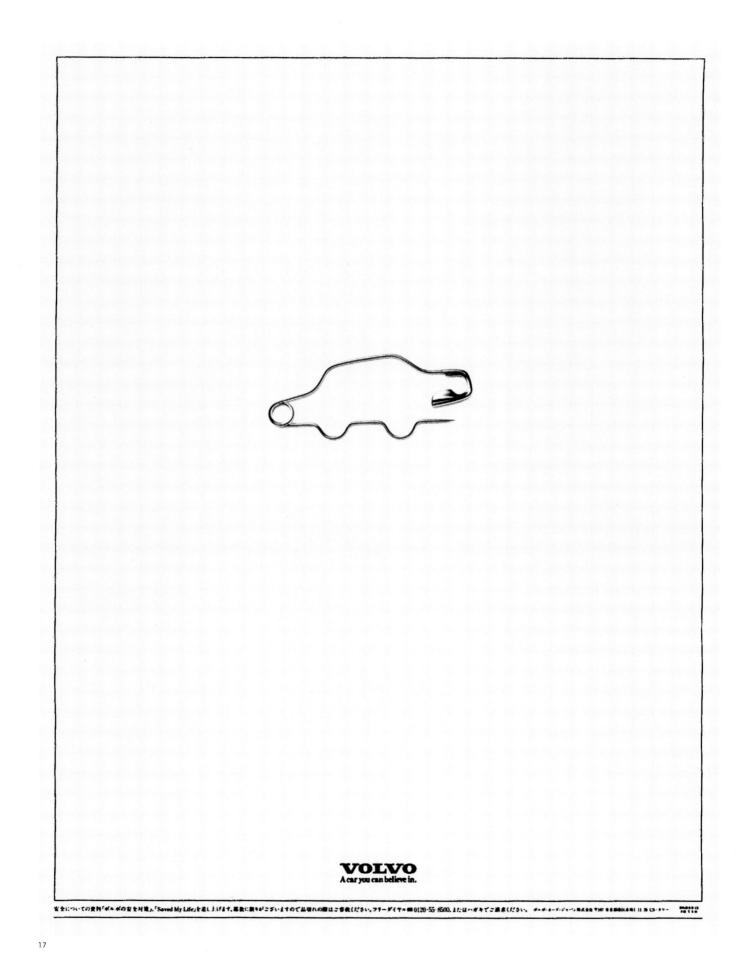

**17. VOLVO**
DENTSU YOUNG &
RUBICAM, TOKYO, 1996
Eschewing words, this ad used a
familiar everyday object to make
a point about the car's safety.
The ad was produced in Japan,
but it would work anywhere.

**18. RED CROSS**
MANDEL MUTH
WERBEAGENTUR GMBH,
FRANKFURT, 1997
In Germany, one agency used
the symbol of the Red Cross
to make a graphic appeal for
blood.

**19. GAMETEK VIDEO GAMES**
CRISPIN PORTER + BOGUSKY,
MIAMI, 1994
The "bloody windshield" ad
was a visually stunning way to
promote a video game filled
with violent car crashes
and mayhem.

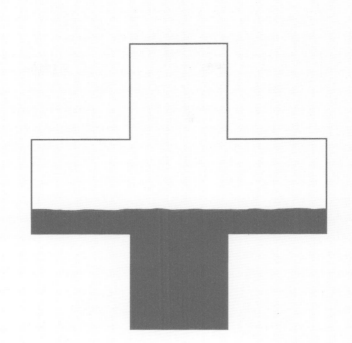

WE NEED YOUR BLOOD.
PLEASE CALL + 02-30 30 96

18

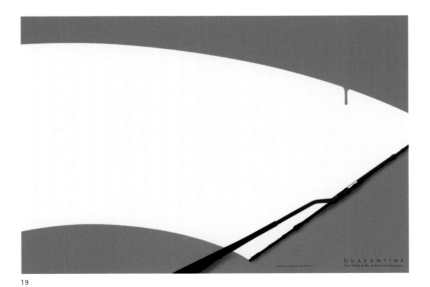

19

A NEW VISUAL LANGUAGE EMERGES.

# INTERVIEW: NIZAN GUANAES

Nizan Guanaes, a native of the Bahia region of Brazil, opened his own ad agency in 1989, and his ads quickly became the talk of São Paulo. But that was just the beginning; Guanaes soon led his agency, DM9 DDB Publicidade, to the top of the advertising world. When DM9 was named ad agency of the year at the International Advertising Festival in Cannes in 1998—and then again in 1999—it marked the first time ever that an agency outside the United States or Europe had earned this distinction. In 2000, Guanaes left advertising as dramatically as he'd entered it, starting a new career on the Internet. But he left a legacy. DM9's style—simple, visually striking, intellectually challenging—has become the hallmark of South American advertising today.

**WHY IS SOUTH AMERICAN ADVERTISING SO DRIVEN BY VISUALS?**

Part of it is that this kind of advertising has become popular in the international advertising-award shows. When you enter your work in award shows, you're being judged primarily through Anglo-Saxon eyes. And you're at a disadvantage because people won't get your local references. Most of the time, our copy is destroyed by translation. It is the visual part of our work that survives. Everyone understands advertising that has visual impact.

**WHAT ABOUT THE EFFECT OF THIS KIND OF ADVERTISING ON CONSUMERS?**

Today, consumers are in a hurry. The advertising must stop them. Painting is visual and has been stopping people throughout the centuries. Same with sculpture. So this idea of the stopping power of visuals is not new; it has been demonstrated in many other art forms. But it's new to advertising. It's a kind of a poster language, and you're seeing it around the world. It makes sense because we are more and more a visual society.

**DO CLIENTS ENCOURAGE YOU TO DO MORE OF THIS KIND OF WORK, SO THAT THEIR MESSAGES CAN BE USED GLOBALLY?**

Yes. For example, our campaign for Parmalat [featured in Chapter 11] has gone through eleven countries, including China. And we don't have to change it much, because it's so visual. But even if the campaign were running only in

Brazil, this country is like several countries in itself—you have some parts that are highly developed and urban, others that are rural. So you want the advertising to cross those boundaries, too. But you can't do visual advertising for every client. If you are advertising something that is very new, and complex, with a lot of features to explain, then it would be irresponsible to do this kind of visual work. On the other hand, if you have a product that people already know, and maybe you have just one point to make . . . then it's powerful.

**SOME OF THESE VISUAL PUZZLES CAN BE SUBTLE— FOR EXAMPLE, YOUR AD FEATURING THE BENT NAIL FOR THE BOTERO EXHIBIT. DO YOU EVER WORRY THAT THE AUDIENCE WON'T GET IT?**

Sure, sometimes people don't. But it's important to make the puzzle challenging so that people will become more involved. You make the consumer's intelligence the password to the ad. And the more you do these kinds of ads, the more you are able to figure out what people will get and what they will miss. I also show the ads to the people around me; if they can't figure out what's going on, I move to another idea. The secretaries in the office must respond to the advertising. If it's going to have an impact, it must do so first with them.

**IS ADVERTISING BECOMING MORE OF A UNIVERSAL LANGUAGE?**

Yes and no. The danger of producing ads for the international community is that you can lose touch with your own culture. I think it's important that some of our ads not be universally understood—some should be made only for our people. I don't think all advertising should become a kind of international currency. But often the international language is appropriate. If I'm selling jeans, no one wants Brazilian jeans—everyone wants American jeans. They want a German beer. A French perfume. So if you're advertising these things, you should be influenced by the culture that the product comes from. And in other cases, the advertising should be about the local culture. When I travel through countries I love to watch their advertising, because you understand so much about a society from the ads.

**WHAT IS THE PUBLIC ATTITUDE TOWARD ADVERTISING IN BRAZIL THESE DAYS?**

People love it. You find them talking about it, and even singing jingles, in bars. Brazilian advertising is funny, fresh, and light. It's related to the spirit of our people—this is a very musical, sexy, easygoing country. So you cannot have dull, serious advertising.

But at the same time, I believe this is not art—people don't meditate on advertising. Do you know anyone who runs home in the evening to watch the ads? I believe advertising is mostly irrelevant to people—and that's why I take it seriously. Because once you understand how irrelevant our work is to people, then you realize that you must work very hard—using emotion, intelligence, humor—to somehow change that and make it relevant to them.

**WHO WERE YOUR CREATIVE INFLUENCES?**

First of all, Bill Bernbach. There's a lot of visual power in the DDB work for Volkswagen. Ogilvy was another guy who influenced all of us. And then you have the new-generation people like Wieden & Kennedy and Goodby Silverstein. I used to tell people at the agency, "You must remember what Bernbach and Ogilvy said, but you must also forget it—because we live in a new world."

Generally, though, I try not to think like an advertising person, because if you do that, you start to pay attention to things people don't care about. To have an impact on people, you must think like them. And I believe the most important thing for an advertising person is to win the "birthday-party survey." Someone at a party asks what you do, and you tell them you're in advertising, and then you mention five or six ad campaigns you've done. If the person doesn't know any of these campaigns, you're screwed. It doesn't matter what the judges in Cannes say—if you lose the birthday-party survey, you're dead.

Folha de S. Paulo Newspaper. Illustrating life with words for 77 years.

20. **FOLHA DE SÃO PAULO**
DM9 DDB PUBLICIDADE,
SÃO PAULO, 1998
This series of ads for a Brazilian
newspaper used newsprint
type to recreate famous images,
including this memorable
photograph of an execution
in Vietnam.

A NEW VISUAL LANGUAGE EMERGES.

(Be careful with the Kaminomoto)

21

**21. KAMINOMOTO HAIR GROWTH,**
THE BALL PARTNERSHIP, SINGAPORE, MID-1980s
A before-and-after demonstration of a hair-growth product with a playful twist. The series also featured an ad that showed hair sprouting on a cue ball.

**22. TRIUMPH LINGERIE**
WIRZ WERBEBERATUNG AG, ZURICH, 1996
The ad becomes a game: by turning the page upside down, the reader sees a visual metaphor of the product's benefit.

**23. STREN FISHING LINE**
CARMICHAEL LYNCH, MINNEAPOLIS, MINNESOTA, 1995
Instead of proclaiming the fishing line as strong, the campaign showed off its strength—with a bit of playful exaggeration.

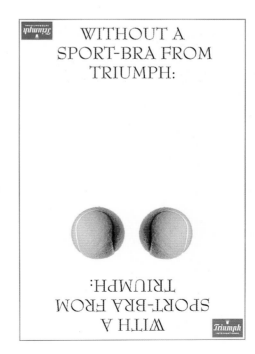

22

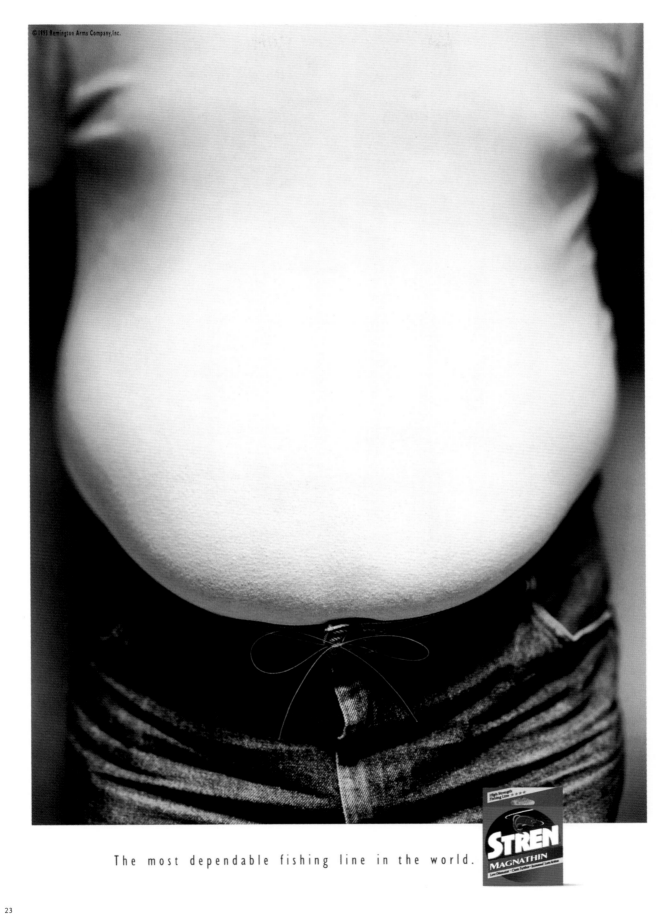

© 1995 Remington Arms Company, Inc.

The most dependable fishing line in the world.

23

A NEW VISUAL LANGUAGE EMERGES.

Botero
at the São Paulo
Museum of Art.
From March 17 to May 17.

24

than to their own local culture. (To some extent, Wilhelm acknowledges, universal ads are also designed to win international advertising awards as much as to influence consumers.)

Whatever the motives behind this style, it is becoming clear that ad agencies in Asia, Australia, South Africa, and particularly South America have proved highly adept at constructing visual riddles, which might also be called "picture plays"—a new version of an old advertising tool, the word play. For example, to make the point that H&R Block accountants are thorough, the company's Australian agency wove its copy into the shape of a comb. Japan's Dentsu Young & Rubicam featured an image of a safety pin, with no words, in its advertising for Volvo. A South African ad for the deaf showed a picture of a telephone handset receiver—upon closer inspection, one notices that the earpiece has no holes in it. Singapore's Ball Partnership agency used a baguette, cut

into pieces, to draw a comparison to airline flights that are interrupted by too many stops. Even a mundane product like Preparation H lends itself to this lively and playful approach: Bates Hong Kong created a suggestive series of visual analogies that captured the feeling of hemorrhoids by showing an image of a bicycle whose seat is a saw blade. On a similar note, a laxative advertiser in Uruguay used a corkscrew to make the key point about its product.

While visual-analogy ads can sometimes be obvious and unimaginative (certain symbolic objects, such as razor blades and magnets, have already been overused), the best practitioners of this style of advertising, such as the Brazilian agency DM9 DDB, which was brought to international prominence by its former creative director Nizan Guanaes, have tended to challenge the audience with the subtlety and sophistication of the picture-plays. Consider, for example, one of the agency's ads for the São Paulo Museum of

Art's Botero exhibit: The ad shows a bent nail on a wall, surrounded by broken plaster. It's left to the reader to figure out that the nail couldn't support the heft of Botero's paintings, which feature chubby figures as their subjects. Similarly interactive is a Swiss lingerie ad showing a stark image of two tennis balls, and inviting the reader to play a game that requires turning the ad upside down. And another lingerie ad, this one from the Johannesburg agency TBWA Hunt Lascaris, promoted the enlarging effects of a Wonderbra by showing a pair of sunburned feet—with only the tips of the toes reddened.

While American ads don't go in for picture-plays quite as much, the most popular campaigns in recent years have been minimalist—stripped down to a single striking image and few, if any, words. The "Think different" campaign for Apple, the relaunch of the Volkswagen Beetle, and the "Curiously Strong" series for Altoids breath mints represent three of the most

BE PREPARED **PREPARATION H**® HEMORRHOIDAL *OINTMENT*

25

PAUL INCE WEARS
PREDATOR TRAXION.
KEEP OUT.

26

**26. ADIDAS**
LEAGAS DELANEY, LONDON,
1998
By the late 1990s, Delaney had
taken a more visual route,
turning images of agile soccer
players into barbed wire.

**27. SIMS SNOWBOARDS**
HAMMERQUIST & HALVERSON,
SEATTLE, WASHINGTON, 1997
The ad evokes a famous image
from the 1989 Tiananmen Square
uprising in China—but this
time, it's a lone snowboarder
defying oncoming snow plows.

**28. NIKE**
KESSELSKRAMER,
AMSTERDAM, 1996
Another example of advertising's
new visual language, this Dutch
ad is a reminder that fancy
sports equipment is not
necessary for all athletes
(but shoes are a must).

In a courageous act of solidarity, a lone snowboarder stands up for freedom. Story on 2C.

Sims Snowboards

27

28

A NEW VISUAL LANGUAGE EMERGES.

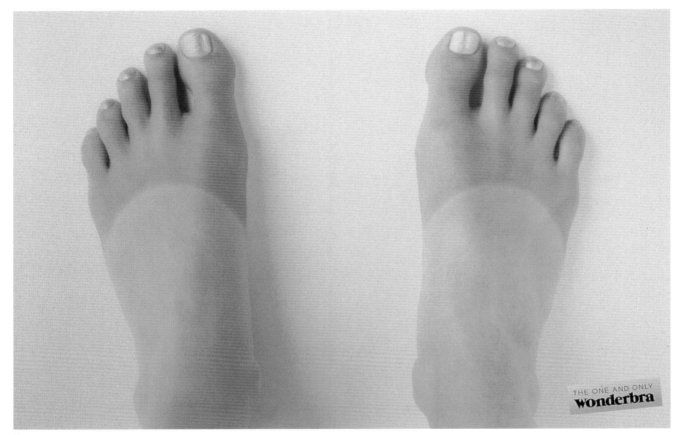

29

29. **WONDERBRA**
TBWA HUNT LASCARIS,
JOHANNESBURG, 1998
The "sunburned feet" ad
promoting the powers of
Wonderbra is another playful
visual puzzle; South Africa
has taken a shine to such ads
because they cross cultural
barriers easily.

30. **MCDONALDS**
PALMER JARVIS DDB,
VANCOUVER, 1997
This Canadian campaign used
the visual power of the company's
"Golden Arches" symbol in new
and surprising ways.

"He's extraordinarily engaging," says **Rob B...** Judge Alex Kozinski ("Wise Guy," page 17...) keeps trying to get my e-mail address to con... his on-line gag line." While Kozinski's intel... charm may lead him to a seat on the Supr... Boynton feels that for the moment, the judge... where he belongs. "Right now, he has the be... the world," says Boynton, "and he only has t... spotlight with two other judges." Boynton... for *The New Yorker* and the *Atlantic Monthly*...

**Elizabeth Kaye** believes the often... Watergate women ("All the President's Wo... 206) were virtual mirrors of what was in m... country. "Their faces, filled with termin... ble disappointment," she says, "were a... where we were all headed, for what Water... do to us all." Kaye is a contributing editor... and the author of *Mid-life: Notes From th...* *Mark* (Addison-Wesley).

Since one of the first movies photographer **Nic...** ever saw was *Taxi Driver,* working with Rob... (cover) was a bit daunting. "He's such a dedic... says Knight, "that it's nerve-racking to perfo... of him." Knight, who works regularly for both... *British Vogue,* was impressed if not shocked b... concentration and energy. "He really worked... shoot," he says, "although I would have been... he'd just turned up and socialized."

"He definitely has his father's charisma and... al power," says **Stephen Rodrick** of Jes... Jr. ("Son of a Preacher Man," page 176), "b... hard translating fame and celebrity in... Rodrick, a senior editor at *Boston,* still be... Jesse the Younger has a promising politi... ahead of him. "Although some people feel... paid his dues yet," he says, "I think he'll... have an influential role in Democratic politi...

"You'd be hard-pressed to insult either a politi... dealer," says **Michael Lewis,** who studied... have the dubious honor of having both of the m... ligned careers imaginable ("Wheeler Dealers... "They can turn almost anything into a com... Lewis, the author of *Liar's Poker* (W.W. No... senior editor at the *New Republic,* understand... siliency. "Perhaps it's because they spend their... rejection," he says, "it's like the construction w... stand on the street and ask women to sleep... They feel that eventually someone will have to...

©T&CO. 1995

# TIFFANY & CO.

If you think watching a volcano
in a movie is frightening, imagine
watching one in a rearview mirror.

**The world's most interesting magazine.**

33

32

successful American print campaigns of the 1990s, and all speak the new succinct language of visual advertising. Meanwhile, the smaller campaigns from the regional agencies have continued to rely on imagery: The best ones have included a wordless series from Minneapolis's Carmichael Lynch for Stren fishing line, in which we see the product tested in memorable ways; an ad from the Seattle, Washington, agency Hammerquist Saffel & Halverson for Sims snowboards, which captures the rebel spirit of the product by evoking the 1989 Tiananmen Square uprising in China with an image of a snowboarder defiantly standing in the path of snowplows; and a long-running Fallon McElligott series for *Time* magazine, which uses a simple red box, strategically placed in certain photos, to make a point about the magazine's ability to cut to the essence of news events.

If any countries have been resistant to the visual movement, they are probably Germany

and the UK, where copy-driven advertising is still popular. "Germans are analytical and like information from their advertising," explains Guido Heffels—though some of the country's cutting-edge creative agencies are bucking that trend. The UK, meanwhile, has always had a fondness for clever and witty copywriting— but even so, there's a growing recognition by top creative directors like John Hegarty, of Bartle Bogle Hegarty, that such a strategy may have to change now, with the growing emphasis on global communication. Hegarty says the language-driven advertising "obviously becomes a problem if you're going to talk to lots of people in different countries. Consequently, we now have to think of advertising as being more driven by the image. This doesn't mean you can't use words—only that you have to think about the words you're using in a different way. You have to think about reducing your ideas down, so that even people who don't understand

the particular language can capture an essence of what the idea is about." Hegarty has practiced what he preaches in his own advertising for Boddingtons Cream Ale—in which the creamy quality of the beer is conveyed by, for example, visualizing ice cream cones made of beer (this campaign is featured in Chapter 11). Another recent acclaimed British ad featured nothing more than a picture of a parked Mercedes-Benz with skid marks in the street alongside the car, suggesting the car's effect on passersby.

While such ads can be baffling, the audience for today's advertising seems to relish the challenge of figuring out what's the product, what's being said, and where's the punchline. "Younger people tend to read this visual shorthand faster, because they're used to looking at a barrage of images," says Myrna Davis of the Art Directors Club of New York. "We've shown some of these ads to older art directors, and they shake their heads. But younger people look at it,

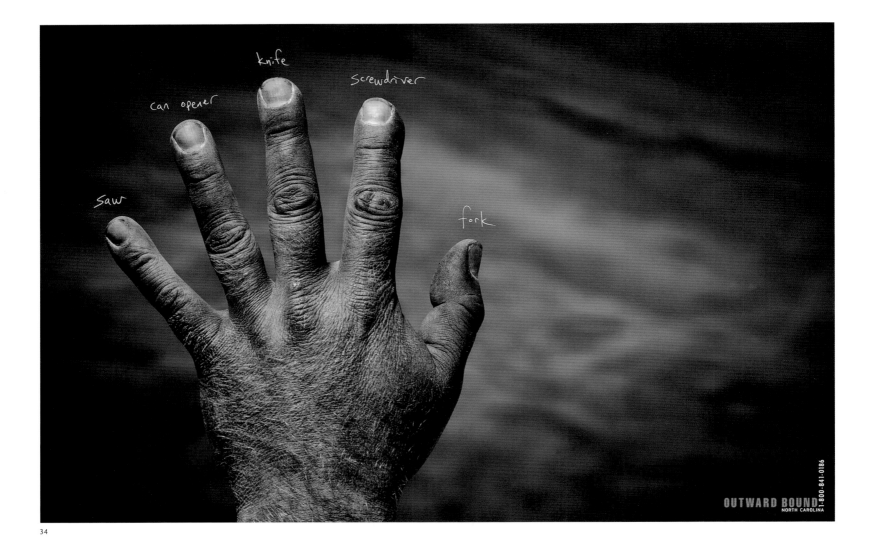

34

There is no noise.
No pistons.
No valves or exhaust.

Just the whir of an AC motor.
And the wind.
And your thoughts, of course.

As you drive the electric car.

EV1. From General Motors.

1.800.25ELECTRIC http://www.gmev.com

35

**34. OUTWARD BOUND**
LOEFFLER KETCHUM
MOUNTJOY, CHARLOTTE,
NORTH CAROLINA, 1997
To promote this wilderness
survival program, ads used
simple imagery to show how a
few days in the woods can change
the way you look at things.

**35. GENERAL MOTORS EV-1**
HAL RINEY & PARTNERS,
SAN FRANCISCO, 1996
A series of ads for the EV-1
electric car conveyed the
picture of serenity, making the
clean, quiet car seem at one
with nature.

36

and say right away, 'Oh, yes, I get it.'" To this segment of the audience, Davis says, "a lot of the information that used to seem essential in ads now just seems too literal and unnecessary."

Is there no place left, then, for the wordsmith in advertising? In fact there is and no doubt will be in the future. As ad historians note, every time someone pronounces ad copy dead, it makes a comeback; advertising loves to contradict itself. However, the ad writers of today are not so much persuaders and closers as they are storytellers; their writing strives to evoke emotion in the same way that powerful imagery does. Resorts to logic are minimized, in favor of reciting from-the-heart poetry for Nike, or spinning yarns about the people who work in the factories for Dr. Martens shoes. And even these ads are becoming rarities in the new landscape.

There are those within the business who worry about the diminishing role of copy in advertising and blame it on short attention spans and MTV. But the trend can also be viewed as a step forward for advertising— a movement away from overexplaining, from the salesman's tendency to talk endlessly about product features and benefits that are not all that special or different from those of the competition. It has been a struggle for advertising's creators to distill and edit down their communications; the client almost always wants to say more, not less. As BBH's Hegarty points out, "Most advertising tries to say too much and ends up doing less. Writing less and saying more requires confidence and courage." If that's so, the new visual language is not only bolder but braver.

At the same time, it provides a fascinating shorthand for what is happening in the culture at any given moment. You could read a long-winded essay about the violence in today's video games—but all you need to see is the American agency Crispin Porter + Bogusky's "bloody windshield" ad to get the point. You could listen to endless pontification on the baby boomers' desperate attempts to cling to their youth—or just look at that Mercedes "rubber duck" ad. Moreover, these ad signposts don't just tell us about our own particular culture; as Amster Yard's Weiss observes, this new strain of advertising acknowledges that people around the world share certain ideas, values, and interests— something that "old" advertising never believed. "Advertising used to try to identify differences in cultures, and then create ads for each group based on those differences," Weiss says. "Now advertising tends to look for the likenesses in cultures—and then communicates those ideas visually." Perhaps the best thing about the new visual language of advertising, however, is that it invites us to solve the puzzle and take part in the process of advertising—leaving room, as Gossage said, for the mouse.

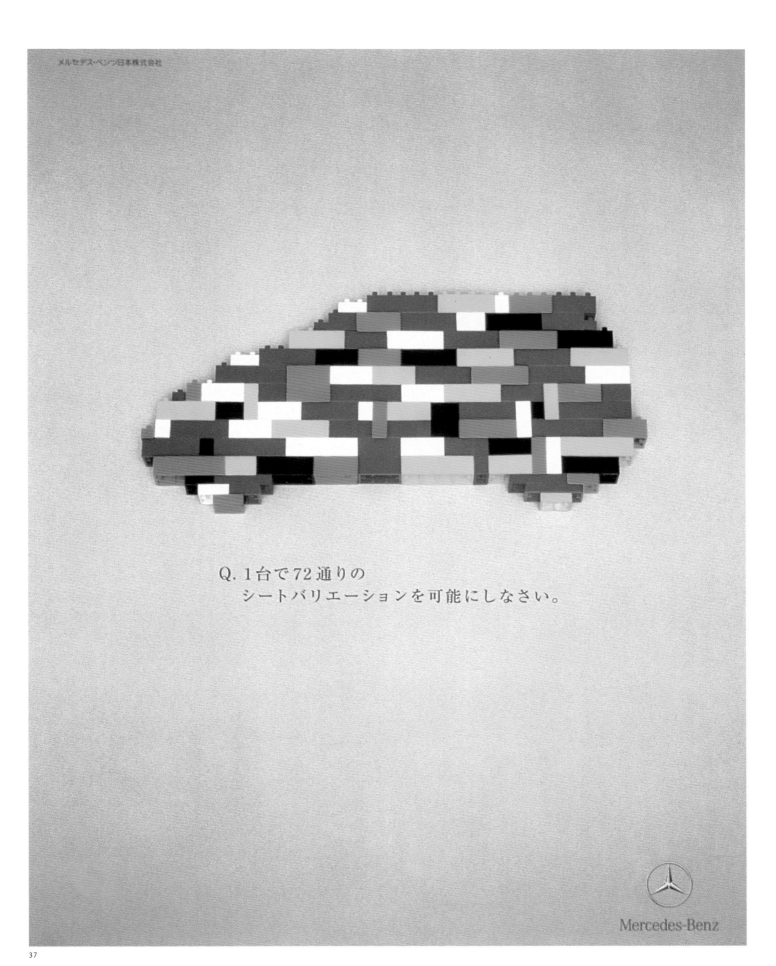

# 4. THE CI
# NEW W
# COMME

NEMATIC
AVE OF
RCIALS.

1

2

T he power of a great print ad often lies in its simplicity: one central idea, elegantly or cleverly expressed. It is advertising in its purest form, and it can be highly effective. But it is not a story.

It was in the medium of television that advertisers were able to take the message and add movement, layers, characters, and stories that came to life in a minute or less. Gradually, the best commercials seemed to transcend television, becoming more cinematic in style and scope. Unlike so many episodic TV shows, a commercial could tell a complete tale, with a point to it. At the same time, a commercial's characters, seen only in brief glimpses, might have a certain mystery about them (what exactly *was* the relationship between those two slackers who put that smelly old chair in the back of their Volkswagen?), which could help to make them more memorable than those legions of cookie-cutter sitcom characters who come and

go each television season. As for style, a high-quality commercial's elaborate sets, innovative camerawork, and at times stupefying special effects tend to have much more in common with film than with television.

It wasn't always so. Commercials in their early days could be charming but were the most rudimentary type of TV fare: In many cases, advertisers were simply presenting on-camera testimonials and demonstrations (the demos, in rare instances, could be dramatic, as in Timex's "Takes a licking and keeps on ticking" campaign, which shot live footage of stunts such as cliff diving), or dancing cartoon characters. Commercials were often shot live, with little or nothing added in the way of production values. With no real story or film style, the early commercials were essentially just print ads brought to TV, often shot by industrial-film directors and TV-show cameramen.

But that began to change during the Creative

Revolution of the 1960s. As agency copywriters and art directors began coming up with richer, more complex concepts that evolved beyond conventional sales pitches, testimonials, and demonstrations, they saw the need to bring the ideas alive, visually, in commercials. That would require talented commercial directors, and the first wave of them included a number of still photographers, led by Howard Zieff. They were visual stylists who "began to bring the beautiful, lush look of print ads to commercials," noted the longtime *Advertising Age* journalist Anthony Vagnoni, a student of the commercial-production world. Vagnoni notes that these photo artists also had a great eye for casting characters; rather than using models or celebrities, they brought to the screen talented actors and quirky faces, such as the owlish Jack Gilford, who became the star of Cracker Jack commercials. Moreover, what quickly became apparent was that this new generation of commercial directors had a latent

3

talent they'd never been able to fully use in their photographic work—they could tell rich, moving stories on film.

Zieff was, in many ways, the trailblazer. "He basically invented the modern comic commercial, with its emphasis on character development and comic timing," says Vagnoni. Doyle Dane Bernback veteran Roy Grace also notes that "at a time when everyone in commercials looked like Tab Hunter or Doris Day, Zieff looked for more real-seeming actors, who were often ethnic." Two of his best-remembered ads from the 1960s are now considered classics of advertising: Alka-Seltzer's "Spicy Meatball" and Volkswagen's "Funeral." The former was remarkably sophisticated for its time. The scenario featured a commercial-within-a-commercial (a self-referential style of humor that wouldn't be widely popular in ads until twenty years later), in which an actor is shown having to eat the same food

and recite the same line, take after take, until he gradually begins to fall ill. Even more impressive was Zieff's "Funeral" spot, which follows the members of a funeral procession; the commercial's voice-over is the reading of a will, which reveals that the deceased has left his greedy relatives and business partner precisely what they deserve—and bequeathed his entire fortune to a levelheaded nephew who drives a Bug. In one minute, a complete story unfolds, with a moral, villains, and heroes (not just the nephew but the little car, too, of course).

If Zieff invented the modern character-based commercial, Joe Sedelmaier took it to the next level. An art director who had kicked around American ad agencies for years, Sedelmaier had begun directing short films on the side and earned modest recognition at film festivals. Eventually, he brought his directorial talents to commercials, and immediately began to put a

unique stamp on all of his work. It almost didn't matter what product was being sold—hamburgers, airline tickets, business-to-business delivery services—Sedelmaier found a way to incorporate the pitch into a surreal, zany world of slapstick performances by nonactors with sad-eyed, hangdog expressions on their faces. Camera angles were skewed for a slightly off-kilter effect, and dialogue was sometimes uttered with a complete lack of conviction or polish, which only served to make the lines funnier. "Most of my stuff wouldn't be funny on the page," Sedelmaier acknowledged; indeed, in his commercials, the magic was not so much in what a character said but *how* it was said. In the famous commercial for the Wendy's hamburger chain, shot by Sedelmaier, all the actress Clara Peller had to say was "Where's the beef?"—and the audience couldn't help laughing.

4

Some accused Sedelmaier of creating the advertising equivalent of a freak show, populated by bizarre and hapless characters. But there was a method in the madness: "There is no time to build character in a commercial," the director told *Adweek*, "so you have to find characters." He looked for those characters in unexpected places: Peller, for example, was a retired manicurist who never would have survived a typical casting call given her grating voice and soggy enunciation. Another of Sedelmaier's most famous characters, the "fast-talking man" for Federal Express, John Moschitta, had been spotted performing on the TV show "That's Incredible." The agency behind the campaign, Ally & Gargano, came up with the idea of connecting Moschitta's weird talent to the speed of Federal Express deliveries, and the well-scripted ads by copywriter Patrick Kelly deftly satirized business-world jargon. (Typical

rapid-fire banter from the fast-talking man: "In conclusion, Jim, Bill, Bob, Carl, Frank, Luke, Dork, Ed, and Ted, business is business and in order to get something done you have to do something and in order to do something you have to get to work so let's get to work.") But what lives on in the mind's eye is the droopy-eyed, slouching Moschitta sitting stiffly at his desk, phone jammed against his face, with Sedelmaier's unforgiving camera zooming in from above.

Sedelmaier also had an important effect on advertising because of the power he wielded on the sets of commercial productions. After shooting ads for J. Walter Thompson early on, he broke away from the agency, set up his own production company, and started calling the shots himself—exercising complete control over casting, often re-writing the scripts of ads sent to him by agencies. In doing so, he began to usher

in the age of the director as the swaggering hired gun, and the new star of advertising.

By the 1980s, other directors were beginning to cast a large shadow in the ad world. Advertisers had witnessed the full power of the big, emotional storytelling commercial with 1979's famous "Mean Joe Greene" Coca-Cola spot, directed by Lee Lacy, in which a young fan discovers the softer side of a ferocious American professional football player. Hungry for more of these mini-epics, the big brands turned to directors like Steve Horn, known for shooting lush, sweeping vignettes (*Esquire* magazine dubbed him "The Thirty Second David Lean") for Coca-Cola, AT&T, and Kodak. Meanwhile, Pepsi emerged as a company that particularly believed in blockbuster movie-style commercials, shot by directors like Rick Levine and Bob Giraldi. It was Giraldi who would produce for Pepsi one of the decade's most lavish, expensive commercials to

5

date—a singing, dancing Michael Jackson extravaganza that borrowed its style from a Giraldi music video done previously for Jackson.

While the Hollywood-style blockbuster commercial was taking center stage in America, an art-film style of commercial-making was emerging in Great Britain, led by a group of cinematic auteurs like Ridley Scott (best known at the time for directing the 1982 film *Blade Runner*), his brother Tony Scott, Alan Parker, Adrian Lyne, and Hugh Hudson. A number of these directors cut their teeth producing commercials in the basement of the renowned British ad agency Collett Dickenson Pearce, where they developed a different sensibility from that seen in American commercials; British ads could be darker, moodier, more experimental. They were being made by directors who had one foot in the film world. While Americans like Sedelmaier, Horn, and Levine were dedicated

full-time to commercials, the British directors easily traversed the boundaries between movies and ads. In the UK, it seemed, there was no stigma attached to shooting ads, as there was still in the U.S. at that time—perhaps because by the 1980s, commercials in England were generally considered wittier and more stylish than most American advertising, and had earned the respect of the public and the film community. The same would eventually happen in America, with Hollywood embracing ad directors—but not until later, in the 1990s. And the Brits, interest-ingly enough, would play a significant role in making commercials respectable in Hollywood.

Ridley Scott, in particular, became a pivotal figure in this phenomenon. Scott had first made his mark in British commercials with his stylish work for Benson & Hedges cigarettes. Gradually, his commercials began having an impact in other countries, too: One of his most famous

was a 1979 commercial titled "Share the Fantasy," for Chanel N° 5 perfume. The spot was awash in atmospheric mystery: As a woman sat poolside, a man appeared at the far end and began to swim toward her, while a voice-over purred, "I am made of blue sky and golden light, and I will feel this way forever." The ambiguity of the commercial (was the man real?) seemed to work in its favor, if you didn't find it too pretentious. American commercial producers took notice, and before long Scott and other British directors were being brought over to inject art-film style into American ads.

One of Scott's most important new clients in America was an upstart computer company named Apple. The company's co-founder Steve Jobs and its stellar Los Angeles ad agency, Chiat/ Day, sensed that a seminal moment had arrived in America. The computer revolution was beginning to take hold, and Apple was ready to

6

THE CINEMATIC NEW WAVE OF COMMERCIALS.

7

7. **BARTLES & JAYMES**
HAL RINEY & PARTNERS,
SAN FRANCISCO, 1985
Director Joe Pytka introduced
two deadpan characters named
Frank and Ed to promote these
wine cooler drinks in the U.S. in
the mid-1980s.

8. **HBO NETWORK**
BBDO, NEW YORK, 1996
In this Emmy Award-winning Joe
Pytka commercial, famous lines
from movies (as in "I'm mad as
hell and I'm not going to take
it anymore!" from *Network*)
sprang from the mouths of
animals like this chimpanzee.

stake its own claim with an important new product, the Macintosh. At the same time, the advertising world was stirring from the creative dormancy of the late 1970s, with Chiat/Day proclaiming itself the pirate leader of the new creative movement in the 1980s. And the final ingredient in this combustible mix was Scott, an audacious filmmaker who saw no reason that an American commercial couldn't aspire to cinematic art. From all of this would emerge a commercial that ran just one time nationally—but would change advertising forever.

Viewers of pro-football's Super Bowl in January 1984, by now used to dramatic albeit coherent and generally upbeat commercials, had to be taken aback by what appeared onscreen midway through the game. The commercial opened on a futuristic, dreary scene, reminiscent of Scott's *Blade Runner,* but it quickly became apparent that it was referencing George Orwell's novel *1984:* It showed an auditorium full of expressionless people with shaved heads mesmerized by a giant TV screen image of a Big Brother character ranting about "pure ideology" and "unification of thought." Gradually, a heroine appeared, toting a sledgehammer and running from masked authority figures; she eventually burst into the auditorium and hurled the hammer at the screen, smashing the image of Big Brother. The spot closed with the line "On January 24th, Apple Computer will introduce Macintosh and you'll see why 1984 won't be like *1984.*"

The commercial was as much of an advertising breakthrough as Volkswagen's "Think small." had been twenty years earlier, though in different ways. If Bernbach's campaign had been a triumph of logic, wit, and subtlety, "1984" relied on emotion, abstractness, and over-the-top theatricality. VW advertising always left the audience with a smile, but here was a commercial that was mysterious (was Big Brother intended to represent IBM? If so, what nerve!), dark and gritty in tone. And yet it worked, driving $4.5 million in sales within six hours. Meanwhile, the commercial was like an adrenaline rush for advertising's creative community: In effect, the creators of the spot, Chiat/Day's Lee Clow, Steve Hayden, Brent Thomas, and Jay Chiat, were the hammer-throwers shaking up the advertising establishment. And, like the hunted character in the spot, they found themselves in peril: The client, nervous about the spot beforehand, never gave approval, but the agency and Scott completed it anyway. There were calls to fire Chiat/Day, and even a last-minute attempt by Apple to pull the plug on the spot just prior to the game. It ran only because Apple was unable to sell off the Super Bowl airtime it had purchased. The artfulness of the ad, and the sense of intrigue and legend surrounding it, all helped to fuel the cult of creativity that blossomed in advertising in the

late 1980s, as young artists flocked to the offices of Chiat and other creative agencies.

The commercial had a couple of other important aftereffects: It established the Super Bowl as the premiere showcase of advertising in the United States. And it made it clear that a commercial, like a popular film, could become a national cultural event. But to create such an event, it was generally agreed, you needed not just a big idea but a big-time director like Scott. Ridley, much in demand after "1984," could do only so much ad work, however, particularly since he was pursuing a film career. By the late 1980s, a new generation of cinematic stylists and storytellers began to fill the vacuum and create the mini-movies that would often debut on a certain Sunday in January, between the punts and passes.

Leading the pack was Joe Pytka, who gradually supplanted Scott as the director that every advertiser wanted to hire. If Scott was advertising's auteur, Pytka, a native of Pittsburgh,

Pennsylvania, became the ad world's Spielberg, blending stylistic film vision with a common touch. There was nothing, it seemed, he couldn't do. He shot lush, warm-and-fuzzy vineyard landscapes for Gallo wine, but for the same client he produced a hilarious bit of banter between a couple of deadpan characters named Bartles and Jaymes. (On all of these spots, Pytka worked for the West Coast adman Hal Riney—one of the ad-agency pioneers in the advancement of richly cinematic commercials.) Pytka could evoke an ethereal world of streams and frolicking French schoolchildren for Perrier, or he could present cold, hard-edged slice-of-life scenes for the John Hancock insurance company. He was a master storyteller, as evidenced by the 1985 Pepsi spot "Archaeology"; in it, an archaeologist of the future embarks on a dig and uncovers a relic—which, it gradually becomes clear, is a Coke bottle. But Pytka could also do song-and-dance bits, built around musical stars like Ray Charles

(the famous "Uh-huh" commercials for Pepsi) or celebrity athletes like Bo Jackson, whom he immortalized in the frenetic commercial "Bo Knows." Lacking a star, Pytka could succeed with chimpanzees; a memorable HBO ad featured apes mouthing famous lines from movies, such as "I'm mad as hell and I'm not going to take it anymore," from the 1976 film *Network*. And if you couldn't afford a trained animal, Pytka could make an interesting ad out of an egg frying in a pan: he did just that in the memorable public-service commercial that declared, "This is your brain on drugs. Any questions?". All of this made him an advertiser's dream, though he was also, quite often, an agency or client's worst nightmare: Continuing in the Sedelmaier tradition, Pytka demanded complete control over his commercials, and—as an intimidating man who was a muscular six-foot-six with a shock of wild hair—he was known to frighten clients or agency creatives who tried to interfere too much.

10

**9. (PREVIOUS SPREAD)**
**APPLE COMPUTER**
CHIAT/DAY, LOS ANGELES,
1984
A scene from "1984," the land-
mark commercial directed by
Ridley Scott. Was the "Big
Brother" figure on the screen
supposed to represent IBM?

**10. LEVI STRAUSS**
FOOTE CONE & BELDING,
SAN FRANCISCO, 1984
The South African director
Leslie Dektor brought a new
authentic "street" look to
commercials in the mid-1980s,
with his handheld "shaky-
cam" style.

**11. LEVI STRAUSS**
FOOTE CONE & BELDING,
SAN FRANCISCO, 1995
Director Michael Bay, who
would later shoot Hollywood
films such as *Armageddon*,
created this mini-drama,
"Elevator Fantasy," in which
two strangers on an elevator
imagine going through
life together.

("I use fear and intimidation," said Pytka of his approach to dealing with clients. "It works for the Catholic Church, and it works for me.")

While Pytka ruled the roost in America, around the world top directors began to emerge in somewhat unlikely places. South Africa had developed a thriving ad culture by the late 1980s, and several directors there made their mark locally and then set sail for America—though none had a bigger impact than Leslie Dektor. A South African documentary filmmaker, Dektor can be thanked (or cursed) for popularizing the cinema-verité technique in commercials that came to be known as "shakycam." Dektor made the style popular with his mid-1980s commercials for Levi's 501 jeans, in which the camera jerked roughly from one character to another, yielding images that were blurry and off-center. The commercials, which featured blues singers and street scenes, were unscripted; Dektor would ask actors to improvise, and, as *Adweek* magazine

noted, he relied on nonintrusive film techniques, such as long-lensed cameras.

This kind of highly stylized advertising was a further evolution of what Scott had begun with the gritty "1984"—but while that commercial had a surreal sensibility, Dektor's advertising strove for absolute realism. The anti-slick quality of his ads was intended to make the commercials seem more spontaneous, more authentic. This style was catching on elsewhere on America's West Coast in the early-to-mid-1980s. The upstart San Francisco agency Goodby Berlin & Silverstein produced a groundbreaking, hilarious documentary-style commercial for the local Mill Valley Film Festival, in which the town's butchers, mechanics, and sanitation workers are shown matter-of-factly exchanging opinions about Godard, Wim Wenders, and the merits of the film-noir genre. (The commercial was a precursor to the artificial-reality "mockumentary" style ads for the sports cable channel ESPN and

others that would become one of the hottest advertising trends of the 1990s.)

These new-look commercials of the mid-1980s—fast-moving, jittery, and rough around the edges—were also partly an outgrowth of MTV, whose jump-cut visual style was highly influential. Hot music-video directors like David Fincher and Dominic Sena soon were much in demand among advertisers. However, not everyone approved of the shakycam and jump-cut ads, which could make you dizzy with their frenetic motion. "I watch them and I feel like I'm in a nuthouse or something," Sedelmaier commented. "It's like the guy running the camera is on something."

While the South African Dektor was busy shaking things up, the India-born director Tarsem Singh was turning commercials into smooth, silent fantasies. Tarsem had been influenced by the visual extravagance, vibrant colors, and spiritualism of Hindi films, as well

11

THE CINEMATIC NEW WAVE OF COMMERCIALS.

# INTERVIEW: TARSEM SINGH

Born and raised in India, Tarsem Singh became one of the most sought-after commercial directors in Europe during the 1990s. His highly cinematic, storytelling commercials for Levi's, Nike, Coca-Cola, and other brands include some of the most stylistic and memorable ads ever put on film. Intended for a visually sophisticated modern international audience, Tarsem's commercials rarely feature any type of sales pitch—or any dialogue at all. And they can be mysterious and unsettling. One chilling Smirnoff ad used a vodka bottle as a window to the inner nature of characters walking through the scene (a normal-looking passer-by was revealed to be a serpent when viewed through the bottle). For Nike in Amsterdam, Tarsem staged an epic soccer game between the forces of good and evil—and created perhaps the most frighteningly realistic Mephistopheles ever to show his face in an ad. In 2000, the director released his first feature film, *The Cell*.

**DOES COMMERCIAL DIRECTING TODAY REPRESENT THE STATE OF THE ART IN TERMS OF FILM TECHNIQUE?**

Yes, it's usually ahead of where feature films are. Movie effects that people say are cutting-edge, as in *The Matrix*, are actually happening in advertising at least five or six years beforehand. It used to be that a lot of the directing technique coming into advertising started out in music videos—but right now the budgets for music videos seem to have gone lower and lower, so a lot of the technical stuff has gone out of them.

**YOU RECENTLY MADE YOUR FIRST MOVIE. DO YOU THINK COMMERCIAL DIRECTORS MAKE GOOD FILM DIRECTORS?**

Not necessarily. The classic problem of people coming from advertising and trying to do films is that the sum is less than the parts. A commercial director may shoot a lot of great scenes, but the whole movie doesn't seem to be greater than the scenes. There are exceptions. If you look at [director Ridley Scott's film] *Alien*, the small scenes are great, but the whole film is also a great film that climaxes.

**YOUR COMMERCIALS HAVE OFTEN BEEN WORDLESS AND AT TIMES RATHER SURREAL. IS THAT YOUR PREFERRED STYLE?**

They have been more visual than anything else. That was the kind of work I wanted to do, and it's the reason I went to Europe as opposed to doing ads in America. In America, the emphasis is first on comedy and second on dialogue. I wasn't interested in doing commercials that were all about dialogue. And the only place that allowed you to work visually is Europe—because there, when you create an ad it has to be able to run two hundred miles away, where people don't speak the same language. So the idea has to be done visually. When I started working on Levi's in Europe, I found that this was the kind of advertising they were looking for. And it kind of became like the days of silent cinema. What I also like more about European advertising is that you're usually doing the sixty-second format, not thirty seconds. I think sixty seconds is the amount of time needed to at least get some sort of feeling into something.

**HOW MUCH DO YOU THINK THAT COMING FROM INDIA HAS INFLUENCED YOUR STYLE?**

I would say quite a bit. I came to America when I was twenty-five. Before that all my upbringing was Indian. I ended up with the techniques of the West. But the color and eye coordination of the Indian cinema—which are very vibrant—have somehow come creeping into my work. It's not something I was aware of until I sat back and watched my reel and thought, "You know what? This doesn't look very American." And somehow that's come from my background being what it is. I never sat down and said, "I'm Indian, so this will have to be done a certain way."

**WOULD YOU SAY THERE'S A MYSTICAL SIDE TO YOUR WORK THAT COMES OUT OF THAT BACKGROUND? SOME OF YOUR COMMERCIALS SEEM OTHERWORLDLY.**

I've been an atheist since fifth grade. So I wouldn't say there's a mystical side to what I do. But the visual aspects of religious themes interest me, not religion itself. If it's something you grow up around, as I did, then it probably influences you even if you aren't aware of it. In the West, I have a slightly different perspective than the next guy because my upbringing is so different from the people here.

**TO WHAT EXTENT ARE TOP DIRECTORS SUCH AS YOURSELF IN CONTROL OF THE ADVERTISING PROCESS? ARE YOU GIVEN A LOT OF FREEDOM BY THE AGENCIES AND THE CLIENTS?**

I have been, which is great for me. If the commercial is visual, I want the agency to present the idea to me in one line. If you can give me the idea that simply, then it's my job to plot it out and create the storyboards. I've never done a commercial where someone gave me a step-by-step storyboard and then I just shot it. I tell them, "No, you need to put your idea down in one line, and I'll make the visuals work for it." For instance, on the Smirnoff ad, the agency gave me a brief that said, "Smirnoff is an alternative world inside a bottle." That's the kind of brief I'm looking for. I can bring everything to it.

**ARE CLIENTS EVER CONCERNED THAT YOUR WORK IS TOO ABSTRACT?**

Almost never. Because I don't think a client would come to me for hard sell. My commercial reel is such that you wouldn't think of me if you had to do a commercial about getting a cold and it's just full of people coughing. And I made a conscious effort in the beginning of my career, starting with the show reel I made in school, to let people know the kind of work I do. If you're looking for hard sell, a million guys can do that. I wanted to position myself as something else.

**DO YOU THINK OF ADS AS BEING AN ART FORM?**

I think *art* is a four-letter word. I never use it for anything; it means too many different things to me. There are some photographs that I think are artistic and some commercials I think are artistic, but I don't know what that word really means. It's used so loosely that anytime someone calls something art, I just think it's the kiss of death.

12

**12. ROLOS**
AMMIRATI PURIS LINTAS,
AMSTERDAM, 1995
Director Rogier van der Ploeg
spun a tale of a lifetime in thirty
seconds: A bratty child is mean
to an elephant, and many years
later, the elephant gets even.

**13. COCA-COLA**
FALLON McELLIGOTT,
MINNEAPOLIS, MINNESOTA,
1994
Another "silent film" from
director Tarsem Singh, this time
featuring a swimming elephant
who journeys to a float, deposits
some peanuts, takes a Coke,
and leaves.

13

as by the surrealism of Salvador Dalí and David Lynch. And so one could expect just about anything in a Tarsem commercial; for an MTV Asia promotion, he once filmed a live animal sacrifice, shot with an overhead camera as a slaughtered lamb bled to death and traditional Indian music played in the background (the spot never ran). His subsequent work was more tranquil, though no less mesmerizing: For Coca-Cola, he constructed an entire commercial around muted scenes of an elephant swimming, with much of the ad shot from beneath the water. As advertising was becoming more of a global form of communication in the 1990s, Tarsem was the ideal international ad director; his wordless, dreamlike commercials needed no translation—which is not to say they didn't leave some viewers baffled.

In Europe, where Tarsem was doing much of his best work, a number of other directorial talents flourished. The French, always at the forefront in cinema trends, produced some important "new wave" commercials, most notably from the director Jean Paul Goude, whose Perrier commercial featuring a feral woman and a lion facing off over a bottle of water became the talk of the Cannes advertising festival. In Germany, home-bred filmmakers like Wim Wenders tried their hand at commercial-making, with the kind of interesting results one would expect. And Dutch directors like Rogier van der Ploeg proved adept at visual storytelling with commercials like the Rolos candy classic "Elephant"—in which a bratty young boy taunts an elephant and then pays the price many years later when the elephant in a passing parade, spots the grown-up man in the crowd and remembers.

Back in the UK, some of the directors who earlier had helped launch the wave of cinematic commercials continued to flourish, including Hugh Hudson—who produced the most winning smile ever seen in an advertisement. Hudson choreographed four thousand people, wearing red, white, and blue caps, to form a giant living face shot from overhead by an airborne camera; the movements of the crowd then change the image, by adding first a smile and then a wink; further movement transforms the face into a living map of the world, to make the point that British Airways "brings people together" from around the world. Not all British commercials were as feel-good as that one; the work of Tony Kaye—who emerged as one of the hottest British directors of the late 1980s and early 1990s—could be downright disturbing and at times bewildering. One of Kaye's best-known commercials, for Dunlop tires, featured a night-marish fantasy in which a car driving alone on the road is terrorized by a Buddha-like demon and his evil army, as they set all manner of deadly traps and obstacles in the car's path. In *Advertising Age*, Vagnoni called the commercial "arguably the most surreal, abstract bit of

14

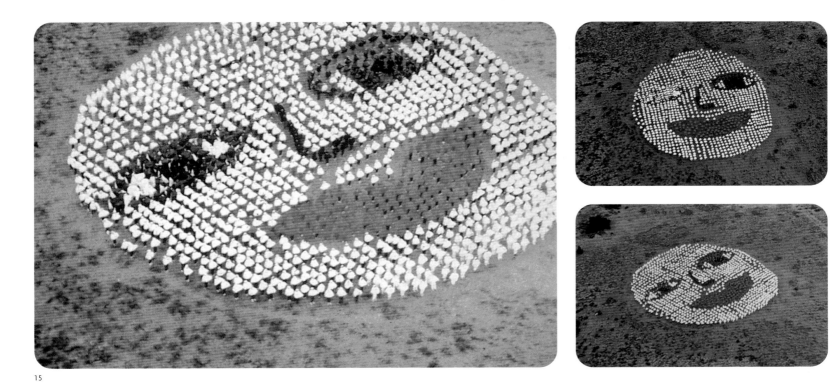

15

14. **MILL VALLEY
FILM FESTIVAL**
GOODBY BERLIN &
SILVERSTEIN,
SAN FRANCISCO, 1983
This early 1980s commercial
was among the first to blend
satire with cinema verité-style
camerawork. A decade later,
the "mockumentary" approach
was much in vogue.

15. **BRITISH AIRWAYS**
SAATCHI & SAATCHI,
LONDON, 1990
"Happy Face," directed by Hugh
Hudson, was an amazing bit of
choreography in which thousands
of people form a human face,
then make the eye wink.

16

16. **BLACK CAT WHISKEY**
OGILVY & MATHER, BANGKOK, 1996
This commercial brought the kung-fu theatrics of Asian film to ads, in a wild story about gangsters and street rumbles.

17. **HEINEKEN**
BATES HONG KONG, 2000
The American film director Oliver Stone shot this Asian commercial in which a key bit of dialogue is obscured by the sound of a blender. Stone is one of many film directors who have "crossed over" into advertising.

impressionism ever produced by a major agency for a major brand." The stunning visual power of the ad did not happen by accident; Kaye shot the commercial in black-and-white, then computer-colored it, frame by frame, to achieve the most vibrant effect. To some this was evidence of Kaye's genius, while to others it demonstrated that commercials were perhaps becoming overstylized and self-indulgent (it didn't help that Kaye was yet another enfant terrible of the ad-directing fraternity, known for spending huge sums in production, refusing to compromise on the content of his ads, and engaging in eccentric behavior; once, when he was chosen to give the prestigious Design & Art Directors president's lecture in London, Kaye stunned the audience by appearing onstage dressed as a Hasidic Jew and singing "My Way").

By the mid-1990s, it was clear that Kaye, Tarsem, and others had ushered in what Vagnoni called "the age of the visual stylist—

in which the commercial is no longer so much about great storytelling or memorable characters, but instead is all about sumptuous images that stay in your mind."

Hollywood soon realized that the power of those images could extend beyond commercials and into feature films. By the late 1990s, Kaye, Tarsem, David Fincher, and the fast-rising ad director Kinka Usher were being signed up for movies. The lines between Hollywood and Madison Avenue were coming down; not only were commercial directors making films, but highly regarded filmmakers like Joel and Ethan Coen, Oliver Stone, and Errol Morris were bringing their talents to ads. Some worried about the effect the commercial directors might be having on feature films; the director Michael Bay, who made the transition from directing Coke and Levi's ads to shooting big-budget Hollywood blockbuster movies like *Armageddon*, was cited by some as living proof that ad

directors would suck the substance right out of films. "The problem is that in commercials, you're trained to tell a story visually in thirty seconds," commented film director Barry Sonnenfeld. "So these guys are very good at creating a visual style and using special effects and quick-cut editing. But there's not much room in commercials for emotion or character development or plot. They often don't know how to deal with any of that."

At the same time, esteemed filmmakers were often criticized for what seemed like half-hearted efforts in advertising. Pytka, who once compiled his own reel of obscure commercials shot by Martin Scorsese, Jean-Luc Godard, and Federico Fellini, noted that the ads were "were uniformly dreadful." Why? According to Pytka, film directors often underestimate how difficult it is to make a good commercial. "They don't take it seriously," he says. "They treat the ad like a jokey scene in a movie." (There have been

As natural as curiosity

17

THE CINEMATIC NEW WAVE OF COMMERCIALS.

18

18. **DUNLOP**
ABBOTT MEAD VICKERS,
LONDON, 1993
This tire ad, from the controversial British director Tony Kaye, featured a surreal, nightmarish fantasy: A car on a lonely road is terrorized by demons.

Simplify.
HONDA

19

20

**19. HONDA**
RUBIN POSTAER &
ASSOCIATES, LOS ANGELES,
1996
Directed by Joel and Ethan Coen,
and reminiscent of their film *The
Hudsucker Proxy*, this ad features
a harried businessman who
flees to a pristine white place.

**20. NISSAN**
TBWA/CHIAT/DAY,
LOS ANGELES, 1996
"Toys" answered the question:
What would happen if G.I. Joe
hooked up with Barbie? Kinka
Usher directed it more like a
music video than an ad.

exceptions: Errol Morris's recent black-and-white commercials for Miller High Life, celebrating duct tape and all things macho, have been highly praised, as has a Honda commercial by the Coen brothers that re-created the visual style of their film *The Hudsucker Proxy*.)

Regardless of whether the new highly visual ad directors came from the world of film or cut their teeth on sales pitches, some in the ad creative community felt that these directors' emphasis on style was not necessarily good for advertising. The American creative director Greg DiNoto credits advertising's star directors with producing memorable ads but noted that their flashy approach "has hurt advertising, too, by making otherwise vacuous concepts all sparkly and beautiful and seductive and easy for agencies to sell to advertisers. All show and no go." The joke around the ad industry, by the mid-1990s, was that when an advertiser lacked an idea, the fallback plan was "Get me Pytka."

That criticism notwithstanding, the commercials that most resonated with the public in the late 1990s were style-driven, not concept-driven. The Gap's minimalist white-background commercials with swing dancers and country line dancers and sullen models singing "Mellow Yellow" to the camera were devoid of what most ad people would call a concept—they were pure style, and their effectiveness derived from the way director Matthew Rolston framed his shots, as well as from the sophisticated film techniques he used, such as stop-action film sequences in the "Swing" commercial. That technique subsequently ended up in the 1999 movie *The Matrix*, demonstrating that now the movies were borrowing tricks and techniques from the cinematic ads, instead of the other way around.

Another of the most arresting and talked-about commercials of the late 1990s was Kinka Usher's "Toys" for Nissan—in which dolls resembling G.I. Joe and Barbie race around the

living-room floor in a tiny car. Again, the spot was loved not so much because it was a strong idea as because Usher had produced a marvelous little movie, one that could be watched again and again. That commercial—and countless others like it—proved that in the new cinematic world of advertising, style *was* substance.

Meanwhile, if "Toys" exemplified the perfect advertising mini-movie, it also exhibited other traits of the new and improved commercial of the 1990s, beyond just cinematic flair. The ad borrowed from pop culture (the sound track was a song from the American rock-music group Van Halen) and from other forms of expression; it looked more like a music video than an ad. It had a hip, ironic sense of humor. And it buried the sales pitch so deeply that it was impossible to find it. All of which raised the question: Was this any way to sell cars? In the mid-to-late-1990s, advertising had not only "gone Hollywood"—it had gone thoroughly postmodern, as well.

# 5. NIKE
# POSTMO
# REVOL

I n the 1960s and 1970s, the creative insurrectionists in New York had begun to subvert some of the conventions of advertising, replacing empty slogans and jingles with more candid and provocative statements, and injecting a strong sense of attitude and style into ads. It proved both popular and effective, and subsequently the heirs to Doyle Dane Bernbach—including British and Australian agencies that had studied Bernbach and adopted his conceptual approach, as well as the American regional agencies like Minnesota's Fallon McElligott—managed to spread the ad revolution, and in many ways advance it with their own refinements.

But they didn't radically change the new advertising model that DDB had helped invent, and by the mid-1980s, there was a restlessness in advertising, a sense that the sound concepts and clever headlines of modern ads had lost some of their ability to surprise. By this time, the consumer audience was evolving, becoming more media-literate with the arrival of MTV and other cable channels, booting up personal computers for the first time, growing hungry for sensory material that challenged it in new ways. Because of these factors—and perhaps also because advertising tends to reinvent itself every so often with bold new packaging—the business was ripe for another revolution. And Dan Wieden had the perfect anthem for it.

Wieden, a quiet Northwesterner who ran a small agency in Portland, Oregon, with his partner David Kennedy, did not seem like much of a rebel. In fact, he hadn't set out to change advertising; he drifted into the field reluctantly and apathetically, after he'd tried writing Beat poetry. "I never liked advertising," Wieden acknowledged years later. He had no taste for the glad-handing ways of the business, nor for the inanity of much of the work the industry produced. And so when he eventually began forming his own small agency, it was not surprising that Wieden would surround himself with others who shared his "anti-advertising" sensibility. His partner Kennedy, a talented art director, was a castoff from several larger agencies. One of Wieden's first hires was Jim Riswold, a perennial college student who read Nietzsche, worshiped the gender-bending rock star David Bowie, and was known to lie on the floor in his office, meditating. Wieden's agency was a small group of advertising misfits located somewhere northwest of nowhere, registering not even a blip on Madison Avenue's radar. Until, that is, the debut of Wieden + Kennedy's first major national TV commercial for its new client Nike, appropriately titled "Revolution."

The commercial featured rapid-fire, grainy scenes that seemed to have been edited almost randomly. For consumers used to seeing slickly produced commercials with linear story lines, there was the shock of the raw; you had to

NIKE AND THE POSTMODERN AD REVOLUTION.

2

2. **HONDA SCOOTERS**
WIEDEN + KENNEDY,
PORTLAND, 1984
Before, "Revolution," this
commercial broke new ground;
it had a rough-cut style and an
anti-hero spokesman in the
underground rock figure
Lou Reed.

3. **NIKE**
WIEDEN + KENNEDY,
PORTLAND, 1989
By the late 1980s, the Nike ad
style had evolved into sophisti-
cated filmmaking. The "Bo
Knows" commercial, centered on
professional American athlete Bo
Jackson's multisport prowess,
moved with dazzling speed.

3

squint to see what was going on. There was no voice-over, and in fact the commercial contained no words at all, a radical departure (*Where was the sales pitch?*). Perhaps the most striking thing about it was the sound track: Wieden + Kennedy played the famous Beatles song "Revolution," which immediately stirred controversy. From a legal standpoint, there was haggling and an eventual lawsuit over rights to the song (which had been purchased from Michael Jackson, who had previously obtained rights to some of the Beatles' music). But the real debate triggered by the spot was not so much legal as cultural: What right did advertising have to co-opt a Beatles song, and particularly this song, which was an anti-establishment, countercultural anthem?

It was only the beginning of a debate that would continue for years, with Wieden + Kennedy in the thick of it. With the "Revolution" ad, the agency signaled to the world that adver-

tising in the late 1980s and subsequently in the 1990s was about to stake new ground—right at the center of American and world culture. In the ads that followed from W+K and other hip agencies, there was a tendency to borrow freely from sources that previously had been off-limits to advertising—not just rock-and-roll but literature, film, art, history. These new complex commercials were dubbed "postmodern advertising" by some journalists and academics because they seemed to share many of the identifying characteristics of postmodern art and architecture—they mixed old and new styles, borrowed from other forms of communication, blended high and low culture, deconstructed themselves, were filled with inside references, and often adopted an ironic and self-aware tone.

"Revolution" was the noisiest shot, but in fact, Wieden had been experimenting with a new kind of advertising a couple of years earlier

for a smaller client, Honda Scooters. Partly by accident and partly from gut instinct, the agency created a commercial in 1984 that seemed to break the mold at the time—though the ad is now largely unknown or forgotten outside advertising circles. Like "Revolution," the Honda Scooter ad used grainy film footage and a hip sound track (in this case, Lou Reed's provocative "Walk on the Wild Side") with no sales pitch. The star, Reed—an underground American rock musician with a bad reputation and a complete lack of affect—was about as unlikely a commercial endorser as one might find. The ad came about more or less by happenstance: Riswold was a fan of the musician and wanted to use him, for fun. As for the rough, cinema-verité film look, it was patched together in the editing room—partly because of problems with the original film that was shot. Wieden recalls that when his producer Larry Bridges finished editing the spot and

IS IT THE SHOES?

IS IT THE SHOES? IS IT THE SHOES? IS IT THE SHOES?

Air Jordan from Nike.

4. **NIKE**
WIEDEN + KENNEDY,
PORTLAND, 1989
Basketball star Michael Jordan
is paired with filmmaker Spike
Lee. Lee's silly question—"Is it
the shoes?"—acknowledged
that it really wasn't the shoes
that made Jordan special.

# REEBOKS LET U.B.U.

5

showed him the rough cut, "We just looked at each other and said, 'Jiminy Christmas, what the hell is that?' We knew we'd stumbled on a different way of communicating in sixty seconds." The author Randall Rothenberg has described the Lou Reed spot as a seminal work that may have been the first postmodern ad (though Chiat/Day's slightly earlier "1984" commercial also had its share of "po-mo" qualities, including an oblique message, an artistic film style, and a story line that borrowed from author George Orwell). In any case, the commercial didn't have much impact on the marketplace—W+K subsequently lost the account—but its style and originality very much impressed Nike and led to the far more well-known "Revolution" ad.

After "Revolution," Wieden and Nike's collaboration took off as they produced, over the next few years, a series of dazzling ads all connected by a single line of copy that Wieden

had written in about fifteen minutes in his office one day. The line, "Just do it," was one of the most ambiguous advertising slogans ever penned. What did it mean? Just do what? (There were all kinds of far-fetched theories; the American journalist John Leo suspected that Nike's message might contain some dark agenda, commanding urban kids to go wild and wreak havoc—an interpretation that astounded and mildly offended Wieden when he was told of it.) Ad conspiracy theorists aside, most people grasped the essence of what Wieden was saying: Be active, get off your couch, stop talking about doing something and get started on it. Wieden had written a simple and stirring call to action, though it was left to the individual to decide what specific action to take.

Like the Doyle Dane Bernbach advertising of old, Nike commercials were usually rooted in a strong, surprising idea, and they were invariably clever. But that was where the similarities

ended. With DDB, the big idea was almost always linked directly to product or company attributes—smaller is better, number two tries harder, and so on. With Nike ads, the big idea was often only tangentially connected to the product—and the idea was just the starting point in the creation of an elaborate, complex, and hyperstylized piece of work that, by completion, didn't look much like a commercial at all. In the ad "Bo Knows" (dreamed up by Riswold and a few others in a bar), the idea was rooted in the fact that one of Nike's endorser athletes, Bo Jackson, had made headlines by playing two professional sports simultaneously. Riswold then mused, "What if Jackson tried to play every sport? And then what if he tried to go beyond sports, taking on, say, guitar-playing? Would he succeed at everything?" The frenzied commercial, directed by Joe Pytka, showed Jackson's sometimes comical attempts at tennis, hockey, basketball—with cameo critiques by other

6

**5. REEBOK**
CHIAT/DAY, NEW YORK, 1988
The postmodern style began to
show up in other ads, including
those of Nike's competitor,
Reebok. But the U.B.U. campaign
was considered too strange at
the time.

**6. BLACK STAR BEER**
WIEDEN + KENNEDY,
PORTLAND, 1992
Wieden + Kennedy also took a
postmodern approach with some
of its other brands; campy Black
Star beer ads were designed to
look old-fashioned and fake.

athletes, some of whom are clearly skeptical of the whole endeavor. The commercial ends with Jackson playing a guitar riff miserably, prompting the rock-and-roll musician Bo Diddley to declare, "Bo, you don't know diddley." The commercial then closes with the Nike logo and the words "Just do it" flashed onscreen. Like most Nike ads, the commercial didn't seem to be promoting anything, other than the growing legend of a particular athlete; Nike shoes are not mentioned in the commercial at all. The spot bore other hallmarks of Nike advertising: inside references to sports, rock music, and pop culture; a willingness to poke fun at the endorser Jackson; a jagged and uneven film style that was almost dizzying. But "Bo Knows" was nearly impossible for television viewers to ignore. The American filmmaker Spike Lee observed at the time that, along with the much-hyped release of the movie *Batman*, the commercial had taken American culture by storm in 1989.

Lee himself would soon be swept into the Nike ad whirlwind, as he began appearing in commercials pairing himself and the basketball star Michael Jordan, with Lee playing a character, Mars Blackmon, he'd created in his first film, *She's Gotta Have It*, in 1986. In the commercials, Lee's character became a kind of anti-spokesman, badgering the star Jordan, making ludicrous statements (Mars insisted that it "must be the shoes" that enabled Jordan to defy gravity, inviting the audience to laugh at this silly proposition), and even calling attention to the advertising process itself: In one ad, Mars yells out the window, "Shut up, we're shooting a Nike commercial." For an ad to acknowledge its status as an ad wasn't entirely novel; in earlier times, everyone from Groucho Marx to the radio pitch-characters Bert and Harry Piel sometimes joked about doing ads as they were doing them. And the self-mocking pitchman was used perhaps most famously in the mid-

1980s with the character Joe Isuzu, whose outrageous claims and promises in ads were acknowledged, in subtitles, to be lies. But Nike ads brought self-referential advertising to a new level, telling the audience, in effect, "We know this is an ad, and you know this is an ad—so let's have fun with it." As Wieden said, such ads were "like pulling back the curtain and showing the little man behind Oz."

On one level, that made the ads more "honest" than most. But critics took a different view. The agency was accused of cannily co-opting the culture and cynically using icons of hipness to sell shoes. In his book *Where the Suckers Moon*, Randall Rothenberg suggests, in effect, that some of the creative people at W+K may have sold out their own countercultural values when they placed rebel heroes like Reed in ads. Other critics noted that the use of irony and "honest" self-deprecating humor in the ads simply served as cover, enabling the

# INTERVIEW: JIM RISWOLD

Few copywriters in the late 1980s and 1990s have had as much influence on advertising as Jim Riswold of Wieden + Kennedy. As the preeminent writer and creative director on the Nike account, Riswold has been credited with helping to introduce a postmodern style to ads. He has also written several of the most famous commercials of the past twenty years—including "Bo Knows," featuring Bo Jackson, and "I Am Not a Role Model," featuring Charles Barkley. And the author David Halberstam credits Riswold with helping to turn Michael Jordan into a global icon.

**WHAT WAS WIEDEN + KENNEDY LIKE IN THE LATE 1980S?**
It was a time when we weren't afraid to make glorious mistakes. And boy oh boy, did we make a bunch.

**THE AD YOU DID FOR HONDA SCOOTERS FEATURING LOU REED HAS BEEN CITED AS A BREAKTHROUGH IN BRINGING AN "UNDERGROUND" SENSIBILITY TO ADS. WHY DID YOU CHOOSE REED?**
Everybody knows celebrities have been used in advertising since time immemorial. However, what I think made the Lou Reed spot different at the time was that it used a persona non grata celebrity.

The very things that made Reed off-limits to any sane advertising professional are what appealed to me: his outspokenness, his troubles, his 24-hour sunglasses, his choice of subject matter, his grating personality, his aloofness, his coolness, his ego, his sexual ambiguity, his darkness; in short, his Lou-ness. He has the guts to stand for something, and the audacity to be Lou Reed on his terms. Maybe people who admired Mr. Reed, warts and all, saw the commercial as speaking to them. Maybe they appreciated being welcomed to the wonderful world of consumerism.

I don't know; partly I did the ad because I just wanted to meet Lou Reed.

**WHY WERE THE "SPIKE AND MIKE" COMMERCIALS [PAIRING BASKETBALL STAR MICHAEL JORDAN AND FILMMAKER SPIKE LEE] SO SUCCESSFUL?**
I think they gave America a glimpse of what Michael Jordan as a person was like. They were a counterpart to the Jordan we saw on sports reports every night—Jordan the total predator, the assassin who went out and laid waste to enemy teams. Opposing teams got the killer, but the fans watching these ads got the charmer, the smile, a man of humor and intelligence.

**YOU SEEM OPEN TO USING ALL KINDS OF PERSONAL INFLUENCES IN YOUR ADS—THE KIND OF MUSIC YOU LISTEN TO, WHAT YOU'RE READING AT THE TIME, OR FILMS YOU'VE SEEN. WHY DO YOU CHOOSE TO INCORPORATE ALL OF THIS INTO YOUR ADS?**
I have never had an original thought in my career. Everything I have ever done has been borrowed, reformulated, regurgitated, turned upside down or inside out, played back at a different speed, and sometimes just plain stolen from either popular culture, music, history, art, literature, the back of cereal boxes, Hegelianism, an athlete's life, a bedtime story my grandmother once read me—whatever. Anything and everything is fair game when it comes to stimulus. (My lawyers have asked me to point out that this is not plagiarism; it is appropriation.)

But, hopefully, what my complete lack of originality did was open up an unlimited number of resources from which to make completely original ads. And, more important, maybe it led to more meaningful and enjoyable ways for people to hear an advertiser's message.

**AS YOU KNOW, ONE CRITICISM OF MODERN ADVERTISING IS THAT IT CO-OPTS THE CULTURE—FOR EXAMPLE, BY BRINGING LOU REED OR JOHN LENNON INTO ADS, YOU'RE TAKING SOMETHING THAT WAS PURE AND AUTHENTIC, AND PUTTING THE TAINT OF COMMER-CIALISM ON IT. WHAT'S YOUR FEELING ABOUT THAT?**
Die-hard fans of the long-dead John Lennon hated the "Instant Karma" Nike commercial. Some brain-damaged fans of Lou Reed were up in arms that I shared their Lou with the non-brain-damaged world.

Even my mother was upset with my transla-tion of "I am Spartacus" into "I am Tiger Woods."

To all these criticisms—yes, even to my mother's—I reply by asking these people to get off their high horses. We're not talking about sacred texts here; we're talking about a song, a book, a TV show, or a movie. These are part of popular culture, and so is advertising. It should be allowed to draw upon all the inspira-tions that the rest of popular culture does. To all the Lou Reed fans I may have upset by "bastardizing" him (never mind that he could have turned down the offer to be in the ad) I reply, "I got to meet him and you didn't." And to my mother (whom I love deeply): It could've been worse; it could've been "I am Cap'n Crunch."

**YOUR ADVERTISING HAS BEEN CALLED POSTMODERN. WHAT DO YOU THINK ABOUT THAT?**
What does postmodernism mean?

Seriously, when I read some weighty commentary about my work, it makes me wish I were half as smart as some author thinks I am.It confounds the hell out of my intellectual sisters, who, upon reading these things, exclaim, "He's really stupid! We know; we had to grow up next to him!" While my sisters were up to their necks in Euclidean geometry, I spent my adolescence with the likes of Monty Python, Andy Warhol, "SCTV," and "Saturday Night Live." (This was before I tried to make myself smart by studying nineteenth-century German philosophy.) I learned from these people not to take anything too seriously.

There is no better place to apply this philosophy than advertising. When did adver-tising deem itself so damn important? Was there a sentence I missed on the tablets Moses brought down from Mount Sinai referring to the sanctity of advertising?

Thanks to the Warhols and Pythons of the world, I was fortunate enough to stumble into a career in advertising with a healthy dose of cynicism. I was doubly fortunate to work for Dan Wieden and David Kennedy, who were equally cynical about the advertising profes-sion. That cynicism and "it's only advertising" attitude allowed us to create some truly wonderful advertising.

NOT AMERICA'S FAVORITE PAPER

**We built this bank
one service charge
at a time.**

**HUMUNGOUS BANK***

*Your money is our money.*

*If you think the big banks are getting bigger at your expense, it's time you talked to Richmond Savings. We believe in rewarding our customers
with fewer charges. Not to mention service that's second to none. After all, that's how we built our business. We're not a bank. We're better. **RICHMOND SAVINGS**

9

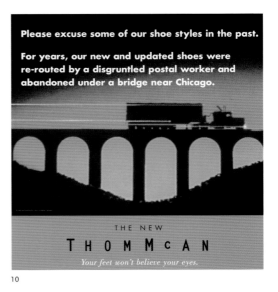

**Please excuse some of our shoe styles in the past.**

**For years, our new and updated shoes were
re-routed by a disgruntled postal worker and
abandoned under a bridge near Chicago.**

THE NEW
**ThoM McAN**

*Your feet won't believe your eyes.*

10

**7. (PREVIOUS SPREAD)**
**ENERGIZER**
CHIAT/DAY, LOS ANGELES,
1989
In this campaign, the Energizer
Bunny appeared unexpectedly in
the middle of fake commercials
for ersatz products.

**8. THE VILLAGE VOICE**
MAD DOGS & ENGLISHMEN,
NEW YORK, 1996
The Mad Dogs agency
sometimes attacked the
products it was promoting;
here, New York's *Village Voice*
newspaper takes a beating.

**9. RICHMOND SAVINGS BANK**
PALMER JARVIS DDB,
VANCOUVER, 1987
This ad campaign promoted a
fictional bank, Humongous,
along with facetious headlines
like this one; the point was to
make the real client, Richmond
Savings, look good in comparison.

**10. THOM MCAN SHOES**
MAD DOGS & ENGLISHMEN,
NEW YORK, 1994
Once again, Mad Dogs makes
fun of its own client: the ads
apologize (and offer lame excuses)
for Thom McAn's previously
unstylish shoes in order
to introduce a revamped
product line.

advertising to slip past the guard of even
the most savvy, cynical consumers. Yes, Nike
advertising *seemed* to be offering moments of
pure entertainment sans the annoying sales
pitch, but in fact the pitch, the link to the
product, was always lurking somewhere under
the surface. As media-studies professor Mark
Crispin Miller pointed out, the modus operandi
of ironic advertisers like Wieden + Kennedy
was to wink at the audience and flatter its
intelligence with clever inside jokes—all for
the single purpose of closing the sale. Seen
in this light, postmodern advertising could
be considered even more manipulative, and
perhaps more dishonest, than the old-fashioned,
straightforward advertising that didn't bother
to cleverly disguise itself.

It's difficult to know, without actually crawl-
ing inside the heads of Wieden and his staff,
whether the creation of Nike ads was as

cynically calculated as some critics suspect.
But for their part, W+K staffers insist the
agency had no hidden agenda. "My sense is
that we were just having fun," Wieden says.
"I think our best work has never been trying to
appropriate pop culture and turn it into advertising. It was simply a reflection of people
who have contemporary brains and taste,
just exploring things that they liked, things that
turned them on." That seems entirely credible,
and in fact likely: Rather than being a result of
cold calculation, the Nike postmodern style
of advertising was more likely the product of
near-complete creative freedom. Nike had given
Wieden license to reinvent advertising—and,
for the most part, didn't even subject the
agency's ideas to standard focus groups or
other testing. Wieden, in turn, created a free-
wheeling work environment in which he
encouraged his staff to be open to outside

influences beyond the narrow world of advertising (he sometimes held seminars at the agencies, bringing in artists or musicians). He
hired offbeat people like Riswold, who were
far more interested in film, philosophy, and
rock music than in advertising. And Riswold,
in turn, seemed to see the agency as a creative
playground in which he could use his sandbox—
Nike ads—to salute cult heroes, play underappreciated songs, and introduce hip new
artists. (Riswold came up with the Spike Lee
idea after seeing a trailer for *She's Gotta Have
It*; "That would be cool," he thought.)

In the end, what mattered was the results.
The Nike commercials were both effective—the
company vaulted past arch-rival Reebok and
never looked back—and thoroughly enjoyed by
the public. Moreover, they set the standard for
advertising in the 1990s; as the *Adweek* columnist Barbara Lippert noted, just about every

11

11. **LITTLE CAESARS PIZZA**
CLIFF FREEMAN & PARTNERS,
NEW YORK, 1994
Postmodern ads often make fun
of advertising itself; this spot
ridiculed focus groups, showing
that they tend to be comprised
of likeminded participants.

12

12. **DIESEL**
LEO BURNETT, COPENHAGEN,
1988
In this commercial for the hip
Italian clothing company, a man
blows his nose on a shirt to
make the point that the
clothing is so cheap, you
can do what you like with it.

13. **LEVI STRAUSS**
TBWA/CHIAT/DAY,
LOS ANGELES, 1998
An acknowledgment that fashion
advertising relies on models—
but at least the famous people
who wear Levi's are tough, like
Marlon Brando.

advertiser developed a case of "Nike envy." To be fair, however, Wieden + Kennedy was not the only agency breaking new creative ground at the time. Goodby Berlin & Silverstein, a small San Francisco shop, had been among the first to experiment with cinema-verité-style documentary commercials; the agency's ad promoting a local film festival was shot with a handheld camera and had an air of authenticity that was rare in ads at the time. Goodby would later create a campaign for the Chevy's restaurant chain that would feature rough-and-tumble low-budget commercials shot and aired on TV all in the same day—the idea being that the ads should be "made fresh each day," just like the restaurant's food. The partners Jeff Goodby and Rich Silverstein—one a veteran of *Harvard Lampoon* magazine, the other from *Rolling Stone*—seemed to share Wieden's "outsider" mentality and his general distaste for most advertising. Though Goodby was not a "post-

modern agency" per se (many of its subsequent commercials, including the famous "Got Milk?" vignettes, featured more classic approaches, albeit brilliantly written and executed), it was nevertheless central in the development of the new advertising in the 1990s.

A little farther down the California coastline, Chiat/Day in Los Angeles was at the forefront of postmodern advertising, perhaps even a step ahead of Wieden. Having been the first to produce the commercial-as-art-film ("1984" for Apple) and the first to shoot a commercial-as-music-video (the rousing "I Love L.A." spot, in which singer Randy Newman cruises the city in his car, promoting Nike sponsorship of the 1984 Summer Olympics), Chiat/Day also produced a campaign for Reebok that tried to take on Nike with a style even more experimental and abstract. Under the banner of "Reeboks let UBU," the ads featured oddball characters, lines from Ralph Waldo Emerson, and the surreal

cinematic style of Italian films: "We mixed it all together to see what we'd get," says the creative director on the campaign, Marty Cooke. The result was advertising that was undeniably intriguing but also baffling. It might have been quite at home in the "Oddvertising" environment of the late 1990s (see Chapter 6), but it arrived in the marketplace a few years earlier and landed with a thud. However, another of Chiat/Day's innovative campaigns from the same period, for Energizer batteries, was a hit. The campaign introduced the Energizer Bunny, a relentless toy rabbit that managed to trample conventional advertising; commercials would start off seeming like a typically banal ad for a make-believe product—only to have the scene interrupted by the battery-powered bunny, unexpectedly and inappropriately marching into the scene.

Following the lead of these three West Coast agencies, much of advertising had by the early

# OUR MODELS CAN BEAT UP THEIR MODELS.

NIKE AND THE POSTMODERN AD REVOLUTION.

**14. PLAYLAND**
PALMER JARVIS DDB,
VANCOUVER, 1996
In an ad for an amusement
park, this Canadian agency
communicated ideas by
metaphor; the blender is a
whirling ride.

**15. BRITISH SCHOOL OF
MOTORING**
LOWE HOWARD SPINK,
LONDON, 1997
Making fun of an old advertising
convention, this ad used the
side-by-side laundry comparison,
but this time, the solution to
stains is in the prevention, not
in the laundry detergent.

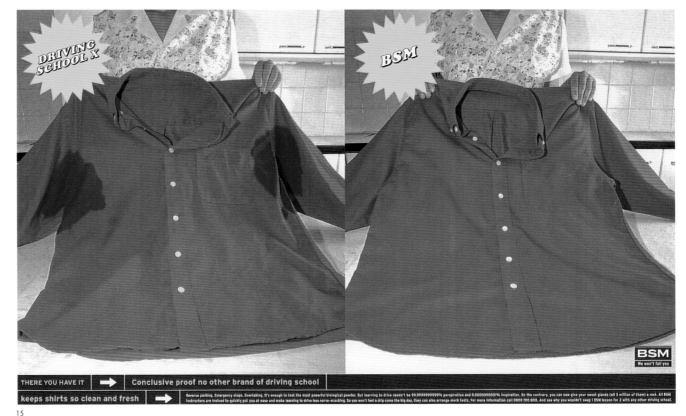

15

to mid-1990s embraced at least some elements of postmodernism: Ads were suddenly awash in irony and seized every available opportunity to break with the conventions of advertising. A new "anti-advertising" approach became the standard way to pitch products. Often, such advertising would demonstrate its candor by gently laughing at the product or brand being advertised. In its late 1990s ads for Thom McAn shoes, a brand that had been popular in the 1970s but had long since fallen out of fashion, the New York agency Mad Dogs & Englishmen created a campaign that offered lame apologies: "Please excuse some of our shoe styles in the past," one ad read. "Through a fluke computer error, the office supply store repeatedly sent us the wrong desk calendars and we still thought it was 1976." Mad Dogs' ads for *The Village Voice* also made the client the butt of its jokes; under the facetious headline "America's favorite newspaper," one ad showed a club-wielding man attacking a rolled-up copy of the *Voice*. (Mad Dogs' creative director Nick Cohen had a history of making light of clients and products: Early in his career, when Cohen was asked to create a promotional poster for a performance of *A Midsummer Night's Dream,* his ad summed up the Shakespeare classic with the tabloid-style headline "Fairy Queen in Donkey Sex Scandal Drama.") Perhaps no client was more ruthlessly parodied in its own ads than the unfortunate Humongous Bank, whose ad agency DDB Palmer Jarvis of Vancouver portrayed the bank as a selfish entity whose own slogans were damning: "We're not just interested in money. We're interested in people with money," read one of the bank's ads. Of course, the agency could afford to be critical of Humongous Bank since the institution didn't actually exist; it was created by the agency as a humorous straw horse, on behalf of a smaller bank that was DDB Palmer Jarvis's real client.

When not joking about their own products, ads were publicly deconstructing the process of advertising. The soft drink Sprite and its agency Lowe & Partners began producing commercials that mischievously exposed the fakery of ads, from bought-and-sold endorsers to outrageous claims; the ads concluded with the line "Image is nothing. Obey your thirst." The behind-the-scenes practices of advertising, both real and imagined, were also played for laughs in a series of ads for Seagram's gin; the ads mischievously resurrected the decades-old suspicion that ads contained subliminal messages, as Seagram's challenged readers to find the secret symbols planted in these new ads. Meanwhile, a series of Little Caesars pizza ads ridiculed focus groups and the tendencies of researchers to assemble like-minded people for their studies; the commercials featured focus groups composed entirely of chimpanzees or *Star Trek* fanatics or other homogeneous oddballs.

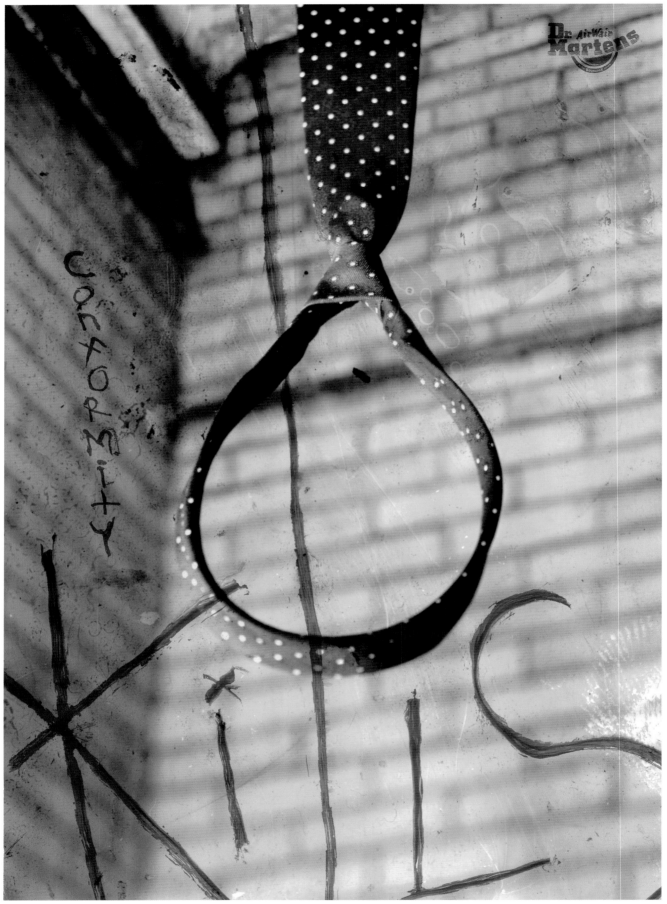

17

16 AND 17. **DR. MARTENS**
CORE, ST. LOUIS, MISSOURI,
1995
The brothers Todd and Eric
Tilford became the new "angry
young men" of mid-1990s
advertising, with harsh
headlines like "Conformity Kills"
and a rough style of design.

Stella Artois. About as sophisticated as a beer can get.

18

18. **STELLA ARTOIS**
CAMPAIGN PALACE,
MELBOURNE, 1992
An Australian campaign
opted for less glamorous
spokesmodels in the form of
gap-toothed peasants.

19 AND 20. **MEZZO MIX**
AMMIRATI PURIS LINTAS,
SWITZERLAND, 1996
An example of "don't believe
the hype" advertising in these
ads for a European soft drink:
the audience is supposed to
admire the advertiser for being
cool enough to admit that ad
promises are fake.

All the other girls have found boyfriends. They're having fun, going out, and even your best girlfriend would rather be with him than you. You've asked all the boys in your class, but they won't even give you a second look. All that's going to change. Drink Mezzo Mix and you'll have a boyfriend in no time. **Mezzo Mix. Coke and orange and everything will be cool.**

19

You broke into your kid sister's piggy bank to buy skin lotion, but they still call you pimple face. All you want to do is get to know a nice girl. But none of them take any notice. And if you try rappin' with them they just whisper and giggle. Don't panic. Drink Mezzo-Mix and the girls will be lining up to go with you. **Mezzo-Mix. Coke and orange and everthing will be cool.**

20

The Hans Brinker
Budget Hotel
Amsterdam
(31) 20-6220687

**\* not included**

21

21. **HANS BRINKER BUDGET HOTEL**
KESSELSKRAMER, AMSTERDAM, 1997
Postmodern ads can be surprisingly candid: this Dutch ad, for a low-budget hotel, delights in pointing out all of the hotel's deficiencies.

22. **SCHLAFLY BEER**
CORE, ST. LOUIS, MISSOURI, 1995
Ads by Todd and Eric Tilford often had a weathered look, intended to make them seem grittier and more authentic.

The best beer didn't come from a brewmaster in Munich or a pub in Dublin. It came from a bucket down the street.

22

Even the models posing in ads weren't safe from the postmodern agency's barbs: One Levi's campaign showed movie stars in tough poses and declared, "Our models can beat up your models." By the 2000 Super Bowl, one advertiser had turned its ad into a joke about the high cost of advertising during the game; the commercial, for the E-Trade on-line brokerage, was intentionally low-brow (it starred a dancing monkey wearing an E-Trade shirt) and closed with the admission "We just wasted two million bucks."

All of this self-referential irony could seem, at times, like mere navel-gazing by advertisers. One also had to wonder whether all the self-flagellation by advertisers, while a logical way to deflect public cynicism about ads, might also suggest a lingering self-loathing on the part of ad creators—many of whom noisily profess to "hate advertising" even as they make their living in it.

The dismantling of the accepted conventions of advertising was occurring not only in the U.S. but around the world. The influence of Nike, a global force by early 1990s, was felt everywhere, though particularly in Europe, where Wieden + Kennedy set up outposts starting with Amsterdam. Moreover, in some sectors of the world, a postmodern way of thinking about advertising had already developed independently. In Scandinavia, Australia, the UK, and elsewhere, advertisers had established a tradition of not taking themselves, or their products, too seriously. The British, in particular, had long embraced the philosophy that an ad's primary challenge was to entertain and amuse the public—and if that required self-deprecating humor or a bit of playful ad-bashing, so be it. One British ad for Amstel beer, by Howell Henry Chaldecott, facetiously pleaded with consumers not to buy the product. The British agency St. Luke's poked fun at

advertising research in a series of ads for Ikea, and Lowe Howard Spink used a classic scenario, the side-by-side laundry demonstration, to make a humorous point about the British School of Motoring ("driving school X," we are shown, causes severe underarm-perspiration stains in shirts).

Australia seemed to particularly embrace this new "nudge and a wink" approach to advertising. An Australian ad for Stella Artois beer used a doctored photograph to place the beer in the hands of toothless peasant women; the headline read, "About as sophisticated as a beer can get." An Australian hospital's ads adopted the blaring bargain-promising headlines of a classic retail ad in their appeal for public donations to help pay for lifesaving medical equipment (demonstrating that ironic humor might be used even in ads dealing with somber subjects). Postmodernism also played well in Switzerland, Sweden, and the

It has a heel cleft for STABILITY. It has a sculpted midsole for STABILITY. It is the most STABLE shoe Nike has ever made. It's STABLE, OK? Now will you RELAX?

23

23. **NIKE**
WIEDEN + KENNEDY,
AMSTERDAM, 1994
23. **NIKE**
WIEDEN + KENNEDY,
AMSTERDAM, 1994
Typography went wild in the
mid-1990s, as the influence of
graphic-design rebel David
Carson began to show up in
ads. Here, Carson seems to be
making the type scream.

24. **NIKE**
WIEDEN +KENNEDY,
AMSTERDAM, 1992
W+K art director Jelly Helm—
who would eventually leave
advertising and become a harsh
critic of it—felt the ads would
seem more real if they were
handwritten.

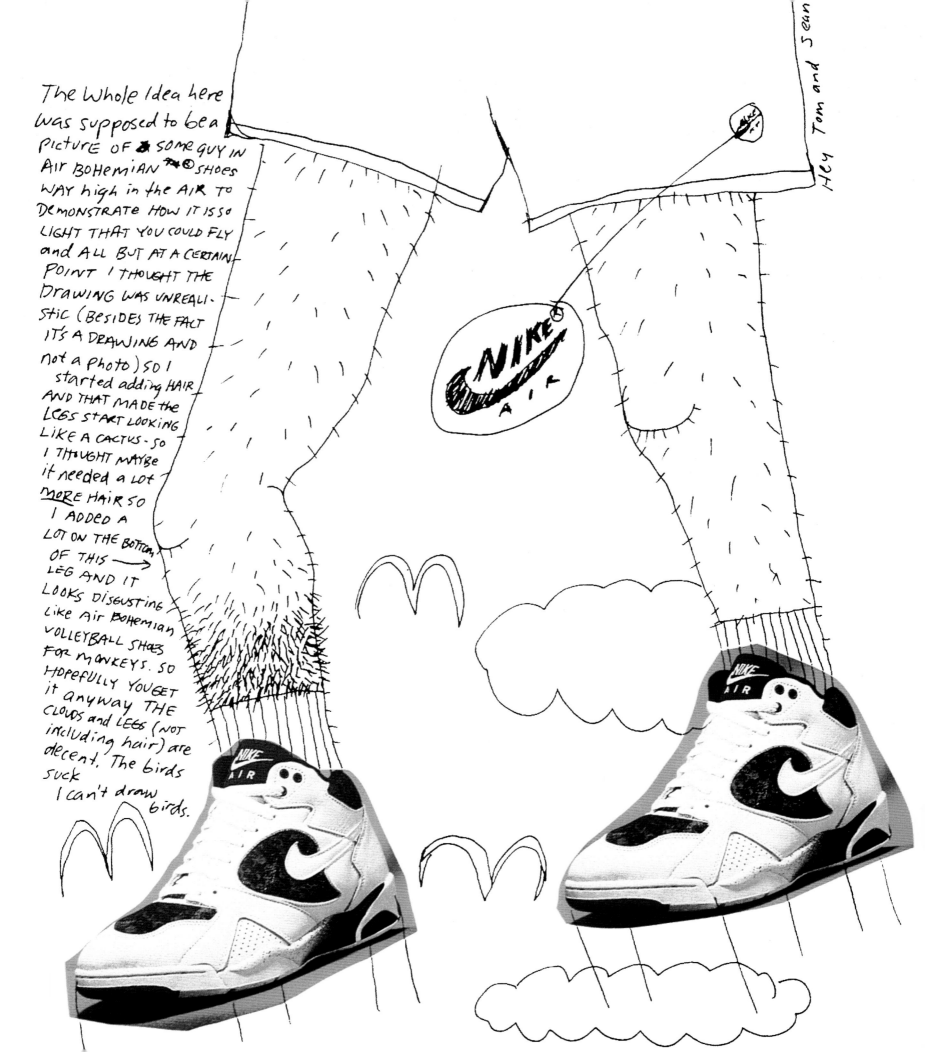

25

Netherlands, all of which had long featured irreverence in their ads. A Swiss ad for Mezzo Mix soft drink dripped with sarcasm, as it showed illustrations of unattractive kids and promised that the product would make them popular with their peers. Meanwhile, the Dutch agency KesselsKramer constructed an entire ad campaign based on the inadequacies of its client, the Hans Brinker Budget Hotel in Amsterdam. One picture shows a luxurious hotel room, full of wonderful amenities—but asterisks are stamped all over the photo, mark-ing the large bed, the minibar, the balcony, and so forth; as we learn from the ad's fine print, the asterisk means that none of these amenities are included with a room at the Hans Brinker. Irony and anti-advertising were not embraced everywhere, however; such approaches tended to fall flat in Asia, notes the Singapore ad writer Jim Aitchison, because "people here are not as cynical about ads. If

you tried to run an ad that mocked itself, the public's reaction would be 'Why are you show-ing me an ad like that? It's a waste of money! Either run the ad or don't, but don't talk about the ad being an ad!'"

Littering an ad with asterisks, as the Hans Brinker ads had done, would have been unthinkable in the past—if only for purely aesthetic reasons. After all, weren't ads supposed to be visually pleasing? Not in the postmodern ad world, which seemed to adopt the philoso-phy that beauty isn't truth—it's just phony advertising gloss. A new school of ad designers believed that a feeling of authenticity could be achieved by presenting more jarring, rough imagery. The New York–based graphic designer David Carson—who specialized in using typog-raphy to wreak havoc in ads and magazine lay-outs—became a large influence in advertising in the early 1990s, and particularly had an impact on ads being produced in Amsterdam.

Carson himself designed a series of Dutch Nike ads that seemed to use type to scream at the reader. Before long, advertisers around the world were aping the Carson style, using unusual typefaces in outrageous ways. Technology was a factor in driving this trend, according to the design writers Steven Heller and Julie Lasky. "Postmodern design styles were boosted by the development and prolifer-ation of desktop computers in the late 1980s," Heller and Lasky wrote in the book *Borrowed Design*. They noted that the newly available technology enabled postmodern designers to play easily and inexpensively with typefaces and mixed fonts, while also layering and manipulating photographs.

Again, part of the objective of all this image manipulation was to make ads that didn't look like ads—so, in effect, digital trickery was used to rough up advertising. Agencies like CORE in St. Louis and Pyro in Dallas,

and that's when I realized that Old Yeller, my most loyal friend, the dog that had saved my mama and my little brother and me from bears and wolves and wild boars, had rabies. My arms were shaking and my eyes were blurry with tears as I raised my rifle and aimed it right between Old Yeller's big, trusting eyes. And then, as my finger tightened on the trigger, I discovered that my best friend wasn't really rabid at all but had just been eating some soap, so I hugged that big yeller dog and he licked my face and we wrestled around in the grass and then ran off into the sunset together.

THE END

EVERYTHING TURNS OUT BETTER ON DOMTAR PAPER.

27

run by the brothers Eric and Todd Tilford, seemed to revel in the obscurity of their visuals, using fractured type, and dark, blurry photographs— which somehow ended up yielding elegant, artful ads. Some in advertising dismissed this as style for style's sake, but Eric Tilford argued that the raw style of his ads was more than an affected look—it was an attempt to make the ads feel as real and weathered as the outdoorsy brands that CORE represented.

If CORE was trying to capture a weather-beaten look in its ads, others were going for more of a homemade feeling. In one series of ads created by Wieden + Kennedy's Amsterdam office, the art director Jelly Helm achieved a startling effect by using handwritten scrawl in place of type. Similarly, a series of Tanqueray gin ads from the New York agency Deutsch, featuring a character named Mr. Jenkins, featured a purposely clumsy cut-and-paste

collage look; while the Sausalito agency Butler Shine & Stern created ads for Miller's Outpost that looked like a handmade school newspaper. All around the world, one could find similar examples of deconstructed ads, designed to look amateurish—including hand-drawn ads from Dentsu for Tokyo Gas. In some cases, it looked as if advertising was reverting to child-hood—all stick figures and scrawled writing. Of course, this advertising was not nearly as naive as it seemed; as Myrna Davis of the Art Directors Club of New York points out, all of the deconstructed and defaced ads of the 1990s were designed to project "an attitude of hipness and street authenticity. With these ads, the attitude is the message."

While some within the advertising creative community felt that the new computer-generated looks in ads were gimmicky, the real debate at the heart of postmodernism revolved around the tendency to appropriate or co-opt.

While it was generally seen as acceptable for a postmodern artist to refer to, or borrow from, other sources (Andy Warhol, of course, was known for borrowing from the commercial world in his art), it was quite a different story when advertisers did it; understandably, questions of exploitation and commercialization were raised, particularly when the ads borrowed from sources considered sacrosanct. It wasn't enough that the Mona Lisa became a pitchwoman in a number of ads—some advertisers even took liberties with Leonardo da Vinci's rendering (Fallon McElligott fattened Mona up a bit, for a Prince spaghetti-sauce ad). Shakespeare was quoted and at times rewritten. Even *Old Yeller,* the sentimental, much-loved American children's tale, was given a new twist—a hilariously upbeat happy ending—from the Minneapolis ad agency Hunt Adkins, making the lighthearted point that "everything turns out better" when printed

30

on a certain brand of paper. In terms of
co-opting rock music, it might have seemed
Nike's "Revolution" had gone about as far as
one could go—but then in the mid-1990s
Mercedes-Benz came out with a commercial
whose soundtrack was Janis Joplin singing,
"Oh Lord, won't you buy me a Mercedes-Benz"
(lyrics that had originally been written by the
late Joplin as an ironic statement against
status symbols). Elsewhere around the world,
Elvis Presley was given a 1990s-style goatee
by a Finland agency promoting a nightclub,
and Fellini's film *La Dolce Vita* became the
basis of a European campaign for Martini
liquor. Was nothing sacred? Apple Computer
answered that question in the late 1990s,
when its "Think different" campaign began
featuring Gandhi and the Dalai Lama in ads.

Cultural guardians did not take kindly to
all this. Michiko Kakutani, a *New York Times*
book reviewer and culture critic, wrote,

"Advertising implacably forges ahead like one
of those indestructible sci-fi monsters, nonchalantly co-opting the very techniques used
against it. Just as it has co-opted rock-and-
roll alienation . . . and Dadaist jokes, so it
has now co-opted irony, parody and satire."
The end result, Kakutani concluded, is "a blurring of the lines between art and commerce."
To the charges that it has co-opted the culture,
advertising's creative community has a reasonable response: The culture belongs to everyone,
including ad creators. "Advertising is a reflection
of our shared experience as human beings,"
says Bob Kuperman of TBWA/Chiat/Day. "I
see no problem with using anything that
makes up that shared experience."

The debate on this issue has continued in
the new millennium and probably will not be
resolved soon. But as the 1990s progressed,
the cultural watchdogs weren't the only ones
expressing concerns about the new advertising.

Marketing traditionalists, including the
guardians of some of the world's foremost
brands, were beginning to raise another issue:
Just how far could the postmodern approach
to advertising go before it strayed too far
from the fundamentals of selling products?
Was it possible that the growing emphasis
on "anti-sell" statements and self-conscious
style was losing touch with basic logic and
strategy? They were reasonable questions from
the people paying the bills for the world's
advertising. And they would be amplified in
the late 1990s, as many ads strayed even
further from logic and rationality—and
moved into the wide-open, anything-goes
realm of "Oddvertising."

# 6. THE
# "ODDVER

RISE OF

RTISING."

1

1. **OUTPOST.COM**
CLIFF FREEMAN & PARTNERS,
NEW YORK, 1988
A pack of wolves was turned
loose on a marching band (with
cinematic license) in a bizarre
bit of stunt advertising for this
attention-hungry dot-com
company.

n a 1998 commercial for the Web site Outpost.com, the opening scene looks like a bit of classic advertising Americana: The camera follows a high school marching band, in full regalia, as members play their instruments and form the letters Outpost on a football field. So far so good, but as the ad's narrator explains, Outpost wanted to add something to make the commercial "more memorable." And so, the narrator deadpans, "we decided to release a pack of ravenous wolves." In the next scene, the wolves are shown attacking the band members, who drop their instruments and run for their lives. Laughing, the narrator concludes, "That's good stuff."

Welcome to the strange new world of "Oddvertising," where anything can happen in an ad—and quite often does. Beginning sometime in the mid-1990s and accelerating as the new millennium arrived, advertisers and their creative agencies increasingly began using advertisements to present extreme scenarios, offbeat characters, and at times baffling messages. Is this any way to advertise a product? Lately the answer to that question, both in America and around the world, seems to be a resounding yes.

"People have a real yearning for the unexpected in advertising now," observes the New York ad executive Cliff Freeman, the creator of the Outpost "Wolves" commercial. If it's a strange twist that viewers crave, Freeman— who has emerged as one of the leaders of the new Oddvertising—rarely disappoints. When his Outpost ads weren't unleashing wolves on marching bands, they were firing tiny rodents from a cannon. Freeman's infamous "Gerbils" commercial—not all that widely seen, yet probably one of the most influential American ads of the late 1990s—featured the same deadpan announcer, once again presiding with no shame over a shocking stunt intended to help viewers remember the Outpost name. This time, the "Outpost" letters were printed on a wall, with a hole in the O. The cannon was used to attempt to fire gerbils through the hole—although the first few shots were off-target, causing the critters to bounce off the wall (which didn't seem to bother the sadistic narrator in the least). One of the strangest aspects of the Outpost ads was that they didn't even bother to explain who the sponsor was or what products it offered; such dry, straightforward information seemingly had no place in advertising that was pure, unadulterated absurdity.

Freeman took a similar approach in some of his advertising for other clients. To promote hockey telecasts on the Fox TV network, ads posed the question, "What if other sports were like hockey?" We were then shown the outrageous answer as, in one ad, a golfer quietly and studiously lined up his putt—when suddenly a competing golfer charged onto the green and

2

BILLIARDS WOULD BE BETTER
IF IT WERE HOCKEY.

began attacking with his club, hockey-style. Still another Freeman ad, for the Fox Sports Web site, started out looking like a heart-wrenching public-service commercial, with a close-up view of a man's toes fumbling with a baby's diaper. Did this mean the man's hands were disabled? Not at all—the camera gradually revealed that the whole time, his fingers were busy tapping away on his computer keyboard as he visited the Fox Sports Web site.

The mischievous Freeman has not been the only one veering off the straight and narrow path of logical advertising. Bizarre ads have been surfacing all across the American advertising landscape, promoting brands large and small. In Adidas and Nike commercials, deranged sports fans were shown stalking athletes. The happy families once prevalent in commercials began to give way to the likes of the "Jukka brothers," stars of Fallon McElligott ads for MTV (like backwoods characters from the film

*Deliverance,* the Jukkas live in a remote cabin, watch only MTV, and occasionally whack one another on the backsides with paddles). In Budweiser's advertising, computer-generated lizards joked about committing murder. In presenting surreal or outrageous scenarios, many of the new ads typically adopted a deadpan tone of voice—with a number of ads using the format of an absurd documentary (or "mockumentary"), a style made popular by the commercials of the ESPN cable television network. Mockumentary ads could transport viewers into an imaginary world or subculture where characters behave obsessively and where the featured product or service—a sneaker, a TV channel—sometimes served as the object of obsession.

Oddvertising has marked a dramatic shift from the linear, easy-to-follow ads of old, and frequently leaves viewers shocked or mystified— though the best of these ads are usually amusing and intriguing, as well. The fever has not been

limited to American advertising. It has surfaced in the ads of the United Kingdom—which dabbled in Monty Python–style absurdity years ago but have now moved further into what the British ad executive John Hegarty calls "the new era of irrationality." One of Hegarty's own recent campaigns for Levi's exemplified the trend: Revolving around a mysterious man who is always shown accompanied by a living yellow puppet named "Flat Eric," the series of ads defied explanation. The stolid man and the frenetic puppet exchanged meaningful glances but never spoke as they traveled around, getting haircuts together, while being pursued by police for reasons never made clear. The mystery seemed to reel in viewers, as "Flat Eric" became a popular phenomenon, first in the UK and then in Germany. Another British campaign, for Tango orange drink, featured an orange-painted bald man who roamed around slapping people's ears for no good reason. And a popular ongoing

3

**THE SPORTSCENTER NEWSROOM, 10:47 A.M., AUGUST 23, 1995.**

Putting a live sports news and information show on the air three times a day is never easy, and at SportsCenter there are plenty of distractions to make it even more difficult. Here, anchor Steve Levy, who's preparing for the 6:30 show, finishes his cup of coffee while Olympic Champion Mary Lou Retton works out a new routine behind him.

**THIS IS SPORTSCENTER.** Mornings, primetime, late night.

©1995 ESPN

4. **ESPN NETWORK**
WIEDEN + KENNEDY,
PORTLAND, 1995
The One Club of New York
called this the ad campaign of
the decade. Using a "mockumentary" style, it took the
audience behind the scenes
at the sports network.

THE RISE OF "ODDVERTISING."

Polo Automatic 

5

6

7

### 5. VOLKSWAGEN
BMP DDB, LONDON, 1997
This campaign baffled the UK by
showing a series of photos of a
left shoe abandoned in the road
(by drivers who had been freed
from having to step on a clutch).

### 6. VOLKSWAGEN
ARNOLD COMMUNICATIONS,
BOSTON, 1997
The intrigue of Oddvertising: in
this TV commercial, we don't
know who these two men are or
why they picked up this old
smelly chair on the street.

### 7. VOLKSWAGEN
BMP DDB, LONDON, 1998
The wedding photo was ruined
because the photographer was
focusing on VW's low prices in
the background; the same series
featured distracted pedestrians
colliding with streetpoles.

THE RISE OF "ODDVERTISING."

8

**8. SONY VIDEO GAMES**
TBWA GGT SIMONS PALMER,
LONDON, 1999
This ad, a big winner at the
International Ad Festival in
Cannes, showed hard-core video
game fanatics displaying the
look of video game control
knobs in an eye-catching way.

**9. URGE SOFT DRINK**
LEO BURNETT, OSLO, 1997
If you don't understand the
headline, you're not alone; the
campaign used the obscure
vernacular of skateboarding
culture.

9

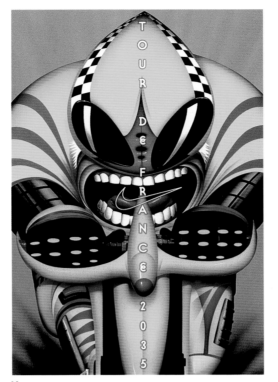

10

11

10. **NIKE / TOUR DE FRANCE**
KESSELSKRAMER,
AMSTERDAM, 1997
By the mid-1990s, the art used
in ads became more abstract,
impressionistic, and even a little
scary, as in this Dutch Nike poster.

11. **WHY EYEWEAR**
PALMER JARVIS DDB,
VANCOUVER, 1997
Turning the world upside down:
An old ad trick finds new life in
the era of Oddvertising.

British campaign for Volkswagen Polo depicts silent and strange little vignettes in which the characters are so surprised to learn of the car's low prices that they suddenly lose consciousness, dropping their faces into their food and walking into lampposts.

While odd advertising has been popping up around the world, some countries, such as Australia, seem particularly predisposed to it. Ads from Down Under have been over the top for years, though the new extremity of the trend can be seen in a commercial for the Australian "Ladies Masters" golf tournament—in which dominatrix female golfers tee up the ball on a man's nose and swing away (the ad ends with a shot showing a disembodied nose on the ground). One of the most popular Australian commercials of the late 1990s was a madcap bit of slapstick for Toyota entitled "Bugger!," wherein a series of mishaps involving a Toyota vehicle cause the commercial's characters to

repeatedly yell, "Bugger!"—the only dialogue in the ad.

Even markets that are generally considered more conservative have been experimenting with wild, offbeat approaches. For example, France has traditionally favored elegant, stylish advertising— which makes it all the more striking to encounter a French Orangina ad featuring a homicidal, chainsaw-wielding man dressed as a piece of fruit. And while Asia has the reputation of being a "straight-arrow" ad market, certain countries, such as Thailand, are embracing outrageousness. It's not uncommon to see wild Thai commercials starring transvestites painted silver. And Japan, whose advertising has long featured quirkiness, seems to be pushing new boundaries. An extremely popular ad campaign for Sega was not just peculiar but almost sadistic: Acknowledging that the company's past products were inferior to those of its competitors, the commercials featured a real-life

senior executive who was repeatedly humiliated on-screen as punishment for Sega's past mistakes. (In one ad, the man, Yukawa Hidekazu, overheard kids saying that "Sega video games suck." After drowning his sorrows at a bar, the drunken Yukawa got beaten up and lay sprawled on the ground while an off-camera voice said, "Come on, Mr. Yukawa, get up!") The campaign turned Yukawa into a pop celebrity in Japan.

As the Oddvertising fever spreads globally, the question arises, "Why are so many ads going a bit mad?" To some extent, eccentric behavior and quirky characters have been seen in commercials since the 1970s era of Charmin bathroom tissue's Mr. Whipple and his compulsive squeezing. The difference is really a matter of degree: Today's odd commercial characters have more of an edge to them and can seem genuinely deranged; Mr. Whipple's innocent fetish pales in comparison to the behavior of a 1990s ad character played by Dennis Hopper in Nike

13

12 AND 13. **NIKE**
WIEDEN + KENNEDY,
PORTLAND, 1997
Telling strange tales: In this
series, a goalie loses his job and
becomes homeless—all because
Nike skates made it easier for
his nemesis to score goals
against him.

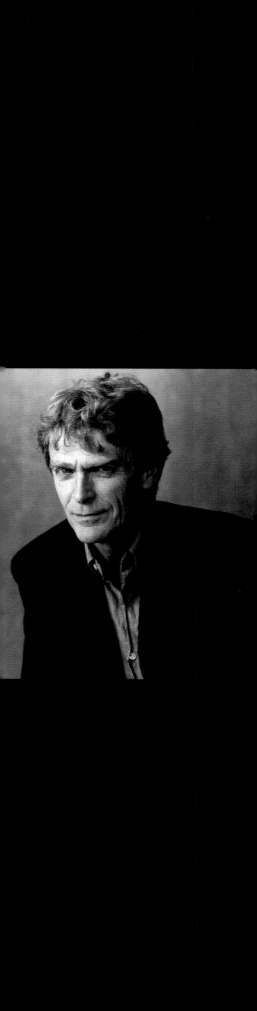

# INTERVIEW: JOHN HEGARTY

As creative director at the preeminent London ad agency Bartle Bogle Hegarty, John Hegarty has had a hand in creating many of the UK's most popular and innovative ad campaigns of the 1980s and 1990s. But no Hegarty creation has had a bigger impact than Flat Eric, a puppet that appeared in a series of commercials named the best advertising of 1999 by England's *Campaign* magazine. The success of the Flat Eric ads, which rapidly spread through Europe, seemed to defy rational explanation—as did the ads themselves. They featured very little dialogue, no coherent storyline, and a series of bizarre scenarios that followed the puppet and his human companion as they cruised in a car and bopped to "dirty house" music, were pursued by police, got a haircut, and somehow ended up in a mortuary. Hegarty himself isn't entirely certain why Eric became a cultural phenomenon—though he thinks it may have something to do with advertising's new "era of irrationality."

**WHEN AND WHY DID IRRATIONAL ADS LIKE "FLAT ERIC" START TO BECOME MORE POPULAR?**
You have to look at the history of this. First, advertising went through a period of being dominated by the "Unique Selling Proposition," which was based on the fact that technology was playing a greater part in the manufacture of products. If you go back to the 1950s, science seemed to have the answer to everything, and advertising used that as a means of promoting brand difference—new Colgate with extra fluoride, and so forth. But after a while, it was obvious that everybody had the technology, and no one company could stay ahead of the crowd. And then we moved toward the Emotional Selling Proposition, where the emotional value—how someone felt about that brand—became the point of difference.

But more recently, I think we've entered a new period, relying on what might be called the Irrational Selling Proposition. In the 1990s, advertisers found ourselves in a situation where a lot of it just wasn't working—there was too much, and people had become acutely able to filter it out. So increasingly, you had to do things to capture people's imaginations. Often that meant talking to a young media-literate

audience in a unique way. That could involve absurdity—because absurdity might provide a stimulation that people want.

In a sense, we're now saying a brand is about fun, and it has an element of irreverence about it—and that's what you try to capture with the advertising. With "Flat Eric," what we were doing is laughing at Levi's own culture; for a long time, Levi's ads had heroes who were muscled, handsome pinups—and now we wanted to break that mold and say, "Here is a hero who's a fluffy puppet. And if Flat Eric can be a hero then you can, even if you've got a pimply face, with thick glasses." People may look at that and ask, "Where's the logic?" The logic is as simple as that—he's fun. He's not taking things seriously, and Levi's is not taking its advertising overly seriously. We know that there's a game in progress, and we want you to enjoy the game.

**IS PART OF THE APPEAL THE MYSTERY OF THE ADS, THE FACT THAT WE DON'T REALLY KNOW WHAT'S GOING ON WITH THESE TWO CHARACTERS?**
Yes, that's a big part of it. You don't want to spell things out too much; you want to let the audience fill out the story for themselves, though we gave them little clues and ideas to work with. When the policeman pulls them over in one ad, you see their driver's licenses—very briefly, you have to look quickly to get it—and that's how you learn that he's called Flat Eric. And on the license, if you look really closely, you can barely make out his date of birth. But it was enough that on the Internet, we started getting birthday cards for him. You give people lots of clues and allow them to get to it. The trouble with most advertising is that it completes everything for you. Which means there's nothing left for you to do, and consequently, your mind is off doing something else while the commercial is on.

**ISN'T THERE A DANGER OF GOING OFF-TRACK WITH ODD ADS LIKE THIS?**
Of course. The danger is that one can look at the Irrational Selling Proposition and say, "Well, this is a license to do anything." But it's not. There always should be a line of logic there—and you have to be careful how you

track that line of logic, because if you don't have that there, then you will produce stuff that has no bearing on the brand. In the case of "Flat Eric," the logic is that Levi's is spoofing its own culture.

**IN THE U.S., THERE HAS BEEN A BACKLASH AGAINST SOME OFFBEAT, ENTERTAINMENT-DRIVEN ADS; SOME MARKETERS HAVE REJECTED THEM AND CALLED FOR MORE OF A HARD-SELL APPROACH.**
Well, they're right in a sense. There are some people creating ads now who are trying a little too hard to be wacky or edgy. It's like everything—imitators come along and don't quite understand the process that was going on originally. And they end up with the trappings of it but not the real meaning of it. We shouldn't be trying to be wacky. However, we should be trying to be entertaining. If you do that, you involve someone in the process and draw them into your sphere of influence. And then you want to link that back to the brand in some way.

I also must say, I've always disliked these terms *hard sell* versus *soft sell*. People use the term hard sell as an argument that's turned against creativity—that creativity doesn't sell. But in fact, great creative advertising has always sold better than conventional *hard-sell* advertising. The problem with the hard-sell ad is that it doesn't intrigue me, it doesn't seduce me, it doesn't create an ambience that I want to enter into. It just shouts at me. It might make the company sales director feel comfortable, but the consumer increasingly is rejecting it. Because in the end, if it worked—if advertising were that simple—we'd all be doing it that way.

In a world of strange tastes,
there's always Bass Ale.

15

14. (PREVIOUS SPREAD)
**BASS ALE**
WEISS WHITTEN STAGLIANO,
NEW YORK, 1997
Fetishism takes center stage in
this ad for a distinguished
British beer.

15. **NIKON**
FALLON McELLIGOTT,
MINNEAPOLIS, MINNESOTA,
1996
A photographer gets KO'ed by a
kangaroo: A good argument for
zoom lenses.

16. **DEJA.COM**
DINOTO LEE, NEW YORK, 1999
The dot-coms, in particular,
tended to feature odd scenarios;
many believed it would help
them to penetrate media clutter.

commercials, in which Hopper is shown stalking athletes and sniffing their shoes in the locker room when no one is looking. The other difference now is the prevalence of bizarre ads: A decade ago, they were rare and served as curiosities. The American fashion designer Calvin Klein, for example, was among the first to dabble in strangeness, producing "Obsession" ads in which emotionally tormented characters spoke in obtuse, highly artificial dialogue— which often ended up being the object of well-deserved ridicule or parody. (Klein's particular brand of Oddvertising was different from today's in that it seemed to take itself so seriously; the ads borrowed more from Ingmar Bergman than from Monty Python, and that pretentiousness drove viewers to distraction.) But in today's environment, Klein's ads begin to seem almost coherent and not all that unusual. There are now so many "offbeat" ads that the word no longer is appropriate; such ads now *are* the beat.

To some extent, the mainstreaming of oddness could be seen as just another step in the evolution that began with Doyle Dane Bernbach's reinvention of advertising. At the heart of much of DDB's work was the element of surprise— designed to give ads a twist, a look, an attitude that caught the public off-guard. That continued to be a primary objective of creative advertising in the 1980s and early 1990s, as the American ad executive Jeff Goodby notes. "It's become more and more important for advertising to be intriguing in some way, and to give people the sense that they don't know where the story is going," says Goodby. As that became increasingly difficult to do, advertisers had to resort to ever more unusual stories, situations, and characters in order to surprise the audience.

Bartle Bogle Hegarty's John Hegarty believes that in the 1990s, many advertisers began to fully realize that the public could no longer be reached with rational messages, neatly packaged and presented. "People were just filtering it out," says Hegarty. "Increasingly, you had to do unusual things to capture people's imaginations. Lots of the old rules have gone by the boards." What campaigns like "Flat Eric" are now presenting, Hegarty says, is not so much a coherent message as "an attempt to talk to a young, media-literate audience in a unique way." The ads may seem illogical, but, Hegarty adds, "I could argue that they are logical in their own way—they're part of the irrational selling proposition that has emerged in the 1990s."

Cliff Freeman believes that a big factor driving this trend has been a profound change in the attitudes of sponsors, including larger clients like Budweiser, Miller Brewing Co., and the Mars candy company, all of whom have gravitated toward more unconventional ads. "Even the big clients are loosening up," Freeman notes. Engulfed by more competition, greater product parity, and fragmented media, "they're

17

**17. LITTLE CAESARS PIZZA**
CLIFF FREEMAN & PARTNERS,
NEW YORK, 1995
Cliff Freeman was a pioneer of
wild and crazy advertising; the
"Training Camp" commercial,
showing the rigorous training
of pizza delivery boys, became
a new classic.

**18. ECAMPUS.COM**
DEVITO VERDI, NEW YORK,
1999
More dot-com madness: In this
ad, an American college student
and fraternity boy shows off
his ability to recite the entire
alphabet—while burping.

18

realizing that nobody can play it safe anymore,"
he says.

In fact, advertising in recent years has come
to be led by a different kind of sponsor. In the
past, large and conservative packaged-goods
companies, like Procter & Gamble, controlled
much of the airtime and set the general tone for
advertising. But today, some of the biggest
advertisers—and certainly the most influential—
are younger, more daring entrepreneurial companies like Apple Computer, Nintendo, and Nike,
who are much more inclined to produce quirky
advertising designed to project a hip image.

If there is a single category of advertiser that
most favors the shoot-from-the-hip style of
Oddvertising, it is the Internet-based companies—the so-called dot-coms—whose outrageous
imagery and messages began to flood the airwaves and the print media in the late 1990s.
The aforementioned Outpost led the charge, but
other dot-com clients were just as willing to

present bizarre scenarios. The Web site
Ecampus.com ran ads showing college students
belching, and depicted one student so strapped
for cash he cooked up his goldfish for food.
Another site, for Beyond.com, created ads
featuring a stay-at-home businessman who
paraded in front of his neighbors in the nude.
The emphasis on egregious behavior in the
dot-com ad market was partly driven by
desperation. In a crowded, rapidly growing
marketplace filled with no-name newcomers,
these companies needed to take drastic measures
to draw attention to themselves. As many of the
dot-com clients approached their agencies, they
made it very clear what was needed: Get us
noticed, by any means necessary. Outpost, for
example, specifically challenged Cliff Freeman to
"do whatever it takes to drive people to the Web
site." It was a wide-open challenge that Freeman,
and many other top creative people in advertising,
eagerly embraced. However, the result, as

*The New York Times* noted in mid-1999, was
often not a pretty sight: "Dot-com advertising
seems to be the place where practically no bodily
function is too private and no rude behavior is
too coarse to be featured in a spot."

The rush of these dot-com ads was the most
obvious manifestation of the booming Western
economies of the late 1990s, but those strong
global economic conditions also seemed to foster
offbeat advertising in a variety of other markets
and product categories. The American ad executive Andy Berlin believes that the boom times
emboldened advertisers, giving them confidence
to take more risks. The noted Massachusetts
Institute of Technology economist Paul Krugman
also observed a link between economics and wild
ads. "When TV commercials get funny, that's
a sign of excessive optimism," Krugman noted.
Advertisers loosen up because, Krugman says,
"when the market is very bubbly, they think they
can get away with that. The point is to get the

JOE BOXER®

Change Daily.

19

attention of people who have plenty of money to spend." On the other hand, "when things turn bad, they just repeat the product [name] fifteen times," Krugman says, echoing Mary Wells's famous "Hard times demand hard selling" statement. Certainly, the larger ad budgets of the 1990s allowed for the kind of ad experimentation that usually isn't attempted during leaner economic times.

While sociological and economic factors fueled the rise of Oddvertising, its spread can also be attributed to an even more powerful force in advertising: imitation. Advertising creators are never shy about jumping on bandwagons; one of the plagues of the industry is that creative people study award-show annuals to see what played well the previous year—then shamelessly begin creating similar ads themselves. In this case, several bizarre mid-1990s campaigns caught the fancy of the public and the advertising creative community, and subsequently kicked the trend into high gear.

Freeman was a pivotal player, and his impact was felt long before the Outpost campaign. In the early 1990s, his agency's highly successful campaigns for Little Caesars pizza could take the simplest, most mundane idea and turn it into wild theater of the absurd. For example, when Little Caesars decided to offer pizza delivery, Freeman created a commercial called "Training Camp," a behind-the-scenes mini-film that purported to show how the company was rigorously training its pizza deliverymen (the trainees are drilled, over and over, on how to outrun dogs and how to kick the car door shut while carrying pizzas in both hands).

Another highly influential campaign came from Wieden + Kennedy. For the cable-TV sports channel ESPN, W+K set out to create ads showing that ESPN sportscasters lived, breathed, and were completely immersed in the world of sports. Inspired by the mock-documentary film *This Is Spinal Tap*, the agency created a series

of commercials that supposedly took the viewer behind the scenes at ESPN headquarters to reveal a sports fantasy world: The channel's sportscasters casually mingled at the office with superstar athletes, as gymnasts danced atop ESPN desks, a basketball star played the piano for tips in the company lounge, and a pole vaulter used his pole to carry around neckties for the sportscasters.

With the popularity of the ESPN campaign (lauded by *TV Guide* as one of the top television ad campaigns of all time), a wave of similar mockumentary-style ads began to surface. A campaign for the Seattle Supersonics basketball team, from the agency WongDoody, showed the team's star players trying to get closer to their fans by visiting ordinary people's homes—then agreeing to help with household chores like washing the dishes. Mockumentaries weren't limited to sports ads; the format was also used to freshen up ads featuring old-fashioned characters

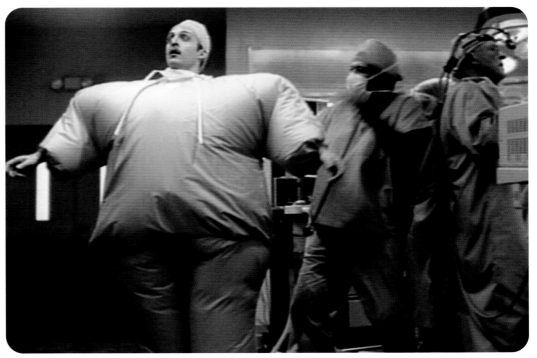

20

19. **JOE BOXER**
ODIORNE WILDE NARRAWAY +
PARTNERS, SAN FRANCISCO,
1998
For this free-spirited underwear
company, OWN+P's creative
director said he wanted to
show "slices of life"—but a bit
twisted. He explained, "We
developed a campaign we called
'Norman Rockwell on acid.'"

20. **LEVI'S JEANS**
FOOTE CONE & BELDING,
SAN FRANCISCO, 1995
The commercial "Doctors" was
set on an operating room table;
as a patient lay in critical
condition, doctors danced to
the rhythm of the EKG machine.

21

21. **LEE JEANS**
FALLON McELLIGOTT,
MINNEAPOLIS, MINNESOTA,
1998
A new kind of ad hero: Buddy
Lee, a tiny doll with a big head,
saves the day in ridiculous ways.

22. **MENTOS**
PAHNKE & PARTNERS,
AMSTERDAM, 1992
Tapping into the power of
"badvertising," Mentos ads
were cheesy and awkward—
and the MTV crowd loved to
laugh at them.

23. **LEVI STRAUSS EUROPE —
STA-PREST**
BARTLE BOGLE HEGARTY,
LONDON, 1999
Flat Eric, the orange puppet, was
a mystery that intrigued Europe
(in the U.S., a poor imitation
called "Bad Andy" failed to
generate the same appeal).

22

23

like Tony the Tiger. One series featured interviews in which people speculated on the existence of the animated tiger (as one man is interviewed, the viewer catches a fleeting glimpse of Tony rushing past a window in the background). A similar series of ads followed a team of people trying to track down the elusive Energizer Bunny.

Part of the appeal of the mockumentary, aside from the absurd humor, was that the ads tended to have an intentionally raw, cinema-verité film style—distinguishing them from the more polished big-budget ads that viewers were accustomed to seeing. With Oddvertising, bad can be good: Often, the more awkward and amateurish an ad seems, the better it may play to a younger audience that responds to camp and kitsch. The best example of this—and another seminal ad in the emergence of the genre—was an accidental hit campaign that came to America from Europe in the mid-1990s. The candy

Mentos arrived from Holland as a relatively unknown brand, with ads produced in-house by a Dutch production team. The ads featured ludicrous scenarios that always ended with one smiling character giving the camera an overly enthusiastic thumbs-up signal. In an age of cynicism, such pure hokiness seemed to have emerged from a time warp. Making matters worse—or in this case, better—the campaign had been exported to America complete with awkward English translation; for example, the candy was referred to as "the fresh-maker." The ads were so amateurish that it was difficult not to laugh at them, and they soon became a cult hit, joyfully ridiculed by young fans on the Internet.

Naturally, more sophisticated advertisers soon tried to imitate the "schlock as chic" appeal of Mentos, creating intentionally bad ads. Commercials for the clothing retailer Old Navy, starring a motley collection of grade-B American celebrities like the actress Morgan Fairchild,

combined silly scenarios, stiff dialogue, and hokey songs. But they lacked the innocent charm of the Mentos campaign, demonstrating that it's actually hard to make something so bad it's good. Some advertisers also tried to inject camp appeal into their ads by giving them a nostalgic, unsophisticated, and old-fashioned tone—harking back to the days when advertising was chock-full of phony optimism. One of the more successful retro-campaigns was for Altoids breath mints, invoking images and featuring graphic design that seemed to be from a bygone era. Meanwhile, Lee Jeans even resurrected an old mascot, the Buddy Lee doll, and made the doll the star of a series of mockumentary commercials.

If Mentos had successfully exported "bad is good" appeal, Diesel, another European brand, used advertising surrealism as its international calling card. Perhaps never had a single ad campaign managed to bewilder so many people all around the world: With highly stylized

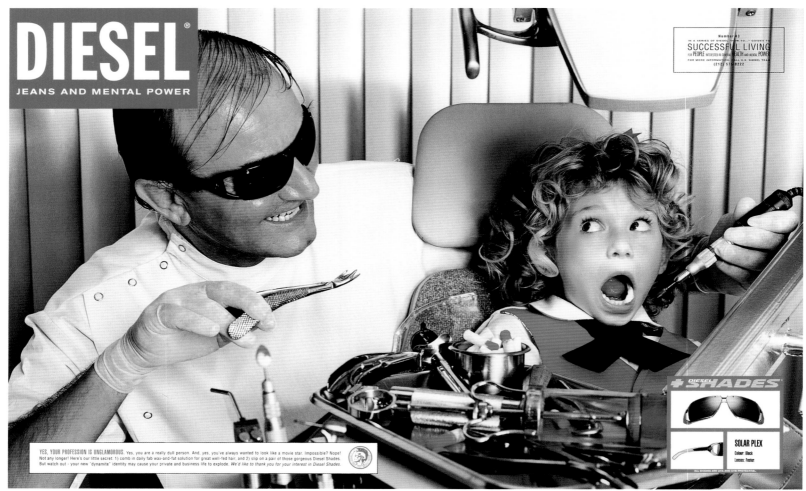

24

25

24 AND 25. **DIESEL**
PARADISET DDB,
STOCKHOLM, 1992–95
Absurd scenes, stylized
photography, and ironic copy
were the hallmarks of this
campaign. The ads were
mocking something, but it
wasn't clear what.

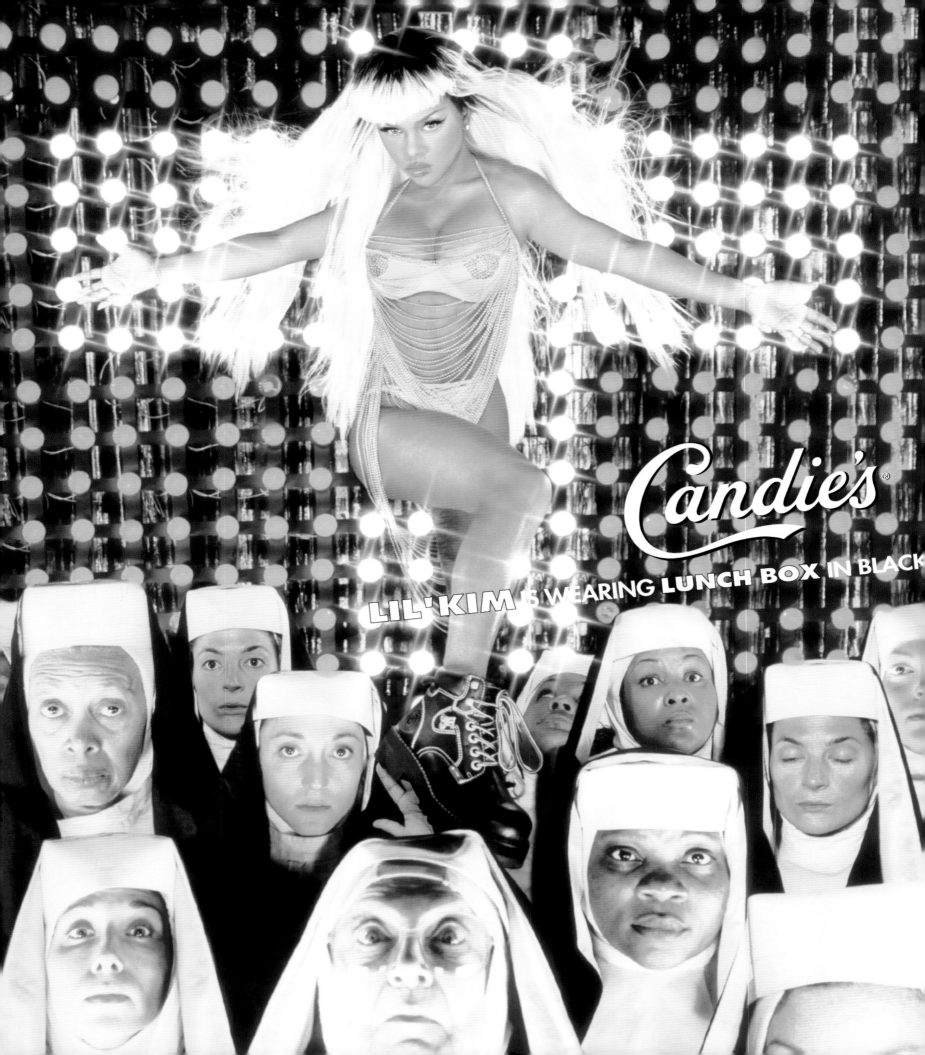

27

**26. CANDIE'S**
IN-HOUSE AGENCY,
NEW YORK, 1998
The photographer David
LaChapelle, who worked on
Diesel campaigns, specialized in
artificial, over-the-top imagery.
Here, he poses a sexy American
hip-hop star among nuns.

**27. CAMEL CIGARETTES**
GYRO, PHILADELPHIA,
1998–99
Camel used the Oddvertising
approach to make smoking
seem hip. In this ad, nothing is
to be taken seriously, including
the warning label.

images of politicians in diapers, evil dentists, and sun-worshipping senior citizens, the ads promised to dispense life lessons (how to get rich, how to get a suntan, how to control wild animals), but the copy dripped with irony. Diesel ads seemed to be mocking something—American commercialism? Vapid fashion models? The self-righteous, socially conscious ads of its competitor Benetton?—but the target wasn't particularly clear. For all their postmodern absurdity, the ads could also be maddeningly pretentious and heavy-handed in their attempts at satire, which probably only added to their abrasiveness and ultimately their effectiveness. Loved or hated, the ads for this Italian fashion company would not be ignored. The agency behind the campaign, Sweden's DDB Paradiset and its creative director Joakim Jonason, seemed to specialize in this type of overstylized, incomprehensible advertising, creating similar work for other clients in Europe.

A number of brands around the world tried to copy the Diesel style, and did so, in part, by hiring the photographer who had shot some of the ads in the campaign, David LaChapelle. LaChapelle had a knack for shooting real-life images that looked cartoonish and surreal, and he brought that style to ads for the Italian motor-scooter company Aprilia, as well as to his work for Bass Ale and Candie's clothing. One of LaChapelle's more noteworthy campaigns was for Camel cigarettes—for whom he created wild, orgiastic scenes that exaggerated the classic cigarette-ad depictions of frolicking cheerful smokers; even the Camel headline, which screamed "Mighty tasty!," was intentionally fake and campy.

But nowhere was the Diesel influence more significant than in the advertising produced by Miller Brewing Co. in the late 1990s. Miller—which had long been one of the most important advertisers in America, dating back to its famous "Tastes Great, Less Filling" celebrity campaign

that ran during the 1970s—opted to take a big gamble when it put its advertising in the hands of the creative agency Fallon McElligott. Fallon, in turn, gave the assignment to a Swedish creative team that had worked on Diesel before being hired and brought to America by Fallon. The campaign that Linus Karlson and Paul Malmstrom created for Miller Lite bore touches of Diesel's absurdity and self-referential humor. Early ads were introduced by a fictitious adman named "Dick," who was sarcastically described as "a creative superstar." The vignettes that were presented—supposedly the work of Dick—were as weird as anything previously seen in American advertising. One ad featured a cheesy magic act that concluded with the magician's female assistant suddenly sprouting mice under her arms; another was a short silent film that followed a man with no pants; a third was a singing tribute to a menacing costumed character called Evil Beaver. What did any of this

28. **KICKERS CLOTHING**
MOTHER, LONDON,
LATE 1990s
Despite appearances, this ad
ran in England, not Asia; the
advertiser knew that bathroom
humor is a universal language.

29. **RED KAMEL CIGARETTES**
GYRO, PHILADELPHIA,
1998–99
Red Kamel, a spinoff cigarette
brand geared to younger
smokers, featured campy scenes
that seemed to spring from the
World War II era, though the ads
ran in the late 1990s.

strangeness have to do with beer? It was a good question, and soon it was being asked by more than a few people.

The campaign became a lightning rod for controversial debate within the American ad industry in the late 1990s. It was one thing for a trendy European fashion brand like Diesel to embrace surreal, absurdist advertising; for a mainstream brand like Miller to do so was considered marketing heresy by some, including many of the company's beer distributors—who began to demand that Miller return to more conventional advertising.

The Miller uproar triggered a larger discussion within the ad industry about offbeat advertising. By the late 1990s, ads had so much freedom to explore and experiment that the period was one of unfettered creativity—at least, this was the optimist's view. Advertising seemed to have become a form of sponsored entertainment that could be highly expressive or individualistic. In

effect, companies were hiring offbeat storytellers to create brief skits or tales, often in an absurd style; the clients simply attached their logo onto the end of the sketch, but otherwise didn't inject much selling into the theatrics. This new advertising was certainly daring in that it was apparently unafraid to present unconventional themes and characters. And since it was unencumbered by sales pitches and logic, the story could go anywhere. Ad creator Freeman observed in 1998 that "the opportunities to try something different or unusual are probably greater now than they've ever been." And he defended the outrageousness of the new ads as a reflection of real human behavior, which was, for the first time, being depicted more honestly in advertising. "Offbeat ads might be tapping into feelings and desires to just let go," he said, "and to laugh at things we weren't supposed to laugh at in the past."

But others saw problems with the trend. The violence, antisocial behavior, profanity, and

cynicism in some of the ads seemed to have "moved beyond irreverence—it's kind of nihilistic," observed Marty Cooke, a creative director with the M&C Saatchi agency. The creative director Woody Kay of the Boston agency Pagano Schenck & Kay noted, "The increasing volume of mean-spirited humor and cynicism is a bit depressing. Humor and irony seem to have bullied sincerity and emotion into submission." And the veteran New York ad executive Jerry Della Femina described the new wild advertising's relationship to consumers as follows: "We don't sell them anymore; we stun them."

One of the biggest critics of the trend was *Advertising Age* publisher Rance Crain, who continually argued that ads were losing all touch with reason and strategy. "The technique most in vogue today is sheer unabashed outrageousness," Crain wrote, adding that "the creative people have taken over the asylum and we're all being held captive."

29

30

31

**30. MAGIC RADIO**
MOTHER, LONDON,
LATE 1990s
This campaign used special
effects and hyper-saturated
colors to achieve absurd results;
here, dogs appear to move to
the music on the radio.

**32. OHIO THEATRE**
MAD DOGS & ENGLISHMEN,
NEW YORK, 1991
Small clients and unusual
offerings lent themselves to off-
beat humor in ads. In this ad for
a musical, we learn what made
Frankenstein sing.

**31. VODKA SOURCE**
MOTHER, LONDON,
LATE 1990s
Murder and mayhem were
played for laughs in this campaign, which featured a couple
of perky, beautiful Swedish
women who also happened to
be cold-blooded killers.

**Frankenstein. The Musical. Feb 22 - Mar 10. Ohio Theatre.**

32

Crain and other critics particularly focused on the Miller Lite campaign, noting that the brewery's sales were not performing well during the "Dick" campaign. Similarly, Freeman's Outpost ads were cited as an example of an outrageous campaign that initially drew attention but didn't help the Web site generate much sales; the "flying gerbil" was quickly grounded. Also coming under attack was the Nissan "Toys" commercial, a highly entertaining spot in which dolls resembling G.I. Joe and Barbie come to life and ride across a living-room floor in a toy car; the ad contained no sales pitch at all, which, even in an era of soft sell, was still highly unusual for automobile advertising. Echoing Clara Peller's famous cry about the missing beef in the Wendy's burger, Crain and other marketing traditionalists screamed, "Where's the strategy?" To which creative-siders like the American copywriter Mark Fenske countered: If the strategy were easily visible to pundits like Crain, then it would also be far too transparent to consumers. "When the strategy clearly shows through in an ad," Fenske observed, "that's about as effective as fishing with a hook that has no worm on it."

In the end, for Miller Brewing at least, dollars were the deciding factor. Because of its flagging beer sales, Miller pulled the plug on the "Dick" campaign, and by mid-1999, had returned to an updated variation on its classic "Tastes Great, Less Filling" strategy. (These new "conventional" ads didn't produce stellar sales results, either—which led some observers to wonder whether perhaps Miller's problems went beyond the advertising.)

The backlash seemed to be extending to other marketers. While offbeat ads continued to proliferate at the close of the century, a simultaneous trend saw some advertisers returning to more classic approaches. Volkswagen, in its relaunch of the Beetle, created a campaign that borrowed some of the style and sensibility of the great DDB campaign of the 1960s. Old familiar characters—including Kentucky Fried Chicken's Colonel Sanders and Charmin's Mr. Whipple—were brought back from the dead. Camel cigarettes abandoned its wacky "Mighty Tasty" campaign, and opted for a more old-fashioned theme. And even some of the wild-and-crazy dot-coms (including Outpost, which parted company with Freeman) began to tone down their ads somewhat.

But the overall advertising landscape remained a wild and untamed frontier as the new millennium arrived. For a new generation of advertisers, it seemed to be a world of "anything goes"—though, of course, it wasn't really. As the battle-scarred veterans of advertising controversies attest in the next chapter, the fact is that even in the "brave" new world of Oddvertising, there are certain boundaries that ads can never safely cross.

# 7. PUSH THE LIMITS

SHING
MITS.

1. **PERSONAL CONDOMS**
KIRSHENBAUM & BOND,
NEW YORK, 1987
By the late 1980s, advertisers
were taking more risks; K&B
was a small agency that gained
notoriety by creating cheeky ads
like this one.

2. **DEMOCRATIC NATIONAL
COMMITTEE**
DOYLE DANE BERNBACH,
NEW YORK, 1964
This ad for U.S. President
Lyndon B. Johnson used scare
tactics—an image of an atomic
explosion—to discourage voters
from choosing the opposition.
But it was a rarity, and
controversial, at the time.

1

f one were to think of advertising as a living creature that has evolved and adapted through generations, it would seem that the species started out relying on aggression—repeatedly clubbing its hard-sell message home in those early days—then gradually developed more of a reasoning mind that could even, occasionally, express thoughts abstractly. But as this evolution took place, there was one part of "Adman" that was slow to develop: the backbone.

Fear has always been uppermost in the minds of advertisers. The guardians of the world's great brands long worried that their advertising might somehow alienate consumers or send the wrong message about a product or, worst of all, stir up controversy that could yield bad publicity for the brand. Because of this, many advertisers imposed strict limitations on what the ad creators could do, and repeatedly tested and retested ads to make sure no one could possibly be offended. In most cases, the ad creators hardly needed to

be reined in: Acutely aware that any misstep could cost them the account, they tended to be just as cautious as the brand managers.

But this approach began to change somewhat in the 1960s, as some of the Creative Revolution agencies started producing more provocative advertising—partly to draw attention to their clients and partly to make a name for themselves. Bill Bernbach was, again, at the forefront in challenging advertising conservatism; he seemed to understand early on that while controversy might not necessarily be good, it wasn't always a bad thing, either. In 1964, Bernbach produced a commercial with imagery that was unthinkable in advertising: To promote the presidential campaign of Lyndon Baines Johnson against the more militaristic candidate Barry Goldwater, Doyle Dane Bernbach showed a little girl picking petals off a daisy—then ended the spot by showing the mushroom cloud of an atomic explosion. The commercial shocked America and drew a

fair amount of criticism, perhaps justified: Was it fair or even conscionable to suggest that Goldwater wanted to blow up the world? But it hit the message home, and Americans chose the LBJ brand in November.

But even though the 1960s produced some examples of advertising derring-do, it was limited and short-lived. Subsequently, throughout the 1970s and early 1980s, "advertisers began subjecting everything we did to tests," says DDB's Roy Grace, and much of the testing was designed to weed out any possible controversial elements in ads. It wasn't until the mid-to-late 1980s, and particularly the 1990s, that attitudes toward controversy in ads truly began to change. Increasingly, some advertisers began to actually court trouble. Among certain ad agencies, it suddenly became a badge of honor to have produced ads that made clients nervous and set tongues wagging. The Los Angeles agency Chiat/Day, run by the maverick ad executive Jay Chiat and

VOTE FOR PRESIDENT JOHNSON
ON NOVEMBER 3.

2

AN AUTHENTIC ITALIAN RESTAURANT WHERE NO ONE'S BEEN SHOT.

YET.

Positano
250 Park Avenue South
N.Y.C.
212-777-6211

Advertising Agency: Kirshenbaum & Bond

3

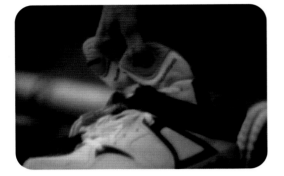

4

**3. POSITANO RESTAURANT**
KIRSHENBAUM & BOND,
NEW YORK, 1987
K&B wasn't afraid to use ethnic
humor in its ads; this one for a
New York restaurant makes fun
of the Mafia's reputation for
gunning down mobsters in
Italian eateries.

**4. REEBOK**
CHIAT/DAY, NEW YORK, 1989
Death comes to advertising:
This TV commercial showed two
bungee jumpers; only the one
wearing Reeboks survived. It was
pulled off the air after viewers
complained.

his artful creative lieutenant Lee Clow, forged its identity as a creator of "dangerous" ads; the agency even hoisted a pirate flag in its offices as a warning signal to the world. The creative staff at Chiat insisted that they never actually sought out trouble—rather, they claimed, it was usually a by-product of speaking more candidly and boldly in ads. "We're not consciously trying to stir controversy," Clow said. "But somehow, we touch nerves."

When showing its risky ideas to clients who were understandably nervous, Chiat/Day would push and push (sometimes threatening to resign the account) until eventually the client agreed to run a daring ad—the "1984" commercial for Apple Computer being one of the more noteworthy examples of this. Occasionally, the controversial spots backfired on the agency and its clients: The successful "1984" was followed up the next year with another Apple commercial called "Lemmings," which showed a group of

blindfolded businessmen following a Pied Piper (IBM, perhaps?) and eventually marching off a cliff. The ad had an impact, certainly, but this time the effect was more depressing than exhilarating: America wasn't quite ready for depictions of mass suicide on Super Bowl Sunday. (Even after this experience, Chiat/Day had no fear of showing people falling to their deaths in commercials: A few years later, the agency produced a Reebok ad in which two bungee jumpers fling themselves off a cliff; the one wearing Reeboks bounces back up on his tether, while on the other side, all that remains is a pair of empty sneakers on a rope. It ran for a short time, drew heavy criticism, and then was pulled off the air.)

But even if their controversial ads sometimes fell flat, creative agencies and their attention-starved clients reveled in the attention they attracted. A controversy could turn an unknown ad creator and his obscure clients into media

stars overnight, as Richard Kirshenbaum proved in the late 1980s. A cofounder of Kirshenbaum & Bond, a tiny New York agency whose early clients included a local shoe store and an Italian manufacturer of condoms, Kirshenbaum had to operate on a limited budget—his small clients couldn't afford to buy much ad space or television time. But he found a way to thrust them in the spotlight nonetheless. One of his condom ads featured a full-frontal view of Michelangelo's *David*, with the headline "Who's better equipped than the Italians to design the world's best condoms?" For his shoe client, Kenneth Cole, Kirshenbaum created ads that ridiculed public figures of the day, including the vice president of the United States, Dan Quayle (one ad showed Quayle, notorious for his poor spelling, under the headline "Don't Forget to Vot").

Such ads prompted a blizzard of media coverage, both for the clients and for the agency. Kirshenbaum would subsequently describe this

Calvin Klein Jeans

6

**5. CALVIN KLEIN JEANS**
IN-HOUSE AGENCY, NEW YORK, 1980
Calvin Klein was constantly pushing the boundaries; his famous Brooke Shields ads sexualized the teenager.

**6. BRAATHENS SAFE AIRLINE**
LEO BURNETT, OSLO, 1993
In the commercial "Naked Lunch," a man arriving home early from a business trip decides to surprise his wife—but he's unaware that her parents are also in the house.

## THE SUGGESTED RETAIL PRICE OF THIS SHIRT IS $125. WE HAVE A SUGGESTION FOR WHOEVER SUGGESTED IT.

We also have a suggestion for you. Come into Daffy's where you'll find men's, women's and children's fashion & designer clothing 40-75% off, every day. New York City; Manhasset, NY; Philadelphia; Elizabeth, East Hanover, Paramus and Wayne, NJ; and Potomac Mills Mall, VA.

**DAFFY'S**
CLOTHES THAT WILL MAKE YOU, NOT BREAK YOU.

7

phenomenon as "the multiplier effect"—meaning that as ads attracted heavy news coverage, their exposure level was multiplied without additional expense; an advertiser might spend a million dollars running K&B's ads and end up with $10 million worth of publicity. (This theory, of course, does not distinguish between good and bad attention, abiding by the Oscar Wilde philosophy that the only thing worse than being talked about is not being talked about.)

Agencies like Chiat/Day and Kirshenbaum & Bond weren't the only ones living on the edge in the 1980s; some sponsors were out there, too. It seemed that no one understood the multiplier effect better than fashion designer Calvin Klein, who drew early attention by putting an adolescent Brooke Shields in jeans ads and having her deliver the sexually suggestive line "Nothing comes between me and my Calvins." That was just the beginning for Klein, who, throughout the 1980s and 1990s, continued to push the

boundaries of sexual explicitness in advertising. *Advertising Age* critic Bob Garfield called Klein "the pioneer of 'shockvertising,'" noting that the designer's modus operandi was to "inflame the many in order to impress the view. Klein didn't create ads, he created Molotov cocktails—he'd toss them out there to see what would happen."

Of course, it remained risky to do this (as Klein would discover firsthand with the infamous "kiddie porn" controversy of the mid-1990s, discussed later). But by the 1990s, a growing number of advertisers could justify taking these risks because of their desperate need to generate attention in a landscape that made it hard to stand out. With the media increasingly cluttered by expanded cable channels, the Internet, and an explosion of advertising in all forms, an interesting reversal took place in the minds of at least some marketers, who now began to feel, in the words of Mary Stow of London's Howell Henry Chaldecott Lury & Partners, that "the biggest

risk is to be safe—because if you're safe you're invisible and you waste your money." One of Stow's agency partners, Steve Henry, advised fellow ad creators, "Get your work banned." To Henry, having ads occasionally struck down by the British media or government was taken as a healthy sign that the Howell Henry agency was doing its job right. It was a way of thinking that began to take hold at creative ad agencies around the world. "We try to be on the edge all the time, and sometimes a bit over the edge when a brand needs shock therapy," said Johan Kramer, of the Amsterdam-based agency KesselsKramer, whose commercials for a healthcare service featured men and women walking through the ad naked. (Actually, those ads didn't shock Kramer's fellow Dutch citizens all that much; "it's hard to be controversial here, because we're very liberal in Holland," he says.)

In fact, much of Europe, and parts of Asia, have tended to be far ahead of America in terms

8

To ensure our Belgian chocolates

# LOSE

none of their smoothness,
we strictly

# CONTROL

their temperature and humidity.

**Häagen-Dazs**

Dedicated to Pleasure

9

9. **HAAGEN-DAZS**
BARTLE BOGLE HEGARTY,
LONDON, 1991
This early 1990s campaign
shocked England by taking on
two taboos at once: not just sex,
but interracial sex.

10. **LEVI STRAUSS EUROPE**
BARTLE BOGLE HEGARTY,
LONDON, 1990
BBH played nudity for laughs in
this ad; it contrasted a pair of
Levi's (which become more
comfortable over time) with
something that doesn't benefit
from aging: the human body.

10

of pushing the boundaries of sexuality in advertising. As far back as thirty years ago, French ads were not only featuring topless women but threatening to go further: In a famous series of outdoor billboards that appeared in the 1960s, the first billboard featured a woman wearing only a bikini bottom, and promised that in the next ad the woman would be shown completely naked; sure enough, she was, although this time the picture was shot from behind. As a French advertising executive from the agency Leo Burnett recently said, when it comes to French advertising, "you can use a breast in anything, provided you can think of a vaguely plausible reason for doing so." Scandinavian advertising has tended to be even more permissive when it comes to nudity and sex, often using these as the basis for commercial storylines. One memorable Norwegian airline commercial, "Naked Lunch," featured a man who arrives home early from a business trip; peering through the keyhole, he

sees his wife sitting quietly, sipping tea. He promptly strips off his clothes and bursts into the room naked with a rose clenched in his teeth—only to discover that sitting across the room from his wife are his in-laws. Even the supposedly staid British—who still have an occasional tendency to "snicker like schoolboys" when referring to sex in ads, according to creative director Gerard Stamp of Leo Burnett in London—have lately been producing a number of ads that deal with sex and nudity in an understated, elegant manner, as in a stylishly sensuous campaign from the London agency Bartle Bogle Hegarty featuring intertwined bare bodies (promoting, of all things, Häagen-Dazs ice cream). Likewise, a number of other advertising markets that might be expected to be more conservative—including Japan and Hong Kong—are apt to feature nudity in ads quite casually, often treating it more as an aesthetic element than as a shock mechanism. Of course, showing geni-

talia is still taboo in ads, though advertisers dance around that in clever ways—as in a Spanish ad that used carefully arranged type to form a penis.

By the mid-to-late 1990s, American advertising, too, had grown more casual about showing sex and skin in ads. Print allowed more freedom than television. Partial nudity in print ads became so acceptable that top-name athletes, like the track star Michael Johnson, began appearing in the buff for Nike, and Nike also showed bare breasts in a 1999 campaign for its sports bras—eliciting a barrage of mail, according to the campaign's creator, Jeff Goodby. ("It surprised me that even today, people could still be freaked out by the idea of breasts in ads," acknowledged Goodby.) Even large, mainstream American brands seemed more willing to move beyond sexual innuendo—a longtime tool of advertisers—toward more explicitness. If nudity wasn't an option on broadcast TV,

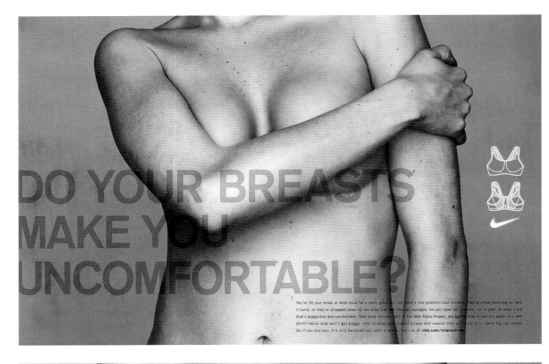

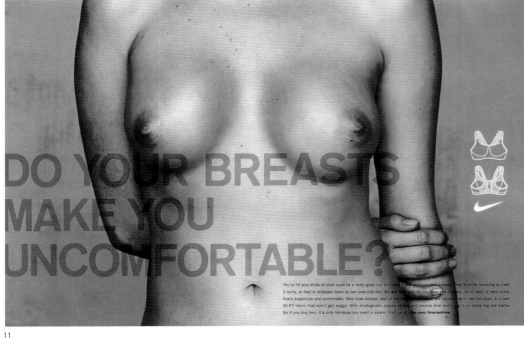

11

11. **NIKE**
GOODBY SILVERSTEIN &
PARTNERS, SAN FRANCISCO,
1999
The advertiser took two
approaches in this ad for a sports
bra: one covered up, one not. The
latter drew complaints, which
surprised ad creator Jeff Goodby.

12. **ALTOIDS**
LEO BURNETT, CHICAGO, 1998
Sadomasochism goes main-
stream: even a perky campaign
like the one in the late 1990s for
Altoids mints was not afraid to
portray a dominatrix.

©1999 Callard & Bowser-Suchard Inc.

12

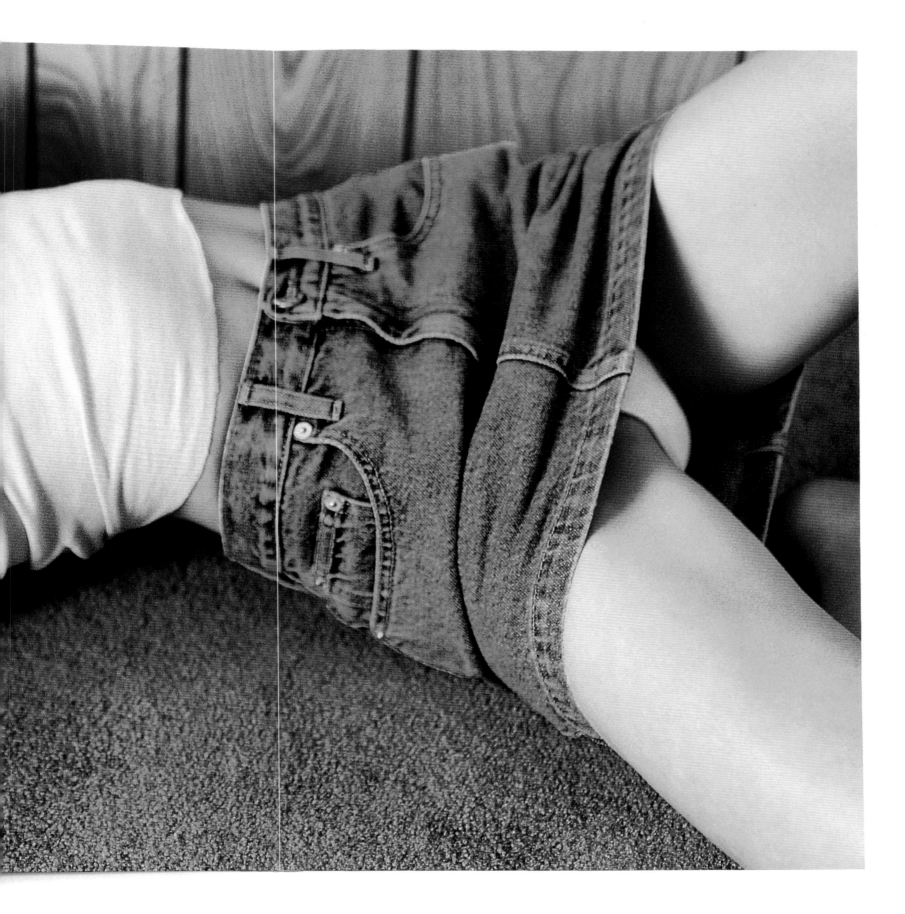

PUSHING THE LIMITS.

14

there were other ways to be sexually adventurous in this medium. To make the point that its hotels had gone through a dramatic overhaul, Holiday Inn produced a commercial whose main character was a transsexual—and it ran the ad during the Super Bowl, though it was subsequently pulled after viewer complaints. Clairol, meanwhile, began running commercials in which a woman groans and sighs as if having an orgasm, though she's actually just washing her hair with Herbal Essences shampoo. (The heavy-handedness of this campaign was, regrettably, a far cry from the slyly suggestive Clairol line "Does she or doesn't she?") Even playful ads for candy were willing to get a little kinky— as in an ad for Altoids mints featuring a cartoonish portrait of a dominatrix, with the headline "Pleasure in Pain," a reference to the mint's reputation for having a strong flavor.

As mainstream advertisers became more sexually daring, the fashion advertisers naturally

had to push even further: fashion ads were more likely to feature images of raw sexuality and even touches of sadomasochism, particularly in the advertising of clothing labels like Guess. Calvin Klein, meanwhile, began to tread in ever more dangerous areas. In 1995, Klein encountered his fiercest controversy when he created a series of ads featuring models who appeared to be teenagers, posing for what seemed to be a seedy pornographic-film shoot. Klein later insisted that the imagery was misinterpreted, but he came under heavy fire before pulling the ads. In the aftermath, the longtime provocateur began to tone down much of his advertising and remarked, "The country has moved to the right, and creatively I don't think this is a moment where people should take too many chances." But it wasn't so much the times, or even the place—in fact, Klein had simply stumbled upon one of the last remaining taboos, which is firmly in place even in more

permissive cultures. Two years ago, a series of French Evian ads created a stir when they showed naked images of children; these portraits were far more innocent and tasteful than Klein's porno-suggestive ads, yet they still caused a public outcry. These episodes served as a reminder, if one was needed, to all advertisers that while sex sells, and children sell, the two should never be mixed in ads.

If it was getting harder in the 1990s to shock the public merely by flashing bare skin in ads, advertisers were finding other ways to the stir the pot. Increasingly, ads began to use more frank—sometimes even profane—language, both in America and in Europe. Here again, standards tended to be a bit looser in Europe, particularly in terms of what was permitted on television. A recent Saatchi & Saatchi commercial for a small London jewelry shop ended with the line "If you don't like it, then f—- off." Another British spot, by Gold Greenlees Trott for Holsten Pils beer,

# RESEARCH SAYS SEX SELLS BEER.

## STEEL RESERVE. THE NOT-TOO-SERIOUS HIGH GRAVITY LAGER.

ALL ANIMALS PICTURED ARE CONSENTING ADULTS OVER THE AGE OF 21. ©1995 STEEL BREWING CO.,LTD., ST. PAUL, MN

15

RUNNERS. YEAH, WE'RE DIFFERENT.

You've never experienced a support shoe like this. The incredibly smooth ride of the Equipment Tyranny is something different too.

16

16. **ADIDAS**
LEAGAS DELANEY,
SAN FRANCISCO, 1999
Nike had tended to glorify
runners, but Adidas focused
on their eccentricities—which
could be downright repulsive.

17. **CANDIE'S**
IN-HOUSE AGENCY,
NEW YORK, 1997
Bathroom humor became prevalent in the late 1990s; American
actress Jenny McCarthy played
along in this notoriously tacky ad.

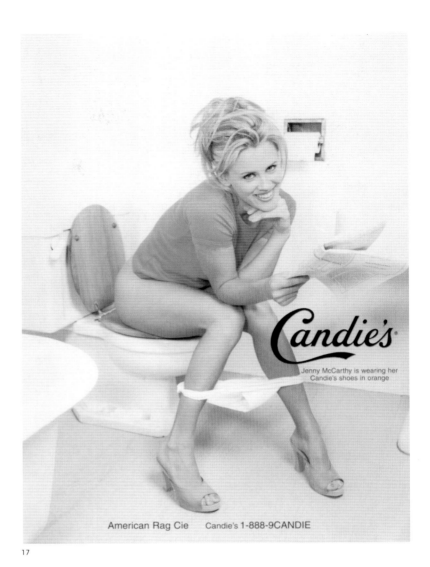

17

featured a comedian who hurled beer bottles as he cursed about additives in beer. Some advertisers have opted for substitutes for profanity, as in a popular American ad for Daffy's clothing that featured an obscene arm gesture being formed by a folded shirt sleeve.

One of the more pervasive trends, particularly in American ads, has been toward scatological humor. A growing number of late-1990s ads began to feature imagery and dialogue revolving around bodily functions. Some were mildly amusing, as in a Polaroid ad displaying photographic evidence of a neighbor's dog soiling the lawn, while others could be more shocking—for example, an Adidas ad featuring a close-up shot of a runner blowing his nose, a Candie's shoe ad showing the actress Jenny McCarthy sitting on a toilet, or a British commercial from Saatchi & Saatchi that showed a man defecating in public (the point of the spot was to persuade people in the London borough of Islington to clean up

after their pets). An ad for the Adam Sandler movie *Big Daddy* featured an image of Sandler and his young co-star urinating against a wall; as *The New York Times* noted at the time, the ad drew surprisingly few complaints from anyone, which led a number of ad executives to conclude that the culture had grown so coarse, it was now actually becoming difficult for ads to offend.

The increase in potty humor in ads has also been accompanied by a growth in the number of ads depicting violence and other antisocial behavior. To promote hockey games in the U.S., the Fox Network showed golfers and bowlers physically attacking one another; the commercials were making the tongue-in-cheek point that these sedate sports would be more lively if they featured the kind of rough action found in hockey. Other recent ads have depicted violence against animals, as in the previously noted Outpost.com ad that showed gerbils being shot through the air (Chapter 6); the ads ended by

advising angry viewers where they could "send complaints." An ad for the long-distance phone service Qwest featured a priest beating a bandaged patient in a hospital bed. For the most part, depictions of violence in ads are not particularly realistic—they tend to be more absurd and cartoonish, in the spirit of the rough horseplay typical of slapstick comedy. But they can be jarring nonetheless and have raised concerns within the ad industry. "There's increasingly a nasty undertone detectable in some of the commercials," observed the renowned British ad executive Adrian Holmes.

Even as they acknowledged the pressing need of advertisers to somehow catch the wandering eye of consumers, some observers considered the proliferation of "shockvertising" an overreaction. However, others pointed out that the new ads were no more risqué than what was being commonly found in other forms of mass communication at the time. In America,

18

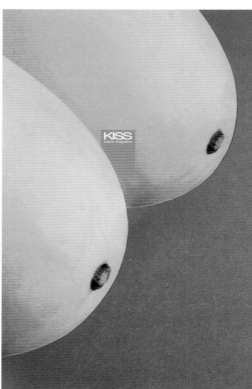

19

**18. BAMBOO LINGERIE**
KIRSHENBAUM & BOND,
NEW YORK, 1992
K&B had fun with stereotypes,
featuring melons in this lingerie
ad, but not everyone appreciated
the joke.

**20. DUREX CONDOMS**
McCANN-ERICKSON,
LONDON, LATE 1990s
Here, a sexy fruit gets equal
opportunity to pitch a product.
You still can't show some things
in ads, but advertisers have
ways around that.

**19. KISS MAGAZINE**
LEO BURNETT, HONG KONG,
1997
Different fruit, similar idea: this
Hong Kong advertiser used the
fruit with less irony, but
produced a striking image.

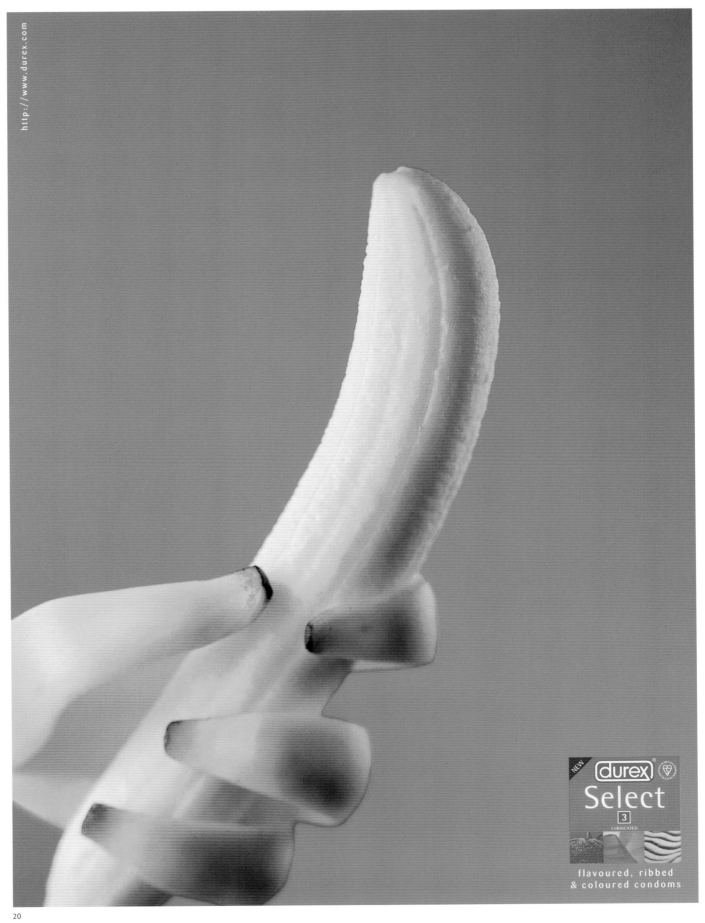

flavoured, ribbed
& coloured condoms

20

PUSHING THE LIMITS.

21

the popularity in the late 1990s of crude and raunchy films like *There's Something About Mary* and TV shows like "South Park," as well as bad-boy magazines like *Maxim,* had a very big impact on advertisers. "I think when you look at the success of a movie like *There's Something About Mary,* that was a big moment in defining how far you can stretch popular culture in a commercially successful piece of entertainment," said Neal Tiles, a top advertising executive with the Fox television network. Rich Silverstein, co-founder of Goodby Silverstein & Partners, observed that at his own agency, the standards seemed to change overnight. "I'm getting scripts every day," Silverstein noted, "where I say, 'We can't do that stuff! It's advertising; you can't swear, can't have a butt joke, can't say 'penis!'" And you just wonder, "Where's this coming from?" And then you watch TV, and every joke is a sex joke. Or you look at the magazine rack

and you see that every magazine is trying to be like *Maxim*—really out there, in terms of sex. If younger people who are writing ads now are finding everything they see—from movies to music to magazines—filled with ramped-up sexual tension, then it's naturally going to find its way into advertising scripts, too. They're just trying to reflect the times. But I'm saying to them, 'It's still advertising, we can't do that!'"

Perhaps the real question is not why young ad creators are pushing these boundaries but rather why clients—who have so much to lose—are out on that edge, too. Why would so many sponsors make the sudden leap from extreme caution to reckless abandon? According to the American journalist John Leo, today's corporations "understand that in-your-face messages that shred social norms can move the merchandise by playing to the current sour, antisocial mood. Thus, the rapid spread of ads

urging us to break all the rules or just make up our own."

But there's more to the trend than just a shift in the cultural mood and standards. A significant contributor is undoubtedly the rise of "targeted marketing" in the current business world—which has all but eclipsed the traditional mass-marketing approaches for many brands. As a growing number of advertisers have narrowed their sights to focus on specific niches of consumers, a side effect has been that many of these advertisers are now less inclined to worry about whether people outside the niche might be offended by certain ads. In effect, what matters now is only the target group. And if the target group happens to be young males—the most sought-after segment among many advertisers—then the content of the ads will be geared to the sensibilities of that group, even if that means offending others in the audience. Such is the

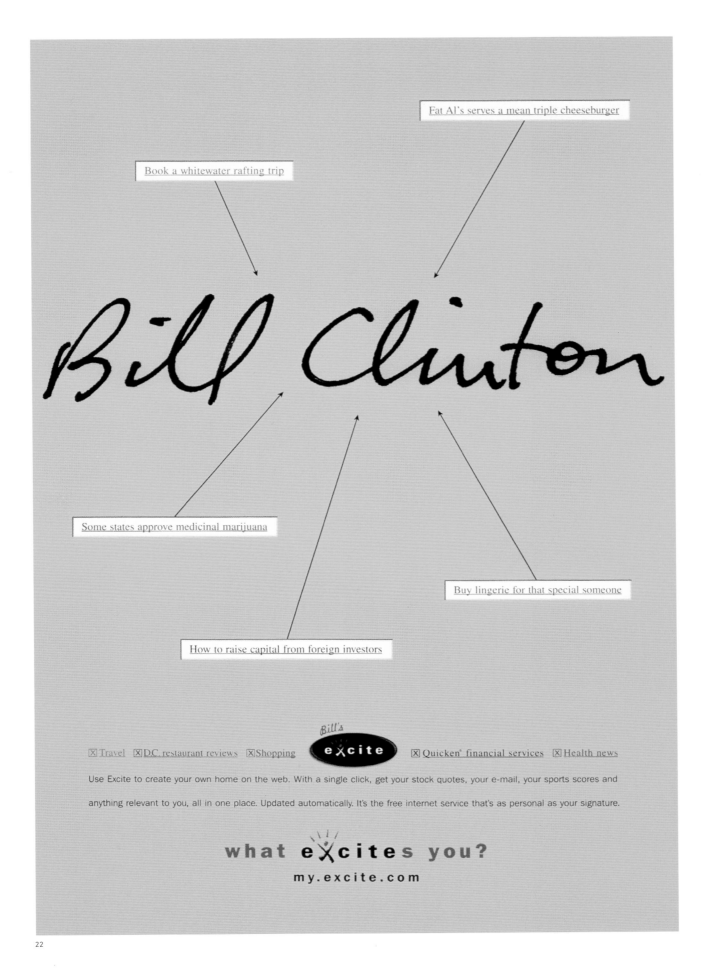

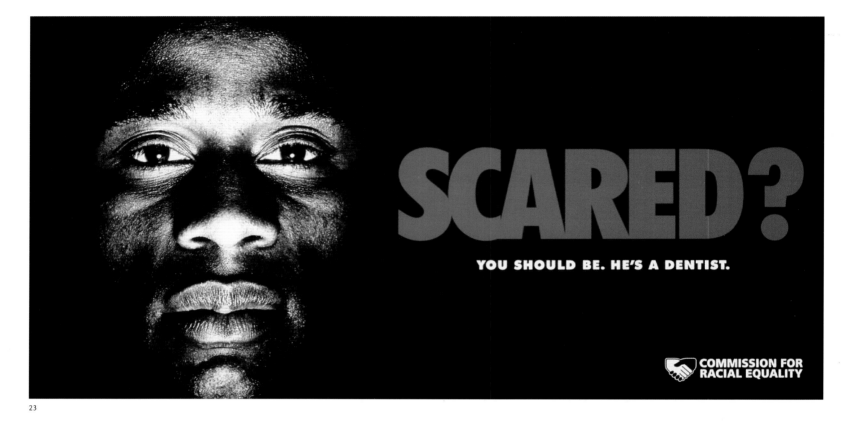

23

23. **COMMISSION FOR RACIAL EQUALITY**
EURO RSCG WNEK GOSPER, LONDON, 1999
Race is a minefield for advertisers. This well-meaning campaign came under heavy fire for offending the people it was trying to help.

24. **ATLANTA'S BLACK PROFESSIONALS**
AUSTIN KELLEY ADVERTISING, ATLANTA, 1997
This ad, on the other hand, took a provocative but less abrasive stand against the "ebonics" language controversy, perhaps because the sponsor was a black professional group.

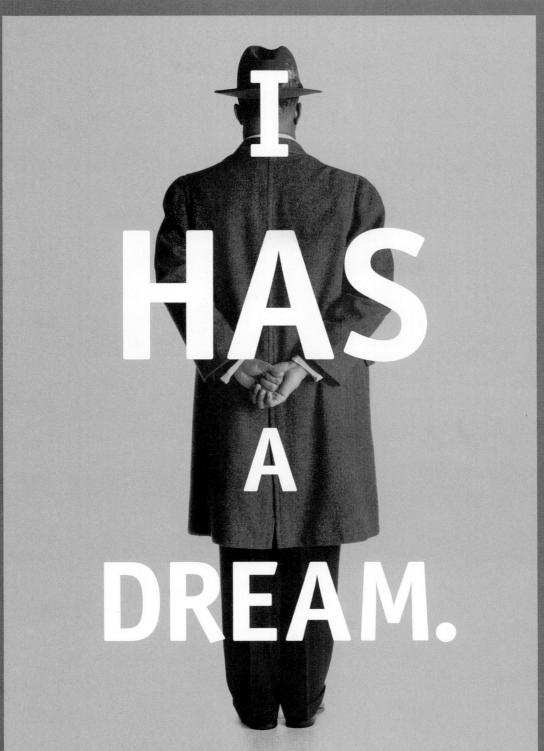

# I HAS A DREAM.

Does this bother you? It should. We've spent over 400 years fighting for the right to have a voice. Is this how we'll use it? More importantly, is this how we'll teach our children to use it? If we expect more of them, we must not throw our hands in the air and agree with those who say our children cannot be taught. By now, you've probably heard about Ebonics (aka, black English). And if you think it's become a controversy because white America doesn't want us messing with their precious language, don't. White America couldn't care less what we do to segregate ourselves.

The fact is language is power. And we can't take that power away from our children with Ebonics. Would Dr. Martin Luther King, Malcom X and all the others who paid the price of obtaining our voice with the currency of their lives embrace this? If you haven't used your voice lately, consider this an invitation.

## SPEAK OUT AGAINST
# EBONICS
This message brought to you by Atlanta's Black Professionals.

25

OF COURSE PEOPLE WITH PIERCED BODY PARTS ARE WELCOME IN OUR CHURCH.

26

Génération Golf

—Mes amis, réjouissons-nous car une nouvelle Golf est née.

27

25 AND 26. **EPISCOPAL CHURCH**
THE RICHARDS GROUP, DALLAS, 1998
Religion, too, is usually considered off-limits to advertisers. But churches have lately begun to use hip, postmodern ads to try to attract a younger crowd.

27. **VOLKSWAGEN GOLF**
DDB, PARIS, 1998
The scene resembles *The Last Supper*, but this gathering is rejoicing because "a new Golf is born." French Catholic bishops sued VW and its agency over this ad.

case at Fox Sports, which aims its ads squarely at young males. "Our main concern when we consider our ads is whether they're right for [our] target audience," says Fox's Tiles. "Because if we try to be appropriate for everybody, then we become relevant to nobody." Tiles acknowledges that Fox gets complaints about some of its wilder, more violent ads, but "usually from people outside the demographic—mothers, older men." The company sees that situation as almost unavoidable because, Tiles says, Fox and many other of today's marketers are faced with a paradox: "We're in a mass medium in terms of how we're consumed, but we're dead set on selling to a specific demographic."

In truth, some advertisers today feel that if an ad polarizes the audience—offending some while impressing others with its bravado—that can actually work to the benefit of the brand. "Being polarizing can be a good thing," says Marty Cooke of the M&C Saatchi agency,

"because it solidifies your core base of customers. If other people don't like what you're doing, that just makes your core supporters like you even more." Calvin Klein, of course, understood this two decades ago, but today even a larger, more conservative advertiser like JCPenney is buying into the same divide-and-conquer niche strategy.

Interestingly, while advertisers now seem to be less afraid of offending the mainstream masses, they're more worried than ever about offending particular ethnic-minority groups. For the most part, the industry has largely cleansed itself of the racial stereotypes that once plagued advertising. But every so often, ads with racist imagery still surface. A noteworthy recent example appeared during the 1999 Super Bowl and promoted a footwear chain by showing a barefoot black Kenyan runner being hunted down by whites, then drugged and forced to wear sneakers. The

spot was so appalling that the client eventually tried to sue the small upstate New York agency that produced it.

The racial minefield in advertising is so treacherous that sometimes ads with good intentions can encounter problems. The London agency Euro RSCG Wnek Gosper recently tried to create a series of public-service ads encouraging people to speak out against racist imagery seen in public. In making its point, the agency tried to be perhaps a bit too clever; Wnek Gosper created a series of outrageous, deliberately racist posters, such as one billboard headlined, "Dominate the race," showing a white man stepping on the hand of a black man while climbing over him on a ladder. After posting the offensive ad around London for a short time, the agency followed up with a subsequent billboard that reprinted the original image along with this message: "What was worse? This advert or

# INTERVIEW: OLIVIERO TOSCANI

As the longtime creative director of advertising for the Italian clothing retailer Benetton, Oliviero Toscani was one of the first—and to this day, one of the only—advertisers to mix social commentary and marketing. Beginning in the mid-1980s, his print and outdoor ad campaigns (featuring his own photographs) presented images of interracial relationships, a bloody baby fresh from the womb, a dying AIDS patient, a priest kissing a nun, a close-up of the bloodstained clothes of a dead Croatian soldier—no subject was off-limits to Toscani. His final ad campaign for Benetton appeared in 2000 and profiled American prison inmates on death row. Toscani is currently the creative director of *Talk* magazine, and he runs Fabrica, a center for communication arts based in Italy.

**WHY DO YOU CHOOSE TO ADDRESS SOCIAL ISSUES IN ADS?**
I think advertising is a social message in itself. Of course—telling people what they are to consume and how they should look and what they should drive. Isn't that a social message?

**BUT YOUR CRITICS SAY ISSUES LIKE AIDS, RACISM, AND WAR ARE TOO IMPORTANT, TOO SERIOUS TO BE DISCUSSED—OR THEY MIGHT SAY, EXPLOITED—IN ADS.**
That's old talk. Advertising is the richest and most powerful medium today, the one where the most money is invested. If it's okay to do very powerful, socially concerned songs and sell a lot of records, and it's okay to do movies the same way, then I don't know why only advertising has to stay stupid. Advertising is the language of production and consumption—two very important activities in the history of humanity. Production means work and consumption means culture. So I don't understand why the language of advertising has to be used in the same old way. I think it's just because advertisers are not smart.

**DO YOU THINK ADS ARE BECOMING LESS FEARFUL OF CONTROVERSY?**
Oh, yes; people now don't always do what the client asks them to do. And I think that, for example, what's happened with Benetton has proved that you can be courageous and stand for your idea, and by doing that the company got

twenty times bigger. I think people appreciate when you stand for something.

**BUT IF PEOPLE DISAGREE WITH YOUR POLITICS, WON'T THEY HOLD THAT AGAINST THE BRAND?**
Everybody thinks that's the case, but it is not true. There are a lot of people who, even if they don't agree with what you're saying, will appreciate that you have the courage to say it. They say, "Look, this is a company that speaks up." For any brand, the most valuable thing is to be known by people. Benetton is one of the five best-known brands worldwide. And it was all done without using television. I never use television.

**WHY NOT?**
I hate television. I think it's very expensive and it's not necessary. [With print ads], you pollute less. A billboard is much more interesting to me. Billboards are simple, as simple as possible. They should appeal to everybody, and everybody can see them and understand them.

**YOUR ADS ALSO DON'T USE WORDS MUCH; THE PICTURE DOES THE TALKING.**
We live in a world of images, we don't live in a world of words. And an image by itself can be a worldwide message—you can use the same picture everywhere, and you don't have to deal with the problem of translation.

**HOW DID YOU DECIDE WHICH ISSUES TO ADDRESS IN YOUR ADS?**
Totally instinct, things I felt strongly about. I don't do marketing research. I look at what the marketing research says, and if you want to have success, you do the opposite.

**HAVE YOU BEEN SURPRISED BY THE DIFFERING REACTIONS IN VARIOUS COUNTRIES?**
Well, every country is different; every one has its own problem. You know there are some countries that don't react at all to a picture—and that same image gets another country really mad. For example, Scandinavian countries never seem to get shocked about anything. Then if you take the ad with the newborn baby—it was a big problem all over Europe, especially in England. But in America it wasn't any problem at all. And then the soldier ad, that ran everywhere except

Germany. The HIV-positive ad upset people in France. By now, we usually know how countries will react based on their political past. For example, "Death Row" was a big problem in America, of course, whereas not in Europe at all.

**SHOULDN'T YOU BE TELLING CONSUMERS AT LEAST SOMETHING ABOUT BENETTON PRODUCTS IN THE ADS?**
Oh, we've done that. That's not difficult. That's something even advertising people can do. But you have to take chances. If you want to interest the world in your message, you have to talk about more than the product—you have to talk about life and death. You have to go for something that might be controversial, that might be rejected, criticized, but so what? That is why you have freedom of speech.

**DO YOU SEE ADVERTISING AS AN ART FORM?**
It could be an incredible art form. When you look back into history and look at Renaissance painting, that was like advertising painted in the church. The painters were called in to express a religious idea, which was like a product—so the painting was there to promote a power, a king, a religion. But those Michelangelos and Leonardos were able to transcend all of that to become art. And we should do the same. I wish advertising's art directors and creative directors, instead of trying to become more and more like salesmen, would move more in the direction of artists. Instead they listen to the marketing men, and for that they give up their art. And that's why advertising is mostly boring and ugly.

UNITED COLORS
OF BENETTON.

28

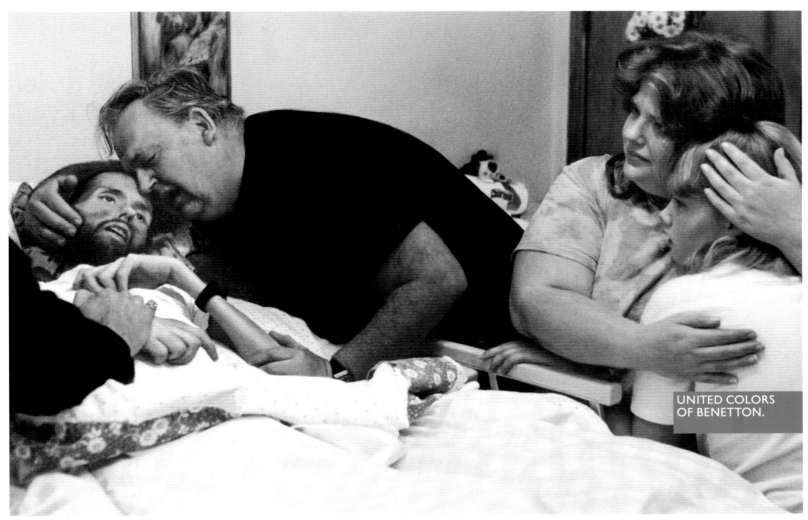

UNITED COLORS
OF BENETTON.

29

**28. BENETTON**
OLIVIERO TOSCANI, MILAN,
1991
One of Oliviero Toscani's
early shockers featured a baby
fresh from the womb and still
bloody—England, in particular,
objected.

**29. BENETTON**
OLIVIERO TOSCANI, MILAN,
1992
Here, Toscani focused on
the death of an AIDS victim
surrounded by his family. Critics
felt the advertiser was exploiting
human suffering.

30

your failure to complain?" But the campaign backfired, as the advertiser was accused of endorsing racist imagery and was compelled to apologize.

Advertisers typically try to avoid misunderstandings like that by handling the subject of race very carefully in ads—perhaps too carefully, according to some critics, who believe the ad industry is currently straitjacketed by its own insecurities and fears. "Political correctness inhibits good advertising," says Rogier van Bakel, the editor of the magazine *Creativity*. He notes that because advertisers are paralyzed by fear of offending members of minority groups, the ads aimed at these groups end up being particularly bland and patronizing. Such ads "shy away from humor and candor," van Bakel says, in favor of "the feel-good, self-esteem-building variety of minority advertising."

Van Bakel and other critics believe that political correctness in advertising has also

taken some of the creative spark out of ads directed to women, many of which have shied away from irreverent humor in favor of relentlessly upbeat and "empowering" messages. But even in the enlightened and empowering 1990s, it still wasn't hard to find ads that ogled women's bodies—and sometimes got into trouble for it. A case in point was the "Swedish Bikini Team" ad campaign for Stroh's beer, which created an uproar in the U.S. in the early 1990s. The ads presented over-the-top scenarios in which a group of men, typically fishing or camping in the middle of nowhere, were unexpectedly visited by beer-toting, dancing, bikini-clad women in blonde wigs. While the campaign's creators took pains to point out that the ads were intended to be tongue-in-cheek, critics weren't buying that line; as one skeptic noted, it seemed clear that Stroh's was trying to "have it both ways," presenting titillating and sexist images of women, while also suggesting, in

very postmodern fashion, that it was all just an inside joke. The controversy seemed to have a significant after-effect on beer advertising; this onetime bastion of sexist imagery began to rely less on exploiting women's bodies in ads and more on bathroom humor (was this progress?). But as the beer advertisers reduced their own "cheesecake" quotient, the new-era lingerie brands like Wonderbra and Victoria's Secret produced ads that, at times, seemed almost indistinguishable from pinup magazine centerfolds. (Wonderbra, to its credit, at least acknowledged its own naughtiness with playful and outrageous headlines accompanying all those body shots: "Hello Boys!" screamed one billboard that briefly became the talk of London in the mid-1990s.)

If advertisers had come to tread lightly around issues of race and gender, they were even more careful when it came to religion. Those few advertisers that took on churches as

31

**30. BENETTON**
OLIVIERO TOSCANI, MILAN,
1991
While many advertisers avoid
the minefields of race and religion, Toscani has not. He insisted there was "nothing sinful"
about his ad showing a priest
and nun kissing.

**31. BENETTON**
OLIVIERO TOSCANI, NEW
YORK, 2000
Toscani's last campaign for
Benetton featured sympathetic
portraits of inmates on death
row. The campaign angered
some who had been
victimized by crime.

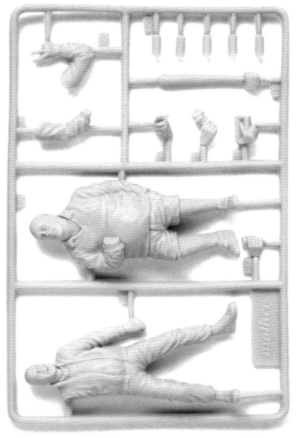

32

clients usually opted for solemn and reverent approaches. Recently, however, some religious advertising has become a bit more humorous. One ad, produced in Texas for the Episcopal New Church, featured an image of Jesus Christ on the cross, with the headline "Of course people with pierced body parts are welcome in our church." And a series of billboards in Florida showed a light touch with the headline "Let's meet at my house Sunday before the game." It was signed, "God." Another ad in the same campaign threatened, "Don't make me come down there." The campaign was designed to encourage young people to attend church, though its creator, Charlie Robb, acknowledged that not everyone appreciated the tone of the ads. European advertising, while often more daring in dealing with sex, is as skittish as American agencies when it comes to religion: In France, a recent Volkswagen ad created an uproar by mimicking *The Last Supper;* the ad

featured people in modern dress posed in exactly the same positions as the figures in Leonardo da Vinci's famous fresco, with the headline, "My Friends, let us rejoice because a new Golf is born." French Catholic bishops sued Volkswagen and its agency.

Like religion, politics is seen as a potentially divisive domain that most advertising agencies and brand marketers avoid. Particularly in America, it's rare to find an advertiser taking a stand on any issue that isn't a reasonably safe one (for example, companies have no problem speaking out against drunk driving—a no-brainer—but hot-button topics like gun control, capital punishment, and abortion are typically avoided). One exception to this rule has been the Italy-based clothing company Benetton, whose advertising in the late 1980s and early 1990s tackled a number of controversial political and social issues, including AIDS, racism, and the ravages of war. Through the stark and

sometimes shocking imagery in his ads, Oliviero Toscani, the creative director of Benetton's advertising, clearly emerged as one of the most outspoken advertisers ever. One of Toscani's more provocative images showed a black woman breast-feeding a white baby; another showed a priest and nun kissing; still another featured the bloodstained clothes of a dead Croatian soldier; and perhaps the most controversial of all Benetton's ads showed a dying AIDS victim.

To some critics, Toscani's advertising seemed exploitive and manipulative; in effect, they argued that he was using the suffering of the world to sell clothes. Toscani's own position was that his ads were simply an attempt to raise social consciousness on certain issues, and to stir debate through the powerful and pervasive medium of advertising. But perhaps the biggest debate he stirred was on the question of whether for-profit advertising can ever

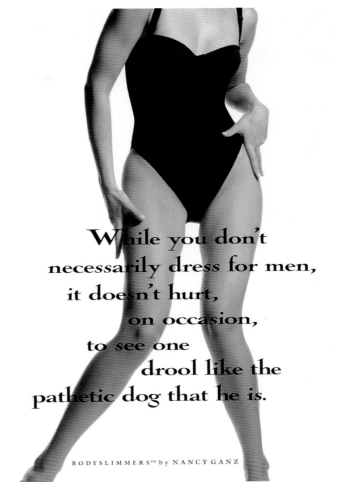

While you don't
necessarily dress for men,
it doesn't hurt,
on occasion,
to see one
drool like the
pathetic dog that he is.

BODYSLIMMERS™ by NANCY GANZ

33

be an appropriate forum for examining serious issues; do advertisers like Toscani have enough objectivity and moral authority to take on the role of journalist or social commentator? The question was never really resolved, though Toscani's aggressive ad campaigns eventually receded from the spotlight. Benetton and Toscani briefly seized the spotlight again in 2000 with an ad campaign opposing capital punishment. In the end, Toscani was beaten back not so much by his critics as by the cold, hard marketplace: Benetton's sales first sky-rocketed, then plummeted, during the course of its controversial campaigns. The vagaries of the fashion business notwithstanding, it's reasonable to conclude that Benetton's shock-politics approach was eye-catching in the short run but gradually turned off consumers who were already getting their fill of painful images on the evening news and didn't need to see more in ads. Still, the legacy of Benetton's

work lives on somewhat in the more recent ads by the clothing company Diesel and also among young European ad-agency creative directors like Johan Kramer of KesselsKramer, who occasionally tries to use his advertising to issue statements about discrimination and other social issues.

Challenging authority or the social structure can be particularly hazardous in some countries, but advertisers still occasionally try it. Kitty Lun, former creative director of the Hong Kong agency Euro RSCG Partnership, notes that while the general public in Asia is usually fairly accepting of sexually frank ads, such ads will often come under fire from governments or activist groups. Lun observes that a recent telecommunications campaign was banned when the commercial tried to make its point—that its mobile phone can access many different networks—by making a comparison to having multiple sex partners. The ad was clever, but "it

really offended a lot of people," says Lun. The Singapore-based ad copywriter Jim Aitchison points out that a recent local ad in which a son was disrespectful to his father became quite controversial. Meanwhile, in Eastern Europe, advertising is still relatively young and finding its voice. A Polish beer ad, for example, ridiculed corrupt Russian military figures; it had only a short run, but the ad developed a cult following in Poland.

It's rarer to find American ads that challenge authority or social convention in that manner. Interestingly, though, American ads some-times trigger social debate unexpectedly, by tapping into deep feelings people may have on a given subject. For example, the ABC television network recently ignited a controversy with a series of seemingly innocuous ads about the guilty pleasure of watching TV. The ads' creators at TBWA/Chiat/Day simply wanted to suggest that perhaps watching TV wasn't such

# Before TV,
# two World Wars.
# After TV, zero.

35

**34. ABC TELEVISION**
TBWA/CHIAT/DAY,
LOS ANGELES, 1997
Another unexpected controversy:
Critics swarmed all over this
humorous campaign because
they felt it was making light of
the mind-numbing effects of TV.

**35. HARVEY NICHOLS**
MOTHER, LONDON, 1998
This department store ad, on the
other hand, featured an image
of a dead cat (albeit computer-
generated), and surprisingly few
people took issue with it.

an awful thing to do, and they did so with headlines that defended TV-watching by way of ironic statements: "Don't worry, you've got billions of brain cells," one ad said reassuringly, while another noted, "You can talk to your wife anytime." In the ensuing weeks, the American media swarmed all over the ABC campaign, which was accused of being overly cynical and of promoting illiteracy. The campaign seemed to touch on strong opinions people had about two separate issues—the effects of watching TV and the use of cynical irony in ads. All of which stunned ad-agency president Bob Kuperman, who says, "We never thought the ads would cause so much intellectual masturbation."

Similarly, Nike and its agency, Wieden + Kennedy, were taken aback by the criticism of an Olympics ad that declared, "You don't win silver, you lose gold." The ad was accused of promoting a win-at-all-costs attitude that ran counter to the Olympic spirit of competition.

But agency founder Dan Wieden claimed the ad was just misunderstood: "The confusion may have been that it was thought to be Nike's voice saying these words, rather than the voice of the athlete," said Wieden. "The whole idea of the campaign was that the Olympics is war minus the killing—for an athlete, just before that gun goes off, it's a very uncompromising moment."

The ABC and Nike campaigns may be testaments to the truly unpredictable nature of ad controversy. Ad-agency executives tend to agree that it's perhaps more difficult than ever to gauge exactly what will upset today's more desensitized consumer. "It always surprises me," said Mark Waites of the British agency Mother. Waites pointed out that he once put a close-up picture of a dead cat in an ad, and braced for complaints—but they were minimal. He also ran a truly incendiary self-promotion for his agency, in which he created a mock ad offering an artificial-fireplace log designed to

look like an American flag—the idea being that America-haters could use this product for the dual pleasure of burning the U.S. flag every time they sat in front of the fireplace. "I thought that would be controversial, but people seemed to get the joke," Waites said. However, when he created another mock ad, offering collections of toy warriors designed to look not like soldiers but like English soccer hooligans, Waites was inundated with complaints by faithful football fans. The bottom line, Waites has learned, is that advertisers can never predict when controversy will rear its head. "The things you think will upset people end up being fine," he said, "and the things you don't worry about are the ones that end up causing the most trouble of all."

# 8. THE
## OF ADVE

FACES

RTISING.

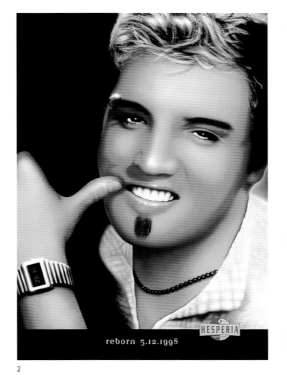

reborn 5.12.1998

HESPERIA

2

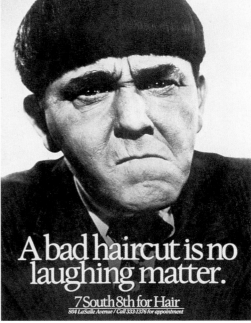

A bad haircut is no laughing matter.

7 South 8th for Hair
804 LaSalle Avenue / Call 333-1376 for appointment

3

A s the messages of advertising changed in recent years, so did the messengers who brought them to us.

Historically, the face that advertising turned to the world was apt to be famous, wholesome, warm, and inviting—in America, it was Bob Hope for Texaco gasoline in the 1960s, or, a decade later, Bill Cosby for Jell-O. Elsewhere around the world, popular mainstream stars, from the comic actor Paul Hogan in Australia to the soccer star Pele in South America, all played a similarly straight-forward, if somewhat disingenuous, role: Smile for the camera, hold up the product, say something laudatory. When not relying on star endorsers, many advertisers, particularly in the U.S., opted for another classic approach: hiring lesser-known actors to portray benign, lovable, fictional characters—such as Mr. Whipple, known for squeezing Charmin bathroom tissue, or the Maytag Repairman, "the loneliest man in town"— who became part of an ongoing story that

revolved around the product. It was a wink-and-nod form of communication with the audience, which knew, of course, that the Maytag Repairman wasn't real, and also suspected that Cosby probably didn't really love Jell-O all that much. Still, there was a feel-good aura surrounding such images, and those familiar faces helped infuse brands with a personality.

Indeed, the classic advertising characters and spokespersons, who continued to dominate ads well into the 1970s and early 1980s, managed to "put a human face on nearly every product," noted Robert Thompson, director of Syracuse University's Center for the Study of Popular Television. "Almost in a Walt Disney–like fashion, Madison Avenue anthropomorphized products— so that toilet paper became Mr. Whipple," Thompson said. "It was a very effective way of getting the audience to identify with people, not just products."

Fast-forward to the present, and one finds

that faces are still at the center of most advertising—though now they are as apt to be snarling as smiling. Hope and Cosby have given way to people like Dennis Rodman, the mischievous, tattooed, cross-dressing basketball star who has appeared in ads for that most wholesome of all products, milk. And while fictional characters still populate ads, they, too, have changed; no longer pleasant and benign, ad characters became "edgier," to use a favorite buzzword of ad creators. Their ranks now include the likes of Stuart, the featured character in a series of commercials for the Ameritrade on-line trading service—a rude, punkish, wild-haired office boy who bullies the boss and wreaks havoc at work. Stuart actually seems quite civilized compared with the 800 Call Collect Guy, played by the actor David Arquette in a series of ads for AT&T, who is often seen stalking and screaming at other characters in the ads. On one level, this new, slightly twisted face of advertising is yet

4

4. JACK IN THE BOX
KOWLOON W. S.C. AGENCY,
LOS ANGELES, 1998
In this late 1990s campaign for
a Southern California-based
hamburger chain, the company
spokesman had a ping pong
ball for a head and a penchant
for violence.

5. AMERICAN EXPRESS
OGILVY & MATHER,
NEW YORK, MID-1990s
American comedian Jerry
Seinfeld met his hero in this
commercial. Like a number
of contemporary endorsers,
Seinfeld maintains an ironic
distance from the product.

another desperate try by sponsors to somehow be heard above the din of growing ad clutter. But at the same time, it's also an attempt to associate with more contemporary, rebellious, break-the-rules attitudes and behavior.

The modern pitchman need not be stark raving mad but must, at minimum, be somewhat cynical. The comedian Jerry Seinfeld, for example, has maintained a pleasant demeanor in his ongoing ad campaign for American Express. Nevertheless, Seinfeld embodies the new-generation ad spokesperson—far removed from Hope and Cosby in attitude. Like many of the trendier spokespersons who have emerged in recent years (the sardonic American comedian Dennis Miller is another example), Seinfeld keeps his skeptical persona even in ads, and always maintains an ironic distance from the product. Today's modern endorsers rarely smile for the camera and almost never do old-fashioned testimonials praising the product. Often they simply

do their personal "shtick" in commercials, allowing the brand to tag along for the ride. If this suggests a certain reluctance on their part to commit to the product, that's perfectly acceptable—that skepticism, hesitance, and candor, along with Rodman-like personal flaws, all come together to form advertising's version of the anti-hero, the perfect postmodern pitching machine.

The evolution of the face of advertising began in the 1960s, when up-and-coming American creative agencies—some of which were staffed by ethnic New Yorkers—tried to bring more diversity and authenticity to the casting of their ads. "We wanted to show in our ads that not everyone was blond and beautiful," said Roy Grace, formerly of Doyle Dane Bernbach, now of Grace & Rothschild. That agency's ad campaign for Levy's rye bread broke new ground by featuring the faces of ordinary people, including Asian-Americans and African-Americans. By the 1970s and early 1980s, a number of advertisers

began using so-called real people in ads—though this was something of a misnomer, because the models and performers were usually actors who just happened to look like imperfect ordinary people. In any case, the ad landscape soon featured people who were balding or over-weight, or others with exaggerated features that made them look sad or silly (as noted in Chapter 4, the commercial director Joe Sedelmaier specialized in ads starring unglamorous characters—including his most famous, Clara Peller, from the Wendy's "Where's the Beef?" ads).

But the ground truly shifted in the mid-1980s, as several convergent trends began to take hold. By this time, a growing number of advertisers had begun to accept the notion that old-fashioned commercials featuring benign mascot characters or overly earnest star endorsers were no longer credible or compelling to an audience that was more savvy and cynical. "The growing feeling was that consumers could

5

6

7

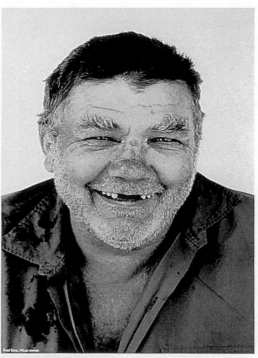

# WE DECIDED AGAINST A VANITY MIRROR.

TOYOTA HILUX
As unbreakable as the people who drive them. *Oh what a feeling!*

Fred Sims, HiLux owner

8

see right through celebrities," said Bill Oberlander, a creative director with the New York ad agency Kirshenbaum Bond & Partners. "To stand apart from all the glamour and all those big stars, ads needed to find anti-stars— people who had more character and integrity."

This accelerated the trend of finding people who didn't look like actors—and who, in some cases, weren't actors—to appear in ads. Kirshenbaum Bond produced one of the more memorable examples with its ad campaign for Snapple fruit drinks, featuring Wendy Kaufman— a heavyset woman with a strong New York accent who had been a telephone receptionist at the beverage company for years. According to Oberlander, the use of Kaufman was an attempt to run directly counter to Pepsi, which was at the time featuring the glamorous model Cindy Crawford in its commercials. "Wendy represented an attempt to zag while everyone else was zigging," Oberlander said. But

Kaufman, who developed a popular following while the ad campaign ran during the early 1990s, also was a good match for the product itself: "She was natural and real," said Oberlander, "and that's what Snapple wanted to stand for."

Increasingly, other advertisers also sought to suggest authenticity and integrity by showing "real people," who sometimes delivered their lines in an unpolished, seemingly unscripted way. One of the most successful regular-guy pitchmen to emerge during the 1990s was Dave Thomas, the top executive of the Wendy's hamburger chain. Thomas certainly was not the first unglamorous, hardworking company boss to appear in his own ads: Frank Perdue of Perdue Chicken had paved that ground years earlier, and Perdue—whose bald, droopy-eyed, beakish head made him look as if he might actually have some chicken genes in him—proved that one didn't need a pretty face to capture the hearts of consumers. But Thomas took the anti-star

movement even further; whereas Perdue had come across as somewhat glib and clever in his ads, Thomas seemed as if he had no business being on TV. Overweight, blandly dressed, slightly marble-mouthed—the *Advertising Age* columnist Bob Garfield once called Thomas "a steer in a half-sleeve shirt"—Thomas became legendary in the ad industry for his ineptitude as a performer (one commercial script requiring him to say "*Muchas gracias*" necessitated four hours of retakes before Thomas got the line right). And yet in spite of all that, or more likely because of it, he was a huge hit with the television audience. Jim McKennan, who wrote the original commercials starring Thomas, noted that he had "an Everyman quality" that "appeals to people on all kinds of levels."

Real people could sell hamburgers and soft drinks, but, predictably, there was far less interest in featuring unattractive faces in ads for clothing and cosmetics. After all, these were the marketers

**Beatrix Lindveld
leest Het Parool.**
Abonnee sinds oktober '88

9

mother
earth
loves my face

Introducing Ceramide Herbal®
Botanical Supplement for the Face

Each capsule of Ceramide Herbal® helps
prevent the signs of aging with twelve of
our purest, most potent natural ingredients.
An herbal infusion with ginkgo and echinacea
helps strengthen the skin's defenses against
environmental damage, and helps keep it
looking healthy and young.

Elizabeth Arden
embrace yourself

10

**9. HET PAROOL NEWSPAPER**
KESSELSKRAMER,
AMSTERDAM, 1997
The ordinary woman as ad royalty:
This campaign dressed up
housewives and secretaries,
who happened to be named
Beatrix, as Holland's queen
of the same name.

**10. ELIZABETH ARDEN**
J. WALTER THOMPSON,
NEW YORK, 1999
Advertising's "beauty myth" was
being challenged by the late
1990s; cosmetics ads still
featured pretty faces, but sometimes allowed for so-called
imperfections such as freckles.

**11. MARLBORO**
LEO BURNETT, CHICAGO, 1984
Representing the classic macho
face of advertising, the Marlboro
Man endures—though some
advertisers have suggested that
he may be in poor health.

that had, for many years, propagated advertising's so-called beauty myth by showing only
flawless faces (and bodies) in ads. But even the
beauty-myth-makers had to acknowledge that
new consumers wanted at least a bit more
authenticity in ads. Influential research studies
in the late-1990s by the firm Lubin Lawrence
revealed that women had simply had enough
of ads projecting standards of beauty that were
seen as unreal and unattainable. And while this
did not spur the makeup companies to sign up
women like Wendy Kaufman, the industry did
take a few tiny steps away from perfection. In
1999, the cosmetics company Lancôme actually
made news when one of its fragrance ads
featured a woman with freckles on her face.
At the same time, ads for Elizabeth Arden
cosmetics started portraying women who,
while physically attractive, looked less like
fashion models and more like fully functioning
human beings; the copy downplayed beauty with

lines like "My best feature is my big beautiful
sexy brain."

The trend toward bringing more natural,
authentic faces to ads became popular in many
ad markets around the world. KesselsKramer
produced one of its most popular and successful
ad campaigns for a Dutch newspaper when it
dressed up frumpy-looking, stocky, and even
buck-toothed housewives to look like royalty (the
women were chosen because they had the same
first name as Queen Beatrix of Holland). And in
Australia, one of the most wildly popular ads in
recent years featured a Toyota truck owner with
a flat nose, unshaven face, and gap-toothed grin,
appearing under the headline "We decided
against a vanity mirror." Aside from being funny
and visually arresting, the ad also made a point—
that the trucks are designed for rough customers.

Of course, even as "real people" in ads were
gaining popularity, celebrities never went out of
vogue. Advertising had been hooked on stars for

too long to give up that dependable quick fix;
many still followed the old advertising maxim
"If you have nothing to say about a product, hire
someone famous to say it." The British ad executive Frank Lowe, founder of the Lowe group of
agencies, has noted that stars "are a shortcut
to getting attention." And, in fact, they're more
than that. According to the *Journal of Consumer
Research,* as consumers process information
from an ad, they often "use information about
the celebrity to make inferences about the
product. This transfer of information from
celebrity to product is, in part, what makes the
endorsement effective."

Star-worshiping in ads is not strictly
American or even Western: In recent years,
Chinese companies have begun to associate their
products with celebrities and mythic figures
(this in spite of the fact that Chinese culture has
historically been less hero-driven than Western
culture). Hong Kong film stars have proved

Come to where the flavor is.

© Philip Morris Inc. 1983

Marlboro Red or Longhorn 100's—
you get a lot to like.

FILTER CIGARETTES
Marlboro
Marlboro 100's

ANGOLA
## Deadly Rite of the

*A new offensive produces the sa*

Caked in grime, ragged in their new-grown beards, the South Africans had finally begun to withdraw. The last of some 2,000 soldiers were making off with booty ranging from Soviet-made guns to Russian-language maps. Some of their trucks were still decorated with Christ-mas tinsel. But the condition of the 30-mile-long column was hardly festive. At the village of Mupa, they had to put up a rickety bridge across a swollen river; far-ther south, they drove past a treasure trove of Soviet-made equipment, includ-ing recently developed AGS-17 automatic grenade launchers. After five weeks of "Operation Askari," the South Africans reported knocking out 25 Soviet-made tanks, giv-ing chase to two Cuban battal-ions, and killing 400 enemy troops. Their own casualties were 21 dead, more than in any other campaign since 1975. Said Lieut. Ian Gleeson: "It was an extended operation and a hard slog."

So ended the annual dead-ly rite of the rainy season. Ev-ery year, before the heavy sum-mer storms, the South Africans launch punishing raids into southern Angola to pre-empt attacks by the black nationalist guerrillas of the South West Africa People's Organization (SWAPO). And every year, once the rains provide them with fo-liage cover and vital water sup-plies, the rebels cross the bor-der into northern Namibia, hoping to bring an end to South Africa's 17-year control of that nation. This year, for the first time, South African troops came into direct confrontation with those of Marxist Angola, supported by some of the country's estimated 26,000 Cuban soldiers and advisers. After five years of tortuous U.N. negotiation, the Angolan-Namibian situation is still at a violent stalemate: Angola refuses to dis-miss its Cuban troops until South Africa withdraws; South Africa refuses to with-draw until the Cubans are dismissed. Meanwhile, South Africa will doubtless continue assisting the insurgent National Union for the Total Independence of An-gola (UNITA) in its attacks against the An-golan government.

The latest offensive showed just how stagnant and how strenuous the evenly matched tug of war has become. Last Au-gust UNITA forces, reportedly supported by South African air strikes, captured the strategic town of Cangamba in southern Angola. During the following two months, SWAPO guerrillas swarmed through north-

Going thr
*Fighting w*

TIME, JANUARY 23, 1984

# INTERVIEW: JERRY SEINFELD

His long-running TV series, *Seinfeld,* was one of the most popular and influential shows in the history of television. But the American comedian Jerry Seinfeld has also made his mark on the world of advertising in his ongoing role as the spokesman for American Express credit cards. Seinfeld doesn't just appear in the ads, he helps create them, working closely with Ogilvy & Mather creative director David Apicella. In fact, Seinfeld's interest in advertising runs so deep that he has considered starting his own ad agency.

**WHY DID YOU CHOOSE TO DO ADS FOR AMERICAN EXPRESS?**
I had always kind of liked the company; they had a certain dignity about them. At the time I decided to do this, [comedian] Jay Leno was doing Doritos ads, and I remember that anytime he went onstage, people would yell out, "Hey, Doritos, hey, nachos"—and I figured that was the last thing I needed. I didn't see that kind of downside to American Express.

And creatively, they were pretty wide open. They didn't really have any set form they wanted to fit me into, and they were willing to let me get involved. And I got more and more involved as we went along. They'll usually give us a general idea of what they're trying to do with the ads—and then we'll take it from there. It's not a hard-sell campaign, obviously. They're giving us sixty seconds to create an entertaining commercial that includes the American Express card. They allow us to use the advertising time to explore the art form of the commercial.

**YOU'VE TALKED ABOUT OPENING YOUR OWN AGENCY. WHAT ATTRACTS YOU TO ADVERTISING?**
I've always been interested in it. In fact, I know if I weren't a comedian, I would be in advertising. I like the restrictions of it. It's kind of like stand-up comedy, which is also a very restrictive form to work in—it may seem free, but you actually have to have the utmost discipline to create something funny in a very small space. In stand-up, you have to bring up an idea, get to the funny part of it, and resolve it—in about forty seconds. Good comedy writing has a very spare, elemental feel to it. And advertising has the same kind of restriction, in that you're working with a very finite amount of time and space. I just enjoy that smallness. It's kind of a haiku.

**IN TERMS OF CELEBRITIES' WILLINGNESS TO APPEAR IN ADS, IT NOW SEEMS THAT EVEN THE MOST CUTTING-EDGE PERFORMERS ARE EAGER TO DO THEM; THE NEGATIVE BAGGAGE THAT USED TO COME WITH PITCHING PRODUCTS SEEMS TO BE ALMOST NONEXISTENT TODAY. IS THAT TRUE?**
It depends on the ad. When I see celebrities in ads where I know they walked on the set, were handed a script, and just read what was written, I consider that very treacherous territory. For a celebrity, I think there is still a huge potential penalty for appearing in the wrong ad. I'm not going to mention names, but there are people doing things they should not be doing. And it's mostly because the celebrity looks at the offer simply as, "Here's how many days it will take, and here's how much they're paying." And they judge it on that basis, which to me is lunacy. The only thing that should count is, How will I appear in this exposure? Will I be entertaining and come off the way I want to come off to the public in everything I do? Just taking the money is almost always a mistake.

**WE'RE SEEING LOTS OF ADS WITH OFF-THE-WALL HUMOR THESE DAYS—GERBILS SHOT FROM CANNONS AND OTHER "ODDVERTISING." ARE YOU IMPRESSED BY THE EDGINESS OF HUMOR IN ADS RIGHT NOW?**
I'm very impressed by it. I think some people feel it's all kind of happened at the same time. Like that Internet company that had the great ad where they released the wild pack of wolves on the marching band. . . . I remember them being the first Internet company to have really funny, unusual ads, and everyone seemed to talk about it, and then there was just an avalanche of it. Of course, then it began to get to the point where people couldn't distinguish one ad from another—the oddity became sameness. The ad that impresses me most is for Budget rental cars, where they send people to Mount Everest, and then they show corpses at the end. I mean, come on—this is something that really happened! That is nervy to do that in an ad. I don't know how you get a client to sign off on that.

**YOU USED TO JOKE ABOUT LAUNDRY-DETERGENT ADS THAT CLAIMED THEY COULD GET MESSY BLOODSTAINS OUT OF CLOTHES [THE PUNCH LINE: IF YOU HAVE MESSY BLOODSTAINS ON YOUR CLOTHES, LAUNDRY MAY NOT BE YOUR BIGGEST WORRY]. HAVE YOU OBSERVED ANY OTHER CURIOSITIES IN RECENT ADS?**
Well, advertising has always been some of the easiest fodder for the stand-up comic. I'm doing a bit now about ads for prescription medicines where they don't tell you anything about the drug. Someone comes on and says, "My doctor says Lipitor." And that's it. And I'm saying, "Well, what's wrong with this guy; is he going to be all right? What's Lipitor? I'll take it—just tell me what it is!"

**HOW MUCH IMPACT WOULD YOU SAY ADVERTISING HAS ON POP CULTURE, COMPARED WITH, SAY, MOVIES OR TV SHOWS?**
It's an incredibly powerful forum. You can come up with a great idea for an ad, and two months later, everyone will be talking about it. The only other medium you could do that in is series television. Movies can't pick up on the culture that quickly, because the [production] pipeline's too long. I think that because advertising works so much faster than everything else and goes through so many ideas, it really forces everybody else to keep up. As a medium of the moment, of the current zeitgeist, advertising is absolutely at the forefront. And that's what attracts me to it—I love to be at that moment.

12

12. **ART DIRECTORS CLUB OF
NEW YORK**
BILL OBERLANDER,
NEW YORK, 1996
Advertising has been resurrecting
its classic characters, sometimes
for camp appeal. Kirshenbaum
Bond art director Bill Oberlander
parodied the trend by showing
tired old versions of Mr. Whipple,
the Doublemint Twins, the
Coppertone girl, Mr. Clean,
and the Jolly Green Giant.

13. **VEJA MAGAZINE**
ALMAP BBDO, SÃO PAULO,
1994
Nothing and no one is sacrosanct; in recent years, the Pope,
the Dalai Lama, and Jesus Christ
have all been featured in ads.

Do like a million
subscribers:
receive the world
at your door.

veja

13

particularly popular, but some ads have also featured Western icons like Michael Jordan and Mickey Mouse.

But even as celebrities have maintained their longstanding appeal to advertisers, there has been a change in the kind of stars in demand. One of the more intriguing recent trends has been the rise of what might be called the "semi-star," who is only slightly famous. Increasingly, ads have featured endorsers who are known to only a small segment of the population. A recent ad campaign for American Express included the Hollywood film-studio executive David Geffen—an important figure but not necessarily a recognizable one—as well as the architect Frank Gehry (whose face is far less familiar than some of his buildings) and a leading advertising executive, Lee Clow of TBWA/Chiat/Day. The ads didn't bother to identify the subjects, leaving the audience guessing. "We wanted interest and intrigue," said an American Express spokesperson,

Emily Porter. "Being recognizable is important, but being almost recognizable plays into the mystique we wanted to create." Oberlander of Kirshenbaum Bond, whose agency's ads for Rockport shoes featured such "undiscovered heroes" as a hot young Web site designer from the company Razorfish, said, "Sometimes advertisers are looking for undiscovered talent, so you can ride their wave when they explode." Another advantage to using semi-stars is that it can lend ads an "underground" sensibility—suggesting that the advertiser is in tune with that which is too cool to be widely known.

A different way to move counter to the mainstream is for advertisers to select stars with a controversial reputation—the "bad boy" (or bad girl) approach that has made Rodman and others increasingly popular. Not long ago, this would have been unthinkable in advertising; one of the ironclad rules of the business was that advertisers should avoid trouble and, therefore, troublemak-

ers. Endorsers had to be squeaky clean and were dropped at the first hint of a scandal. But by the late 1990s, that rule was turned on its head by some advertisers. Suddenly, a scandal could actually lead to an endorsement contract. The American basketball player Latrell Sprewell found himself in demand as a spokesperson after a highly publicized incident in which he choked his coach. Monica Lewinsky, one of the most scandal-tainted figures in recent history, was quickly signed to an advertising contract by a leading American weight-loss center. And Nicholas Leeson, the rogue stock trader who was infamous for causing the financial collapse of the British bank Barings, was recently featured in the advertising for a Swedish on-line stock-trading company (in the ads, Leeson warns of the dangers of gambling on the stock market—and, of course, he would know).

Why would a company want to associate itself with scandal? To start with, the mere

14

announcement that a celebrity involved in one will appear in ads brings instant news coverage and public attention (another example of Kirshenbaum's multiplier effect). Moreover, "if you're an advertiser and you want to say you're cutting-edge and not stodgy, then you do the opposite of what old-fashioned advertisers do," said Syracuse University's Thompson. "Putting Monica Lewinsky in your ads is a bold statement. It says, 'We're not part of the establishment.'"

The strategy seems to be particularly popular among fashion advertisers trying to show their rebel side to a youthful consumer audience. A few years back, the Philadelphia ad agency, Gyro, featured the mass murderers Charles Manson and Jeffrey Dahmer in its ads for a clothing merchant, Zipper Head (the copy: "Everyone has the occasional urge to go wild and do something completely outrageous"). The ads drew an avalanche of complaints, but they also turned a spotlight on both the brand and the agency. Is

it possible to push the boundaries beyond Manson? Believe it or not, Adolf Hitler has starred in a number of ads, including one of the most famous Brazilian commercials in recent years. The spot, for a São Paulo newspaper, opened with an extreme close-up of dots forming an unrecognizable image as the voice-over recited, "He made the economy grow . . . he invested in the arts. . . ." As the camera continued to pull back, it became clear that the dots formed the image of Hitler's face. The point of the ad: Knowing only a few facts about a person or story can be misleading if you're not shown the whole picture.

But even the more daring advertisers of today have their limits. O. J. Simpson, who had been such a huge star years ago in his work for Hertz car rental and other clients, has been persona non grata in the ad world since his infamous California murder trial. And the basketball star Magic Johnson, who announced

in 1991 that he had contracted the AIDS virus, seemed to lose some of his luster for advertisers thereafter. One of Johnson's sponsors, Converse sneakers, publicly voiced its support—but also backed off from producing new ads with Johnson after the news broke.

Perhaps no one took a greater fall from the heights of advertising stardom than the American pop singer Michael Jackson. During the 1980s, Jackson had been the featured attraction of one of the biggest ad campaigns ever, for Pepsi-Cola, and reportedly earned $15 million in the process. But after allegations of child molestation surfaced, Jackson's pitches for Pepsi dried up, and the sponsor didn't renew his contract. At the time, even the notoriously daring advertising man George Lois said of Jackson, "I'm supposed to be outrageous, and I'd be too chicken to touch him." (Actually, there were a couple of advertisers willing to feature Jackson in their ads—but now they cast him as the object of

15

16

**14. AND 1 ATHLETIC WEAR**
CRISPIN PORTER + BOGUSKY,
MIAMI, LATE 1990s
After NBA basketball star Latrell
Sprewell was suspended for
choking his coach, he starred in
these commercials. "Some
thought we were glamorizing
thuggish behavior," says ad creator Alex Bogusky, "but we felt
Sprewell deserved another
chance."

**16. MATTEUS.COM**
TBWA, STOCKHOLM, 2000
Nicholas Leeson, the rogue
stock trader blamed for the
1995 collapse of Barings bank,
emerged from the scandal as
the new ad spokesman for an
on-line stock trading company.

**15. PRICELINE.COM**
HILL, HOLLIDAY, CONNORS,
COSMOPULOS, NEW YORK,
2000
Actor William Shatner, the
original Captain Kirk in the
1960s TV series *Star Trek*,
helped resurrect his career by
making fun of himself in these
ads, but Priceline's stock price
eventually plummeted.

THE FACES OF ADVERTISING.

everyone
has the occasiona
urge to go wild and do
something completel
outrageous
when you fight this urge
it builds up within yo
until one day you snap

south street
new hope
ardmore

ZIPPER HEAD

extreme clothing

17. **ZIPPER HEAD CLOTHING**
GYRO, PHILADELPHIA, 1991
When this upstart clothier and its
mischievous agency wanted to
draw attention, they put famed
murderer Charles Manson in
their ad. It worked, but also
caused problems.

Folha de S. Paulo. Há 77 anos retratando o mundo com palavras.

19

ridicule. One ad from the Gyro agency, the mischief-makers behind the Manson ad, promoted a tanning salon with a picture of Jackson's bleached, surgically altered face and the headline "Some people are just too white.")

While advertisers were generally more willing to take a chance on endorsers who were controversial enough to have a rebel image and an underground following, there was an evolution taking place on the other side of the bargaining table, as well—underground stars, cultural rebels, and icons of hip were becoming far more receptive to the overtures of advertisers than in the past. Suddenly, it seemed, no one was too cool or too independent-minded to consider doing a little shilling on the side.

In fact, the whole notion that appearing in ads was a form of "selling out" became almost quaint in the 1990s. Even the most anti-establishment performers—rebel rock stars or menacing hip-hoppers—were ready and eager

to pitch products. As the raucous musician Kid Rock told a newspaper reporter, "I'm about to start hitting everyone up for money. I want to be like NASCAR, where people are going to pay me to wear stuff. If they call that sellin' out, they don't understand. If I want to make a difference, I need the money. I've never seen too many hippies make a difference—no one listened to them because they didn't have any money." This represented both a new "commercial chic" attitude and a new level of greed, as the advertising executive Marty Cooke of M&C Saatchi observed. "Years ago, the idea of someone like Bob Dylan doing a commercial would have been unthinkable," Cooke said. "Now the whole purpose is to sell out. You adopt an anti-establishment stance—until you get the big commercial offer."

How did the act of appearing in an ad become so acceptable, even among cultural rebels? "In the continuum of what is hip, commercials went through a complete change in the 1990s,"

noted Syracuse's Thompson. "It used to be if a star did ads, it meant their career was over. But now for a young, cool actor or musician to do a commercial, it can be a great career move." Appearing in ads "doesn't have the stigma it once had," Liz Rosenberg, Madonna's spokeswoman, recently observed. As commercials became more stylistic, artful, and entertainment-driven in the late 1980s and early 1990s, with some beginning to seem more like miniature films than product plugs, they gradually became a more acceptable forum for many performers. If a star chose the right ad vehicle— one with a hip Nike style, perhaps directed by a Hollywood-style storyteller like Joe Pytka, with a humorous script, lively music, and a cool, ironic sensibility—the result was nothing to be ashamed of.

In fact, as Rosenberg noted, "It's a way of [gaining] exposure without having to tell your life story to a reporter all over again." Plus, she

**THE FACES OF ADVERTISING.**

Neil Overend, World Champion
(C) 1996, Specialized Bicycle Components, Inc.

20

added, it was unlike an interview with the press; "you can have control over an ad shoot—and that's what artists want." Certainly, today's ad stars are far more in control of the commercial process than ever before. Most refuse to recite a sales pitch—many stars in ads don't even talk about the product at all. Stars in recent years have been wary of hyping products not only because it's "uncool" but also because it is potentially dangerous for them: The singer Pat Boone once came under fire from the U.S. Federal Trade Commission just for reading aloud lines from a script that contained unsubstantiated claims about an acne medicine. Consequently, many contemporary star-driven ads are much more about the performer than the product; the ads represent a vehicle within which to sing a hit song, do a comedy routine, or act out characters. For some stars, an ad may offer a chance to soften or lighten their public image (in his ads for the Internet company Priceline,

former *Star Trek* television star William Shatner was able to rejuvenate his popularity by making fun of his own image as a hammy actor and woeful would-be singer). For others, ads can serve to enhance and build upon the star's own growing legend.

In terms of the latter, no one has done a more masterly job than the basketball star Michael Jordan. When Jordan entered professional basketball, he announced that he wanted to be the best-marketed player in the game— and by the mid-1990s, he was the most popular advertising figure in America and one of the most popular in the world, earning ten times as much money for his ads as for his ballplaying. The phenomenal marketing success of Jordan owes much to his unparalleled playing skills and charismatic personality, but he was also helped immensely by the ongoing ad campaign created by Nike and its ad agency, Wieden + Kennedy. The ads presented Jordan as a kind of mythic

hero of the sports world, but they also showed his human side; some of them explained, in Jordan's own voice, what motivated him, how he managed to overcome self-doubt, why he loved to challenge and push himself. ("I've failed over and over and over again in my life," Jordan acknowledged in one ad, "and that is why I succeed.") Each new campaign seemed to add another chapter to his unfolding life story, which continued in ads even after he retired in 1998. In effect, Nike advertising was, and still is, Jordan's official biographer.

Jordan wasn't the only athlete that Nike tried to mythologize through ads. The football star turned baseball player Bo Jackson was presented as a multisport miracle in the memorable "Bo Knows" commercials. And the sometimes-surly basketball star Charles Barkley became a heroic clown prince in Nike ads, mugging his way through a mock-opera spot called "Barkley of Seville." When not clowning, Barkley also

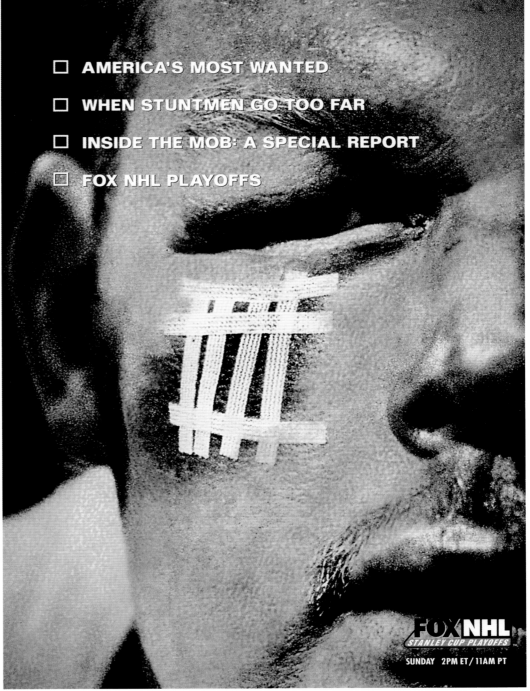

AMERICA'S MOST WANTED

WHEN STUNTMEN GO TOO FAR

INSIDE THE MOB: A SPECIAL REPORT

FOX NHL PLAYOFFS

FOX NHL STANLEY CUP PLAYOFFS

SUNDAY 2PM ET / 11AM PT

21

**20. SPECIALIZED BICYCLES**
GOODBY SILVERSTEIN &
PARTNERS, SAN FRANCISCO,
EARLY 1990s
Who says the face of advertising
must be clean and fresh? A little
dirt doesn't hurt, especially when
the audience is outdoorsmen.

**21. NATIONAL HOCKEY**
**LEAGUE (NHL) ON FOX**
CLIFF FREEMAN & PARTNERS,
NEW YORK, 1999
Here, the face is battered and
bruised, though the headline
remains playful. Freeman under-
stood that violence was hockey's
Unique Selling Proposition.

THE FACES OF ADVERTISING.

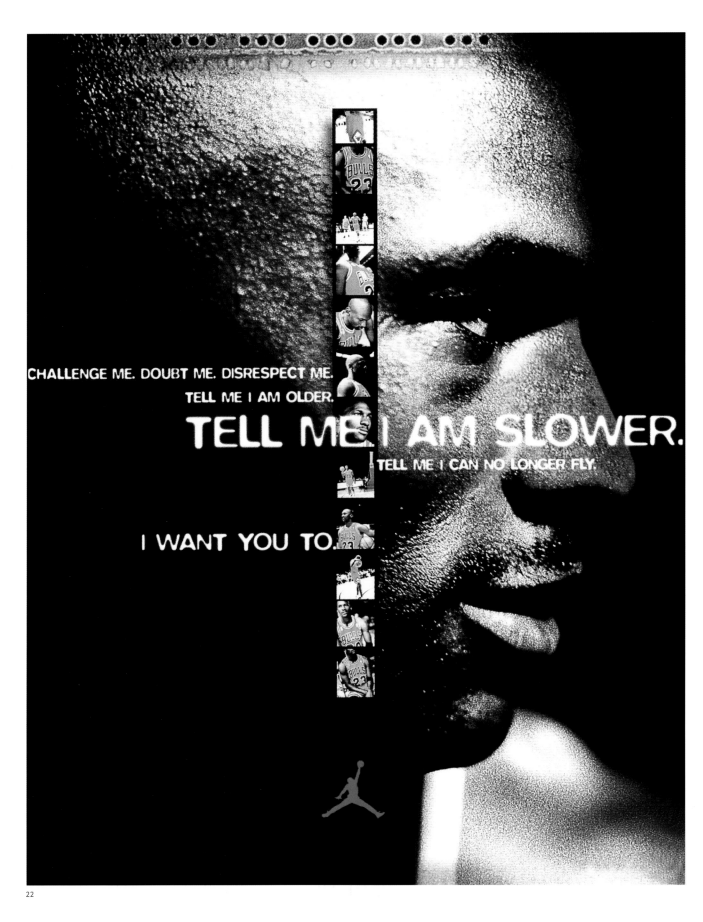

CHALLENGE ME. DOUBT ME. DISRESPECT ME.

TELL ME I AM OLDER.

TELL ME I AM SLOWER.

TELL ME I CAN NO LONGER FLY.

I WANT YOU TO.

22 AND 23. **NIKE**
WIEDEN + KENNEDY,
PORTLAND, 1993
Nike became Michael Jordan's
official biographer, turning him
into a mythological figure while
also showing his human
frailties. When Jordan retired in
1998, he left a gaping hole in
basketball and in advertising.

22

I'VE MISSED MORE THAN 9000 SHOTS IN MY CAREER.

I'VE LOST ALMOST 300 GAMES.

26 TIMES, I'VE BEEN TRUSTED TO TAKE THE GAME WINNING SHOT

AND MISSED.

I'VE FAILED

OVER AND OVER AND OVER AGAIN IN MY LIFE.

AND THAT IS WHY

I SUCCEED

23

# Hello world.

I shot in the 70s when I was 8.

I shot in the 60s when I was 12.

# Hello world.

I won the United States Junior Amateur when I was 15.

I played in the Nissan Los Angeles Open when I was 16.

I won the United States Amateur when I was 18.

# Hello world.

I played in the Masters when I was 19.

I played in the United States Open when I was 19.

I played in the British Open when I was 19.

# Hello world.

I am the only man to win three consecutive

United States Amateur titles.

# Hello world.

There are still courses in the United States that I am

not allowed to play because of the color of my skin.

# Hello world.

I've heard I'm not ready for you.

Are you ready for me?

*Just do it.*

**JUST DO IT.**

**24. NIKE**
WIEDEN + KENNEDY,
PORTLAND, 1998
After Jordan, pro golfer Tiger
Woods became the new god of
advertising. Again, the ads told
the life story of the young man—
sometimes embellished for
dramatic effect.

**25. NIKE**
WIEDEN + KENNEDY,
PORTLAND, 1993
In the early 1990s, temperamental
basketball star Charles Barkley
played the role of advertising's
reluctant hero: "I am not a role
model," Barkley declared in this
famous TV commercial.

unburdened his soul in ads, most famously in a commercial in which he declared, "I am not a role model." (In the ad, Barkley goes on to say that parents, not ballplayers, should be role models for children.) Most recently, Nike has attempted—with very successful, though perhaps not quite Jordanesque, results—to turn the golfer Tiger Woods into the new god of advertising. When he was barely old enough to vote, Woods was unveiled to the ad public with a dramatic campaign entitled "Hello World." With that, the ad version of Tiger's tale began to unfold, in all its exaggerated glory and heartbreak ("There are still golf courses in America that I can't play on," the biracial Woods declared in one ad, which immediately led critics to question whether Woods, a prodigy who practically grew up on lush golf courses and in the spotlight, wasn't being a bit melodramatic with that line). Similar kinds of Nike legend-building have been going on around the world; the Amsterdam

office of Wieden + Kennedy has made larger-than-life figures of a number of European soccer stars in ads like the fiery one headlined "Sudden death: What any team faces without Eric." Who's Eric? For the record, his last name is Cantona and he plays for Manchester—but if you have to ask, you're not the targeted customer.

In recent years, there have been occasional backlashes against highly paid athlete endorsers; the sneaker company New Balance recently ran a campaign defiantly headlined, "Endorsed by no one." But for the most part, sports stars have continued to be a gold mine for advertisers—more effective, experts say, than actors, musicians, or any other type of performer. While all celebrities can, as research has shown, "transfer" positive feelings to the product, star athletes are a particularly rich source of transferable good feelings; when they appear in ads, one advertising creator told *USA Today*, viewers associate the products with the joy of watching

sports—hence, "what you're getting is the borrowed interest of the excitement."

Perhaps the only thing that can rival the athlete for sheer popularity as an endorser is the animal. Dog, cat, frog, chimpanzee: The particular species does not matter (well, perhaps it matters a little—the naked mole rat doesn't get too many endorsement opportunities, except in one ad for a New England zoo with the headline "The naked mole rat. As if being a rat weren't bad enough"). In American ads, talking animals have been the focal point of several of the most popular ad campaigns of the 1990s—including a Budweiser campaign that began with frogs croaking the name "Bud-wei-ser," and evolved into a subsequent series of ads in which lizards engaged in sarcastic banter with one another. But none of them could compete with the "spokesanimal" of the 1990s—the Taco Bell Chihuahua, one of the single most recognizable advertising characters created in recent years.

26

26. **TACO BELL**
TBWA/CHIAT/DAY,
LOS ANGELES, 1998
The Chihuahua's big piercing
eyes had a mesmerizing effect,
but the dog just didn't sell
enough tacos. The company
eventually said "*adios*" to the
corporate icon.

27. **BRITANNICA.COM**
DEUTSCH INC., NEW YORK,
1999
This ad for the on-line encyclope-
dia company delved inside the
mind of author Norman Mailer.

As is often the case with animal ads that strike gold, no one expected much from the Chihuahua—it was more or less a throwaway idea. The creators of the ads, TBWA/Chiat/Day's Chuck Bennett and Clay Williams, had been struggling to come up with ideas when, during an outdoor lunch break, they observed a passing Chihuahua "who looked like he was on a mission," said Bennett. They decided to try one ad about a little dog in search of a taco and thought that would be the end of it. But TV viewers loved it, and thus was born the tale of the Chihuahua on the endless quest for Mexican food. Does anybody really know why the Chihuahua struck a chord? Vada Hill, chief marketing officer of Taco Bell, theorized that it was because the Chihuahua was "a perfect personification of a quirky, iconoclastic, quasi-Mexican brand." More likely, it was the tiny dog's oversize, piercing eyes, which stared into the television camera with a mesmerizing effect

as she mouthed (via computer-generated effects) her lines. In the end, although the dog became a pop-culture phenomenon, it didn't sell enough tacos—and the company opted for a new canine-free ad approach.

The Chihuahua was just one in a parade of pitch-animals in recent years—including the Hofmeister bear and the PG Tips chimp in the UK, the koala bear for New Zealand's Qantas Airlines, Morris the Cat, or the whole menagerie that appeared in a series of ads for the Singapore SPCA—with each animal bearing a sign with a promise to behave well if adopted. Thompson believes that animals sell because, quite simply, they can be trusted: "They're the ultimate innocents," he said. Certainly they're the only performers in ads that haven't been paid off (except, perhaps, in peanuts). They're often adorable to begin with, and by the time advertising's special effects work their magic, piping in funny voices or enabling the creatures to dance,

the end result, Thompson noted, "is like a cruise missile to the heart."

In some ways, these technology-engineered talking animals of contemporary ads have filled a void left by the departed cartoon ad characters of old—creations like Charlie the Tuna and the Jolly Green Giant. However, Thompson asserts that the talking dogs and cats of today's ads—who, with rare exceptions, generally tend to come and go without leaving much of a lasting impression on the culture—are pale substitutes for the old-time ad characters, both animated and human. Those classic ad figures, from Mr. Whipple to Ronald McDonald, "contributed some of the most memorable, richest characters to the cultural pantheon," Thompson said.

And yet many of these characters were partially if not completely abandoned by brands and their ad agencies in the 1980s, as more contemporary, postmodern advertising approaches took hold, favoring elaborate style over simple

This page:
Norman Mailer thinks
he wouldn't trust a
house that didn't have
a ghost or some kind of
indefinable presence in
it. He's also wondering
about the weather in
Provincetown.

go to *supernatural*,
go to *weather*

at **britannica.com**
what's on your mind?

©1999 Britannica.com Inc.

©1997 Time Inc. TIME is a registered trademark of Time Inc. Photo Credit: Reuters/Gary Hershorn/Archive Photos. Internet: http://time.com CompuServe: GO TIME

What kind of bandage can

boxing possibly put on this?

**The world's most interesting magazine.**

Make sense of anything.

Almost.

The world's most interesting magazine.

30

The world's most interesting magazine.

29

28, 29, AND 30.
**TIME MAGAZINE**
FALLON McELLIGOTT,
MINNEAPOLIS, MINNESOTA,
1997
Three faces of *Time* from the
long-running series of ads art-
directed by Bob Barrie. The red
box frames the significant details:
Boxer Evander Holyfield's chewed
ear, Bill Clinton's sweat, and the
angelic face of a child soldier.

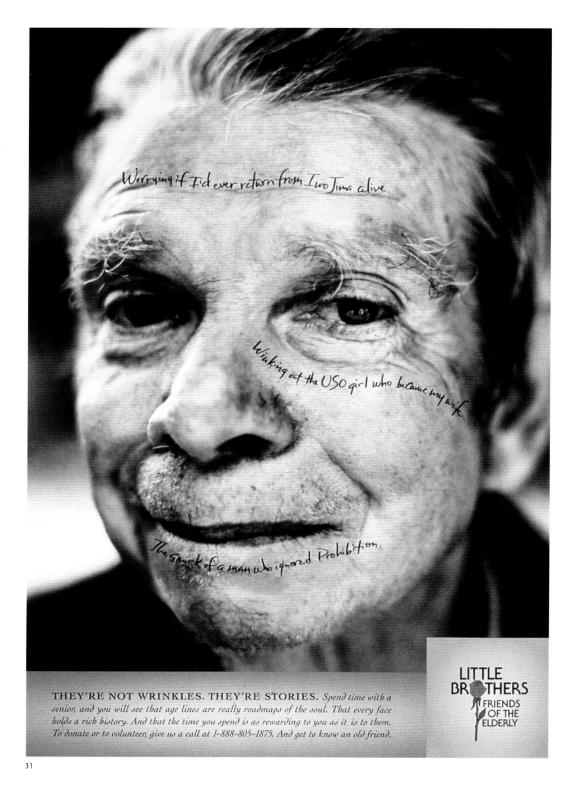

Worrying if I'd ever return from Iwo Jima alive.

Winking at the USO girl who became my wife.

The smirk of a man who ignored Prohibition.

**THEY'RE NOT WRINKLES. THEY'RE STORIES.** *Spend time with a senior, and you will see that age lines are really roadmaps of the soul. That every face holds a rich history. And that the time you spend is as rewarding to you as it is to them. To donate or to volunteer, give us a call at 1-888-805-1873. And get to know an old friend.*

LITTLE BROTHERS FRIENDS OF THE ELDERLY

31

31. **LITTLE BROTHERS**
ODIORNE WILDE NARRAWAY +
PARTNERS, SAN FRANCISCO,
1998
Advertising has traditionally
shunned older faces, although
as this ad observes, there are
stories to be found in those
wrinkles.

32. **THE JOHN FITZGERALD
KENNEDY LIBRARY**
THE MARTIN AGENCY,
RICHMOND, VIRGINIA, 1997
Reliving history through adver-
tising: This series of ads explored
the complex relationship between
Jacqueline Bouvier Kennedy and
the man she married.

Mark Shaw Collection/Photo Researchers

*Jacqueline Kennedy's*
*historic restoration*
*of the White House.*
*Part of a new exhibit at*
**The John F. Kennedy**
**Library & Museum.**
*Boston, Massachusetts.*

32

characters. The assumption was that the new audience was far too cynical for the likes of the Jolly Green Giant. But it was also true that many creative people at ad agencies were eager to leave behind classic ad characters—which were considered both hokey and gimmicky. (Among advertising's creative cognoscenti, Mr. Whipple had become a kind of whipping boy, ridiculed along with old-fashioned jingles and earnest slogans. In the early 1990s, the award-winning American ad writer Luke Sullivan authored a book titled *Hey Whipple, Squeeze This!*—which opens with Sullivan joking about his longtime secret desires to gun down ad characters like Whipple and the Ty-D-Bol man.)

But it would take more than fantasy bullets to kill an icon like Whipple. To the surprise (and dismay) of many in advertising, the character resurfaced in Charmin's ad campaign in 1999, around the same time that a number of other classic ad characters—including the Jolly Green Giant, KFC's Colonel Sanders, and Life Cereal's Mikey—were also being resurrected. Why? "These characters are part of the fabric of these companies, and there's an emotional attachment to them," said Ted Bell, chief creative officer at Young & Rubicam, the agency for KFC. Even after being on hiatus, Bell said, the classic characters remained known to consumers; "you see the Colonel, and it's instant recognition, with no explanation necessary," he said. What's more, Bell added, when the old characters reappeared, the new cynical audience actually seemed to like them. Younger consumers enjoyed them because they were corny and campy; for older viewers, they had nostalgic appeal. In some cases, the resurrected characters were modernized a bit—as with the KFC Colonel, who was brought back in animated form (originally, the character was played by a real person) and injected with a touch of hip-hop style.

It should come as no surprise that advertising would raid the coffins of its own characters; death, it seems, is no impediment to being a successful advertising spokesperson. In recent years, special-effects technology has made it easier for advertisers to seamlessly insert old footage of deceased actors into new commercials, while also putting words in their mouths. Humphrey Bogart, James Cagney, and Louis Armstrong all showed up in Coca-Cola commercials in the 1990s, while Fred Astaire danced with a Dirt Devil vacuum cleaner. A recent South African ad for Dunlop tires featured the face of film icon James Dean, digitally retouched to make it appear as if Dean (who died at age 24 in a car accident) is an old man, alive and perched comfortably behind the wheel of his sports car. The point of the ad? To suggest that if only Dean had driven on Dunlop tires, he might be alive today. And if so, he could frolic with Judy Garland, who was resurrected in a commercial that ran during the January 2000 Super Bowl; using footage lifted from *The Wizard of Oz*, the

Glamour

33

34

**33. MERCEDES-BENZ**
LOWE & PARTNERS/SMS,
NEW YORK, 1997
Marilyn Monroe continued to
land endorsement deals, three-
decades after her death. Here,
the advertiser has transformed
her beauty mark into a
corporate symbol.

**34. DUNLOP TIRES**
TBWA HUNT LASCARIS,
JOHANNESBURG, 2000
In this South African ad, an
image of film star James Dean
(killed in 1955 in a car crash) was
digitally aged to show what he
would look today. The implication:
Dean might still be with us if he
had driven on Dunlop tires.

"WHEN I LOOK AT MY BACKSIDE
I see that it's split in two parts."

Winston Churchill, 23rd February 1947.

"**Q**uand je regarde mon derrière je vois qu'il est divisé en deux parties." OOH LA LA! What he really meant was when he looked at his past he could see it was split in two parts. Maybe our wartime leader should have given us a call. At Wordbank, translation is handled by a national from the relevant country. In fact, we have a network of over 3,000 translators living in their own country, which eliminates the risk of embarrassing mistakes. If you want to make your foreign marketing and advertising make sense, call us on 0800 281 005. You can rest assured, our translators know their arse from their elbow.

**WORDBANK**
WORLD CLASS TRANSLATION

35

# WHY DOES MAN EXIST?

Friedrich Wilhelm Nietzsche, 1882.

BASS HELPS YOU GET TO
THE BOTTOM OF IT ALL.

BASS & Cº PALE ALE
*Bass*

© 1995 Imported by the Guinness Import Company, Stamford, CT

36

Babe Ruth says: "I haven't **felt** this **good** since I gave up **sausage**."

© 1998 Pepsi-Lipton Tea Partnership. Lipton and Brisk are registered trademarks of Lipton. ℠ © 1998 Babe Ruth League, Inc. and the Family of Babe Ruth under license authorized by CMG Worldwide Inc., Indianapolis, Indiana 46256 USA. Major League Baseball trademarks and copyrights are used with permission of Major League Baseball Properties, Inc.

37

**35. WORDBANK**
LEO BURNETT, LONDON,
MID-1990s
Not everything Winston
Churchill said was inspirational:
this series of ads cites mis-
statements resulting from bad
translations. That a British
advertiser would dare to poke fun
at Churchill, however, is unusual.

**36. BASS ALE**
WEISS WHITTEN STAGLIANO,
NEW YORK, 1990
Friedrich Nietzsche probably
never contemplated a future
in advertising, but he is
used here to pitch beer to the
intellectual set.

**37. LIPTON ICED TEA**
J. WALTER THOMPSON,
NEW YORK, 1998
The legendary New York Yankees
baseball player, The Babe,
returns to pitching: Many dead
celebrities have more earning
potential now than when they
were alive.

ad plunked "Dorothy" down in the middle of a Federal Express commercial. (Also during that game's broadcast, the same computer-generation wizardry that raised Garland from the grave was used to lift the paralyzed American actor Christopher Reeve out of his wheelchair and make it appear as if he was walking—to some viewers, this was even creepier than watching the dead rise.)

While the use of deceased stars in ads has been widely criticized, ad agencies are free to use just about anyone in an ad if they can get the star's heirs and copyright holders of their films to agree to it, usually for a fee. The fact is, "many dead celebrities have more earning potential now than when they were alive," *The Chicago Sun-Times* observed recently. Consider the philosopher Friedrich Nietzsche, for example; shunned by advertisers during his lifetime (one can only assume they found him much too dour and seri-

ous), he's a perfect star for contemporary, slightly ironic Bass Ale ads positioning the beverage as the thinking man's beer. Gandhi, meanwhile, serves as a powerful symbol of "thinking differently" on behalf of Apple, as does the late Beatle John Lennon. The fact that some of these figures may have stood for anti-commercialism in their lifetimes doesn't trouble Apple. "The people that we're using in our ads are never used to sell the product," explained Allen Olivo, the company's former ad director. Instead, Olivo maintained, the ads "celebrate who they are, and we try to recognize them for their accomplishments." Perhaps Gandhi and Lennon would have welcomed that recognition—though it seems more likely they would have spurned offers or, at the very least, raised bothersome questions about what Apple does with its profits. No-questions-asked complicity is just one of the benefits of hiring dead pitchmen; they're also

cheaper—advertisers typically spend about only about $10,000 to use a deceased celebrity in a campaign—and far less likely to land in the midst of a scandal (though, given the "Bad is good" nature of some advertising today, that last point might actually be seen as a strike against them).

In the end, this much can be said about what it takes to qualify as a face of advertising in the modern commercial landscape: One doesn't necessarily have to be glamorous anymore. Or wholesome, or even law-abiding. Or well known. Or human. Or, for that matter, alive. In the age of the advertising anti-hero, what's required is only this: the attitude of a rebel, the authenticity of a "real" person, the pure dumb honesty of an animal, and the inner spirit of a legendary sports god. All of which, it turns out, can be bought as easily as the old point-and-smile pitchman of days gone by.

**THE FACES OF ADVERTISING.**

# 9. ADVE
# AS AN A
# SOCIAL

RTISING
GENT OF
CHANGE.

1. **FRIENDS OF PUBLIC EDUCATION**
FALLON McELLIGOTT,
MINNEAPOLIS, MINNESOTA,
1995
Using a minimalist message to make that point that reading is fundamental.

When she was hired to pitch Lucky Strike cigarettes forty years ago, Janet Sackman seemed an ideal advertising spokesmodel—fresh-faced and attractive, with a lilting voice that urged the public "to light up a Lucky." Sackman was so eager to do a good job that she took up smoking (following the suggestion of her employers, she said) so that she'd look more natural when holding a cigarette. That began a thirty-year smoking habit and, eventually, the onset of throat cancer. By the 1990s, Sackman no longer seemed like a likely candidate for a job as spokesperson—particularly since her voice box had been surgically removed as part of her cancer treatment. But then, in 1995, she returned to the advertising spotlight in a dramatic way.

Sackman was hired by the ad agency for the Massachusetts Department of Health, which was working on a series of anti-smoking ads. The agency and its client were looking for someone who could deliver a stirring indict-ment of the tobacco industry—and who better than Sackman? In an unsettling series of radio and television commercials, she apologized to the public—in a strained whisper of a voice— for having appeared in cigarette ads decades earlier. The ads won acclaim and awards throughout the industry, and were a centerpiece in a larger ad campaign that helped drive down smoking in Massachusetts by a remarkable 30 percent in the late 1990s.

Ads like Sackman's anti-smoking commercial represent, in effect, the conscience of advertising. In an industry that is often justifiably blamed for encouraging vanity, excessive spending, overeating, smoking, alcohol consumption, and any number of other bad habits, there is a growing category of ads that seeks to make amends for all of that. Commonly known as public-service advertising, it has billions of dollars and some of the ad industry's most creative minds behind it. And it is confronting virtually every critical social issue imaginable— including, in some cases, problems that were partly caused or at least exacerbated by advertising in the first place.

Increasingly, around the world, advertising is becoming a central part of the public discourse on matters of life, death, and much of what occurs in between. Some examples:

In the United States, more money than ever before is currently being spent on advertising to combat drug abuse, as part of a $2 billion initiative that began in 1998 and runs through 2003. In making such a huge commitment of resources, the U.S. Government has effectively pronounced that the best way to steer kids away from drugs is through advertising.

In the United Kingdom, an ongoing major ad campaign on the issue of child abuse has been so widely and thoroughly disseminated that it

**Stay in school.**

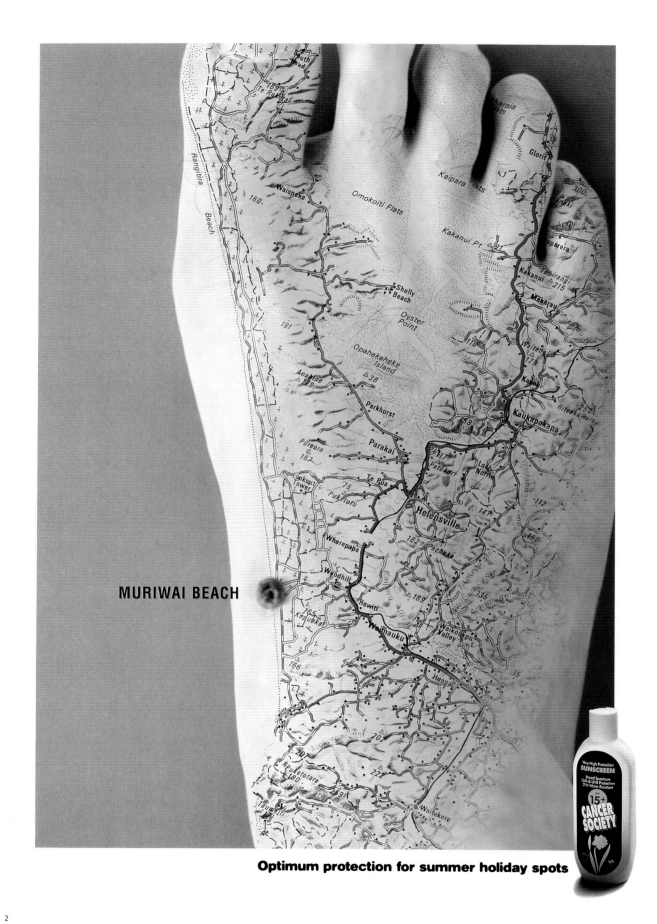

MURIWAI BEACH

**Optimum protection for summer holiday spots**

3

2. **CANCER SOCIETY
OF NEW ZEALAND**
WALKERS ADVERTISING,
AUCKLAND, 1997
In a part of the world where
the incidence of skin cancer is
particularly high, ads are
providing a road map to
prevention.

3. **MASSACHUSSETTS
DEPARTMENT OF HEALTH**
HOUSTON EFFLER HERSTEK
FAVAT, BOSTON, 1995
Janet Sackman, who lost her
voice box to cancer, became a
dramatic spokesperson in
anti-smoking ads.

has reached the attention of some 90 percent of the population. The campaign's ambitious goal: to actually wipe out child abuse.

In South Africa, advertising has taken on a central role in the sensitive and critical debate involving race and politics. In fact, many in the country believe that ads—by way of education or scare tactics, depending on one's viewpoint— were a driving force in mobilizing white support for apartheid reforms.

In Japan, recent public-service ads have attempted to change longstanding customs and behavior, including child-rearing participation among men. Addressing the problem of men neglecting their families to focus on work, one ad campaign showed well-known and respected Japanese men engaged in fathering, with the headline "You cannot call a man who doesn't care for his child a man." (The ads have stirred controversy among

some Japanese men, drawing complaints about meddling in private family affairs.)

Elsewhere around the world, public-service ads have addressed issues that are particularly critical in certain countries: educating on the need for birth control in India, or warning of the rise of xenophobic actions by neo-Nazi groups in Germany, or reminding people to stay out of the sun in New Zealand, whose population has one of the highest rates of skin cancer in the world. A look at a country's social-cause ads can be an eye-opener, bringing to light obscure issues that are unique to a given culture—as in the case of passionate, persuasive ads in Singapore urging citizens to refrain from eating tiger-penis soup (the popularity of this dish has threatened the tiger population).

But as advertising has become more concerned with social issues and causes, that has

in turn raised questions about the propriety and effectiveness of such ads. Skeptics reasonably wonder whether public education on complex social problems can, or should, be undertaken by the same people who peddle corn flakes (or, worse, liquor and cigarettes). And, too, there is the question of motive: If, as some suspect, advertisers address social issues primarily for self-serving reasons—i.e., to burnish their own image—does that diminish the value of the work they're doing in this area? Does it mean, perhaps, that advertising's public-service warnings and advice should be viewed with a wary eye?

It's fair to say that public-service advertising has been at least somewhat self-serving from the outset. In the U.S., such ads began to gain momentum in the early 1940s, after the industry leader James Webb Young, a consultant to the ad agency J. Walter Thompson, suggested that advertisers could offset mounting public criticism of their business by creating ads for good causes.

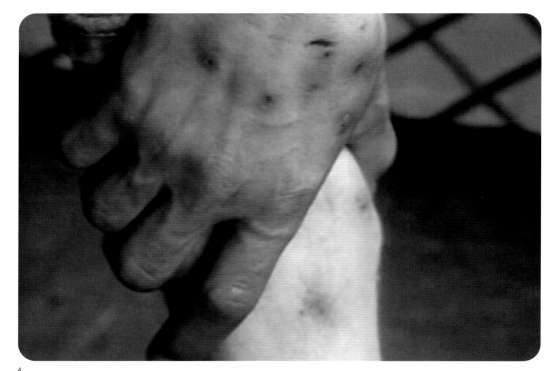

4

**4. PARTNERSHIP FOR A DRUG-FREE AMERICA**
CLIFF FREEMAN & PARTNERS,
NEW YORK, 1995
"Portrait of Lenny," an anti-heroin commercial, provided an unsettling glimpse into the life and mind of a junkie.

**6. PARTNERSHIP FOR A DRUG-FREE AMERICA**
KEYE/DONNA/PEARLSTEIN,
LOS ANGELES, 1987
From a decade earlier, the original and wonderfully simple "Fried Egg" spot, which declared: "This is your brain on drugs."

**5. PARTNERSHIP FOR A DRUG-FREE AMERICA**
MARGEOTES, FERTITTA & PARTNERS, NEW YORK, 1997
Back into the frying pan in the late 1990s: a woman shows the shattering effects of heroin. Critics, however, wondered why she was so glamorous-looking.

Young challenged his colleagues to use their persuasion skills "to confound the critics of advertising with the greatest demonstration of [advertising's] power they have ever seen." If ads could accomplish this, Young reasoned, the adversaries and critics of the business "will all be on our side."

The ad industry soon had an opportunity to put Young's plan into action. The onset of World War II led to the formation of an American group called the Advertising Council, which created ads serving the war effort by explaining food rationing, urging people to conserve, and so on. Some of the Council's more famous World War II ads became classics: "A slip of the lip can sink a ship" was one example of pithy Madison Avenue sloganeering brought to the cause, as was the emotional story told in "The Kid in Upper 4"— an ad that presented the thoughts of a fictional soldier on a train as he was heading off to war.

In creating wartime propaganda, these advertisers were not necessarily breaking new

ground— similar work had been done previously in posters and short films not just in the U.S. but elsewhere, most infamously in Nazi Germany. But what was significant about America's wartime Ad Council was that it didn't disband when the war ended—instead, the group turned its attention and persuasive skills to peacetime domestic issues. In the late 1940s, the Ad Council brought to life one of advertising's most famous characters, Smokey the Bear, to educate the public on the dangers of forest fires. The success of Smokey suggested that advertisers could, in fact, use some of the same tools that sold cereal—lovable cartoon characters uttering catchy phrases—to tackle matters of grave importance.

Over the next three decades, advertising on behalf of various social causes developed into a multibillion industry in itself (in 1990, in America alone, roughly $2 billion worth of advertising time was devoted to public service announcements, or PSAs). Who paid for all of

this benevolent advertising? To some extent, the public did, by way of donations to various charities, or through tax dollars that were subsequently allocated by government to address certain problems. However much of the tab for PSAs was picked up by ad agencies and the media; typically, ad professionals donated their time and creative ideas, while broadcasters and publishers donated airtime and pages to run the ads (the only part of the process that cost money was the actual production of the ads).

The creators of these ads realized that making dramatic commercials for important social causes also made them look good—and could help bring acclaim, awards, and new business to their agencies. Still, as PSAs began to proliferate in the 1960s, the spirit of the times was perhaps the primary motivator; as Doyle Dane Bernbach's Roy Grace noted, social activism and creative revolution were in the air. For the writers and art directors at top Madison

5

6

Alex Bishop.
Killed by a drunk driver
on November 8, 1992
on Kent-Kangley Road
in Kent, Washington.

7

# Imagine having your body left to science while you're still in it.

Three animals die every second in U.S. laboratories.

The monkey pictured here was surgically crippled and then forced to use his deadened arm.

Other animals, including rabbits, dogs, cats, pigs, rats, and primates, are routinely blinded, shocked, mutilated, decapitated, and force-fed poisons in tests that could easily be replaced with modern and more reliable methods.

These animal tests are being conducted by the government, universities, medical associations, and private corporations. And always behind closed, locked doors.

If you think these kinds of cruel experiments have no place in the 20th century, please join us: People for the Ethical Treatment of Animals.

PETA is America's leading animal rights organization. By working with medical and legal professionals, the media, members of Congress, and people like you, PETA has been able to stop some of the most horrifying animal experiments, including the one pictured here.

Please send me more information.
Name_____
Address_____
City_____State____Zip_____
__Please send me a free copy of the book *Animal Liberation*
Please accept my tax-deductible contribution of:
__$20 __$35 __$50 __$100 ___other $_____

**PeTA** PETA, P.O. Box 42516
Washington, DC 20015

8

---

Avenue agencies like DDB, Young & Rubicam, and Marsteller, making a public-service message was the ad executive's equivalent to joining the Peace Corps or marching for equal rights. And all of those hot-button issues of the day—war overseas, growing urban poverty, civil rights, pollution, increased drug abuse—offered a wealth of dramatic subject material and inspired a golden era in public-service ads.

It was during this period that some of the most memorable, even haunting images of social advertising were produced. A commercial targeting litter and pollution featured a Native American named Iron Eyes Cody, who was shown paddling a canoe while observing the desecration of the American landscape; the character responded, wordlessly, by shedding a single tear, as the ad's tagline urged, "Keep America beautiful." Protecting the environment became a prevalent theme in ads; the San Francisco ad executive Howard Gossage—

who had long preached that advertising was too important to waste on commercial products— applied his logic and wit to championing the Sierra Club. Other public-service ads at the time took on sensitive issues such as racism and poverty, with heart-wrenching ads for the United Negro College Fund that featured the slogan "A mind is terrible thing to waste," as well as commercials for the Urban Coalition that rendered a stark portrayal of ghetto life. (One particularly unsettling ad trained the TV camera on a rat, while an off-camera child's voice beckoned, "Here, kitty, kitty.") Meanwhile, ads on road safety, urging the public to "buckle up" seat-belts and avoid driving after drinking alcohol, clearly began to alter behavior and shift public attitudes, thanks in part to dramatic imagery: One memorable "Don't drink and drive" commercial showed wineglasses being joined in a toast and shattering to bits. Outdoor ads for Mothers Against Drunk Driving installed parts of

wrecked cars upon the billboard, and topped that with the resounding headline "Sometimes it takes a family of four to stop a drunk driver."

Gradually, such advertising seemed to be developing its own style and tone, distinct from ads that sold products. Perhaps it was to be expected given the seriousness of the subjects, but in the 1970s public-service ads tended to be highly emotional and often harrowing. In a way, these socially conscious ads turned conventional advertising on its head—they dealt in brutal honesty, not upbeat fantasy. If anything, the ads became harsher in the 1980s, as advertising stepped up its own war on drugs with the formation of the Partnership for a Drug-Free America, which, unlike the Ad Council, focused on a single issue and attacked it fiercely. The group's early print ads targeting cocaine use showed close-ups of people pointing guns up their noses. And one of the Partnership's first TV commercials remains one of its most famous:

**ADVERTISING AS AN AGENT OF SOCIAL CHANGE.**

YOU SHOULD BE PROUD OF YOURSELF. YOU'VE GOT "VIETNAM ROSE" (VD). Wear a condom, because next time you won't be so lucky. AIDS CONCERN. Helpline: 2898 4422

9

**9. STD PREVENTION
CAMPAIGN**
LEO BURNETT, HONG KONG,
1997
While American public service
ads tended to shock, Asian ads
were sometimes artfully designed;
this one warned against the
sexually transmitted disease
known as "Vietnam Rose."

**10. PROMOTING
CONDOM USE**
LEO BURNETT, MUMBAI, 1997
In India, this ad served as a
highly visual reminder, avoiding
the need to preach or persuade.

Remember.

SOMETIMES IT TAKES A FAMILY OF FOUR TO STOP A DRUNK DRIVER.

MADD

11

"This is your brain," a voice-over declared as the camera focused on an egg; as the egg was broken and fried, the announcer added, "This is your brain on drugs. Any questions?"

The drug ads seemed tame compared with those produced on behalf of animal-rights activists such as the American group People for the Ethical Treatment of Animals (PETA). These ads included photographs taken inside animal-research laboratories; one showed a laboratory dog with its head in a viselike contraption, and the headline "There's a reason they cut the vocal cords first." Another featured a tortured monkey, as the accompanying headline, written by The Martin Agency's Luke Sullivan, asked the reader to "imagine having your body left to science while you're still in it."

Similar ads could be seen around the world by the 1980s—for example, European advertising for animal-cruelty prevention also featured images of tortured or dead animals. There are, not surprisingly, great differences in the levels

and kinds of public-service ads encountered from one culture to the next. No other country has come close to spending the billions of dollars that the U.S. pours into social ads, and in fact few have established large, powerful PSA organizations comparable to the Partnership or the Ad Council. Many countries take more of an ad hoc approach, turning to ads as a particular social problem is perceived to be worsening. Anti-drug advertising has been getting a lot of play in South America in recent years, but such ads are not nearly as prevalent, for example, in the Netherlands, which tends to have more relaxed attitudes about certain types of drug usage (on the other hand, the Dutch tend to use ads for social engineering—preaching tolerance for people of other races, those with disabilities, etc.). The different ways that ads in varying cultures address common problems, such as sexually transmitted diseases, can be interesting. Hong Kong ads warning against the STD known locally as "Vietnam Rose" featured artful design

and illustration; a campaign in India promoted safe sex by making a logical and sincere case for masturbation ("The best sexual partner you've ever had is someone you've known since you were born," declared one headline).

For the most part, though, the more successful social-issue ads around the world have had one thing in common—a reliance on disturbing imagery and blunt language. A British campaign created by Saatchi & Saatchi for the National Society for the Prevention of Cruelty to Children took the viewer inside a child's bedroom, as the camera showed teddy-bear wallpaper and pictures of the Spice Girls—while the soundtrack eavesdropped on rustling in the bed and a man's voice saying, "Not a word to anyone. It will be our little secret." The campaign brought scores of complaints from viewers across the UK who were upset by it—including victims of child abuse who said that it caused them to relive painful experiences. And one of the most

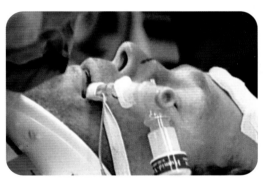

Should you be driving home tonight?

12

11. **MOTHERS AGAINST
DRUNK DRIVING (MADD)**
THE AD COUNCIL, NEW YORK,
1990
Not only is the headline powerful,
but it is accompanied by an
actual car crushed in a drunk
driving accident, which is
attached to the billboard.

12. **AUSTRALIAN ROAD SAFETY**
GREY ADVERTISING,
MELBOURNE, 1996
This campaign brought a new
level of realism to drunk driving
ads; crashes were simulated
on film with jarring force. The
commercials led to dramatically
lower local fatality rates.

# INTERVIEW: DORIA STEEDMAN

As the vice chairman of the Partnership for a Drug-Free America, Doria Steedman oversees a coalition of communications professionals who create most of the anti-drug advertisements produced in the United States—a huge and highly influential body of work, particularly since the Partnership received more than $3 billion worth of donated media exposure for its ads from 1987 to 1999. But the increased funding and visibility has also ratcheted up the pressure on the Partnership to produce quantifiable results and progress.

**FIRST OF ALL, HOW DO ANTI-DRUG ADS GET MADE?**
Sometimes ad agencies approach us, but it usually begins with us contacting them. Once an agency agrees to take on an assignment, we provide a creative brief and a strategy, plus a lot of information about the specific drug involved. Then they come back to tell us what they're working on. The idea is presented to our creative-review committee—40 ad executives who are the best in the business. And the committee either says, "That's fabulous; go do it" or "No, it's not sound; it needs to be changed."

**IN 1998, THE U.S. GOVERNMENT EARMARKED MORE THAN $2 BILLION FOR ANTI-DRUG ADS, RUNNING THROUGH 2003. WHAT DOES THIS MONEY ENABLE YOU TO DO?**
A lot. The money is being used primarily to purchase media, whereas before we relied entirely on donated media. In recent times there was an erosion of what the media were able to give us. Several TV networks told us they were only going to be able to give us ten-second spots. And our chance of getting into prime time—slim always—became close to none. This money has allowed the Partnership ads to be seen in places they've never been before. Also, we now have funds available for research if an agency requests it. And we have a panel of behavioral scientists who can provide their input.

**CAN ANTI-DRUG ADS REALLY CHANGE SOMEONE'S BEHAVIOR?**
We've learned that if we can change attitudes, we can change behavior. When there is sufficient media support, we can affect the two key attitudes—perception of risk, and social disap-proval. When awareness goes up in those two areas, drug use goes down.

**IS ADVERTISING ABLE TO REACH AND AFFECT PEOPLE USING MORE ADDICTIVE DRUGS, LIKE HEROIN?**
We have never tried to convince a heroin user to stop using it—because we have no evidence whatsoever that advertising can do that. We're trying to reach people before it gets to that point.

**ANY SURPRISES YOU'VE FOUND IN TERMS OF WHAT WORKS AND WHAT DOESN'T?**
When we launched an anti-heroin campaign, we learned that it would not be effective to tell young people they were going to die from this drug. Because that was part of what made it so glamorous—the flirting with death and disaster. And, of course, everybody knew of the dangers but said, 'It's not going to happen to me.' So we took a different approach, trying to deglamorize the drug. We showed an apparently beautiful woman—and as she took off her makeup she was revealed to be haggard, and then she removed her top dentures. And we had two commercials set in toilets. The hope was that these images of writhing in a filthy toilet or losing your teeth would be more of a turnoff—particularly to young people who are concerned about appearances.

**FOR YEARS, PUBLIC-SERVICE ADS HAVE BEEN ACCUSED OF RELYING ON SHOCK TACTICS. IS THAT CHANGING?**
I think there is movement away from doom and gloom. And I think the reason is that we have more behavioral science available to us now, and as we learn more about what is effective with young people, then other avenues open up. The newer ads take all kinds of approaches that do not end in toe tags or gravestones.

**SUCH AS A SARCASTIC, CHEERY JINGLE FOR HEROIN?**
Yes, we have a significant amount of advertising that is humorous. Our philosophy has always been "Any way you can get to them, try it."

**WHAT ABOUT CRITICS' CHARGES THAT THERE ISN'T ENOUGH RESEARCH PROVING THE EFFECTIVENESS OF ANTI-DRUG ADS?**
For the past twelve years, we have done an attitude-and-tracking study, where we interview 6,000 kids and 800 parents across the country. There have been many other studies done showing the effectiveness of the ads. And drug use is down in this country, across the board.

**THERE'S A FEELING OUT THERE THAT PEOPLE CREATE PUBLIC-SERVICE ADS FOR SELF-SERVING REASONS, TO GET ATTENTION AND WIN AWARDS. ANY VALIDITY TO THAT?**
If that is true, I have never seen it. I am astounded by how involved agency creative people have gotten in the problem, sometimes going out and meeting kids and taking a personal interest in somebody. This drug problem is one that affects so many lives—so it's less likely someone's going to say, "This doesn't affect me; I'm just in it for an award." Most people working on the ads know someone who has been affected by drugs.

**DO ADVERTISERS SOMETIMES USE TOO MUCH HYPE WHEN ADDRESSING SOCIAL ISSUES?**
All I can say is, not one ad goes out of here unless every claim in it has been proved by the National Institute for Drug Abuse. So if I try to say smoking marijuana makes your nose drop off—because I think that would be effective—the experts will tell us, "You can't say that unless there is the science to prove it's accurate." We know that if we blow our credibility, we've had it. If I spin or hype you on one ad, then you may not believe me on the next one.

**WHAT HAPPENS IF YOU SUCCEED—DOES THE EFFORT GET SCALED BACK?**
In the best of all possible worlds, we'd put ourselves out of business by eliminating the drug problem. I'm an optimist, but I don't know if I have that much optimism. But I do think that if this effort works—when it works—it will be a template for social change that will be extraordinary. Everybody will be able to point to it and say, "Here is proof that you can have an effect on children's lives through advertising."

ADVERTISING AS AN AGENT OF SOCIAL CHANGE.

HOW CAN YOU WORSHIP
A HOMELESS MAN ON SUNDAY AND
IGNORE ONE ON MONDAY?

They could use your prayers. More importantly they could use your help. Call the Coalition For The Homeless at 695-8700 to find out how.

13

13. **COALITION FOR THE HOMELESS**
STREETSMART ADVERTISING, NEW YORK, 1992
Jesus makes a rare appearance in advertising, for a worthy cause. The headline poses a tough question that is hard to ignore.

14. **COALITION FOR THE HOMELESS**
STREETSMART ADVERTISING, NEW YORK, 1992
This commercial won top prize at advertising's One Show; it featured homeless people ironically singing the upbeat song "New York, New York," normally a paean to the city.

14

## IT'S UP TO YOU NEW YORK, NEW YORK.

gripping ad campaigns in Australia in recent years has been a series of anti-drunk-driving commercials that show characters who've been drinking and then decide, against their better judgment and advice from others, to get behind the wheel. The ads then show the ensuing horrific car collisions—presented with jarring force and realism—as well as gory scenes taking the viewer into the emergency room post-crash. A mid-1990s American ad campaign on the same issue took a different, though no less compelling, tack: Rather than showing what happened to the drunk driver, "our attitude became 'Screw the drunks—let's focus on the real victims,'" said Steve Landsberg, one of the creators of the campaign from the agency Wells Rich Greene. So the ads featured children who had been killed in drunk-driving accidents, bringing them briefly to life for the TV viewer by showing scenes from old home videos obtained from the deceased children's families. One spot opened with footage

of a boy learning to swim in the family pool as his mother cheered him on; gradually, the heart-warming scenes are intercut with onscreen text explaining when and how this child died.

Such advertising can be like a punch to the gut of the audience, and that is the intention. The American ad executive Sal DeVito, who created some of the aforementioned PETA work (including the "vocal cords" ad), said, "At first when I was working on that, I tried showing images that weren't as harsh—for example, showing one of these electrocution devices, without the animal in it. But I could see that it wasn't going to be as effective. With something like this, you need as much visual impact as possible. And then you have to balance it with a thoughtful headline, so it doesn't come across as just sensationalism." DeVito added, "I know people don't like seeing these pictures, but it's the reality."

But some question whether the barrage of shocking and disturbing images is the best way

to address difficult social issues. Bob Garfield, a columnist for *Advertising Age,* recently wrote of PSAs, "Let's face it, the damn things are depressing. You're watching TV and at the commercial break, just when you think that you're going to see talking cars or adorable kittens or slow-motion images of women tossing their hair, on comes some gritty black-and-white film about spousal abuse." As the number of public-service ads have increased, the bombarded public can experience something akin to battle fatigue—particularly down in the trenches, in PSA-saturated places like subway trains, where ads about AIDS, child abuse, and rape are often placed side by side. One subway rider recently wrote to *The New York Times,* "Can't something be done to change the unrelentingly downbeat messages on display? Sure, people have problems, but one gets the impression that most of our fellow passengers are addicted, abused, diseased wretches living in roach-infested apartments."

15

**15. BARNARDO'S**
BARTLE BOGLE HEGARTY,
LONDON, 2000
The campaign for a children's
organization used dramatic
imagery to show that some
adults might not be here today if
they hadn't been helped as kids.

**16. SAN FRANCISCO
AIDS FOUNDATION**
J. WALTER THOMPSON,
SAN FRANCISCO, 1995
An attempt to encourage drug
users to participate in needle
exchange programs; the
placement of the words within
the picture turned the ad into
a puzzle.

The spread of such advertising is not limited to bargain-basement ad environments like the New York subway—increasingly the ads have begun to show up even in the priciest advertising slots (in January 2000, the first public-service ad appeared on the multimillion-dollar-a-minute Super Bowl). The Italian ad executive Marco Mignani, of Euro RSCG MCM, works on public-service ads himself but nevertheless recently observed, "On [TV] screens all over the world, anti-drug, anti-alcohol, anti-AIDS commercials follow one after the other; they raise social awareness, but they are powerless to offer an alternative." *Ad Age's* Garfield echoes that view, saying that such ads, for all of their noble intentions and attention-getting tactics, often leave the audience feeling overwhelmed by so many social problems and "powerless to help."

Of course, in many cases, the audience is not powerless; there are volunteer groups to join,

donations to be given, or individual behavioral habits—smoking, drinking, etc.—that can be reformed. The question is whether an ad is capable of providing enough motivation to spark that kind of action. There is evidence that ads can do this—sometimes. For example, since the American public was introduced to Vince and Larry—a couple of crash-test dummies that starred in a long-running "buckle up" ad campaign that debuted in the mid-1980s—American safety-belt usage tripled. Meanwhile, all of those horrifying Australian car-wreck commercials have been tied to measurable declines in drunk-driving accidents, year after year. And a number of local anti-smoking campaigns throughout the U.S. have been linked to declines in smoking rates.

But critics charge that these success stories are scattered, and that evidence of the effectiveness of social-issue ads is scant. Such ads are generally not held to the same rigorous standards as are ordinary soap and cereal ads; while the latter are

expected to produce immediate, measurable sales results in the marketplace, anti-drug ads, for example, are not expected to immediately reduce the number of drug users—only to "raise awareness" of the problem. Moreover, some believe that this type of advertising, for all of its high drama, is far less scientific and sophisticated than ads that sell products, in part because PSAs, with limited funds, typically are not subjected to the same kinds of research and testing as product ads. One study by the Harvard University School of Public Health found that melodramatic scenes in PSAs did not have a lasting impact on young people who viewed them; the study suggested that in order to truly effect behavioral changes, public-service ads needed to abandon shock-and-scare tactics and begin to incorporate some of the more sophisticated marketing approaches used in consumer ads—including product placements, sponsorships, more research and testing of ads, and manipulation of news programs to get the

16

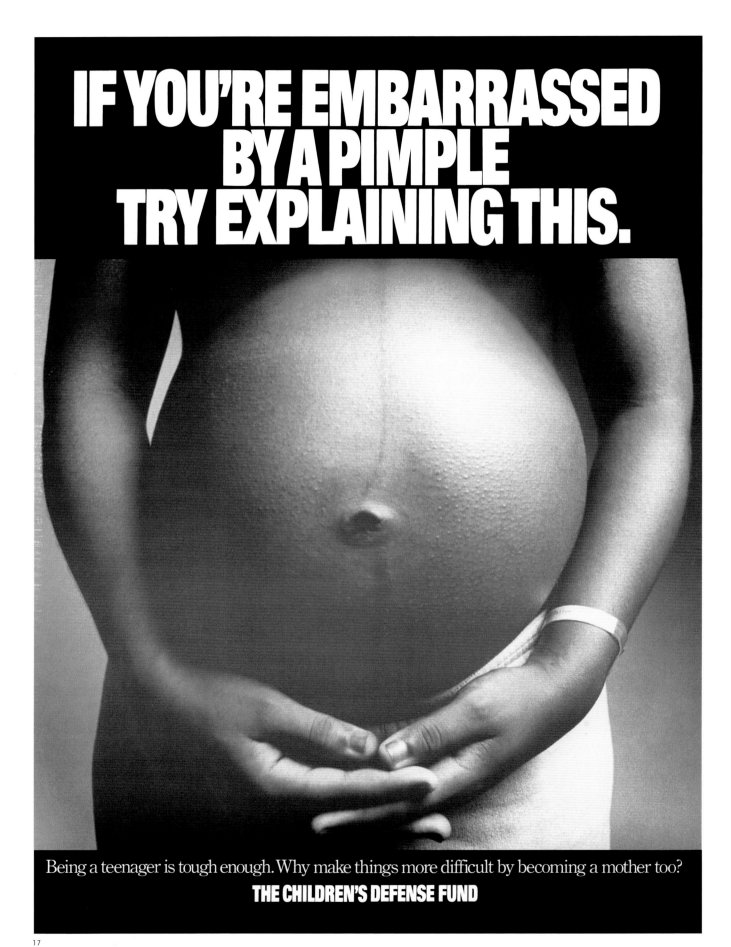

**IF YOU'RE EMBARRASSED BY A PIMPLE TRY EXPLAINING THIS.**

Being a teenager is tough enough. Why make things more difficult by becoming a mother too?

**THE CHILDREN'S DEFENSE FUND**

18

17. **THE CHILDREN'S DEFENSE FUND**
FALLON McELLIGOTT, MINNEAPOLIS, MINNESOTA, 1988
Part of a long-running series of ads attempting to reach disadvantaged youth.

18. **STATE OF THE WORLD FORUM**
SAATCHI & SAATCHI NEW ZEALAND, WELLINGTON, 1998
The photo may be melodramatic, but it makes the point well; this ad became a popular poster.

Water-man.

The human body is 70% water.
Respect and protect this essence of life.
The bodies of water we pollute
will someday be our own.

人間のカラダの70%は水でできています
あなたが汚した水は、いつかあなたを
汚すことになります
きれいな水を次の世代に。

19

**19. WATER CONSERVATION**
DENTSU, TOKYO, MID-1990s
The campaign created a character,
"Water-man," to dramatize the
need to conserve.

**20. KEEP AMERICA BEAUTIFUL**
AD COUNCIL / MARSTELLER,
NEW YORK, 1971
In this classic campaign, a
Native American witnesses the
desecration of nature all around
him and sheds a single, memo-
rable tear.

**21. WORLD SOCIETY FOR THE
PROTECTION OF ANIMALS**
MULLEN, BOSTON,
EARLY 1990s
In the aftermath of the Exxon
*Valdez* oil tanker disaster
in 1989, this picture was
particularly poignant.

20

# Could The Price Of Oil Be Any Higher?

*If you think you pay a high price, consider what our beaches, coastlines and wildlife have to pay. Help us save the animals and clean up the spills. Donate what you can to WSPA, PO Box 190, Boston, MA 02130. Or call (617) 522-7000. We've been providing animal disaster relief for 30 years.*

World Society for the Protection of Animals

21

messages across in a nonadvertising format. (It should be noted, however, that public-service messages can come under fire when they are delivered in such devious ways. When the U.S. government's Office of National Drug Control Policy recently began offering financial incentives and reviewing scripts in an effort to encourage producers of TV shows to weave anti-drug messages into their shows' story lines and dialogue, there was a public outcry—and a sense that the government was treading close to the dangerous areas of censorship and propaganda.)

In fairness, public-service ads shouldn't be expected to do the same job, in the same manner and with similar results, as product advertising; it is, after all, considerably easier to influence purchasing decisions than to change ingrained behavior among smokers, alcoholics, or abusive parents. The more realistic objective is that the ads become part of a public dialogue that gradually shifts public attitude, which in turn can lead to

changes in behavior. But it is a slow and multi-layered process, experts say. Dr. Gregory Connolly, who oversees the Massachusetts Department of Health anti-smoking campaign, acknowledges that the 30 percent decline in smoking achieved by the campaign was the result of a number of combined factors. "One thirty-second ad is not going to affect anybody's behavior," Connolly said. "But a series of ads, integrated with higher prices for cigarettes, clean indoor air [regulations] at the local level, and ready access to cessation services—all that together can result in hundreds of thousands of people quitting. We view advertising as the air cover for our ground troops. It frames the debate."

And that it seems to do well; when it comes to stirring discussion and placing a social issue on the radar of public consciousness, advertising has proved quite effective. When ads in America first targeted the issue of child abuse twenty-five years ago, the subject was still practically taboo. "People

didn't understand it and the media didn't want to get involved with it," according to Anne Cohn, who served as president of the National Committee for the Prevention of Child Abuse. The group started running a high-profile ad campaign headlined, "Child abuse hurts everybody" in 1976, and within five years, public attitudes on the issue had shifted dramatically—a 1982 Harris poll found that nine of ten people felt child abuse was a major social problem, compared with a previous study showing that only one in ten thought so.

Similarly, when the Partnership for a Drug-Free America began to saturate the American media with its messages in the late 1980s and early 1990s—producing a volume of ads second only to McDonald's at the time—the subject, as a result, was on everyone's mind: At one point, 92 percent of American teenagers reported that they had seen the "Fried Egg" spot (some drug users even took to joking, "Let's go fry an egg"). Did that growing awareness lead to

# HERE'S A DEAD DOG. WHERE'S MY AWARD?

**THIS YEAR AWARD WILL BE GIVING LESS TO CHARITY.**

Community service and charity advertising has always been a special case when it comes to awards.

It has its own categories in every major advertising festival around the world. AWARD is no exception. However, we've spotted a problem.

Not only have community service and charity ads been able to enter their own categories, they've also been able to enter the general ones. A small space charity ad, for example, gets three bites at the guernsey; the Community Service and Charity section, the Small Space section and the Newspaper section.

Hardly fair on a packet soup ad that only gets one go. And often resulting in a book that looks more like a Charity Awards Annual.

So we've made a few changes for AWARD'91. Community Service and Charity ads will now only be judged in their own categories. Likewise, Small Space ads.

A minimum size for posters has been introduced to stop press ads being entered on the grounds they were pinned to the wall.

And Christmas cards, wedding invites, birth announcements, etc get their own category and are no longer a direct threat to direct mail for proper clients.

Details of changes are in the 13th AWARD Call for Entries booklet. If you still don't have a copy, call Mary or Sandra on (02) 267 6907 or (02) 267 6916.

But get a move on, the deadline for entries is June 7th. And if you've been pinning all your hopes on getting several gongs for one charity ad, all is not lost.

Just think of the money you'll save only having to enter it once.

**1991 CALL FOR ENTRIES.**

22

**22. AUSTRALIAN WRITERS & DIRECTORS ASSOCIATION**
BROWN MELHUISH FISHLOCK, SURRY HILLS, AUSTRALIA, 1991
A backlash against all the award-winning "help the animals" campaigns, this cynical ad suggested that it had become too easy for manipulative ads to win kudos.

**23. FRIENDS OF ANIMALS**
MAD DOGS & ENGLISHMEN, NEW YORK, 1997
Mad Dogs tried a postmodern approach to public service advertising, relying on irony instead of shock appeal.

changes in behavior and a decline in drug usage? That was a tough claim for the Partnership to prove; even in instances where some types of drug usage declined after the ads ran, as with cocaine in the early 1990s, there were various other factors aside from ads that could be credited. At the time, high-profile cocaine deaths among celebrities and other real-life horror stories in the news media may have had a larger impact than all of those make-believe ads. But various studies, such as one by the Johns Hopkins School of Medicine in 1991, indicated that teenagers exposed to anti-drug ads did seem to come away with a better understanding of the risks involved.

Such advertising can also have a kind of "ripple effect" that is difficult to measure, said Peter Cohen, one of the co-creators of a poignant, award-winning public-service commercial that ran in the early 1990s, featuring scenes of homeless people singing the lyrics to the song "New York, New York." Cohen says that that ad campaign, and others like it, succeeded in generating news-media attention, helped raise the visibility of the charitable organizations involved, attracted volunteers to the cause—and sometimes inspired individuals to take unexpected and spontaneous action. "I am constantly amazed," Cohen said, "by how many stories of goodwill and good deeds I still hear of that were generated by the 'New York, New York' ad we did years ago."

Of course, some of the people who are most affected by public-service ads are the people who create them. The most stark and striking ads tend to draw attention in the news media. And because such ads allow for more human drama than the usual recitations of product features and benefits, they are ideally suited for winning creative awards—which can help advance the careers of the award-winning creators. This not-so-hidden agenda has been the subject of much debate within the ad business (one

Australian creative team, frustrated at seeing shocking PSAs honored with prizes, ran a trade ad featuring a canine carcass and the headline "Here's a dead dog, where's my award?"). Dave Buonaguidi of the British agency St. Luke's believes that "probably less than 10 percent of the people who get involved in the production of [public service] ads give a damn about the end result." They do it, Buonaguidi suggested, because they see an opportunity to make high-profile ads that will, ultimately, boost their salaries.

Even if that's true, should anyone outside the business care? Certainly, the results of this advertising matter much more than the motives behind it—but it's also conceivable that the latter could influence the former. Skeptics in the ad industry believe melodramatic PSAs are sometimes designed for the press and award-show judges, rather than the target audience—which would raise questions about whether such ads may be neglecting their primary function and misusing

23

All in favor
of gun control
raise your hand.

All against,
raise both.

24

ONE BLACK VICTIM. ONE WHITE VICTIM.
IS THIS WHAT RACIAL EQUALITY MEANS NOW?

If we don't begin to build trusting relationships between the races, what you see isn't the past of one American city, it's the future of all of them. Join us for an honest conversation on race, reconciliation and responsibility at a special National Cities Conference, June 16-20 at the Richmond Centre, Richmond, Virginia. Call 804-648-4216.

**HEALING THE HEART OF AMERICA CONFERENCE**

25

24. **FLORIDA COALITION**
**TO STOP GUN VIOLENCE**
CRISPIN PORTER +
BOGUSKY, MIAMI, 1995
Giving new meaning to the
phrase, "target marketing."

25. **HEALING THE HEART**
**OF AMERICA CONFERENCE**
THE MARTIN AGENCY,
RICHMOND, VIRGINIA, 1993
In the wake of the Los Angeles
race riots of 1992, this ad
appealed to all sides for calm.

donated funds and media time. But other ad experts insist that is a nonissue; what wins awards and what helps the cause is usually the same thing. John Hegarty of the London agency Bartle Bogle Hegarty noted that regardless of the personal motivations of people creating the ads, the point is that good talent prevails—and public-service advertising "gives worthy causes access to creative people they could not otherwise afford."

Meanwhile, for many agency creative people, the ads provide a rare chance to say something important and meaningful. As Stuart Elliott of *The New York Times* pointed out, in creating a PSA, "you can pour your heart out—in a way that you can't for dog food." Socially responsible ads have become a defining characteristic of some agencies, including the Amsterdam-based agency KesselsKramer. "We're interested not just in selling a product but in the social meaning of our work," said co-founder Johan Kramer. "People in

advertising should realize they have a big responsibility in creating social patterns." On an individual level, ad people often gravitate toward issues and causes that have special relevance to them. The American ad copywriter Richard Yelland, who has worked on anti-drug ads, said, "A couple of friends of mine had died because of heroin problems, and my partner and I felt desperate to do what we could to help."

Another concern about public-service ads is their tendency to inject some of the less desirable elements of advertising—the propensity to hype and oversell, to glamorize, to put a Madison Avenue spin on reality—into the public discourse on critical issues. One might assume that in the harsh world of PSAs there would be little room for glamorization, but advertising is still advertising. In one Partnership anti-drug ad—in which a young woman viciously wields a frying pan in a kitchen to make a point about the damage that

drugs can cause—the signals sent out by the ad were decidedly mixed. As noted by columnist Frank Rich of *The New York Times*, the woman in the ad doesn't look like an addict but more like "Winona Ryder; she's wearing a tight tank top; there are no visible track marks on her arms; and the kitchen representing her drug-induced hell is right out of the Pottery Barn, if not Williams-Sonoma." When not beautifying the image of problems such as drug addiction, ads can go the other way, creating an ersatz horror show; one recent campaign for battered women in New York showed disturbing images of women's bruised and swollen faces—however, the women in the ads were actresses, and their bruises had been created by a special-effects-makeup artist (the copy, too, could be considered less than authentic, considering that it was written by young male ad writers). Some feel that when ads take on serious, complex social problems in a superficial manner,

26

In the lower section:

**26. NATIONAL ASSOCIATION OF ATOMIC VETERANS**
DOYLE ADVERTISING & DESIGN, BOSTON, 1992
The campaign, from the early 1990s, gave voice to a group of victims who had remained silent for decades.

**27. NORTH KOREA FAMINE RELIEF**
SAATCHI & SAATCHI, SINGAPORE, 1998
Using propaganda to counter propaganda, the advertiser took on those who tried to deny that there was a crisis in North Korea.

**28. VIRGINIA HOLOCAUST MUSEUM**
THE MARTIN AGENCY, RICHMOND, VIRGINIA, 2000
Each ad featured a bold headline and told the story of a concentration camp victim, incorporating objects and personal artifacts to provide depth and detail.

27

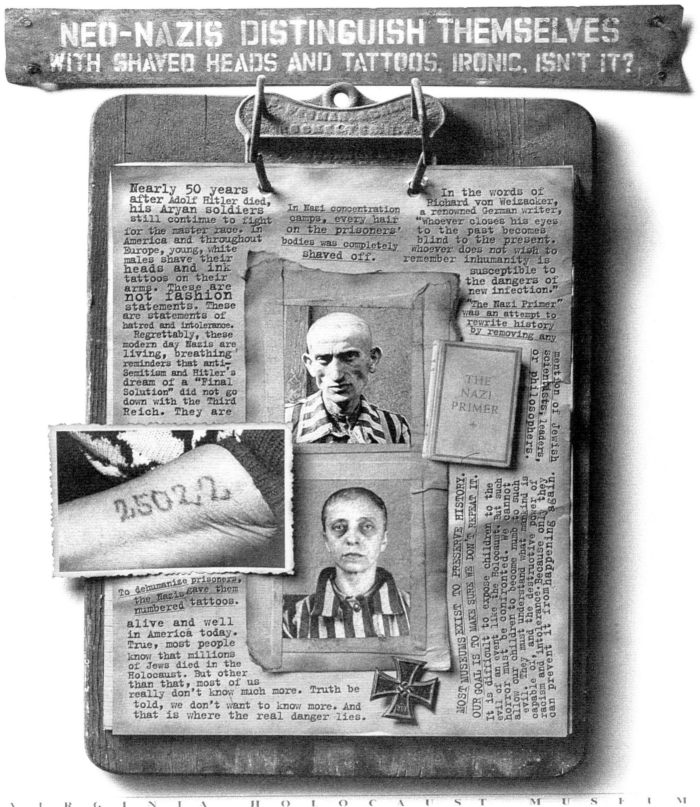

**NEO-NAZIS DISTINGUISH THEMSELVES WITH SHAVED HEADS AND TATTOOS. IRONIC, ISN'T IT?**

Nearly 50 years after Adolf Hitler died, his Aryan soldiers still continue to fight for the master race. In America and throughout Europe, young, white males shave their heads and ink tattoos on their arms. These are not fashion statements. These are statements of hatred and intolerance.

Regrettably, these modern day Nazis are living, breathing reminders that anti-Semitism and Hitler's dream of a "Final Solution" did not go down with the Third Reich. They are

In Nazi concentration camps, every hair on the prisoners' bodies was completely shaved off.

In the words of Richard von Weizacker, a renowned German writer, "Whoever closes his eyes to the past becomes blind to the present. Whoever does not wish to remember inhumanity is susceptible to the dangers of new infection."

"The Nazi Primer" was an attempt to rewrite history by removing any mention of Jewish scientists, leaders, or philosophers.

THE NAZI PRIMER

To dehumanize prisoners, the Nazis gave them numbered tattoos.

alive and well in America today. True, most people know that millions of Jews died in the Holocaust. But other than that, most of us really don't know much more. Truth be told, we don't want to know more. And that is where the real danger lies.

MOST MUSEUMS EXIST TO PRESERVE HISTORY. OUR GOAL IS TO MAKE SURE WE DON'T REPEAT IT.

It is difficult to expose children to the evil of an event like the Holocaust. But such horror must be confronted. We cannot allow our children to become numb to such evil. They must understand what mankind is capable of, and the destructive power of racism and intolerance. Because only they can prevent it from happening again.

VIRGINIA HOLOCAUST MUSEUM

The Virginia Holocaust Museum was established in 1996. The museum is not intended to answer why the Holocaust happened. Rather, its sole mission is to teach tolerance through education. The startling exhibits trace the steps of the Ipson family from Lithuania's Kovno ghetto to a 9 x 12 x 4 foot underground hiding place where thirteen family members lived. Guided tours are available by calling 804-257-5400. The Virginia Holocaust Museum is located at 213 Roseneath Rd., Richmond, Virginia. Museum hours: Monday through Friday, 9 am-5 pm, Saturday, 2 pm-5 pm; and Sunday, 1 pm-5 pm. Admission is free.

28

HELP CURE SPINAL CORD INJURIES. Send your donation to The Canadian Paraplegic Asso

ion, 520 Sutherland Drive, Toronto, ON M4G 3V9. (416) 422-5644. Or visit info@cpaont.org.

29. **THE CANADIAN PARAPLEGIC ASSOCIATION**
BUTLER SHINE & STERN,
SAUSALITO, CALIFORNIA, 1998
This ad altered a universal symbol
to convey an optimistic message.

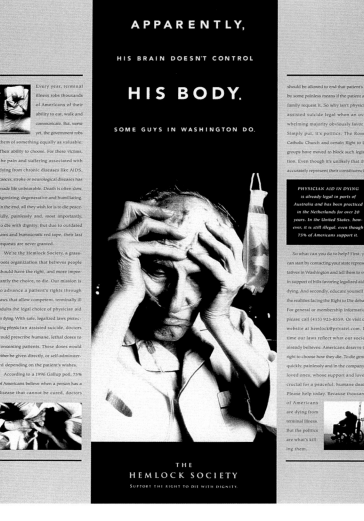

APPARENTLY,

HIS BRAIN DOESN'T CONTROL

# HIS BODY.

SOME GUYS IN WASHINGTON DO.

Every year, terminal illness robs thousands of Americans of their ability to eat, walk and communicate. But, worse yet, the government robs them of something equally as valuable: Their ability to choose. For these victims, the pain and suffering associated with dying from chronic diseases like AIDS, cancer, stroke or neurological diseases has made life unbearable. Death is often slow, agonizing, degenerative and humiliating. In the end, all they wish for is to die peacefully, painlessly and, most importantly, to die with dignity. But due to outdated laws and bureaucratic red tape, their last requests are never granted.

We're the Hemlock Society, a grass-roots organization that believes people should have the right, and more importantly the choice, to die. Our mission is to advance a patient's rights through laws that allow competent, terminally ill adults the legal choice of physician aid in dying. With safe, legalized laws protecting physician assisted suicide, doctors could prescribe humane, lethal doses to consenting patients. These doses would either be given directly, or self-administered depending on the patient's wishes.

According to a 1996 Gallup poll, 75% of Americans believe when a person has a disease that cannot be cured, doctors

should be allowed to end that patient's life by some painless means if the patient and family request it. So why isn't physician assisted suicide legal when an overwhelming majority obviously favor it? Simply put, it's politics: The Roman Catholic Church and certain Right to Life groups have moved to block such legislation. Even though it's unlikely that they accurately represent their constituencies.

*PHYSICIAN AID IN DYING is already legal in parts of Australia and has been practiced in the Netherlands for over 20 years. In the United States, however, it is still illegal, even though 75% of Americans support it.*

So what can you do to help? First, you can start by contacting your state representatives in Washington and tell them to vote in support of bills favoring legalized aid in dying. And secondly, educate yourself on the realities facing the Right to Die debate. For general or membership information, please call (415) 923-8559. Or visit our website at hemlock@privatei.com. It's time our laws reflect what our society already believes: Americans deserve the right to choose how they die. To die gently, quickly, painlessly and in the company of loved ones, whose support and love is crucial for a peaceful, humane death. Please help today. Because thousands of Americans are dying from terminal illness. But the politics are what's killing them.

THE
HEMLOCK SOCIETY
SUPPORT THE RIGHT TO DIE WITH DIGNITY.

30

they can do more harm than good. For example, a frequent criticism of some child-abuse ads has been that they tend to demonize and shame the abuser rather than reaching out to him or her (as child-abuse experts say the ads must do in order to have a positive effect). Shocking PSAs can occasionally further traumatize victims of abuse, as in the case of the aforementioned British child-abuse campaign. Or they can offend large segments of the population, as with recent South African rape-prevention ads, which alienated males who felt the ads seemed to be suggesting that all men are rapists.

Critics also worry about the blurring of the lines between bona fide public-service ads and hybrid ads that try to promote both a cause and a company at the same time. Increasingly, serious issues and causes are being adopted—or co-opted—by companies with a sales agenda. Nike has earned kudos for using its ads to promote more opportunities for women in sports,

as in the award-winning commercial "If You Let Me Play Sports. . . ." It's hard to take issue with that message, but it's also logical that as more girls and women "play," Nike will sell more sneakers to this demographic. At the same time, Anheuser-Busch increasingly uses ads to promote "responsible" drinking—which can seem like a mixed message from a company that so heavily promotes drinking. Recent commercials by Philip Morris, which owns numerous cigarette brands, have centered on the plight of battered women and the company's contributions to that cause; to a cynic, these ads might seem to be an attempt to divert attention from the public-health problems associated with this company's mainstay product. Perhaps the most obvious example of opportunism could be seen in a campaign from a British power company, which sent out promotional leaflets with the headline "Stop it, daddy, stop it"—yet another dramatic PSA, with the power company announcing its support for the national child-abuse fund.

But here was the catch: Money would be donated to the cause only if the recipient of the ad agreed to switch power companies.

Corporations aren't the only ones using ads to weigh in on social issues; so, too, are political-action groups, special-interest lobbies, private individuals and foundations, and academic think tanks, all of which have been fueling the growth of PSAs. The result, said issue-advertising specialist Victor Kamber, is that "TV has become a battleground of disparate voices, because groups realize the need to appeal to the public to effect change." And as this continues, the public will be exposed to more and more ads pushing something that can't be bought—a philosophy, a choice, a way of life.

Meanwhile, the ads themselves continue to evolve. Some have actually begun to move away from gloom and shock, opting for something more upbeat and contemporary. The Brazilian agency DM9 DDB recently unveiled an anti-gun

# HAPPINESS IS BEING AN ORGAN DONOR.

**OREGON DONOR PROGRAM**

*Feel good knowing you can help someone long after you're gone. Carry an organ donor card.*

31

THE MORE YOU SMOKE THE MORE
COOL GEAR
YOU'LL EARN.
ALL EXPENSE PAID TRIP TO
CANCER CLINIC OF YOUR CHOICE
We'll fly you and a loved one for a week of pampering, exploratory surgery, and round-the-clock attention. Package includes deluxe accommodations. Meals in bed. Flowers. Reservations for the finest OR tables in town.
2000 POINTS
DELUXE
CARRYING CASE
The gear to end all gear. Kick back. Relax. Stretch out in ultimate comfort. In the everlasting elegance of rich burled mahogany with brass fittings. Your friends and relatives will agree, you've never looked more rested.
10,000 POINTS
SPORT DEFIBRILLATOR
Don't let a little coronary put a damper on your whole day. This handy dandy hi-tech gizmo is just what the doctor ordered to recharge the old ticker. And it's waterproof, so it goes wherever (and whenever) you go.
5000 POINTS
SPORT DEFIBRILLATOR
PORTABLE
RESPIRATOR
You've got mountains to conquer. Roads to travel. Take off. Explore the breathtaking beauty around you. Life is yours for the taking. Interchangeable oxygen tanks included.
1000 POINTS
truth
A Generation United Against Tobacco
www.wholetruth.com

32

**32. FLORIDA TEENAGE
ANTI-SMOKING CAMPAIGN**
CRISPIN PORTER +
BOGUSKY, MIAMI, 1995
The ironic ad spoofs promotions
and giveaways by tobacco
companies, showing the less
than appealing things that come
free with smoking. This was part
of a long-running series that
used "Truth" as the campaign's
brand name.

**33. ANTI-SMOKING CAMPAIGN**
ABBOTT MEAD VICKERS,
LONDON, 1993
The British comedian John
Cleese brought a light touch
to a dark subject in this TV
commercial. Some smokers
leave behind piles of ashes,
Cleese observed while emptying
an ashtray. He added, "Of
course, they're not all cremated;
some of them are buried."

33

campaign, asking Brazilians to declare, *"Sou da paz,"* or "I am for peace," which borrowed the basic ingredients of product advertising—star endorsers, a slogan, a jingle (actually a peace song), and even a logo designed for the cause. And it seemed to be working, as more than 1,000 people in São Paulo turned in their guns in the first week of the campaign—far more guns than local police had been able to raise in three years of their own campaigns.

Some of the current ads have even begun to adopt an ironic attitude toward misery and death, using the kind of postmodern "anti-sell" approaches favored in hip commercials for sneakers and jeans. One ad titled "Everybody's Doing It," from the California agency Ground Zero, featured an upbeat jingle and copy promoting the virtues of heroin—while the screen showed images of a dirty, needle-scarred man convulsing on a bathroom floor. The sarcastic slogan: "Heroin, for the rest of your life." Another

ad, from the American Cancer Society, spoofed the typical TV sales offer; just buy enough cigarettes, the gushing announcer promised, and you'll be eligible for gifts including an oxygen mask, a chemotherapy discount . . . and even "a beautiful lung ventilator with matching tracheal tube!" (Some TV stations felt the ad's humor was in bad taste and refused to run it, but the cancer society stuck by it, believing it would appeal to teenagers because of the cutting-edge humor.) Still another popular anti-smoking campaign neatly turned cigarette advertising against itself: On billboards throughout California, the familiar Western-cowboy imagery of Marlboro advertising was recreated, but the ad agency, Asher & Partners, plugged in new headlines that were simultaneously disturbing and amusing. In one ad, a macho Marlboro Man was shown confiding to his fellow cowboy, "Bob, I've got emphysema."

As this more modern creative sensibility takes hold, public-service ads are also crossing

new media frontiers; recently the Ad Council brought Smokey the Bear into cyberspace, where the character has his own Web site. In some ways, the Internet may be the ideal environment for social-cause ads, and only partly because Web pages are inexpensive to produce. More important, this interactive medium allows PSAs to move beyond mere attention-grabbing to deliver more in-depth information on an issue or problem, while also helping to connect people with resources that can provide real help—rather than leaving viewers feeling helpless before an onslaught of grim images on their TV screens. That's not to suggest, however, that public-service ads won't continue to be at least somewhat unsettling, disturbing, and provocative, as the conscience of advertising faces up to its own demons and compels the rest of us to face ours. The adman DeVito noted that harsh problems demand harsh ads, and, he added, "If you can't stand looking at these pictures—well, that's the whole point, isn't it?"

# 10. THE COMMAN

E NEW
DMENTS.

**T**he line wasn't terribly original. It wasn't particularly lyrical. It wasn't even grammatically correct. But when the Los Angeles ad agency TBWA/Chiat/Day coined the phrase "Think different" and placed it on a series of Apple Computer ads featuring the faces of well-known innovators and radicals, the campaign became a late-1990s cultural phenomenon. Interestingly, the line used by Apple echoed a similar "command" issued three decades earlier, when Volkswagen advertiser Doyle Dane Bernbach advised car buyers to "Think small." If those two campaigns represent a couple of the most well-known examples of advertisers telling us how to think, another famous series of ads, from the Nike agency Wieden + Kennedy, put forth a different kind of command, beginning in the late 1980s: Stop thinking about it, these ads barked, and "Just do it."

What connects all three of these slogans, aside from their immense popularity, is that each seems to be urging us to do something much larger and more meaningful than purchasing a product. What these advertisers are really "selling" is a philosophy, a belief system, an attitude, a way of life. Increasingly, these are the kinds of loftier messages to be found in today's ads. These new commandments—sometimes clearly stated, sometimes slightly ambiguous ("Just do *what*," exactly?)—constitute Madison Avenue's instruction book of rules to live by.

Why has so much advertising stopped telling us what to buy, opting instead to tell us how to live our lives? Like so many of the changes in advertising, this, too, can be at least partly attributed to the increase in product parity. As the award-winning ad writer Luke Sullivan pointed out, "It has become more difficult to find and promote a unique benefit to a particular product," and consequently, many advertisers have turned away from the product itself. As Sullivan observed, advertisers have elevated the conversation from mundane product benefits to higher emotional benefits. Hence, an ad for a camera now is less likely to claim that the device takes better pictures, and more likely to urge you (or to gently order you) to get the most out of life by documenting and savoring experiences. And do it now, before it's too late.

Advertising's commandments are constantly changing to reflect cultural shifts and evolving public attitudes—because even as advertising seemingly orders us around, it is always careful to dispense only the kinds of orders that the current society is ready, willing, and, in fact, eager to obey. For example, in years past, ads were more apt to pressure the public to conform and to "keep up with the Joneses." And thus, advertising opened itself up to criticism for preying on insecurities: If you didn't use the right toothpaste or antiperspirant or a strong-enough floor polish, you risked potentially devastating embarrassment and ostracism, such ads suggested. "Ring around the collar," the

Think different.

www.apple.com

THE NEW COMMANDMENTS.

The new, 26 vent Bahlsen Pro™ with advanced Fusion In-Mold™ technology. Some rides are scarier than others.

COURAGE FOR YOUR HEAD.  BELL HELMETS

2

2. **BELL HELMETS**
GOODBY SILVERSTEIN &
PARTNERS, SAN FRANCISCO,
1999
"Have no fear" is the message,
and the helmet helps provide
courage in a testy environment.

3. **QWEST**
J. WALTER THOMPSON,
NEW YORK, 1999
In an era of sweeping change,
advertisers are fostering the
belief that everything can now
be recreated and improved.

line and image used in commercials by Wisk detergent during the 1970s and early 1980s, was a signal to the world—as visible and damning as a scarlet letter—that one had failed at the most basic kind of personal hygiene. During these times, ads often issued one kind of warning or another, as in the famous slogan for the credit-card company American Express: "Don't leave home without it."

In more recent years, however, advertising has tended to adopt a tone that is much more positive and (to use a word that has been beaten nearly to death in ad land) "empowering." According to the research firm Iconoculture, which studies trends and consumer attitudes, contemporary advertisers in the 1980s and particularly in the 1990s gradually realized they were dealing with a much more self-assured consumer, and "so it made more sense to sell through positive empowerment, rather than through fear and insecurity," says Iconoculture's co-founder Larry Samuel. In fact, if anyone had reason to feel insecure in the

new marketplace, it was the advertiser—because increasingly, the customer was in control, with endless options and brands to choose from. Mark Waites, creative director at the British ad agency Mother, observes, "In the 1980s, an ad might have asked, 'Are you cool enough to drink our beer?' Now if you say something like that, people will tell you to screw off." If this newfound consumer confidence was true of the contemporary male, it was even more true of the modern woman—who, by the 1990s, was clearly rejecting old-fashioned ad messages that in any way suggested women could not be as outgoing, adventurous, aggressive, or successful as men.

The new advertising was also tapping into a lifestyle shift in America, Europe, and elsewhere. Buoyed by economic prosperity and greater political freedom around the world, the new-millennium consumers—both male and female—were no longer content with just fitting in and getting by, according to Iconoculture and

other attitudinal researchers. The objective now was to have adventures, to live well and fully, and to make a mark as an individual. All of which has made it a prosperous time to be an advertiser, since this more adventurous lifestyle dovetails well with the selling of everything from athletic gear to sport-utility vehicles.

Responding to this new culture, ads in recent years have done their best to reinforce the spirit of rugged individualism, the desire for complete self-fulfillment, and the hunger for experiences. And in so doing, advertisers have taken on the combined role of therapist and cheerleader—urging us to "go farther" (Isuzu cars) and to "do more" (American Express). Or, if you prefer, "the major brands have become our new philosophers," says the American ad executive Jeff Weiss. In so doing, they have shifted some of the focus of ads away from themselves: Merrill Lynch used to describe itself as "bullish on America," but now urges the rest of us to "be bullish." The Prudential Insurance

**Change** everything.

**Finally, a network with the bandwidth that delivers the promise of the Internet.**
It's called Qwest. And it can make all your expensive IT investments pay off. Because it's the network with
the bandwidth to maximize multimedia applications, put e-business into overdrive, and make your kids start
recognizing you again. Visit our Web site at **qwest.com** to find out about the bandwidth to change everything.

*ride the light*

Qwest

3

Unplug the phone. Mix plaids and stripes. Stop speaking to friends who begin every sentence with "I." Drink 6-8 glasses of water a day. When the oil light goes on in the car, add oil. Take deep breaths. Stay out of dark alleys. Listen when your boyfriend says he doesn't want a commitment. If it's collecting dust, throw it out. Stop feeling guilty. Don't surround yourself with off-white walls. Quit smoking. Don't lie to religious figures. Scratch the itch. Think of the thing you fear the most and do it. In the end, a spotless kitchen floor doesn't matter. Grow your own. Lower-watt light bulbs are more flattering. Move 3,000 miles away from your parents. Open a window. Smile when you say that. Kiss a baby. Go to church. Or a synagogue. Or a mosque. Or a mall. Play gin. Forgive somebody. Television isn't a role model. Laugh. And remember, sometimes all it takes is the right pillowcase. Live better. **IKEA**®

It's a big country. Someone's got to furnish it.™

4

**LUNCH IS FOR SISSIES.**

Dick Durrance designed several of the original runs in Aspen without stopping for lunch. Of course, this was in 1948. Today he sometimes has a sandwich. While he's on the lift.

ASPEN
HIGHLANDS

5

**4. IKEA**
DEUTSCH INC., NEW YORK,
1997
Loading up on the commands,
the furniture company Ikea
sums it up last: Live better.

**5. ASPEN SKIING COMPANY**
COLE & WEBER, SEATTLE, 1994
The advertiser as bully: Mark
Fenske's no-nonsense campaign
for the Aspen, Colorado, ski
resorts chided the audience for
taking it easy. (Another headline
in the series: "April in Paris is
for wussies.")

Company of America's slogan evolved from "Own a piece of the rock" to "Be your own rock."

As advertising's new commandments increasingly reflected and fostered the confident "can do" spirit of the times, the messages have been largely aspirational—and in that regard, they can be viewed as a positive evolution from older ads that played on insecurities and fostered conformity. On the other hand, the new can-do ads are guilty of their own sins: appealing to vanity; encouraging a false sense of confidence bordering on arrogance; applauding behavior and attitudes that can be self-absorbed and antisocial. More than ever before, ad writers have resorted to flattery ("You are strong, you are special, you are one-of-a-kind" is the mantra of the sycophantic ad). And while they are no longer as apt to make false claims about the product being advertised, they've taken to proffering more grand illusions—often overpromising the opportunities and experiences available to today's "empowered" people. Having

death-defying adventures, becoming wealthy, enjoying great sex, answering to no one, having a rock-hard physique, attaining a deeper sense of fulfillment—it's all available to us if we get off the couch and "just do it."

Advertisers have promulgated countless new commandments in the past few years, but the ten that follow have been particularly prevalent. They may not last: Having been ushered in by various trends and economic developments, they could easily be swept away by more of the same. But for now, these commandments represent the dogma of advertising.

## 1. BREAK THE RULES.

It is perhaps the single most dominant message of contemporary advertising, running through ads for cars, computers, financial services, sneakers. No matter how generic and unoriginal their own products may be, advertisers are urging *us* to be different—to become rebels and nonconformists.

Of course, the other shoe drops with the suggestion, implied or stated outright, that the advertiser's products can somehow play a role in helping us to blaze our own trails.

This trend is ironic in that, for so many years, critics of advertising worried that Madison Avenue's overarching "Big Brother" agenda was to promote mindless conformity, with everyone buying into the same mass-marketed products and lifestyles. But now we find the modern advertiser's favorite message is "Reject the status quo. Be a rebel. Think different."

Advertising's rebel yell can be traced back to the 1960s. Led by Doyle Dane Bernbach's "Think small." campaign for Volkswagen, ads began to advance the proposition that a purchasing choice could be a bold statement of individuality and independent thinking, a chance to break from the pack. DDB had been prescient in identifying a burgeoning restlessness of spirit that would become much more apparent in the mid-to-late

@mortar

J.D. Edwards is an **IBM** Business Partner

7

8

6. (PREVIOUS SPREAD)
**ADOBE SYSTEMS**
YOUNG & RUBICAM,
SAN FRANCISCO, 2000
The old woman atop the bridge
conveys fearlessness and a love
of risk: If she can do this, why
can't you? asks this ad for a
computer software manufacturer.

7 AND 8. **IBM**
OGILVY & MATHER, NEW
YORK, 1998–99
To promote IBM's electronic
business services, these ads
used images of "bricks and
mortar" companies that are
"plugged in" to the New
Economy.

1960s—by which time many mainstream advertisers were encouraging consumers to "do your own thing" or "join a new generation," both in America and in Europe. While the 1960s strain of rebellious advertising quieted down somewhat in the more sober late 1970s and early 1980s, the "Break the rules" rallying cry returned in the mid-1980s, this time surging on the momentum of the computer revolution. The author Thomas Frank points to Apple's anti-establishment "1984" commercial as a leader in spreading the message that products could set us free and help us all to be the mavericks we really want to be. From that point forward, Frank believes, the nature of business theory itself was transformed: it became "about revolution, not status or hierarchy . . . about liberation, not order."

Nowhere has this philosophy held greater sway than in California's Silicon Valley, a culture rooted in the notion of breaking away from the established way of doing things, of leaving behind the safe company job to launch a dot-com business in a garage. The technology revolution in the 1990s certainly fueled the current wave of "Break the rules" advertising, and the message is delivered forcefully in the ads of Apple, Adobe, Qwest, and other high-tech companies.

But it isn't just the techies promoting revolution; even mundane, "old economy" businesses like fast-food chains have picked up the rallying cry (Burger King at one point was ending all its ads with the line "Sometimes you gotta break the rules," though the ads never made it clear who was breaking which rules and why). To some extent, the more traditional a company is, the more its advertising now screams about rule-breaking. In an age of too many look-alike products, advertisers are desperate to say, "We're not like everyone else. We're different. We break the rules. (How? By cooking the french fries longer!)."

It isn't just the advertisers who are "desperate to be different," however; it's the customer, too. The "Think different" entrepreneurial spirit "is all around us these days," says Tom Julian, a trend analyst with the agency Fallon Worldwide. "People now believe, 'I have to think out-of-the-box in order to be successful, and I must live my whole life that way.' " Cognizant that the voices in our heads are urging us to be bolder, advertisers are echoing back that command, again and again—sometimes verbally, sometimes through imagery of quirky, off-center behavior. Wearing a Mohawk hairstyle to the office, painting one's face blue, taking a bath in a public place (an image that appears in a Swedish ad for, of all things, Maxwell House coffee) becomes shorthand for "distinctive"—a quality that every brand, no matter how nondescript, must somehow claim for itself.

## 2. HAVE NO FEAR.

Of course, it's not enough just to decide to break the rules; you have to have the courage to act on your decision. And so "Have no fear" is a partner command to "Break the rules," though it also

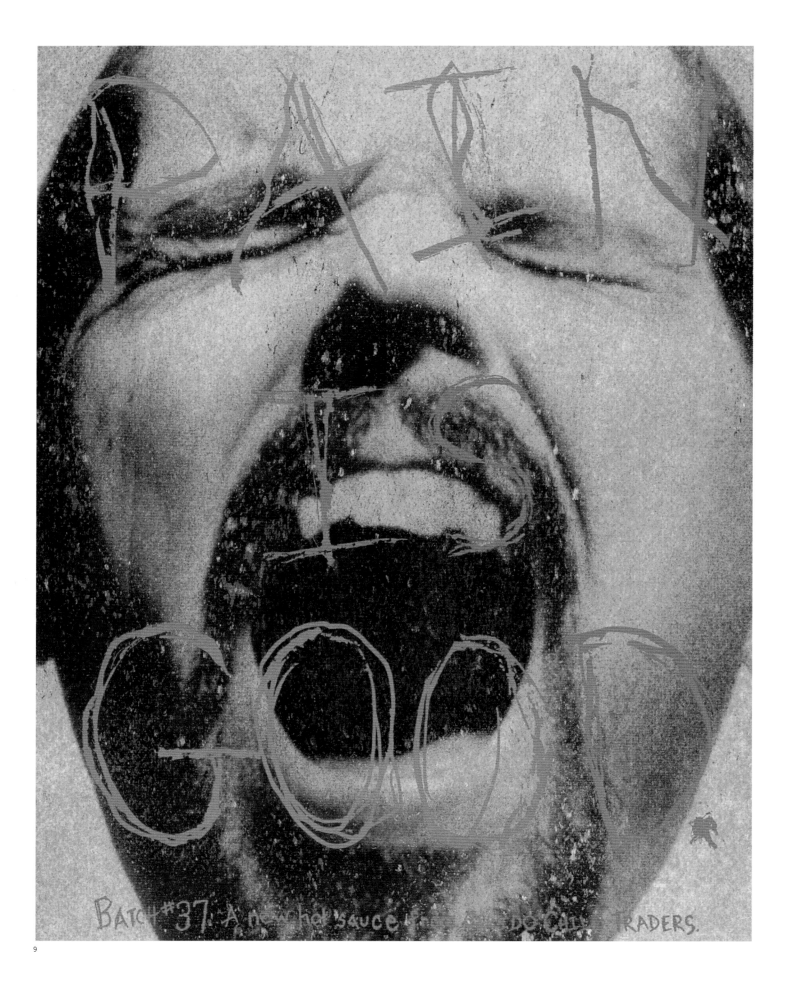

BATCH #37. A new hot sauce f... ...DO CAL... TRADERS.

9

10

9. **CALIDO HOT SAUCE**
CORE, ST. LOUIS, MISSOURI,
1994
"Pain is good," this ad insisted;
when you feel your mouth on
fire, you know you're alive.

10. **PLAYLAND**
PALMER JARVIS DDB,
VANCOUVER, 1999
In "have no fear" advertising,
being a little crazy is encouraged;
it can help you enjoy life's twists
and turns.

LAND ROVER DEFENDER. THE ORIGINAL 4x4.

11

extends beyond taking entrepreneurial chances or dressing differently, and encompasses a whole lifestyle of risk-taking. Jumping off cliffs, braving storms, riding a jeep into untamed territories: These are the challenges that today's advertisers lay before us, like a dare. The big question: Do you have the guts? (After which comes the follow-up question: If you have the guts, do you have the right tires?)

This relatively new strain of kamikaze advertising is partly an outgrowth of the adventure-seeking culture that has evolved in recent years. Julian says today's thrill-seekers "want to experience something so pure that they're much more willing to take risks." And each adventure or experience they live through becomes a social "badge of accomplishment" that can be proudly shown off to others, Julian notes. Meanwhile, ads are offering the encouragement and the road map to adventure. New-millennium advertising has been filled with scenes of people skydiving or jumping off cliffs—

and the participants aren't just wild teenagers. A commercial for the Best Western hotel chain featured an older woman gleefully throwing herself from atop a waterfall because, the ad explained, "you always promised yourself you would." The promise of many of these ads is that "what doesn't kill us will make us stronger."

It's a philosophy that is being espoused by all sorts of product advertisers looking to jump on the "extreme" bandwagon, from a jeans company in Argentina (the brand, Nasa, takes this to a sadistic level with imagery of a bound woman and the headline "Face the pain, don't live in fear of it") to a hot-sauce-maker in the American heartland ("Pain is good," blared the headline of a condiment ad created by the St. Louis agency CORE). Not surprisingly, thrillseeker ads are particularly popular among advertisers peddling adventure-related products, including hiking boots, all-weather jackets, and of course, the sport-utility vehicle—presented in ads as the great

getaway machine, enabling us to break the boundaries of civilized life and explore the unknown. The former ad creator-turned-ad critic Jelly Helm has suggested that the fantasies spun in SUV ads border on recklessness by encouraging suburbanites to buy gas-guzzling trucks that end up being used to simply tool around the suburbs—at a higher cost to both the consumer and the environment. In such ads, "mountains and forests are playgrounds and racetracks for your cars," Helm says. "The entire world is an amusement park in which every natural object or creature exists in order to scratch whatever itch you want."

### 3. JUST BE YOURSELF.

In writing a Nike campaign of the early 1990s targeted at women, the Wieden + Kennedy copywriter Janet Champ began one ad with the line "You do not have to be your mother." If that sounded like something a psychiatrist might say to a patient on the couch, it was in some ways characteristic

# It's what separates us from the animals.

LAND ROVER **DEFENDER 90**

12

**11. LAND ROVER**
TBWA HUNT LASCARIS,
JOHANNESBURG, 2000
Reinvent yourself: This
adventurer crosses borders
and identities, thwarting a
customs official attempting
to read his passport.

**12. LAND ROVER**
GRACE & ROTHSCHILD,
NEW YORK, 1995
Not surprisingly, marketers of
sport-utility vehicles use ads
to encourage exploration and
adventure, even though the
typical SUV owner seems rarely
to venture beyond familiar suburban territory.

I live in a castle on the ocean floor. It is a roomy and convenient castle.

I like it.

My neighbors, fish, recently held an election. I was elected Emperor.

(Much to my surprise.)

I am the "Emperor of Fish." I think I will like this job.

NORWEGIAN
CRUISE LINE

It's

different

out

here.

My life has really changed since I put on a snorkel and mask.

13

13. **NORWEGIAN CRUISE LINE**
GOODBY SILVERSTEIN &
PARTNERS, SAN FRANCISCO,
1994
The sensuous ads suggested
that people could shed their
everyday inhibitions out on the
ocean, where the laws of the
land do not apply.

14. **NIKE**
WIEDEN + KENNEDY,
PORTLAND, 1991
You are not a goddess, and
you're not your mother. Nike's
early-1990s ads urged women to
forget about the expectations
of others.

YOU DO NOT HAVE TO BE YOUR MOTHER UNLESS SHE IS WHO YOU WANT TO BE. YOU DO NOT HAVE TO BE YOUR MOTHER'S MOTHER, OR YOUR MOTHER'S MOTHER'S MOTHER, OR EVEN YOUR GRANDMOTHER'S MOTHER ON YOUR FATHER'S SIDE. YOU MAY INHERIT THEIR CHINS OR THEIR HIPS OR THEIR EYES, BUT YOU ARE NOT DESTINED TO BECOME THE WOMEN WHO CAME BEFORE YOU, YOU ARE NOT DESTINED TO LIVE THEIR LIVES. SO IF YOU INHERIT SOMETHING, INHERIT THEIR STRENGTH. IF YOU INHERIT SOMETHING, IN-HERIT THEIR RESILIENCE. BECAUSE THE ONLY PERSON YOU ARE DESTINED TO BECOME IS THE PERSON YOU DECIDE TO BE.

14

of a reassuring and therapeutic message that advertising in the 1990s began to disseminate, particularly in ads aimed at women. The essence: Don't try to live up to other people's expectations; stop worrying about what others think of you; live life on your own terms.

To propagate such a message (even if cynics suspected it of being as coldly calculating as any other ad message) was almost a kind of heresy in women's advertising, which had for so long fostered the notion that women *should* live up to other people's standards of beauty or accomplishment. Champ and her partner on the campaign, Charlotte Moore, sensed that women were ready for a new kind of individualistic, empowering advertising—and they were right. The Nike women's campaign was heralded as revolutionary within the ad industry, and was embraced by women across America; after it first appeared, Nike was swamped with 100,000 letters, the most ever received for any of its ads. The campaign also

triggered a wave of copycat empowering women's ads by other advertisers, all sharing a similar "Feel good about yourself" theme.

It wasn't the first time advertising had tried to modernize its message to women, but previous attempts at faux-feminist ads had been strident and sometimes woefully off-key. In the late 1970s and early 1980s, as advertisers projected unrealistic images of "Superwomen" who effortlessly balanced career and family life, looking sexy all the while, they only exacerbated that old Madison Avenue problem of holding women to impossible and ridiculous standards. One of the more memorable misfires was a ludicrous 1980 commercial for Revlon's fragrance Enjoli, depicting a woman who could, according to the sultry theme song, "bring home the bacon . . . fry it up in the pan . . . and never let you forget you're a man." In contrast, the campaign from Champ and Moore took a distinct anti-Superwoman approach;

one ad, in fact, bore the headline "You are not a goddess."

In the years since the Nike campaign broke, many other advertisers have come up with their own versions of the "Be comfortable with yourself" message. Another athletic-shoe company, Avia, advised women, "The only competition is yourself." More recently, an ad for Sephora, a luxury-cosmetics-and-fragrances retailer, asked, "Have you ever wondered what other people see? Does it really matter?" And a striking Canadian ad campaign for Special K cereal urged women to be comfortable with their own bodies via a series of ads that ridiculed fashion designers and anorexic models. One ad showed a well-proportioned woman standing next to a pudgy man, with the headline "Ironically, she's the one who's worried about her weight." The ad went on to advise women to "Look good on your own terms." Of course, it also squeezed in a plug for Special K, which might, in the views of some,

It isn't a race. It's not a beauty contest. Your biggest challenge isn't someone else. It's the burning in your legs, and the ache in your lungs, and the voice inside you that yells "can't". But you don't listen, you just push harder. And then the voice stops yelling "can't", and whispers "can". Where there was pain and doubt, you find strength and power and joy. And you discover the person you thought you were is no match for the one you really are.

Our Fitness Training shoes and apparel are designed for your total gym workout. Aerobics, Step, Weights, Machines.

The *FT3100* fits like an aerobic shoe with the comfort of a running shoe. When it comes to Avia Fitness Training shoes, there really is no competition. ∎

FOR MORE INFORMATION, CALL 1-800-555-CASEY

# THE ONLY COMPETITION IS YOURSELF

**AVIA**

15

16

There are feet that have never seen a David Hockney. There are feet that have never walked the streets of Cannes. There are feet unfamiliar with beluga at midnight. Dunham. They get the job done.

15. **AVIA**
CITRON HALIGMAN
BEDECARRE, SAN FRANCISCO,
1993
Nike's empowerment theme
was picked up by many other
advertisers, particularly in the
athletic wear category.

16. **DUNHAM BOOTS**
DOYLE ADVERTISING &
DESIGN, BOSTON, 1990
While ads urged women to be
themselves, they called on men
to "get real," and to choose
authenticity over superficiality
or fads.

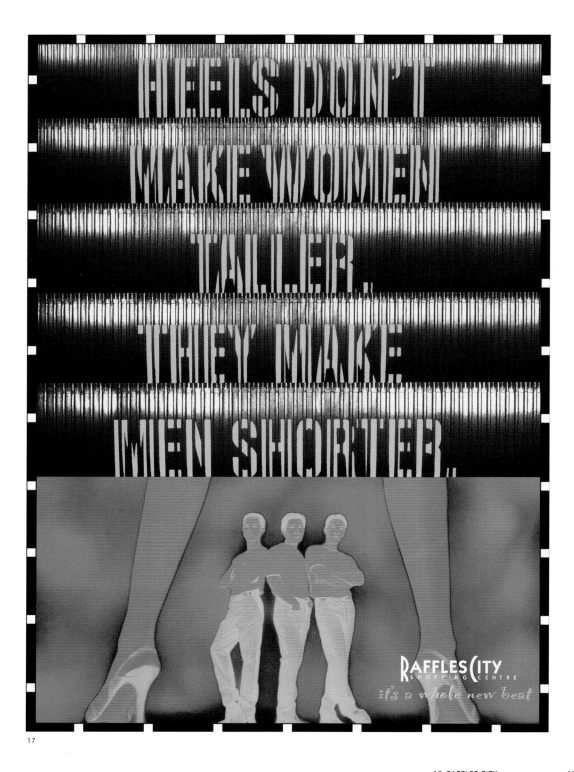

HEELS DON'T MAKE WOMEN TALLER. THEY MAKE MEN SHORTER.

RAFFLESCITY
SHOPPING CENTRE
it's a whole new beat

17

17. **RAFFLES CITY
SHOPPING CENTRE**
LEO BURNETT, SINGAPORE,
LATE 1990s
Ads that fostered group pride—
among women, men, or members
of ethnic groups—sometimes
took a good-humored "us-
against-them" tone.

18. **NORDSTROM**
FALLON McELLIGOTT,
MINNEAPOLIS, MINNESOTA,
2000
This campaign for an American
clothing store urged suburban
American "soccer moms" to
reinvent themselves via trendy
new shoes and garments.

# REinvent THE GIRL NEXT DOOR.

NORDSTROM

reinvent yourself

undercut the noble message slightly. Some critics have also suggested that empowering ads, for all their sensitivity and good intentions, can end up being condescending to women. Still, ads that encourage self-acceptance over the old self-loathing, and that replace the bacon-frying Superwoman with a realistic human being, must represent some kind of progress.

## 4. REINVENT YOURSELF.

This is, according to Syracuse University television professor Robert Thompson, "the first commandment of advertising, and always has been—the notion that you can change your life by way of a particular purchase." True, this message is not entirely new. But it may be more effective now than ever before—because many of today's consumers are predisposed to believe they can change their lives, and their identities, on an almost-daily basis. Fallon's Tom Julian points out that in today's culture of job-hopping, adventure-

seeking, Internet chat rooms, and diversified lifestyles, "people assume more identities than in the past." They're more flexible, more open to new experiences, and constantly eager to improve and enrich themselves, Julian noted. According to Iconoculture's research, many people today are refusing to be defined or limited by boundaries—whether physical, geographic, or age-related. "The popular thinking is that you can change your whole look with cosmetic surgery, or become a new person by taking kickboxing lessons," says Iconoculture's Larry Samuel. Advertising has helped to foster this new mind-set, consistently reassuring us that anyone can be anything. A "soccer mom" can reinvent herself as a hip woman of style, according to a Nordstrom campaign from Fallon; an aging baby boomer can feel like a kid with a rubber duck again, just by buying a Mercedes-Benz.

In some ads, reinvention of the self is linked to the notion of escape—the idea being that if you can just get away from your mundane surround-

ings, you'll discover another side of yourself. That was the essence of a brilliant Goodby Silverstein campaign for Norwegian Cruise Line. The lush, sensuous ads suggested that people could shed their everyday inhibitions—i.e., have more sex, for those not reading between the lines—by setting sail on the ocean, where the laws and restrictions and distractions of the land do not apply. Goodby's campaign was refreshingly candid in its acknowledgment that people tend to think of cruises as an opportunity to rekindle their sex lives; on the other hand, as ad executive Jack Supple of the Carmichael Lynch agency pointed out, the campaign may have been overpromising just a bit. "Will I really feel like being naked more on Norwegian Cruise Lines," Supple wondered, "or will I be fighting an old couple from Missouri for a deck chair?"

Ads also promise reinvention through the acquisition of instant wealth; the latter can come by way of savvy investment or just by playing the

**WALK IN A DEMOCRAT.**
**WALK OUT A REPUBLICAN.**

*Mystic Lake Casino*

19

**19. MYSTIC LAKE CASINO**
HUNT ADKINS,
MINNEAPOLIS, MINNESOTA,
1992
Nothing transforms a person
quite like instant wealth: this
wonderfully witty headline
is also a succinct lesson in
American politics.

**20. BUDWEISER**
DDB NEEDHAM, CHICAGO,
EARLY 1990s
In a popular series of commer-
cials from the early 1990s,
this character found himself
reinvented via mistaken identity.
Was he really rich and powerful?
"Yes I am!" he insisted.

lottery. In the classic commercial "Boardroom,"
created for the New York State Lottery by DDB
Needham, we are introduced to Chuck, the
mailroom clerk—who, after winning the lottery,
turns the tables on his stodgy bosses and begins
barking orders at them. Meanwhile, another
advertisement, by the agency Hunt Adkins for
Minnesota's Mystic Lake Casino, boiled the whole
reinvention fantasy down to one extremely clever
headline, which said simply, "Walk in a Democrat.
Walk out a Republican."

If you're not lucky enough to win the jackpot,
can't afford the sports car or the cruise or even
the Nordstrom makeover, there is one other
option—lie about yourself. That was the tack
taken by a character in a series of humorous
Bud Lite commercials from the mid-1990s. In a
case of mistaken identity, the insignificant fellow
was asked if he was a certain important and
wealthy person, and he responded, with great
conviction, "Yes, I am!" And off he rode in a

limousine, just another one of Madison
Avenue's successful reinventions.

## 5. BE PROUD.

Faced with an increasingly multicultural society,
advertisers have become adept at targeting
consumers according to race, gender, age,
ethnicity, and socioeconomic status. What has
emerged is a new "tribal advertising"—which not
only acknowledges diversity but celebrates it,
urging consumers to identify with their own
particular groups and take pride in them. As is
often the case, advertisers putting forth this
message are playing catch-up with social trends;
group-identity politics has been gaining
momentum on university campuses and in
workplaces for years. "In society at large, the
movement has been away from assimilation, and
toward feeling proud of our own group's heritage
and identity," says Iconoculture's Samuel. Still, for
advertising to move in this direction took some

daring on the part of marketers—who were always
more comfortable showing benign images of a
homogenized society in which everyone played on
the same team. The old approach was designed to
appeal to the mainstream of society—the essence
of mass marketing. The problem was, by the new
millennium, there wasn't much of a "mass" to
market to anymore, so advertisers had to begin to
speak the language of each group.

Ads did this with some trepidation, because,
as *New York Times* columnist Stuart Elliott noted,
"sometimes members of minority groups
appreciate it if an advertiser speaks to them in
their own vernacular, but other times they may
feel that it's pandering." McDonald's was among
the first to use African-American slang in
commercials whose characters referred to the
restaurant as "Mickey D's"—a nickname that was
first heard on the street, then incorporated into
the ads. More recently, Budweiser achieved a
cultural breakthrough with a humorous campaign

20

THE NEW COMMANDMENTS.

**21. BUDWEISER**
DDB WORLDWIDE, CHICAGO,
1999
Crossing the great divide in
"group pride" advertising: The
"Whassup?" campaign used an
African-American expression, a
question that was uttered again
and again, with hilarious results.
It achieved widespread mainstream popularity.

**22. MILLER HIGH LIFE**
WIEDEN + KENNEDY,
PORTLAND, 1998
This campaign, artfully directed
by Errol Morris, was a celebration
of duct tape, greasy foods, and
all things masculine.

21

22

in which African-American characters use the expression "Whassup?" While the ads seemed to be targeted to a black audience, they played just as well with whites and other groups—eventually spawning fan clubs and Web sites. While the "Whassup?" commercials themselves are not deep (aside from the characters shouting the catch-phrase to one another, not much happens in the ads), they may end up having a profound effect by demonstrating that ethnic advertising can have wide, across-the-board appeal. Similarly, advertis-ers have lately experimented with mainstream messages featuring apparently homosexual char-acters; a breakthrough spot was created by the agency Deutsch Inc., for the furniture retailer Ikea and showed two men shopping for furniture together. The commercial treated the subject with subtlety and humor, and proved to be one of the company's most popular ads.

While it's hard to find fault with advertising's long-overdue acknowledgment of the rich diversity

in our midst, group-pride advertising can have its downside; at its worst, it can take on a divisive "us against them" tone. Recent ads targeted to blue-collar types have tended to sneer at yuppies; meanwhile, ads for the upper crust have been perhaps a little too candid in declaring that "greed is good." But the real battleground seems to be in gender-targeted advertising. The past few years have seen a spate of ads whose theme might be "It's good to be a guy." One campaign for Miller High Life, shot by the director Errol Morris, is a droll celebration of beer bellies, greasy hamburgers, duct tape, and other macho signifiers; the ads are stylish, self-aware, and funny, but still seem to have an edge of defen-siveness. Other recent beer ads have shown men finding ways to trick women so they can avoid shopping or so they can watch football games without being nagged. Meanwhile, ads directed to women can be just as guilty of male-bashing; as Elliott noted, there has been a rash of them in

which women belittle men, and occasionally even whack them in the head. "It is becoming adversar-ial," Elliott noted. The newly aggressive "pride" message has even filtered down to little girls and Barbie, whose recent campaign declared, "Girls rule!"

## 6. GET REAL.

The quest for authenticity has become a near-obsession for marketers and their customers. The more that store shelves are packed with product knockoffs and look-alikes, the greater the appeal of those that can claim to be "the original" or "the real thing." Iconoculture's research has found that today's consumer is inclined to choose highly advertised products because they reinforce the feeling of being an individualist, the person who won't settle for generic products like everyone else. Of course, that's not entirely logical—choosing the original, best-known brand could actually be considered more conformist than experimenting with a no-name brand. But the "get real" ads make

# INTERVIEW: ANITA SANTIAGO

Anita Santiago's Los Angeles–based ad agency is one of the top specialists in the exploding field of ethnic advertising, which customizes and targets ads to various minority groups. In particular, Santiago helps advertisers tap into a Hispanic consumer market that spends an estimated $440 billion a year. She brings an interesting background (she started out writing TV soap operas in Venezuela), a keen understanding of Latin culture, and a master's degree in clinical psychology to her work for such clients as Wells Fargo Bank and the California Milk Board.

**HOW HAS HISPANIC ADVERTISING EVOLVED?**
I've been in the Hispanic ad market since the early 1980s, before it was really on the radar of major advertisers. Back then, it was a very minimal effort. It's now more sophisticated, with more strategic thought behind the message, and the production values are way up—because there's more money behind it now.

**IN THIS CHAPTER, WE'RE LOOKING AT SOME OF THE PSYCHOLOGY DRIVING MODERN ADS, INCLUDING NEW COMMANDS LIKE "BREAK THE RULES." WHY DO YOU THINK THAT KIND OF MESSAGE IS RESONATING RIGHT NOW?**
I think it's because such a huge portion of the American population—and the ones with so much of the real power right now—are baby boomers. And advertisers have analyzed the mind-set of the boomer and found someone who's accomplished, who's been at a job for a long time and maybe is tired of following the same routine. I do think the rich part of the U.S. population is going through midlife crises—and those crises are about who you are and who you want to be in society. That's why you see so much "Break the rules" and "Have no fear" and "Control your own destiny." It's because a lot of boomers are almost going through a second childhood right now.

**DO THE SAME THEMES AND MESSAGES WORK IN THE HISPANIC MARKET?**
No, not really. The mainstream American market is very individualistic. The average Anglo person in this country is out to make a name for him- or herself, and a career, and achieve his or her own goals. But in the Latin communities,

it's not so much about *me, me, me*—it's *us*. And people actually give up their own goals for the benefit of the larger community. Because of that, many of these themes, like "Break the rules," don't really work that well with this community. That rebel message represents too much of the me-oriented way of thinking. What connects much better with the Hispanic audience is something like "Show me how to better my lifestyle. Tell me what to do so I can work with this culture, your culture, so that I can improve my lifestyle — that's what I'm here for. And also, let me know that I'm welcome."

**WE'RE ALSO SEEING A LOT OF ADS THAT URGE US TO "BE PROUD" OF OUR GROUP—WHETHER THE GROUP IS MEN, WOMEN, AFRICAN-AMERICANS, JOGGERS, YOU NAME IT. DOES THAT RESONATE WITH THE HISPANIC MARKET?**
Well, there is a lot of pride in Hispanic heritage. But it's not really a matter of coming out and saying, "Hey, I'm proud to be Hispanic." It's more about taking pride in one's accomplishments. For example, you might see an ad with a father handing the car keys to a son—and that says a lot about how you've bettered your lifestyle and that you care for your family. Successful Hispanic advertising tends to be very aspirational and also emotional. You're less likely to see the kind of cool, sarcastic advertising you see for the Anglo audience now— that approach doesn't fly too well.

**SHIFTING TO A DIFFERENT TARGET GROUP, WHAT DO YOU THINK ABOUT SOME OF THE CHANGES WE'VE SEEN IN ADVERTISING TO WOMEN IN RECENT YEARS— SPECIFICALLY, THE KIND OF "EMPOWERING" IMAGES AND MESSAGES PUT OUT THERE BY NIKE AND OTHERS?**
I think it's been a great thing because it really did begin to focus ads on women's uniqueness. However, once again, the "women's empowerment" theme is a very Anglo message and doesn't really ring a bell in the Hispanic market. Hispanic women have a different mind-set— and, of course, I'm generalizing here. But if you tend to have more of an "us"-oriented way of thinking, then as a woman you don't want to separate yourself from family and talk about "doing my own thing." People in the Hispanic culture tend to set their own goals within the

landscape of family goals. The empowering message—"I am woman"—has an attitude that can be almost divisive. And that's not the attitude this audience responds to.

**BY THE WAY, WHY DON'T WE SEE MORE FEMALE CREATIVE EXECUTIVES IN ADVERTISING?**
I go back to my own experience starting as a copywriter, trying to rise up in this business. The battle was so intense to get your thoughts and concepts heard within a world of men. It is a very competitive, rough arena—and it's one in which you are exposed to ridicule. In advertising, anything you do creatively has to be put on the line, usually in front of a roomful of men, who will often shoot it down. And as a woman in these groups, you always run the risk of being perceived as a lightweight, so that adds to the pressure. I think all of this turns off some creative women—they might have great ideas and skills, but they don't want to deal with that part of the process.

**ARE THERE ANY PRODUCTS YOU REFUSE TO ADVERTISE TO YOUR OWN ETHNIC COMMUNITY?**
The beer companies are always waving offers under our noses, and we've turned down millions of dollars in business there—we just won't do it. Not because I don't drink beer and like beer, but I don't want to use my skills to do that, because I know I could sell a heck of a lot of it, and I'm aware of the problems it can cause. And the same with cigarettes; we won't do it—in fact, we did the first Hispanic anti-smoking ads in California. Turning down these products has probably slowed the agency's growth a little. But at least we sleep at night.

plane tickets to the town where she was born: $1,200

train to the house where she grew up: $63

pints at the pub where she met your dad: $8

finally understanding where your mother was coming from:

priceless

Platinum MasterCard® has a high spending limit
for the things that matter.

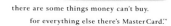

there are some things money can't buy.
for everything else there's MasterCard.℠

23

ARIEL

भारत तेरा रंग कैसा ?                                                    पक्का. एरियल के वादे जैसा !

24

25

23. **MASTERCARD**
McCANN-ERICKSON,
NEW YORK, 1998
Prioritize your life: The "Priceless"
campaign encouraged us to
place a value on what is really
important—even if it means
using a credit card to do so.

24. **ARIEL**
LEO BURNETT, MUMBAI, 1997
The "break the rules" theme
wasn't just a Western phenomenon; this ad from India for
household detergent shows a
woman standing out from the
pack by slipping off her head-scarf.

25. **BARBIE**
OGILVY & MATHER,
NEW YORK, 1998
This ad declares that even little
girls can be empowered, and that
Barbie dolls (somehow) stand
behind them.

26

sure our thoughts don't stray down this path; they do their best to forge the associative link between "real" products and "real" people.

But how does a brand prove it's the real thing? One approach is to trot out the advertising-embellished history of the company, which may take the form of sepia-toned ads showing old bearded fellows from another era, perhaps cobbling shoes by hand; it's the most literal way to say "We're the original," but it's also, frankly, unoriginal. A more popular approach these days is to focus on the customer—not just any customer but a particular subset, the die-hard fanatic. Harley-Davidson sells its authenticity by populating its ads with Hell's Angel–type bikers, who wouldn't be caught dead on anything else; they may not be the most glamorous ad models, but they reek authenticity. Finally, some ads demonstrate the brand's authenticity by taking a down-and-dirty, we-don't-give-a-damn approach. Everlast got rid of the phony models in its ads and showed the

product in nonglamorous ways (such as showing a pair of Everlast shorts on a bird's legs). The unspoken message: We're too "legit" to pitch.

## 7. DON'T BELIEVE THE HYPE.

When the need to seem authentic collides with postmodernism, the result is this: advertising messages that urge us to disregard advertising messages. As described in Chapter 5, the past decade has seen the rise of a whole new genre of ironic, self-referential advertising that often mocks ad conventions; when done with a light touch, as in Wieden + Kennedy's early innovative work for Nike, the result can be engaging. But when "Don't believe the hype" is fairly screamed at the audience as a command, it tends to become, in effect, more hype. One of the leading proponents of this approach has been the soft drink Sprite, whose advertising campaign actually uses another command, "Obey your thirst," as its tag line. But the real point of the Sprite ads is to attack

advertising. The ads make fun of feel-good, overpromising commercials; they mock actors who affect street mannerisms, and they even ridicule one of advertising's most valuable tools, the athlete endorser (a commercial featuring the basketball star Grant Hill shows visions of dollar signs in his head as he does an advertising pitch). Rogier van Bakel, the editor of *Creativity* magazine, describes this approach as "advertising biting itself in the tail and chomping down hard. No one knows where it will end." As van Bakel points out, "this style of advertising plays on cynical, weary anti-advertising sentiments," but at the same time, "it only adds another layer of consumer cynicism. It confirms consumers' perception that advertisers are cunning salesmen who'll say just about anything—including anything 'self-deprecating'— to make a buck." Still, he adds, for the time being, "these messages seem to work quite nicely because they're paying consumers a compliment for being media-savvy 'individualists.'"

**26. IKEA**
DEUTSCH INC., NEW YORK, 1994
In rare instances, group pride ads extended to gays. Deutsch took a bold step forward when it featured male living companions in this mid-1990s commercial.

**27. CISCO SYSTEMS**
GOLDBERG MOSER O'NEIL, SAN FRANCISCO, 1999
"Plug in," was the message from the technology companies, who promised that the Internet would solve all of the world's problems. This ad asked: "Are you ready?"

27

# If your broker's so great, how come he still has to work?

It's time for ✳ E✳TRADE

### 8. PLUG IN.

If there is any category of advertising that should come with a "Don't believe the hype" warning label, it is high technology. In this sector, advertising seems to be irony-free; on the contrary, ads for Internet-related technology have tended to be earnest and full of grand promises. Giant high-tech companies like Microsoft, Cisco Systems, and Nortel have used their ads to assure us that the Internet will soon solve all of the world's problems, provide equal education to everyone, and, in case that's not enough, enable us "to see every movie, ever made, any time of day or night" (a line from a popular commercial for Qwest broadband information networks). Sometimes this message is delivered by the industry's gods themselves: Microsoft chief Bill Gates recently appeared in his own ads promising "the best is yet to come," and that new technology will "anticipate your needs" and "help your children learn." For those who are just lonely and misunderstood, the Internet can

solve that problem, too; log on to Yahoo!, the company's ads show us, and you can search for kindred spirits who share your appreciation of punk rock and quilt-weaving.

Of course, to take advantage of all these wonders, you must "get wired"—hardware, software, high-speed modem, broadband Internet service connection (no one said admission to utopia would be cheap). And the unspoken warning from technology advertising is that if you're not quick about it, you'll fall hopelessly behind everyone else. "The message is 'Your life will be empty and meaningless unless you get on board the technology train,'" observes Helm, because "you are not only deprived of very cool stuff, but your relationships lack meaning, you are less fulfilled as a person, and you are not able to achieve all that you're capable of."

### 9. PRIORITIZE YOUR LIFE.

There's a problem with being so plugged-in,

empowered, and adventurous—you may become overwhelmed by your own life. Addressing this potential hazard is a series of ads that encourage us to always remember what's important: family, friends, helping the poor, relaxing with a cup of Maxwell House International Blend coffee. For those who have trouble sorting out what's really important and what isn't, a recent campaign for MasterCard, by the agency McCann-Erickson, helpfully offered a kind of valuation chart; in the ads, everyday activities like going to a ball game with the kids are deconstructed, with price tags flashed onscreen for each part of the experience (buying the tickets, the hot dog, etc.); the spots end by pointing that the most important part of the experience—seeing your son enjoy his first ball game—is, of course, "priceless."

One of the curious aspects of "Prioritize your life" ads is that they seem to be advocating a return to simplicity—but at the same time, they add to our collective stress overload by reminding

29

I will forgive my husband for snoring. I will stop finishing other people's sentences. I will buy myself sunflowers and anemones. I will send my parents on an Alaskan cruise. I will read everything ever written.

MAKE *EVERY* DAY
GOOD TO THE LAST DROP.   MAXWELL HOUSE®

© 2000 Kraft Foods

31

30. **MAXWELL HOUSE**
OGILVY & MATHER,
NEW YORK, 2000
Prioritizing your life can get
complicated; the woman in
this ad takes a coffee break to
mentally review her to-do list.

31. **DISCOVER BROKERAGE**
BLACK ROCKET,
SAN FRANCISCO, 1998
"Be your own boss," this ad
advises, appealing to the
corporate woman of the 1990s,
who balances career, home,
and family in affluent times.

us there are so many important things we should
be doing. Some ads have even taken to printing "to
do" lists for us. A recent Maxwell House ad
features an Everywoman character who is shown
thinking, "I will forgive my husband for snoring. I
will stop finishing other people's sentences. . . . I
will send my parents on an Alaskan cruise. I will
read everything ever written." She'd better put
down that coffee and get started.

### 10. CONTROL YOUR OWN DESTINY.

The last and most important thing advertisers
would like us to realize is this: In today's every-
man-for-himself world, you can't count on anyone
or anything except yourself (and also the product
being advertised). This is another variation of the
"Go your own way" theme, but it specifically plays
to growing concerns that we can no longer count
on employers or government programs or hired
financial experts to take care of us or guide us—
we must do for ourselves. Iconoculture's Samuel

calls this the "free-agent mentality," and one of its
preoccupations is the building of a nest egg that
will provide for the individual when all else fails.
How do you build the nest egg? If you are a free
agent, "you're not going to do what some financial
analyst might tell you—better to trust yourself
and become your own day trader," noted Samuel.
Cheering on the free agent is today's advertiser,
with slogans like the Ameritrade line "Believe in
yourself." Another on-line-trading company,
E*Trade, created an ad campaign that told people
to "fire your broker." (E*Trade's logic seemed
pretty sound: "If your broker's so great," the ads
wondered, "how come he still has to work?")

The ads for on-line trading certainly seem to
be "empowering," but they've also come under
fire for encouraging people to think of stock trading as a get-rich-quick option. E*Trade's agency,
Goodby Silverstein, tried to counter some of this
criticism recently by creating an ad in which a day
trader sees his stock portfolio skyrocket and

promptly marches in to his boss to quit his job;
by the time he gets back to his desk, his stocks
have plummeted, forcing him to march back into
the boss's office, full of apologies. But that message—suggesting that a real job with a real boss
may actually be worth hanging on to—is an aber-
ration in the ads of the free-agency world. More
typical is the campaign for Discover Brokerage,
which is headlined, "You are the C.E.O. of your
life." The copy reads, "Your life is like a business.
It makes sense that you're the one in charge."
And it concludes with the words "Be your own
boss." That was an appropriate message for the
roaring late 1990s, but as the economy began
to sputter early in the new century, one had to
wonder: Where will the advertisers` who urged us
to "go for it" be found as stocks crash and businesses fail? No doubt they are already crafting a
fresh set of commandments for harder times,
with a newly cautious tone: "Think safety." "Don't
blow it." "Just watch it."

OF CREAM.

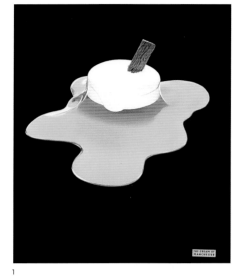

1

2

A great many advertisements come and go, unnoticed. A far smaller number of ads do slightly better than that, generating a brief blip on the cultural radar screen. And then there is that rarest of advertising miracles: the ad campaign that becomes a phenomenon, that permeates the culture down to the grassroots, lasts for years, and, even after it is gone, leaves a mark on the public consciousness. The creation of such ad campaigns is what brand marketers and ad creators lust after. But how does it come about?

To some extent, it is magic and dumb luck. But not entirely. Look closely at the making of any breakthrough ad campaign and you'll usually find there were critical ingredients and particular processes that had to be in place before the magic could occur. Often, it all begins with mind-reading: arcane, meticulous research that probes public attitudes, beliefs, and desires with regard to a particular product.

If the researchers are both good and fortunate, they may derive from this a key insight— a revelation of how people really feel about a product or an activity—that can help start the campaign on the right track. Then comes the hard part: A flash of inspiration is needed, a big idea that somehow speaks to these deep feelings of the audience but does so in a manner that is both original and intriguing. Even if the big flash occurs (and ad creators acknowledge that often, it never does), that's just another starting point; the idea must be sold to clients who are in need of original thinking yet at the same time tend to fear it. Then it must be executed in a way that brings the idea to life. And then it must be released upon the world in a manner that ensures it won't be simply ignored, like so much advertising. What happens after that is beyond the control of the ad creators or anyone else; it is at this point that the whims of the

zeitgeist take over. All the creators can do is wait and watch, to see if their idea is soon being discussed at water coolers and in pubs, joked about on the late-night talk shows, worn on T-shirts, lauded in the press, analyzed by academics, showered with awards. And even if all of that happens, it still won't mean a thing unless the campaign also causes the advertised product to sell like hotcakes.

During the past decade, not many ad campaigns have met all of these challenges. One that has is the California Milk Board series of ads from the San Francisco agency Goodby, Silverstein & Partners, which turned the simple question "Got Milk?" into one of advertising's most popular and powerful catchphrases. On the other side of the world, a separate and very different milk ad campaign created by the Brazilian ad agency DM9 DDB Publicidade, for the dairy company Parmalat, triggered a public

got milk?™

DREAMS OF CREAM.

3

4 AND 5. **CALIFORNIA MILK BOARD**
GOODBY SILVERSTEIN & PARTNERS, SAN FRANCISCO, 1997
The billboard images featured various foods that cry out for milk, with chocolate topping the list (top). The campaign also borrowed freely from pop culture: Snap, Crackle and Pop, from the famous Kellogg's Rice Crispies ads, were left high and dry in the ad above.

6. **CALIFORNIA MILK BOARD**
GOODBY SILVERSTEIN & PARTNERS, SAN FRANCISCO, 1995–96
The campaign's "deprivation strategy" called for stories in which characters run out of milk at the worst times; here, the Trix Rabbit realizes to his horror that he (and his cereal) has run dry.

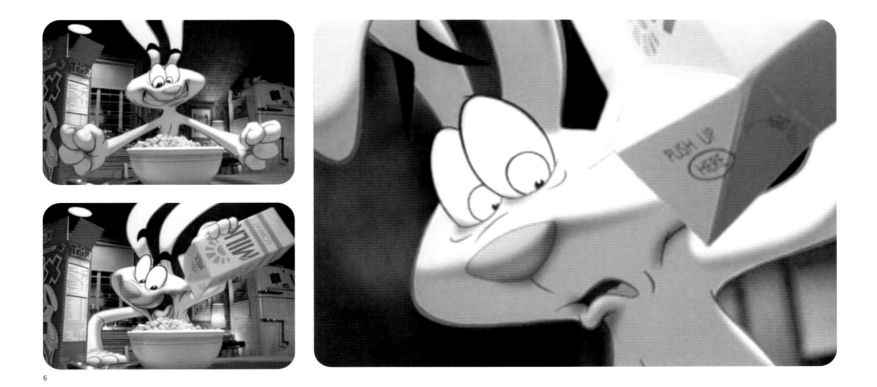

6

frenzy around milk, mammals, and stuffed toys. And in the United Kingdom—where, for some local denizens, beer quickly replaces milk as the source of life—a campaign for Boddingtons by the London agency Bartle Bogle Hegarty presented this beer as if it were a dairy product, and in doing so helped make both the brand and the ad agency legendary.

## GOT MILK?

To some extent, milk is an advertising nightmare. The very things advertisers love to say about a product—"it's new, it's cool, it's different!"—do not apply to milk. It's generic, it's old-fashioned, it's bland. "What can you say about milk? It's white and comes in gallons," observed Jeffrey Manning, director of the California Milk Processors Board. Nevertheless, Manning's task, beginning in the early 1990s, was to try to encourage Californians to drink more milk, and he knew this would not be easy. The one thing

that had worked in milk's favor in the past was that it was thought to be healthful; hence, the old ad line that had been used for years by milk processors declared, "Milk does a body good." But in recent times, the public had become more concerned about fat and cholesterol, and milk is loaded with both. So the old health claims simply did not wash with the audience anymore, particularly in body-conscious California. Milk consumption in the state was plummeting, and had been for twenty years straight.

Manning needed something akin to an advertising miracle to turn this situation around. He called Jeff Goodby and Rich Silverstein. The two admen, who run the agency Goodby, Silverstein & Partners in an old waterfront warehouse in San Francisco, paid a visit to the milk board in the summer of 1993. Their agency was one of four that had been summoned by Manning to bid for the milk account. Goodby arrived with flowing, shoulder-length hair,

a self-effacing manner, and a razor-sharp wit, accompanied by partner Silverstein, a hyperactive exile from *Rolling Stone* magazine, known for riding a bicycle to work each day. The admen and their co-workers were so casual, Manning recalls, "I felt like we were having a cocktail party, not a meeting." Then Goodby slipped Manning a piece of paper with two words on it: "Got Milk?" That question—a minimalist slogan if ever there was one—summed up an entire strategy that Goodby had concocted before coming to the meeting.

In previous brainstorming sessions, the agency knew that it had to find some motivating principle, other than questionable health claims, that could rekindle people's interest in milk. As Goodby and his creative team discussed this, the beginnings of an idea started to surface: Someone made the observation that although milk is generally taken for granted, there is one time when it is fully appreciated—that desperate

**DREAMS OF CREAM.**

g

ot milk?™

7. **CALIFORNIA MILK BOARD**
GOODBY SILVERSTEIN &
PARTNERS, SAN FRANCISCO,
1994
Some photographs in the
campaign did a remarkable
job of pinpointing the moment
when milk is badly needed—
such as right after biting into
a peanut butter sandwich.

**DREAMS OF CREAM.**

8

moment when you reach in the refrigerator and find that it is gone. Goodby and his cohorts immediately felt that this somewhat obvious observation actually represented a hidden truth; it was a feeling widely shared by people, but one that had not been articulated or expressed in advertising. The creative team began to toy with something Goodby would later call "the deprivation strategy"—which would, in effect, remove milk from all the ads and instead focus on its absence. Goodby reasoned that ads highlighting the horrors of being deprived of milk might not necessarily cause people to like milk more—but it just might scare them into buying an extra container just to avoid running out of the stuff.

Before proceeding too far with this somewhat heretical approach (removing the featured product from ads is always considered risky and is a tough sell to clients), the agency turned to its in-house planner, or consumer researcher,

Jon Steel, to find out if the idea was on the right track. In his research, Steel attempts to uncover inner, subconscious attitudes people have about products or brands, the kind of feelings that don't necessarily reveal themselves in standard surveys and interviews. "You have to dig deep for those feelings," Steel said. He conducted a number of unusual field tests involving milk. Steel spied on the ad agency's own employees by slyly planting a video camera in the back of the office refrigerator, to tape the distressed reactions of employees as they discovered there was no milk for their coffee. He also gathered members of the public into focus groups and asked them to deprive themselves of milk for a week and then report back to him. At the next session, "some pretty pissed-off people arrived," said Steel. "Somebody even said, 'When you're without milk, you want it so bad you'd steal it from the baby.'" (This statement would become one of Goodby's commercials, in which a

desperate man faces off against his own baby for the last of the milk, while the sound track plays the theme from the cowboy-showdown film *The Good, the Bad and the Ugly*.)

Armed with research, Goodby was able to sell the deprivation strategy to Manning, who realized the agency "was onto something big," and gave the green light to start making ads. Now came the fun part for Goodby, Silverstein— the creation of a series of ads that incorporated the deprivation theme into the most compelling, imaginative pictures and stories. The print ads were fairly easy: Just by showing food that cries out for milk—cupcakes, chocolate chip cookies, peanut butter sandwiches—they gave the two-word question that much more power. For the TV commercials, however, Goodby wanted to go further, creating a series of exaggerated thirty-second tales of protagonists for whom the missing milk is not just desired but desperately needed, like water in the desert.

got milk?

9

10

DREAMS OF CREAM.

# INTERVIEW: JEFF GOODBY

As co-founder and co–creative director of the San Francisco–based Goodby Silverstein & Partners, Jeff Goodby presides over what some regard as the best ad agency in the world. Goodby also helped produce one of the most memorable ad campaigns in recent years, promoting a certain dairy fluid with the minimalist slogan, "Got Milk?"

**WHERE DID THE IDEA TO USE THOSE TWO WORDS, "GOT MILK?," COME FROM?**
That line by itself never would have seemed like an interesting line. But when I thought of it, I was thinking of it being used in conjunction with all of these shaggy-dog stories, the kind of stories you'd watch and think, "Why am I watching this? What the hell is going on; what's the linchpin of this story?" Then the line at the end would be so tiny but so explanatory of the story that it would be kind of a humorous shock. That's the way I envisioned it.

**THE "DEPRIVATION STRATEGY" YOU USED, WHICH BUILT THE WHOLE CAMPAIGN AROUND WHAT IT'S LIKE TO BE WITHOUT MILK—HOW DID YOU ARRIVE AT THAT?**
That insight came somewhat from the research; someone in a focus group said something like "I never think about milk except when I run out of it." But the idea of the campaign was really having these incredibly elaborate stories about something as mundane, as tediously unimportant as milk. The deprivation strategy was important, but someone could have taken that same idea—that people think about milk only when they run out—and come up with something like "the magic milkman" who rushed in to give you milk as soon as you run out, or some stupid thing like that. I think that the planning community [researchers] gives you the impression that the commercials pretty much write themselves once you have the strategy. That's not the case.

**WHEN DID YOU REALIZE THE ADS HAD BECOME A CULTURAL PHENOMENON?**
When we had our Christmas party at a theater that wasn't in a particularly good part of town, and a few streets from the theater there was an X-rated bookstore. They had a sign out front that said, Got Porn. So I knew it was starting to take off.

**SOME PEOPLE HAVE CITED "AARON BURR" AS ONE OF THE BEST COMMERCIALS EVER MADE, AND AN EXAMPLE OF HOW ADVERTISING CAN BE ART—BEAUTIFULLY CRAFTED, WITH ITS OWN HUMAN TRUTH TO IT, A STRONG CHARACTER, A REVELATION AT THE END. DO YOU LOOK AT THE COMMERCIAL THAT WAY?**
I do. I think that's one of the best commercials we've ever done. And the reason is that it's based on something that is really true but is exaggerated in ways that are very pleasing. The obsession that character has is just esoteric enough to make it interesting. And the exaggeration made it work. I think that some of the things [director] Michael Bay did to it, particularly the wild set he created, with all the weird memorabilia, took the ad further than I thought it would go. The character lived in this crazy kind of apartment that happens to be in the middle of a warehouse—and you don't even wonder why, for some reason. It's a great piece of fantasy.

**DO YOU FIND THAT A GREAT AD CAMPAIGN USUALLY STARTS WITH A MOMENT OF REVELATION AND THEN BUILDS FROM THERE?**
Sometimes a great campaign starts with one really good commercial someone thinks of, and then you try to replicate it, or push it farther. Sometimes you can't do it. An example of that would be the Nissan commercial that Chiat/Day did with the dolls ["Toys"]. The rest of the campaign didn't live up to the promise of that commercial—they just couldn't replicate that feeling down the line. Making a good campaign is much harder than making a single piece of good advertising. You have to start out with a much deeper insight about the workings of a product and the way it really fits into people's lives. And the idea you come up with has to have a kind of depth and breadth that you'll be able to explore further down the line.

**IS IT DIFFICULT TO KEEP A CAMPAIGN LIKE "GOT MILK?" FRESH AND INTERESTING OVER TIME? AND HOW DO YOU KNOW WHEN IT'S TIME TO MOVE AWAY FROM IT?**
It's hard to keep the momentum going. You can change the people who are working on it—that's the easiest trick, and it usually gives you a new perspective on things. But actually, I find creative people and clients are sometimes too quick to give up on a campaign. Because all they've been

doing is thinking about this campaign, and they get sick of it. And the creative people get scared, like, "Maybe we won't be able to think of another round of ads." So the advertising people sometimes just want to start fresh, and they abandon a good campaign—even though the public might be just starting to get into it.

**IN THE PAST, AD CAMPAIGNS OFTEN HAD ONGOING STORY LINES AND RECURRING CHARACTERS. WHY DON'T WE SEE THAT AS MUCH NOW?**
I think some of it is fear on the part of creatives that they won't be able to come up with something else for Mr. Whipple to do, to keep him interesting. Also, I think the research that goes on now doesn't support that kind of campaign. You get research that says something like "Everyone remembers the Taco Bell dog, but they don't remember the burrito that was advertised. So the campaign's no good." So then, the creatives go back and try to come up with some way to integrate the burrito and the dog, with the dog asking for a burrito over and over—and the campaign starts getting bad because of that. Or maybe they start lessening the dog's role, thinking, The research shows that people remember the dog instead of the fajitas—so let's use the dog less. That's what you saw with that campaign. I think research really hurts that kind of campaign. If you took the classic Cracker Jack campaign now [starring the veteran actor Jack Gilford], the researchers would probably tell you, "Well, some consumers don't like to see old people." It's a mistake, because good characters and good stories can last a long time.

11. **NATIONAL MILK PROCESSOR PROMOTION BOARD**
BOZELL WORLDWIDE, NEW YORK, 1998
While the "Got Milk?" campaign ran in California, the national milk board's popular series of ads featured celebrities with milk moustaches (including the pro wrestler Steve Austin). The ads borrowed Goodby's headline, though it wasn't as appropriate in this context.

12. **CALIFORNIA MILK BOARD**
GOODBY SILVERSTEIN & PARTNERS, SAN FRANCISCO, 1993
The commercial "Aaron Burr" takes the viewer into the obsessive world of an American history fanatic who collects memorabilia from the famed 1804 duel between U.S. President Aaron Burr and Alexander Hamilton.

12

The first commercial, "Aaron Burr," featured a wild-haired history buff who is obsessed with the early American politician Alexander Hamilton, and who misses his opportunity of a lifetime—to answer the radio-contest question, "Who shot Alexander Hamilton?"—because he has no milk to wash down the peanut butter sandwich stuck in his mouth. ("Owum Buh!" he screams into the phone, to no avail.) Another early spot was the aforementioned father/baby showdown. A third featured the Trix Rabbit, star of a long-ago series of commercials in which the rabbit was always denied Trix cereal; in the new ad, Goodby created a clever scenario in which the rabbit finally gets the cereal—then is all the more heartbroken to discover there is no milk to pour on it.

The commercials worked on multiple levels, as entertainment and as a selling message. While almost every good ad agency tries to achieve that dual effect with its ads, "no one is able to do it as well as Goodby, Silverstein," said the *Advertising Age* critic Bob Garfield. Garfield pointed out that the "Got Milk?" refrain serves not only as a punch line to the ads' jokes but also as a nagging question that follows consumers all the way to the supermarket. "The agency does all of this so smoothly it's almost sublime," Garfield said.

Perhaps the best ad in the bunch was the commercial titled "Heaven." In the opening scene, we meet a nasty yuppie executive snarling into his cellular phone. Stepping into the street, he's run over by a truck (one of the rare times a commercial has ever shown someone being killed), only to reappear in an ethereal world, where he's surrounded by chocolate chip cookies and containers of milk—Heaven, it would seem. Stuffing his mouth with cookies, he reaches for the milk and finds that each and every container is empty. This prompts him to pause and wonder, "Where am I?"—at which point a flaming "Got Milk?" logo burns itself onto the screen.

Selling such a dark and complex commercial to a client is rarely easy, and "Heaven" was no exception. The idea originated with copywriter Harry Cocciolo. It hadn't tested particularly well in focus groups, but Cocciolo and his partner, Sean Ehringer, kept refining the script and presented it again to Goodby. According to Ehringer, "Goodby's reaction was warm but not overly positive. Kind of like when your kid proudly shows you his first poop in the toilet. I thought it was over, but Harry kept at Jeff [Goodby]. Day after day we would submit tiny changes." Goodby finally became convinced the spot could work. But the client didn't agree. "I didn't like it at first," Manning said. Goodby suspected that Manning was afraid of showing a man killed in a commercial, but Manning says, "I just thought the story was too complex to do in thirty seconds." Now it was Goodby's turn to nag. "Every meeting after that, I'd mention it,"

13

13. AND 14. **PARMALAT MILK**
DM9 DDB PUBLICIDADE,
SÃO PAULO, 1999
One series of ads suggested an
uprising of milk-powered cats
against dogs, and the cats
were winning. A dog shows
the wounds of battle (above),
and a poodle is left a widow
(opposite).

Parmalat
Fortified Milk.
It gives you
more energy.

says Goodby. "I'd say, 'Yeah, this new idea's
pretty cool, but I keep thinking about that
"Heaven" idea.' " He finally won Manning over
by agreeing to direct the commercial himself. "I
said, 'Fine, if you're going to put your rear end
on the line, go do it,' " Manning said.

"Heaven," along with "Aaron Burr," became
one of the most lauded commercials of the
1990s (Goodby even got a call from filmmaker
Steven Spielberg, asking for a videotape of
"Heaven"). *Time* magazine named "Got Milk?"
the best advertising campaign of 1995. The Girl
Scouts of America asked if they could be
featured in the campaign, and Goodby obliged.
Meanwhile, "the phrase 'Got Milk?' became part
of the vernacular in California," says Manning.

But for the client Manning, the real news
was in the sales figures: In 1994, the first full
year the campaign was running, Californians
drank 15 million gallons more milk than the
previous year. It was the first time in two decades

that consumption increased. The California ads
soon started running around the country and
were successful everywhere. And eventually the
question "Got Milk?" was licensed by a separate
national milk-promotion group that had been
running a series of ads featuring celebrities with
milk mustaches. (While the milk-mustache
campaign has been popular with the public
for a number of years, it is generally not well
regarded in advertising's creative community
because of its easy reliance on celebrities; in fact,
the grafting of the "Got Milk?" line onto this
campaign displeased not only Goodby and
Silverstein but others in the ad industry, such as
TBWA/Chiat/Day creative director Lee Clow,
who called it "a bastardization.")

Meanwhile, the original "Got Milk?"
campaign was still running in the new
millennium, as Goodby continued to spin tales
of poor milk-deprived souls. And client Manning
has continued to leverage the phenomenon in

every way possible, licensing the logo for T-shirts
and putting the words on everything from pens
to toy milk trucks. At this point, Manning said,
"'Got Milk?' is more than an ad campaign. It has
taken on a life of its own."

## PARMALAT

While Goodby's challenge was to promote
generic milk, the packaged-milk company
Parmalat and its Brazilian agency, DM9 DDB
Publicidade, had a more daunting task—they
had to persuade Brazilians not only to drink
more milk but specifically to choose Parmalat.
Exacerbating this problem was the fact that, at
the time, few people in Brazil knew or cared
much about the brand.

Back in 1995, Parmalat's own research found
that only 19 percent of Brazilian households
were using the brand. Women, in particular,
seemed to feel no connection to it, which was
understandable—Parmalat's previous

Parmalat
Fortified Milk.
It gives you
more energy.

promotional efforts had been aimed primarily at men. The brand's marketers had chosen to sponsor soccer matches, in an attempt to tie in with athleticism and good health. The problem was, men were not the ones making most household milk purchases—the real opportunity lay in appealing to mothers of growing families. And among this group, "we were still distant from our consumers," said Vania Machado, the brand's marketing manager. Moreover, as in many other places around the world, milk consumption in Brazil had declined in recent years. And those who were still drinking it tended to favor fresh pasteurized milk from local dairies; Parmalat, based in Italy, offered a packaged dairy product that was, in the minds of some, not as fresh.

When Machado presented her case to DM9, she understood what needed to be done but didn't know how to do it. Parmalat had to remind people that milk was an important and

natural source of nutrition; at the same time, the ads had to transcend this informational message and somehow establish a special emotional bond with mothers and their children.

Erh Ray, a creative director at DM9, started out with a vague idea about tying in the notion of "mother's milk" with the ads. The point of that would be "to remind people that milk is the very first source of nutrition for all of us," he said. "This was not only about being fed but being taken care of, being loved, being near a gentle, caring mother—that whole universe of the moment when we first open our eyes to the world."

Ray was trying to come up with a scenario that might capture those sentiments when, on a visit to New York in 1996, he saw the work of the photographer Tom Arma, who specialized in photographs of young children in costume. "When I came back to Brazil I had this idea of using these kinds of photographs, with the kids dressed as animals," Ray said, but he still didn't

have the idea fleshed out. He sketched some rough layouts of costumed children and showed them to his boss Nizan Guanaes. Guanaes looked at the pictures and immediately made the connection to a larger theme: The ads would feature kids portraying various mammals that are nursed on mother's milk. A slogan popped into Guanaes's head immediately: "Parmalat— because we are mammals."

The creative team decided that each ad would feature an Arma photo portrait of a different child in a different furry costume: a panda, a lion, a monkey, a sheep (and in each picture, the child/mammal would be shown clutching a package of Parmalat, of course). The agency knew the images of the cute kids, of varying ethnicities and races, would likely be irresistible to mothers, but they also reasoned that if the ads were crafted in the right way, children might be drawn to them, as well. So the creative team devised a theme song for the

DREAMS OF CREAM.

Parmalat milk. Because we are mammals.

Parmalat milk. Because we are mammals.

Parmalat milk. Because we are mammals.

Parmalat milk. Because we are mammals.

Parmalat milk. Because we are mammals.

15

**15. PARMALAT MILK**
DM9 DDB PUBLICIDADE,
SÃO PAULO, 1996–98
In portraits by photographer Tom
Arma, children were dressed up
in costumes of mammals that
drink milk. The campaign
became the talk of Brazil, and
soon created a feeding frenzy
for stuffed mammal dolls.

commercials that sounded like a lullaby. "The music was our 'secret-sauce recipe,'" said Ray. As soon as Machado saw the first versions of the ads, she knew that the idea was on target. "It was such a simple and obvious idea, and yet it managed to convey everything we wanted," Machado said, noting that the imagery tied up the various themes of nutrition, nature, family, caring, reliability, and more.

The campaign broke on Mother's Day. Ray wasn't sure what to expect but soon found that in his own neighborhood, a buzz was building. "Mothers were talking about the ads from day one," he said. And it just steamrolled from there. "People sang the mammals song, kids wanted to be mammals, at birthday parties the theme was . . . mammals! It was 'mammalsmania' everywhere," Ray said. "And not only here. It spread like a fever to all Latin America, and then all the way to China."

It's hard to figure why something as simple as children in furry suits can trigger a phenomenon. But when it happens, a smart advertiser seizes on the opportunity and leverages it. Parmalat and DM9 did that with one brilliant move: Once the mammal characters had been popularized through ads, the company began offering miniature stuffed dolls based on them—and soon a feeding frenzy was under way. Each day, some 60,000 Brazilians were lining up to exchange $7 plus twenty Parmalat bar codes for a mammal toy. Machado noted that people became fanatical collectors, wanting not just one or two but the entire collection of twenty-one animals. In subsequent ads, the agency started featuring the mammal toys being clutched (along with the milk) by the mammal-kids.

By now, the success of the campaign was being fueled by two separate but intertwined forces: Parents had come to associate Parmalat with nurturing and nutrition; kids, meanwhile, were badgering parents to buy more Parmalat milk so they could collect more toys. Within a year, Parmalat's penetration into Brazilian households jumped by an astounding level— from 19 percent to 96 percent, virtually overnight. Meanwhile, the company was producing and redeeming mammal dolls as fast as it could, eventually selling more than 16 million of them.

As the company saw its milk-market share growing, it began to promote spin-off milk products, such as fortified milk and low-fat milk. But wisely, the ad agency didn't overplay its "mammals" hand. DM9 took a different tack with these products because the target groups were different. The low-fat milk, for example, was geared more to weight-conscious adults, so DM9 came up with a new twist on the animal

Dietalat Parmalat. The milk for people who like themselves.

16

16 AND 17. **PARMALAT MILK**
DM9 DDB PUBLICIDADE,
SÃO PAULO, 1997
For low-fat milk, the pitch was
aimed at body-conscious adults;
this time, instead of children in
cute costumes, slim adults
appeared with cow spots.

theme—this time, the ads featured adults whose bare skin was printed with cow spots. Unlike the cute and cuddly kids in the main campaign, the subjects of these ads were presented as being self-absorbed, reveling in their own bodies. The copy read, "The new light Parmalat. Milk for all those who are really into themselves."

Some of the most striking ads DM9 produced were for Parmalat's specially fortified milk. Here again, the agency wanted to connect with mothers and children, but because the milk was fortified the ads needed a much stronger emphasis on nutrition and physical growth. The agency again returned to the theme of animals, which had worked so well already. But this time, DM9 zeroed in on two particular species: dogs and cats. Obviously, the latter drinks milk, and the former doesn't. And so the creative team of Pedro Cappeletti and Jader Rossetto dreamed up a series of

exaggerated, humorous scenes showing what might happen if cats drank fortified milk—and suddenly grew larger and more powerful than their longtime canine nemeses.

In effect, the campaign presented images of a feline insurrection against dogs but did so without depicting any violence. Nor did the ads offer much in the way of explanation—the ideas were conveyed almost entirely through visual images (one of DM9's proven specialties is the ability to tell a story through still pictures). One ad shows a cat sitting majestically at the entrance to a doghouse; the name "Rex," above the doorway, has been scratched out, indicating that this particular battle has already been won. Another ad shows a dog, wide-eyed in terror; behind him on the wall, we can make out a giant cartoonish shadow of a cat's head. One of the most delightful ads is a DM9 picture-puzzle that is not immediately understandable unless you've

been following the campaign about the cat uprising; the ad simply shows a poodle dressed in widow's garb.

The overall campaign was such a resounding success that by the late 1990s, Parmalat had actually overtaken Coca-Cola and McDonald's as the most recognized and most popular brand among Brazilians. And don't expect its popularity to fade anytime soon. Perhaps the canniest aspect of this campaign is that it has begun to convert customers while they are still toddlers. Discussing the mammal-doll phenomenon with *Advertising Age* recently, Machado acknowledged, "Kids go to sleep cuddling your brand. That's the best branding you can have."

## BODDINGTONS

People may have been drinking less milk in America and Brazil, but when it came to Brits and beer, declining consumption was never an

17

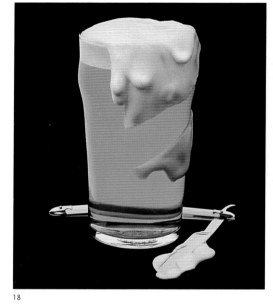

18

19

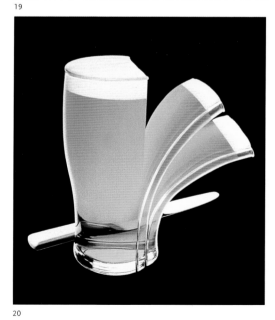

20

21

**BODDINGTONS BEER**
BARTLE BOGLE HEGARTY,
LONDON, 1991–98
BBH constructed three-
dimensional models that looked
like beer glasses transformed
into various creamy objects. The
images weren't explained; each
was a kind of visual puzzle
for the reader to figure out.
Counterclockwise from top left,
"Razor," "Strawberry & Cream,"
"Cream Slice," "Quiff" (Hair
Cream).

22. **BODDINGTONS BEER**
BARTLE BOGLE HEGARTY,
LONDON, 1996
Another image from the beer
glass campaign, "Cream Tea."

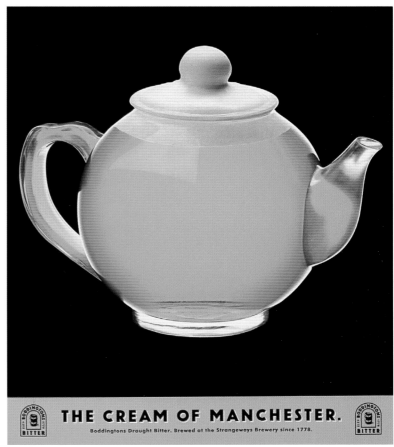

## THE CREAM OF MANCHESTER.
Boddingtons Draught Bitter. Brewed at the Strangeways Brewery since 1778.

22

issue. However, there were plenty of other problems to be faced when Bartle Bogle Hegarty was called upon to advertise an obscure little brew known as Boddingtons.

Though the 200-year-old beer had a faithful following in its hometown of Manchester, that wasn't sufficient for its new owner, the large Whitbread Beer Company—which had acquired the Boddingtons brewery with an ambitious plan to take the beer national. It fell upon Bartle Bogle Hegarty, Whitbread's trusted agency and one of the hottest creative ad shops in England in the 1980s, to pull this off against several obstacles. For one thing, recent history had shown that when big beer companies took over little breweries, they usually ended up ruining the beer—something the public was aware of. "So we had to deal with the assumption that the takeover might ruin this local beer, too," said Martin Smith, the deputy chairman of the BBH agency. At the same time, Smith said, the agency

had to balance two conflicting agendas: "We had to maintain the heritage and authenticity of the beer and at the same time, go national with it— fast. Add to that the fact that half the country didn't care for this kind of beer [known as northern bitter] to start with, and you had a pretty difficult situation."

The first thing client and agency did was venture into the pubs of Manchester to find out what people liked about this particular old beer. What they learned was that the northern English treasure a beer with a thick, creamy head— unlike the thin-headed, weaker variations favored by southerners. The good news for BBH was that Whitbread had new technologies that would enable Boddingtons to maintain its distinctively northern creaminess, even after it was packed up in cans and shipped down south. That settled it for BBH: The advertising would have to focus on creaminess.

Of course, Boddingtons wasn't the only

creamy beer—far from it. Any number of competitors could have staked out this territory beforehand, noted BBH's Steve Kershaw. But they never did. According to Kershaw, the other brewers had "forgotten about the product," focusing their advertising on "male bonding, talking about sex or football." BBH decided to swoop in on this opening. By "owning creami- ness" (advertisers tend to believe they can "own" anything if they just get there first), BBH was able to link various wonderful qualities to the beer—not just richness and freshness and flavor but other connotations of the word cream, such as quality, premium, "cream of the crop." The agency, its executives freely admit, got lucky when it stepped in cream.

Still, just saying your beer is creamy isn't going to impress people much, BBH realized. They had to do something original and evoca- tive with the theme. Quickly, the creative team started playing with images of cream and just

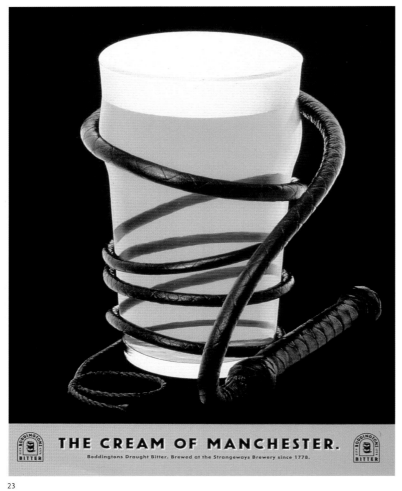

23

23 AND 24. **BODDINGTONS
BEER**
BARTLE BOGLE HEGARTY,
LONDON, 1996
Some of the "picture plays" in
the campaign were trickier than
others. "Whipping Cream"
(above) took a bit of work,
while "Hand Cream" (opposite)
was easier to figure out.

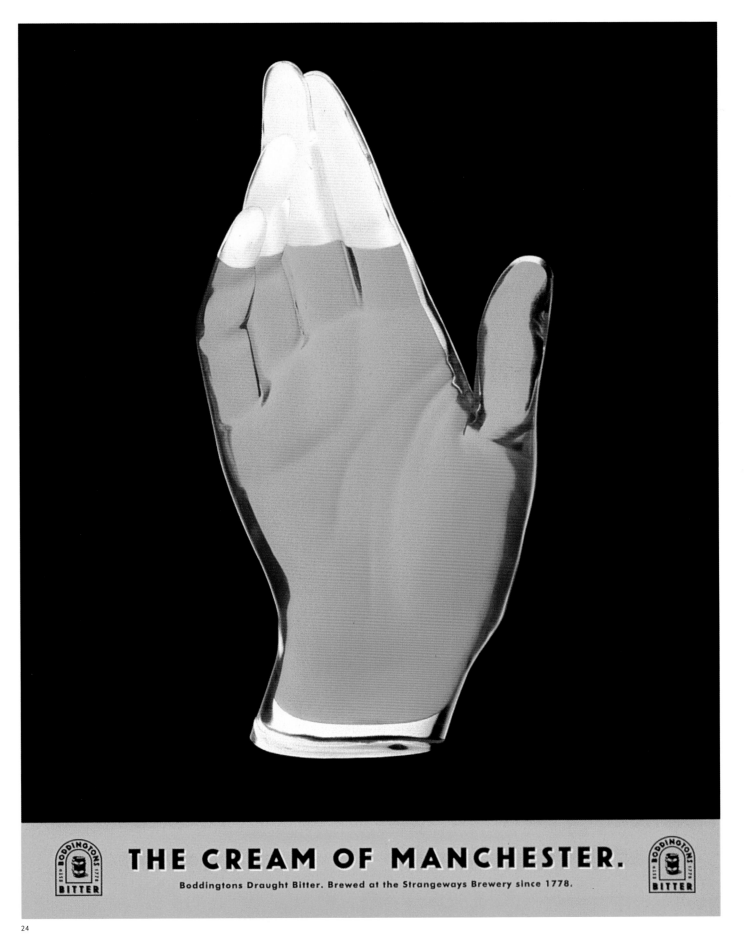

**THE CREAM OF MANCHESTER.**

Boddingtons Draught Bitter. Brewed at the Strangeways Brewery since 1778.

24

THE CREAM OF MANCHESTER.

Boddingtons Draught Bitter. Brewed at the Strangeways Brewery since 1778.

25

BODDINGTONS. THE CREAM OF MANCHESTER.

Boddingtons Draught Bitter. Brewed at the Strangeways Brewery since 1778.

26

one line of copy: "The cream of Manchester." (The agency didn't want people to forget where this beer came from.) That said, there wasn't much point in blathering on about creaminess—better to show than tell, BBH decided. What emerged from the drawing board was a series of playful images that substituted beer for cream: putting beer into an ice cream cone, pairing it with strawberries, turning it into shaving cream.

The picture riddles were undeniably clever, but within the agency, "there was dissension as to whether to present this to the client," said Smith. "It worked as a visual pun, but the taste expectations from some of these images were, frankly, a bit disgusting—who wants to eat a strawberry with a beer? And if you show a beer as shaving cream, does that mean it tastes like soap?" BBH creative director John Hegarty argued that the audience wouldn't draw those conclusions and would understand the game

being played in the ads. Still, just to be certain, the agency decided to get the opinion of real experts—which necessitated, of course, another run to the pub. "Our planner went in there and asked blokes what they thought of these pictures," said Smith (who admits the study "was ad hoc research—it wouldn't have stood up in a court of law"). Nevertheless, the reactions were exactly what BBH was hoping for: "They looked at it and said, 'Yeah, I get that,'" said Smith.

At this point, the BBH team began to feel they might be onto something big. "It was as if we'd created a whole new visual language," Smith said, "and suddenly every pun involving cream was open to us. The possibilities were endless." The agency explored them all, it seemed, from "cream tea" (beer poured in the shape of a teapot) to "cream cheese" (a glass of beer with Swiss-cheese holes in it). Part of what made the ads work was the richness and realism

of the images; rather than using illustrations or trick photography, BBH built lifelike models of the beer/cream objects, then photographed these creations against a dramatic black background. The result looked good enough to eat, or drink, though it was hard to tell which.

The finished work looked more like posters than magazine ads. But how to get those posters into the homes of millions? The agency purchased the back covers of Sunday newspaper magazines, and each week a different image appeared—then lay on kitchen tables or in cafés for days afterwards, inviting people to ponder the puzzle.

In 1992, within eighteen months of the campaign's debut, Boddingtons had become the number-one beer of its type in all of England. Meanwhile, the ads "became a kind of pop-culture art," said Smith, as well as a national pastime of sorts: Since the ads never actually explained the cream allusions being shown, it

**BODDINGTONS BEER**
BARTLE BOGLE HEGARTY,
LONDON, 1993–94
The beer glass was riddled
with holes for "Cream Cheese,"
and transformed into a cone for
"Ice Cream Cone." The glass
disappeared altogether for
"Vanishing Cream."

27

**DREAMS OF CREAM.**

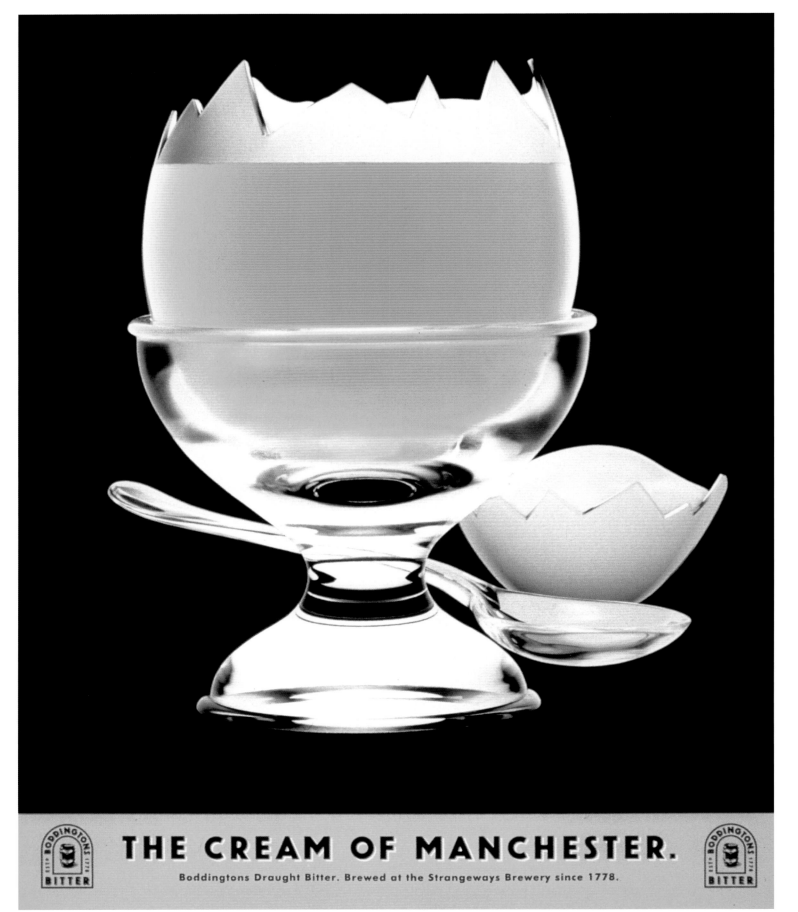

# THE CREAM OF MANCHESTER.

Boddingtons Draught Bitter. Brewed at the Strangeways Brewery since 1778.

29

28. **BODDINGTONS BEER**
BARTLE BOGLE HEGARTY,
LONDON, 1996
In a more complex image,
"Cream Egg ," the beer glass is
transformed into an egg cup
holding the creamy contents.

29. **BODDINGTONS BEER**
BARTLE BOGLE HEGARTY,
LONDON, 1994
In the commercial "Sun Cream,"
sunbathers are shown rubbing
the beer into their bodies;
another TV spot showed a
glamorous woman using it
as a face cream.

was left for the audience to figure out each one—and BBH kept making them a little harder to solve. "People liked it that way," said Smith. "They wanted to be challenged." One slightly kinky ad wrapped the beer glass with a cat-o'-nine-tails (whipped cream). Another had an all-black page, with no beer at all (vanishing cream, of course).

Gradually, the brewer, ecstatic with the success of the print campaign, wanted to bring it to life on television. The first commercial appeared in 1993, picking up on the print advertising's cream theme, but taking it in a quirky new direction. The spot starts out looking like a glamorous cosmetics commercial: A beautiful woman in an elegant setting is massaging her face with what appears to be face cream. Gradually we see that she's actually dipping her hand into a glass of Boddingtons, skimming off the creamy head, then rubbing it into her face. The commercial ends with her distinguished

tuxedo-clad paramour arriving, embracing her, and then declaring—in a completely incongruous broad cockney accent—"By 'eck, you smell gorgeous!" Subsequent spots pulled off equally effective spoofs of advertising for suntan cream and ice cream. The commercials were hip and postmodern enough to appeal to the most sophisticated viewers, but they were particularly well loved in the working-class pubs, where, Smith says, "You'd hear guys at the bar joking to each other, 'By 'eck, you smell gorgeous tonight!'" One more thing that made the commercials stand out: They featured women, something that just wasn't done in British beer ads (traditionally, beer advertising in the UK has almost always featured three men in a pub because, as the British adman Trevor Beattie once observed, "Four or more was a potential riot . . . two could only be a gay couple . . . and one was just sad!").

By the late 1990s, the Boddingtons

campaign was industry legend. In England, it was so recognizable that 84 percent of consumers could identify a Boddingtons ad without any name or logo. In the final stages of the campaign (Boddingtons finally stopped running it after nearly a decade, having finally exhausted the seemingly endless supply of cream puns), the advertiser was so confident of recognition that it did, in fact, pull its name off the ads, leaving just the picture and the "Cream of Manchester" line. "Everyone knew from the look that they were Bodd's ads," said Kershaw, so removing the brand name was one more way to "make the ads work harder and re-engage with the audience." It meant everyone now had to figure out not just the riddle but the identity of the advertiser. Most of them could do this easily, but it still made them feel quite clever, said Kershaw. "But of course, if you asked them they would say it was the ads that were clever. Funny how psychology works in cases like this."

12. TH
GLOBAL H

E NEW
OT SPOTS.

SOMEDAY, COMMUNISM WILL TAKE OVER CAPITALISM.

TILL THEN WE ALL NEED TO EAT.

HOUSE OF MAO

A REVOLUTIONARY RESTAURANT, NOODLE BAR AND CAFE AT CHINA SQUARE FOOD CENTRE. TEL: 5330660.

1

1. **HOUSE OF MAO
RESTAURANT**
OGILVY & MATHER,
SINGAPORE, LATE 1990s
Asian ads like this one reflect
the culture clash and political
shifts taking place in the region
as consumerism takes hold.

2. **ACTAL ANTACID**
OGILVY & MATHER,
SINGAPORE, MID-1980s
By the 1980s, Singapore adver-
tising was becoming increasingly
irreverent, and it was just as apt
to feature Western icons as
Eastern ones.

ACTAL PLUS
ANTI-FLATULENT ANTACID

NO WIND.

2

t was, perhaps, to be expected that the
ad revolution based in New York in the 1960s
would quickly spread to London and throughout
Europe; after all, the heavy interaction between
American and European cultural and business
communities almost guaranteed that the fever
would be transmitted. But how did this particular bug—whose symptoms included an
unshakable urge to apply conceptual thinking,
clever language, and stylistic design to the
selling of products—find its way to places like
Singapore or São Paulo?

In recent years, sophisticated advertising has
been bursting forth from somewhat unexpected
places, in locales far removed from the
advertising epicenters of New York and London.
No one has been more surprised by all of this
than American and European ad creators, who
had every right to assume that creative advertising
was a form they alone had mastered. In the past,
when advertising's creative cognoscenti gathered

annually on the French Riviera to select the
world's best ads at the International Advertising
Festival, the only real mystery each year was
"Would the most-honored ad agency be
American or British this time around?"

But by the mid-1990s, the party in Cannes
was being stormed by outsiders. They arrived
from Asia, South America, and Africa, unveiling
their elegantly simple and striking posters and
their thirty-second TV gems of humor and
pathos—all rooted in ideas and concepts that
needed no translation to connect with an
audience of any nationality. Increasingly in
recent award festivals, the outsiders won over
advertising's most discerning judges and ended
up taking many of the top creative trophies
home with them. More important, their work
was refreshingly different; it was rewriting some
of the rules of advertising communication and
demonstrating that ads from the other side of
the planet could, in fact, be bolder, more styl-

ized, and more innovative than what was being
produced by the most experienced practitioners
of the craft.

On one level, of course, this should have
come as no surprise; good ideas know no
boundaries and are apt to emerge anywhere and
everywhere. But at the same time, modern
creative advertising was a uniquely Western
creation. It had to be carried to far-off cultures
and then nurtured. The major agencies based in
America and Europe were, in many cases, the
ones that initially foisted the advertising culture
on countries with developing commercial
business markets. However, as these big ad-
agency networks put down roots in Asia, South
America, and elsewhere, they tended to export a
bland version of "global advertising" in the
1970s and 1980s. "International advertising was
a creative graveyard," said John Hegarty of the
British agency Bartle Bogle Hegarty. "Nobody
wanted to work on it, and most of the advertising

3

**3. BREAST CANCER
AWARENESS CAMPAIGN**
LEO BURNETT, SINGAPORE,
1997
A new candor in Asian ads: This
commercial shows men ogling
a woman's body, with the line,
"If only women examined their
breasts as much as men do."

**4. TOYOTA / BORNEO MOTORS**
SAATCHI & SAATCHI,
SINGAPORE, 1997
The boy in bubble wrap is
an image targeted at a new
generation of pampering parents.

produced was dull and creatively dead." Hegarty says that such ads "tended to overemphasize cultural differences," while missing the point that a good idea expressed a certain way can often transcend cultural differences.

There were exceptions, however. In a few scattered markets throughout Asia, South America, and Australia, a handful of creative "missionaries" were spreading the gospel of Bill Bernbach and David Ogilvy and the UK's Collett Dickenson Pearce—in effect, putting forth the notion that ads could be more compelling if they were stylish, unpredictable, and relatively candid with the public. In some regions, that philosophy was quickly seized upon by local writers and artists who, for the first time, began to see advertising as a place to express ideas.

Meanwhile, the regional barriers that had at first impeded the spread of the Creative Revolution began to dissolve as a new global culture emerged. The "McDonald's effect," as some called it, was more accurately "the MTV effect"—dominated not so much by big business as by American youth culture. By the mid-1990s, British ad executive Tim Delaney of Leagas Delaney had observed, "one culture is sweeping across the entire planet. It is the only game in town. Whether you go to India, Australia, or South America, agencies with a global perspective are selling American culture. It's going to be the only 'kids culture' in the future."

Delaney noted that the emergence of this common global youth culture played to the strengths of creative advertisers. "It has helped us to find shared interests among people around the world, and connect with them. The big ideas are beginning to work in a way that crosses borders. All of those old rules that made global advertising so dreadful—'Humor doesn't travel,' and so forth—make no sense when you're dealing with a world that is totally media-literate and plugged into one culture. More and more, if you

write great, simple, and true ads, the audience, no matter where they are, will reach for them and embrace them."

This one-world approach has been labeled "global consumer culture positioning" by the *Journal of Marketing*, and is based on the idea of "associating a brand with a widely understood and recognized set of symbols." Put simply, it explains why images of Michael Jordan and Marilyn Monroe show up not just in American ads but in Asian and South American ones, too. As the new advertising popping up in regional "hot spots" around the world has become increasingly multicultural, it is often relying more on visual images than language—enabling the ads to move easily from one country to another. In these markets, "advertisers are realizing they have to live beyond their own borders," said BBH's Hegarty. "Agencies in these places find themselves with a client saying, 'Listen, our ads are going to have to run in eight

**Corolla. For overprotective parents.**
Dual airbags, self-tensioning seat belts, collapsible steering column, energy-absorbing reinforcements in the roof-side rails and pillars, side impact protection beams, rigid passenger safety cell, ABS and shatter-resistant glass. ⊕TOYOTA

4

THE NEW GLOBAL HOT SPOTS.

VISA GOLD. He who has the gold makes the rules.

5

6

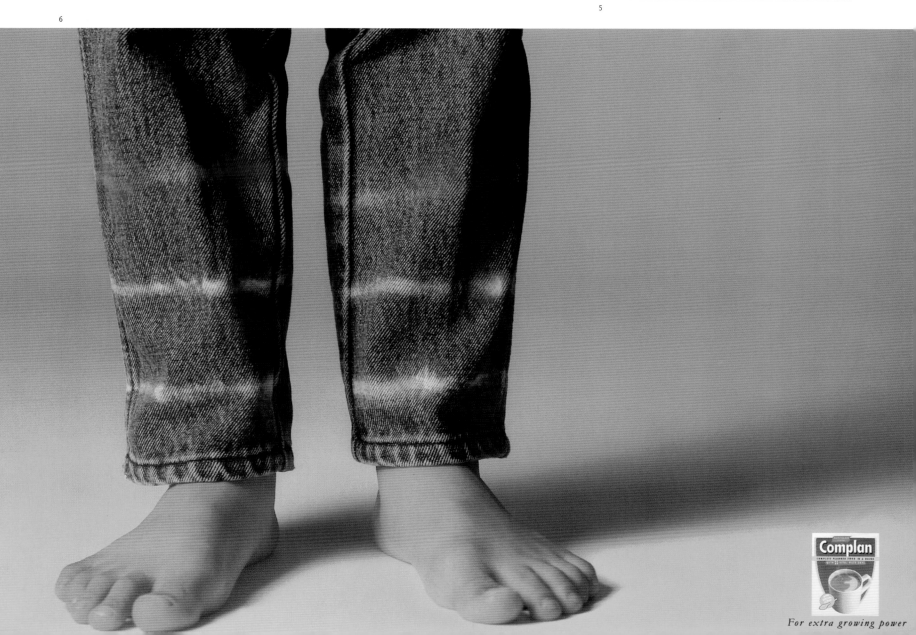

*For extra growing power*

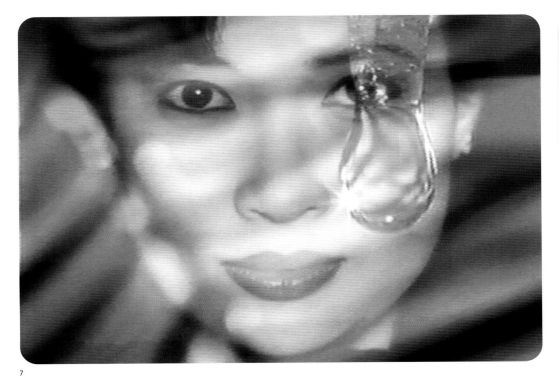

7

**5. VISA GOLD**
BATEY ADS, SINGAPORE, 1996
With the widespread availability
of credit cards in Asia, new
attitudes came to the fore. This
mid-1990s campaign promoted
self-indulgence.

**6. COMPLAN**
CHAITRA LEO BURNETT,
MUMBAI, 1998
Ads in India have tended to be
highly visual; this one makes
its point without a word of
body copy.

**7. SINGAPORE AIRLINES**
BATEY ADS, SINGAPORE, 1994
The "Singapore Girl" campaign
promoting the airline's hostesses
has portrayed women in a
traditional subservient role,
though recent ads have taken
a more modern approach.

different markets, and they all speak different languages.' You have to find a way of reaching all those people, while still creating advertising that communicates to a very advertising-literate young audience." As a growing number of international ad agencies have risen to this challenge, a handful of countries in particular have emerged as new creative hot spots on the continents of Asia, South America, Australia, and Africa.

## ASIA

Asian advertising, which is still relatively young and growing up fast, can confound one's expectations at every turn. In a part of the world often associated with traditionalism and conformity, it's not uncommon to find an ad in Hong Kong or Bangkok that challenges convention, attacks stereotypes, advocates individuality—and flashes some skin, too. (Although in mainland China, some restrictions

remain; recent ads have been censored for mentioning politics or showing women in miniskirts.) But for the most part, ads in Asia increasingly celebrate—indeed, revel in—the consumer culture of spending, status symbols, and self-indulgence. Such ads can seem strangely disconnected from traditional Asian values, as well as from the codes of conduct associated with some Asian countries' Communist history. But in many parts of Asia, including China, attitudes began to change as the public got its first taste of real consumerism in the early 1990s: Branded consumer products flooded in from the West, credit cards became available, the Asian media expanded—all of which helped fuel a burgeoning Asian consumer class.

Naturally, advertising is pouring as much fuel on this fire as it possibly can. But the best Asian advertising does so with a light touch and an awareness of local culture and history. As one restaurant ad from O&M Singapore recently

declared, "Someday Communism will take over Capitalism. Till then, we all need to eat."

Singapore has been at the forefront of creative advertising in Asia. Because the former British colony has had a heavy Western influence and a substantial English-speaking population for some time, it was a natural entry point, along with Hong Kong, for Western advertisers trying to penetrate the Asian marketplace. As a number of agencies put down roots in the early 1970s, Ogilvy & Mather, and in particular the O&M creative director Neil French, seemed to have the most formative effect. "The map in Singapore was changed by Neil French," observed the Asian ad writer Kash Sree. Prior to French's arrival, the local advertising "was all about not making waves," said Sree. "But French brought an irreverent English sensibility." In a very proper society, French's ads spoke candidly about human behavior ranging from sex to flatulence.

8

**8. PETROLEUM AUTHORITY
OF THAILAND**
LEO BURNETT, BANGKOK,
1996
Thai advertising has shown a
quirky wild streak; this TV
commercial, "Lead Devils,"
featured silver transvestites
who invade gasoline tanks.

**9. IKEA**
DENTSU YOUNG & RUBICAM,
SINGAPORE, LATE 1990s
Humor is not used as widely in
Asian ads as it is in the West,
but certain targets and situations
are always ripe for laughs—one
being the dreaded mother-in-law.

He also started mining the local talent base, and found a treasure trove of "local writers who'd been unable to really express themselves in advertising before," said Sree. At the same time, an influx of talented ad creators from Australia and India arrived in Singapore; one was the Australian Ian Batey, who, along with his compatriot Jim Aitchison, turned a Singapore start-up called Batey Ads into a creative powerhouse. All of the Singapore agencies operated on relatively modest budgets; that necessitated an emphasis on print advertising and strong, simple ideas. Some of the advertising had a traditional flavor to it; for example, Batey Ads created one of the most enduring advertising icons to come out of Asia, "the Singapore girl," for Singapore Airlines.

But what's surprising is some of the less conventional attitudes and messages that regularly surface in Singapore advertising. Just as Western ads are urging consumers to "break

the rules" and assert their individuality, you can find a similar noncomformist message in the ads of Singapore—where it takes more backbone to make such a statement. A Visa Gold campaign from Batey Ads encourages all sorts of tiny rebellious acts such as putting caviar on your hot dog (the point being "I have money and I shall do as I damn well please"). One recent Singapore ad for a hair salon even took a postmodern, ironic approach to praising individuality: "When you have groovy hair," the headline declared, "it doesn't matter that you've zero originality."

At the same time, a feminist sensibility has been creeping into many Asian ads. Leo Burnett in Singapore, whose creative director is a woman, Linda Locke, recently produced a campaign for Raffles City stores with headlines like "Heels don't make women taller. They make men shorter." Another campaign from the same agency, for breast cancer awareness, shows a

woman on her way to work and encountering men who constantly ogle her cleavage. The point of the ad: "If only women examined their breasts as much as men do."

One can offend audiences easily in Asia without realizing it, Kash Sree points out; he recalls a Singapore promotional campaign that involved giving out green hats—which seemed innocent enough, except that to the local culture the green hats were associated with cuckoldry. And using humor can be a risky proposition. "Self-deprecation is not an Asian trait," according to Batey. "Asians want to gain face, not lose it. If you surround your brand with negative irony, they will walk away in droves. Call your car a lemon, for example, and the Asian grapevine will spread the word that it's for losers." Batey noted, however, that certain situations and targets are always ripe for laughs—one being the dreaded mother-in-law. Dentsu Young & Rubicam in Singapore scored big with an Ikea

# There's more than one way to hang your mother-in-law

In appreciation of her contribution to family harmony, IKEA suggest you put the good woman in her proper place.

After all, with a wide selection of frames in all shapes and sizes, you're bound to find one that fits your favourite subject.

Be it a large poster frame in loud colours to brighten up the bedroom. Or a dainty design in soft shades to liven up the living room. IKEA has a frame for every corner and for every pocket. It's really the simplest way to personalise your home.

However, if you don't have a mother-in-law to frame, you could always hang yourself.

**$9** FIFFIG frame, 9 x 9 cm, unfinished wood

### Freeze Frame
Bring your mother-in-law for a free 50 x 70 cm caricature by Einstein, this Saturday and Sunday (2pm to 6pm, 1st Level, Market Hall) and she could go home rather animated.

### Aspiring Picassos
A chance for kids 10 and below to show off their talent this Saturday and Sunday (12 noon to 6pm, 2nd Level). All they have to do is draw a family portrait. And they'll receive a little gift from IKEA, on top of a chance to win a $30 IKEA gift voucher. All winning drawings will be displayed in the atrium. Framed, of course.

### Salmon Blitz
What better way to end a visit to our gallery then digging into our simply irresistible Norwegian salmon dishes, available at special prices till 23 June. Savour Baked Salmon, Salmon Pudding, Gravad Lox and Salmon Sandwiches at prices between $2.50 to $5.50 at Restaurant & Café IKEA.

**$69** ROMB poster frame, 70 x 100 cm, solid wood, assorted colours

**$45** STAFFLI floor easel, H208 cm, solid wood

**$19** JUFFE frame, 10 x 15 cm, brown

**$15½/2-pc** CADJA picture frame, 9 x 13 cm, 8.5 x 8.5 cm, multi-coloured

**$15** RULJANGS frame, 18 x 24 cm, brown, solid wood

**$11** REM frame, 18 x 24 cm

**$3⁵⁰/3-pk** RAKET frame, 10 x 15 cm, unfinished solid wood

**$19/each** POSTERS 70 x 100 cm, assorted designs
**$15/each** POSTERS 50 x 70 cm, assorted designs
**$12⁵⁰/each** POSTERS 40 x 50 cm, assorted designs

**$55** RESPONS poster frame, 70 x 100 cm, gold or silver

**$18** TIDDUBBEL picture light, white, brass or black

**$14** RATT triple frame, 10 x 15 cm, unfinished wood

**$14** CLIPS rimless frame with clips, 40 x 50 cm

**$9⁶⁰** MADDE frame, 9 x 13 cm, multi-coloured

**$9⁹⁰/2-pk** REKORD frame, 13 x 18 cm, gold or silver

**$9** RAMSA collage frame, outlay dimension 40 x 50 cm, dark red

**$6** RASTA frame, 13 x 18 cm, solid wood

**$5/3-pc** FLUKT frame, 8 x 12 cm, 3.5 x 4 cm, assorted colours

**$19** BATTIS double frame, 10 x 15 cm, assorted colours

**$11** RINGEN cardboard frame, 10 x 15 cm

**$8/4-pk** BLUDDER frame, 3 x 5 cm, assorted colours

## IKEA GALLERY WEEKS • FROM NOW TILL 23 JUNE
### IKEA®
OPENING HOURS: 10AM TO 10PM. 317 ALEXANDRA ROAD, SINGAPORE 159965 TEL: 4740122

9

# INTERVIEW: KITTY LUN

As the former creative director of Euro RSCG's renowned Hong Kong agency, Kitty Lun was one of the most respected creative leaders in Asian advertising and one of the highest-ranking female executives in the region. With a flair for design and a willingness to take on controversial themes (her ads for Chinese modern art shocked some in the Hong Kong ad community), Lun represents a new generation of Asian ad creators who are helping to modernize advertising throughout the continent.

**WOULD YOU SAY ASIAN ADVERTISING HAS HAD A CREATIVE REVOLUTION OF ITS OWN IN RECENT YEARS?**
Yes, in different places and at different times. Thailand was one of the first Asian markets to awaken to the need for its own creative style. In the 1980s, a unique brand of Thai advertising emerged with emphasis on local culture and Thai humor. During that time, Hong Kong and Singapore were supposed to be the most sophisticated ad markets, but the style in those two countries was very much influenced by the West. Global clients ruled. Even ads developed locally took on the globally accepted formulas. I am not saying there was no great creative work—but it lacked a unique local culture. Most creative directors in Hong Kong and Singapore were expatriates. So Thailand's revolution came as a breath of fresh air. After Thailand came Taiwan. A new style emerged there—very unique, highly art-directed and MTV-ish, with messages always focused on social issues. Western rational approach was not emphasized. The revolutions I'm referring to are a departure from conventional Western wisdom of what an ad, or an idea, should look like. They represent a completely different-thinking path, a kind of Oriental way of thinking. Usually not linear and not rational, hence very lateral and amazing. The next market to watch would be China.

**A LOT OF ADVERTISING AROUND THE WORLD, ESPECIALLY PRINT, HAS BECOME VERY SIMPLE AND VISUAL—OFTEN USING ONE STRIKING IMAGE WITH FEW WORDS. HAS THIS CAUGHT ON IN ASIAN ADVERTISING?**
Yes, especially in Singapore and Hong Kong. Singapore consumers are very sophisticated and can understand the simplicity and can draw their own conclusion with minimum clues given. Also, Singapore was groomed by a group of very sophisticated admen from the West who favored this kind of approach. And when done cleverly, these ads win awards easily—hence attracting younger creatives to do more of the same.

**AMERICAN ADVERTISING HAS COME TO FEATURE MORE WILD SCENARIOS, BIZARRE CHARACTERS, OFFBEAT MESSAGES—"ODDVERTISING." DOES THIS KIND OF APPROACH WORK IN THE ASIAN MARKETS? THE COMMON PERCEPTION IS THAT THE AUDIENCE THERE MIGHT BE MORE CONSERVATIVE.**
Japan was probably one of the first to use Oddvertising. Years ago, Japanese advertising started to catch the eye of the world, with award-winning Cup Noodles commercials—not much of a strategy, very left-field, very unusual. And Thailand and Taiwan are very used to this kind of offbeat approach—even more so than the West. Many people have a perception that China is a conservative market. However, time and again, the consumers surprise us. After all, a piece of communication is more than just science. It is art that appeals to the emotion, the soul, the aesthetics. Chinese consumers react mostly the same ways as consumers around the world. They react with their hearts. They may not be as worldly, because the country was not exposed to the outside world in the last century. But being such a virgin market, they are even more open to unusual ideas.

**IS IT UNUSUAL FOR A WOMAN TO BE A TOP AD EXECUTIVE IN ASIA?**
Actually, I find the opportunities are good. The best person gets the job, period. In fact, we find a higher proportion of women in top creative and management positions in Hong Kong, Taiwan, and China than in the U.S. and in Europe. With advertising being seen as a "soft" business, it is a female-dominated industry over here.

**WHAT ABOUT PORTRAYALS OF WOMEN IN CHINESE ADS—WOULD YOU SAY THEY ARE PROGRESSIVE OR MORE OLD-FASHIONED AND TRADITIONAL?**
The answer is both. The portrayal of business-women is pretty progressive, and comparable to anywhere in the world. However, there is still a large number of ads portraying women as the "plaything." It was particularly true a few years back when cognac and beer were big players in the industry. Also, in traditional household products like cooking oil, rice, and detergent, women are still confined to the standard good-housewife image. For cosmetics, shampoo, and other beauty products, women are still portrayed as trying to look their best for their men. Apart from being a social and sexist issue, it is also a creative issue—it's about finding new ways to represent the users of these products.

**OBVIOUSLY, MANY AMERICAN ADS ARE BASED ON THE IDEA OF PEOPLE TREATING THEMSELVES WELL AND INDULGING DESIRES FOR EXPENSIVE THINGS. DO CHINESE ADS TEND TO HAVE CERTAIN ATTITUDES ABOUT SHOWING WEALTH AND SELF-INDULGENCE— MIGHT THAT BE CONSIDERED INAPPROPRIATE IN SOME ASIAN CULTURES?**
No, it is extremely appropriate. This is the market for conspicuous spending and indulgence. The higher the price tag, the bigger the "face." It is always glorified as "aspiration"—and the ad agencies are often forced to present products in a light much superior to what they really are. Categories that do this include real estate, selling dreams rather than homes; luxury goods— watches, jewelry, designer labels like the rest of the world; self-indulgent products like chocolates, airlines, and hotels. Advertising people often struggle to present things in a more earthy, back-to-basics light. But it is very seldom that clients have the insight to portray the true value of the products. However, that situation is improving now.

Roger Daly. Age 67.
Retired milkman.

10

11

**10. AUSTRALIAN MILK ASSOCIATION**
CLEMENGER, MELBOURNE, 1998
This risqué Australian campaign used sex to sell milk, portraying the milkman as a door-to-door Romeo. The milk is what keeps his juices flowing.

**11. KADU CLOTHING**
ANDROMEDA, SYDNEY, 1994
Shocking imagery has been part of Australian advertising for years; this ad showed a disemboweled shark, whose contents included a human skeleton.

ad for picture frames, showing a wall filled with photographs, in a variety of frames, all containing the same scowling woman's face; it was headlined, "There's more than one way to hang your mother-in-law."

A couple of places in Asia where humor is more welcome and usually wilder are Thailand and Japan. In the past few years, Thailand has earned a reputation for quirky outrageousness in its commercials, which have been known to feature spontaneous kung fu brawls, slapstick humor, and even silver-painted transvestites (known as the Lead Devils, these characters created by the Bangkok office of Leo Burnett invade cars filled with the wrong type of gasoline, and can be dispatched only by fueling up with the right kind of gasoline). According to Rutaiwan Wongsirasawad, creative director at JWT in Bangkok, "You can make fun of the product, of yourself—nothing is out of bounds." Even the country's military leaders aren't shielded

from the barbs of advertisers; in one popular commercial from Bangkok's Results agency, an army general tries to talk a kidnapper into giving up his hostage—and ends up getting a hole blown in his stomach. Then, a working-class hero named "tractor man" comes to the rescue in his Mitsubishi tractor, which plows right into the kidnappers' hideaway. Bhanu Inkawat, regarded as one of the creative leaders of Thai advertising, says the wild humor in ads "is based on the comic-book and slapstick-comedy style we grew up with. You can see this kind of entertainment everywhere, in the coffee shops across the country, on the TV game shows."

The advertising of Thailand has been compared to that of Japan, which is known for bursts of wild humor and outrageous antics—though Japanese advertising can also be subtle and stylish. In either case, Japanese ads have long tended to favor emotional appeals, fantasies, and soft sell, rather than straightforward

sales pitches. Having embraced industrialization and capitalism relatively early, Japan was well ahead of other countries in Asia when it came to mastering the craft of advertising; in fact, it had its own ad creative revolution back in the mid-1960s, just a few years after the American one. Subsequently, Japanese ads became very image-oriented—they tended to promote the company, not the product itself, and gently tried to forge bonds of goodwill. Critics from abroad often said that Japanese ads didn't sell at all, but Jun Yoshitake, a top executive at the Dentsu agency, explains that for Japanese consumers, who have a strong tendency toward brand loyalty, the soft sell was often preferable. Hard-sell pitches could be seen as a form of bragging.

In recent years, Japanese ads have lost some of their stylishness, and have come to rely more on celebrities and on quick sales pitches packed into the now-popular fifteen-second commercial

12

format. Yoshitake attributes this to the economic downturn in Japan, which pressured advertisers to gravitate toward hard sell. But there are still bright spots and surprises, as in the slapstick humor of a long-running campaign that always ends with the bizarrely enthusiastic exclamation "Hungry? PotNoodles!" And a recent Dentsu commercial for a cable movie channel shows there's still room for lively storytelling. The commercial opens with a dinner scene in which a Japanese expatriate in America informs his blonde girlfriend that he must return to Japan immediately. In an overly dramatic manner, he slowly journeys back to his homeland, while we hear his girlfriend screaming over and over, "Why? Why?" In the end, the truth is revealed: He's gone back because he misses the Wowow TV channel.

If Japan is slumping creatively these days, other Asian countries are picking up the slack. India, for example, produces lively commercials

that borrow heavily from the country's thriving "Bollywood" film industry and tend to feature "lots of music, chaos, and beautiful women," Aitchison observes. Kash Sree adds, "Whereas jingles have lost their power in the West, you can sell almost anything with a song in India." India has also served as a rich source of English-language copywriters for Asia. The country that gave us Salman Rushdie (a onetime advertising writer himself, before he gave the craft up for novels) has also produced a host of other copywriting stars, who "have beaten a path to Hong Kong and Singapore," Aitchison notes, because they can earn much more money there than back in India.

Many believe the next stage in the evolution of Asian advertising will be a rediscovery of local culture. After a decade of trying to copy and learn from Western advertising, says Inkawat, the Asian ad community is now feeling more confident and secure in its own identity. He

thinks that will be reflected more and more in the Asian ads created in days ahead. "I believe every country is now looking inward for its inspiration, for insights and stories from its own culture, rather than looking toward the U.S. or England like before," said Inkawat. "It's a good sign of progress."

## AUSTRALIA

Down Under, they're still talking about the dancing penis. An Australian commercial featuring a singing, dancing penis (promoting a gay radio station in Sydney) not only attracted attention locally but ended up stealing the show at a recent gathering of the International Advertising Festival in Cannes. It wasn't the first time that those randy and mischievous Australians had shocked the international ad community.

Each year, it seems, Australian advertising pushes the boundaries of good taste a little farther, which recently prompted one Australian

WHAT THE BITCH WHO'S ABOUT TO STEAL YOUR MAN WEARS.

13

hey! sister• by Bendon

MADE FOR HUMANS

14

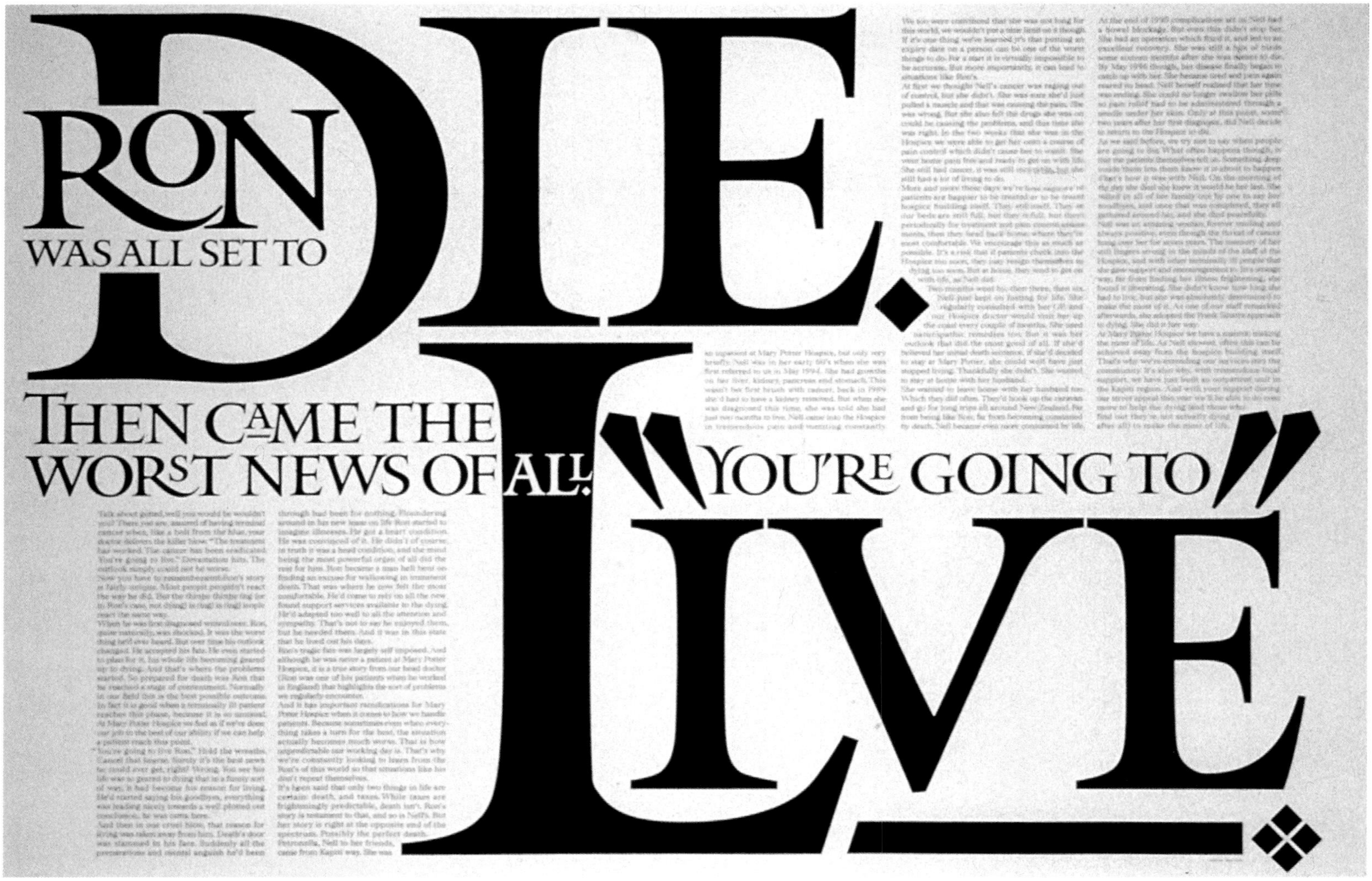

DIE.

RON WAS ALL SET TO

THEN CAME THE WORST NEWS OF ALL. "YOU'RE GOING TO LIVE"

16

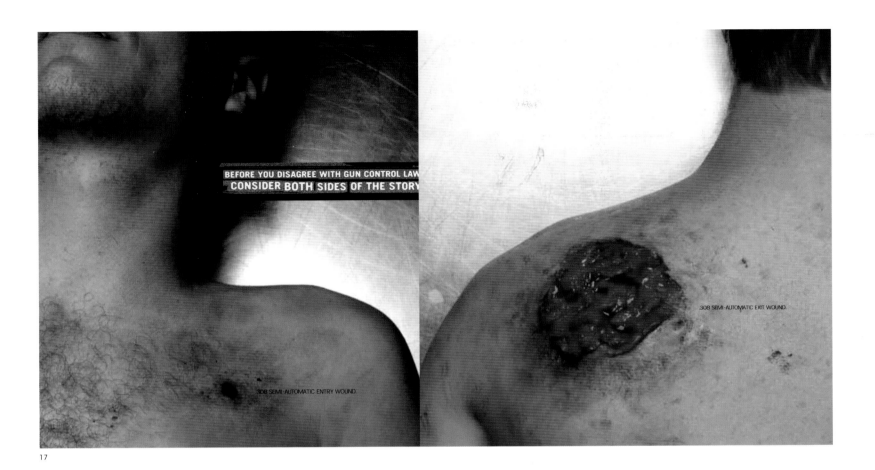

BEFORE YOU DISAGREE WITH GUN CONTROL LAW
CONSIDER **BOTH** SIDES OF THE STORY

.308 SEMI-AUTOMATIC ENTRY WOUND.

.308 SEMI-AUTOMATIC EXIT WOUND.

17

expatriate, Paul Bernasconi, to wonder aloud in an *Advertising Age* editorial, "Why is Australian advertising so hilariously obnoxious? How do they get away with it?"

The examples abound, as Bernasconi pointed out. An infamous commercial from Campaign Palace featured a semi-naked girl who rids her underwear of ants with the help of an aggressive anteater. Another showed a transvestite cleaning a public toilet, then declaring it "fit for a queen." One of Bernasconi's favorites: "a beer commercial showing a man in a confessional box tricking a priest into revealing the names of wayward women."

Even the most wholesome of products, milk, is promoted with a healthy dose of sexual innuendo in Australia. A hugely popular ad campaign from the Clemenger Melbourne agency features a spry 67-year-old retired milkman who continues to make his rounds— but it's not milk he's delivering to the house-

wives at each stop. Another ad in the series acknowledges the cliché of the milkman as door-to-door Romeo, and points out, "It was never the postman, always the milkman." The only explanation for this, the ads suggest, is the power of milk.

When not using outrageous or risqué humor, Australian ads have been known to feature shockingly gritty scenes: An award-winning print ad for Kadu clothing company showed a photograph of a disemboweled shark, with the ingredients of its stomach (including a human skeleton) spilling out on the ground. And a long-running series of commercials promoting traffic safety, from Grey Advertising in Melbourne, presents some of the most devastatingly realistic simulations of car accidents ever seen on television—showing not only the bone-jarring collisions but also the ensuing bloodshed and tears in the hospital emergency room.

It's not entirely clear why Australian

advertising has tended to be so bold and occasionally shocking. Bernasconi theorized, "Australia is an island, physically and culturally. And as such, within a very short time, Australians have developed into a breed apart. We have our own sense of humor. . . . We brandish our crudeness like a sword, repelling the creeping sameness, the choking homogeneity of the rest of the English-speaking world. We wear vulgarity and brashness like a badge, declaring to the world that we will not be Canadianized. And as America and Britain continue to dominate the global conversation, we make our voice heard by behaving like the spoiled bastard child that we are. . . . We misbehave."

Whether the contributing factors are geography, genetics, or something else, Australian ads have been attention-grabbers since the local ad creative community first started to take shape, back in the early 1970s, under the guidance of Lionel Hunt, who came

The world's never going to be like this.
Lose weight with Sanavita.

Sanavita. You'll eat less and
lose weight healthily.

18

from the UK and helped set up the pioneering creative agency Campaign Palace. From the outset, the advertising was—and to some extent remains—derivative of the English irreverent style. As Rob Dow of Grey Melbourne said, "Australians tend to follow the UK style with subtle wit rather than the belly laugh." At the same time, Australian advertising was also heavily influenced by America, which may have contributed to its brassy, in-your-face sensibility.

The frankness of Australian ads extends beyond sex or blood and guts. Ads to women have tended to be refreshingly candid. One award-winning fashion ad from a few years back bore the provocative headline "What the bitch who's about to steal your man wears." Another, for the body-pillow mattress, engaged in a bit of playful male-bashing by describing the product as "the perfect male substitute. Warm, cuddly, and totally brainless." And advertisers in the region have been willing to challenge the beauty

myth: the New Zealand underwear marketer Bendon created a campaign featuring young models who bore the scars of real life, including a woman with her arm in a plaster cast and using an asthma inhaler. The advertiser said that local teens "do not necessarily relate to the cover girl and supermodel look. . . . The images they find most powerful are those closer to their own individual reality."

A surprising level of candor about race can be seen in some Australian commercials. In pitching suntan lotion, Young & Rubicam in Sydney featured black characters who are amused by the fact that Caucasians get burned in the sun and need sunscreen "to get the protection the black man has naturally." After one character concludes, only half-jokingly, that "Mother Nature must be black," the commercial closes with the ironic tag line "For whites who want equality."

Though the public seems to enjoy provocative ads, there is the occasional backlash.

For example, a Johnson & Johnson TV campaign for Meds tampons seemed innocuous enough; the ads posed the question "What tampon does your lady use?" and showed men reacting in various ways—some grimace at the query; some laugh; some actually answer the question ("Meds. If she's busy, I buy them for her," said one very progressive fellow). Yet the campaign was pulled from the air after a barrage of complaints—mostly from women. And the Australian Standards Council called the ads "a bit gauche."

Australian advertising's brashness is tempered by a sense of style; the region is known for its elegant design, particularly in New Zealand—which is heavily influenced by the Australian culture but at the same time exhibits its own flair. The agency Saatchi & Saatchi in Wellington has specialized in arresting imagery that seems to scream out its messages. Its work includes an eye-opening type treatment for a

THE ABUSE YOU YELL
AT YOUR KIDS STAYS IN THE
FAMILY FOR GENERATIONS

You're useless. You're dumb. I wish you'd never been born. Shout verbal abuse like this at your kids and you don't just hurt them, you teach them to be abusive parents too. Break the cycle. Call 0800 222 999 for a free parenting booklet that will help.

NEW ZEALAND
CHILDREN & YOUNG PERSONS
SERVICE

HONDA 97.

WHERE MY HEAD
WAS AT WHEN I DECIDED
TO BUY A HONDA.

**HONDA**
A WORLD OF EXCITEMENT

20. **HONDA**
DM9 DDB PUBLICIDADE,
SÃO PAULO, 1997
Selling a motorcycle by showing
a train: DM9 focuses not on the
product itself but the feelings
associated with it.

21

local hospice, as well as a child-abuse ad that features a screaming mouth within a screaming mouth within a screaming mouth, and the headline "The abuse you yell at your kids stays in the family for generations." Even more than Australia, New Zealand is a cost-conscious ad market, and there's little opportunity for elaborate Hollywood-style production and special effects. Given those limitations, says Saatchi New Zealand art director John Fisher, "a strong idea becomes even more important here, because it can get the job done even if the production values aren't quite where you'd want them to be in an ideal world."

## SOUTH AMERICA

In the 1990s, South America, and particularly Brazil, fell madly in love with advertising. Suddenly, commercials were being passionately discussed in bars. Students who formerly might have opted for a career in medicine or

engineering now wanted to make ads. And award-winning admen became local celebrities, "granted the status of pop stars," observed the veteran Brazilian adman Washington Olivetto.

The love affair has, over the past few years, produced a body of creative advertising that has been sweeping international award shows and introducing a new language in the ad world. As befits the region it springs from, South American advertising tends to be bold, colorful, emotional, and playful. But what is perhaps most striking about it is the economy with which it communicates big ideas. The advertising produced by São Paulo's DM9 DDB Publicidade, the preeminent agency in the region over the past few years, often conveys emotion through one simple image: A picture of ketchup coming out of a bottle is all that's needed, in one ad, to suggest that this particular condiment will set your mouth ablaze. And the agency used nothing more than a picture of a

man trying to squeeze out of a car door in a tight parking space to make its case for a diet soft drink.

When asked why his ads invariably tried to say so much by saying so little, DM9's longtime creative director Nizan Guanaes blamed it on Brazil. "I live in a simple country," Guanaes said, noting that Brazilians have no desire to wade through tedious explanation and no tolerance for ads that take themselves too seriously. "No one here wants to spend a lot of time reading an ad," Guanaes said. "They want to know immediately what it is about."

That may explain the prevalence of visual riddles and puns in South American advertising, running the gamut from subtle and emotional (a car key being passed from one hand to another in a Volkswagen ad headlined "Forever") to obvious and a bit tacky (a Colgate mouthwash ad that turns a human mouth into a toilet seat). There is another explanation for all of these ads:

Drink Diet Guarand.

They tend to fare well at international award shows and have reaped top prizes for the agencies that created them. "In the 1990s some professionals, eager to be well renowned, started producing advertising for festivals only," said Olivetto, who runs the Brazilian agency W/Brasil. The hallmark of such ads, he noted, is their tendency to be "preeminently visual, easily understandable in any language, but inappropriate to the Brazilian reality. I myself consider this to be extremely bad and unreal, so much so that I have labeled this 'ghost advertising.' "

Olivetto's opinion on such matters cannot be discounted, considering that he is regarded as South America's creative ad pioneer, the Bill Bernbach of Brazil. He served as creative director at the agency DPZ, which first began draw attention in the late 1970s and early 1980s with advertising that blended humor, emotion, and sensuousness—traits that are "typical of the Brazilian people," Olivetto said. While Olivetto

and his peers were developing their own approach, they also drew on the influences of Doyle Dane Bernbach as well as British advertising. The blending of these all of these styles, Olivetto said, "gave birth to a type of advertising that aims at selling but is also conscious that entertainment is necessary."

Olivetto, after moving on to form W/Brasil, also helped to train a new generation of South American creative leaders, including the young copywriter Guanaes. During the 1980s, Guanaes was already experimenting with a postmodern style of advertising that seemed light-years ahead of the kinds of ads previously seen in South America. One of his ad campaigns for a local bank parodied other hyperbolic commercials by using the character of a bank spokesman who made boastful claims about the bank; as it became clear he was exaggerating, the character desperately tried to cover up and make excuses. Guanaes was practicing "anti-advertising"

before most of his peers had even grasped straightforward advertising.

Guanaes was just one of a handful of talented young creative leaders who were poised to take the mantle from Olivetto in the 1990s. As both creative fervor and entrepreneurial fever began to rage in Brazil, a third factor fueled the 1990s ad revolution—the Brazilian economy, which had suffered through years of hyperinflation, kicked into gear in the mid-1990s and created a thriving consumer market. Brazil emerged as one of the top-selling markets in the world for a vast array of consumer products, from beer to detergent to TV sets. By the mid-1990s, *Advertising Age* noted, "global marketers rushed in to win the hearts and wallets of Brazilian consumers."

These big agency outsiders from America and Europe—including the Saatchis, BBDO, and the DDB network—realized the way to do that was to align themselves with Brazil's most talented admen. That led to the formation of

Those who destroy forests

don't only kill trees.

To help or join,
**call:** (0xx11) 887-1195
**fax:** (0xx11) 885-1680
**Internet:**
www.matatlantica.org.br
**e-mail:**
amata@ax.apc.org

**FUNDAÇÃO S.O.S. MATA ATLÂNTICA**

23

Those who destroy forests
don't only kill trees.

To help or join,
cell: (0xx11) 887-1195
fax: (0xx11) 885-1680
Internet:
www.matatlantica.org.br
e-mail:
amata@ax.apc.org

FUNDAÇÃO S.O.S. MATA ATLÂNTICA

24

23 AND 24. **SAVE THE
FOREST CAMPAIGN**
F/NAZCA SAATCHI & SAATCHI,
SÃO PAULO, 1998
The campaign could have shown
trees, or it could have shown
endangered animals; by showing
animals carved from trees, the
image is far more striking
and effective.

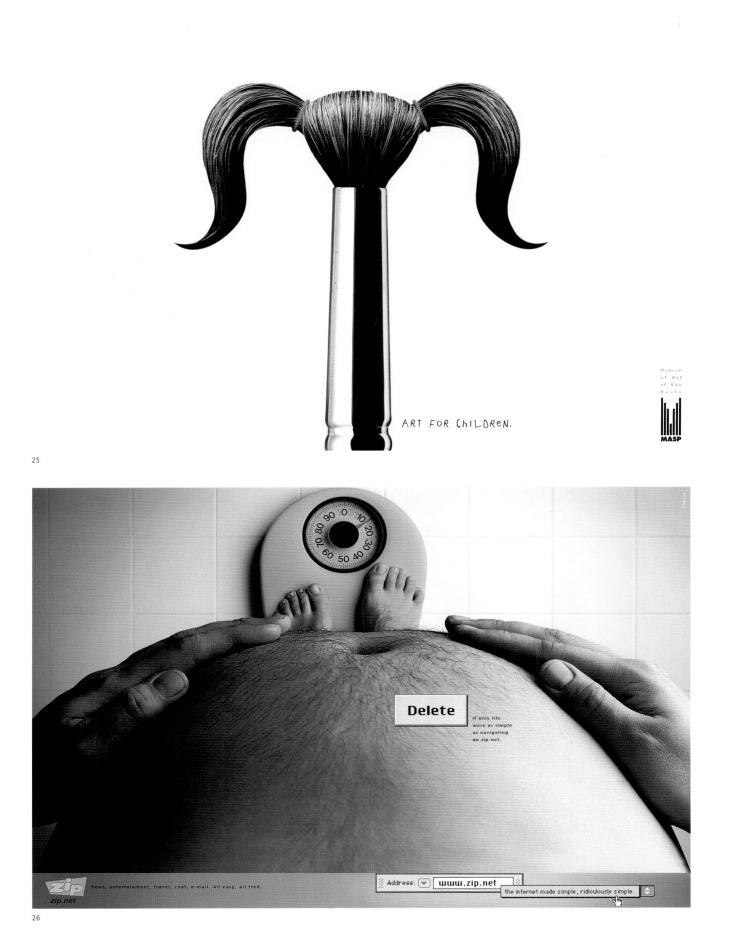

ART FOR CHILDREN.

Museum
of Art
of Sao
Paulo

MASP

25

Delete

If only life
were as simple
as navigating
on zip.net.

zip
zip.net

News, entertainment, travel, chat, e-mail. All easy, all free.

Address: www.zip.net

the internet made simple, ridiculously simple.

26

Forever

27

### 25. SÃO PAULO MUSEUM OF ART
W/BRASIL, SÃO PAULO, MID-1990s
South American ads are designed to travel across cultural and language barriers. Here, the paintbrush with ponytails becomes the headline.

### 26. ZIP.NET
F/NAZCA SAATCHI & SAATCHI, SÃO PAULO, 1999
As in North America, dot-com ads below the equator tend to suggest that technology can solve even the most intractable problems; this campaign made fun of that notion.

### 27. VOLKSWAGEN
ALMAP BBDO, SÃO PAULO, LATE 1990s
Instead of using text to discuss tradition, family values, and a sound automobile, the agency decided to let the picture do the talking.

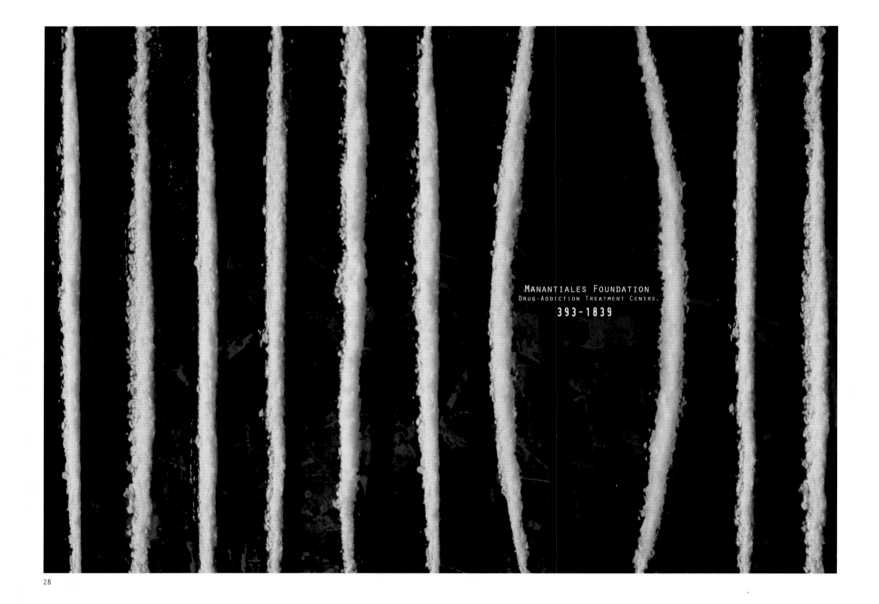

MANANTIALES FOUNDATION
DRUG-ADDICTION TREATMENT CENTRE.
393-1839

28

29

30

agencies such as DM9 DDB, Almap/BBDO, and F/Nazca Saatchi & Saatchi—all well funded by the international networks but still operating under the autonomous creative leadership of local ad stars like Guanaes, Marcello Serpa, and Fabio Fernandes. With resources and creative freedom, the revolution was under way—and it wasn't limited to Brazil. Argentina also emerged as a red-hot creative market, producing ads that were often just as visually striking as the work from Brazil.

Not all South American advertising has achieved the level of sophistication found in Brazil and Buenos Aires. That was made painfully evident recently in Peru, where a late-1990s controversy erupted over an overtly racist commercial that showed Africans preparing to eat white tourists—then opting for Nabisco pudding instead. In fact, several well-known brands had to deal with fallout when a news report uncovered a number of ads featuring

caricatures or stereotypes of blacks (in a Goodyear ad made in Peru, a pitchman compared the thickness of tires to the lips of his black partner). Even in Brazil, it sometimes seems that the attitudes expressed in the ads are not as advanced as the style; a recent commercial that sensuously compared a glass of beer to various parts of a woman's body, including hips and legs, was elegantly and stylishly art directed, but the idea itself was outdated. If the region can overcome such lapses—and resist the temptation to overindulge in the occasional gimmickry of some visual-pun ads designed for award shows— South America may be central to the future of global advertising.

## SOUTH AFRICA

When the apartheid system came tumbling down in South Africa, it had an unexpectedly liberating effect on the country's advertising community. Previously, explains the Johannesburg adman

John Hunt, "we lived in a very strict Calvinist society, and we knew all about barriers and how to confine things, how to split things into black and white." Hunt believes that those confining attitudes—not to mention the old regime's tendency to stifle dangerous ideas—kept advertising from being as freethinking and creative as it could be. "Then came 1994 and the celebration of freedom of the new South Africa, and advertising was ready to blossom," Hunt said. "With the liberalization of South Africa, there was also a liberalization of advertising norms and trends. The old censorship—'Don't show certain things, or talk about certain things'—gave way to a new freedom. There was a whole lightness of attitude that emerged." Today, South African ads are known worldwide for their stylishness and their sense of humor. "We've learned to laugh at ourselves," says Hunt. "Before, we were so busy having our wrists slapped, we weren't too hot on humor."

31

perso___          ___ssenger.

31. **VIRGIN ATLANTIC**
NET#WORK AGENCY,
JOHANNESBURG, 1998
This TV commercial—which
teased the viewer with pornographic scenes partially blocked
by the back of someone's head—
touted personalized TV screens
on Virgin flights.

32. **LAND ROVER**
TBWA HUNT LASCARIS,
JOHANNESBURG, 1999
Selling a car like a condom: The
headline is familiar, but not in
this context.

33. **CITY PRESS**
J. WALTER THOMPSON,
JOHANNESBURG, 1996
The provocative headline (making
the point that this South African
newspaper has enjoyed big
readership gains among blacks)
shows a surprising candor about
sensitive racial issues.

Hunt's agency, TBWA Hunt Lascaris, has been one of the driving creative forces behind the rise of South African advertising in the past decade. But he's had plenty of company. Agencies like Ogilvy & Mather Rightford Searle-Tripp & Makin, the Jupiter Drawing Room, and Net#work have also joined in, forming a vibrant creative community.

Like Brazilian advertising, ads in South Africa tend to be visually bold and direct—the ideas are conveyed with minimal explanation. "That might have something to do with the fact that we have eleven official languages in South Africa," said Hunt. "We also have extreme wealth to extreme poverty—a little like Brazil, I guess—so when you're selling something, you've often got to catch all those different people. You tend to be simple, be visual, make the point, and then get the hell out."

Examples of this can be seen in Hunt's own advertising for clients like Nando's chicken

restaurants. To inform the public that this purveyor of spicy food was now serving kosher food as well, the agency simply showed a picture of a red pepper—with the tip sliced off. To convey the driving power of one of its clients' four-wheel-drive trucks, Hunt Lascaris showed the vehicle being driven off by newlyweds—but instead of dragging the customary tin cans, the speeding truck has huge kegs tied to its rear bumper.

But South African advertising is interesting these days not just because of its cleverness. Many of the ads are providing a mirror—surprisingly faithful to reality, at times—of a society adjusting to sweeping changes. Advertising has, in fact, been in the midst of the country's social upheaval. In the election leading up to government reform, ad agencies played a role in assuring the public that there was no reason to fear change. As it became clear that apartheid was ending, Schweppes used in its

advertising the line "Everything you wanted to know about mixing in the new South Africa." And finally, after Nelson Mandela came to power (partly on the strength of Hunt Lascaris's advertising), advertising helped white-owned companies overcome some of the ill will felt by black consumers. For example, one government-owned oil company that had been linked to the apartheid regime was advised by Hunt Lascaris to start addressing blacks in its ads; the resulting commercials showed a black child dreaming of being a soccer star, and it proved popular with both whites and blacks.

By the mid-1990s, it was normal for advertisements to show racial mixing—which had been practically taboo in the old days (as one local ad executive explained in the press, ads used to cut from showing blacks to showing whites, but "now we can show a more extended interaction," he said). Of course, portraying integration in ads wasn't simply an act of goodwill by

RIBBED FOR EXTRA PLEASURE.

THE BEST 4x4xFAR

32

# Circulation up 94%.

# An explosion you can categorically blame on the Blacks.

From 134 389 (ABC July-Dec 1991) to 261 057 (ABC July-Dec 1995). It makes us the biggest Black newspaper in the country. And it makes sense to buy a page in it, don't you think? Call City Press for the damage.

33

THINK YELLOW

34

34 AND 36. **YELLOW PAGES**
JUPITER DRAWING ROOM,
JOHANNESBURG, 1996–97
In one Yellow Pages campaign,
the agency constructed familiar
shapes from paper; in a separate
series of ads, type was used to
create the images (in the ad on
the opposite page, the names
of businesses form the shape
of a key ).

35. **NANDO'S RESTAURANT**
TBWA HUNT LASCARIS,
JOHANNESBURG, 1998
The agency used this picture
to announce that Nando's
restaurant was now serving
kosher food.

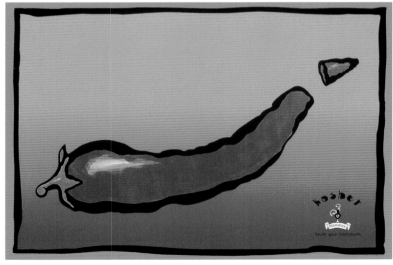

35

FURNISHED ACCOMMODATION, ABATTOIR EQUIPMENT, ACIDS, ACCOMMODATION AGENTS,CHEMICALS, CHEMICAL MANUFACTURERS, ESTATE AGENTS, ABATTOIRS, PROPERTY ADMINISTRATORS, FERTILISERS, COLLECTORS, LITHOGRAPHIC PLATES, EQUIPMENT & CHEMICALS, PORTABLE ABLUTION FACILITIES, ACCOMMODATION ESTABLISHMENTS, PHARMACEUTICALS, HYDROCHLORIC ACID MANUFACTURERS, APARTMENTS, TOILETS, FLATS & HOUSES TO LET, ACOUSTIC CONSULTANTS, HOLIDAY FLATS, CHALETS & HOUSES, HOSTELS, ABRASION RESISTANT MATERIALS, HOTELS/RESIDENTIAL, ACOUSTIC MATERIALS & TREATMENT, HOTELS/TOURIST, BOARDING HOUSES, ASBESTOS PRODUCTS, WEAR RESISTANCE ENGINEERING, RESORTS, BUILDING MATERIALS, CEILINGS, ABRASIVE BLAST CLEANING, ACCOUNTANTS & AUDITORS (PUBLIC), PROTECTIVE COATINGS, CORK PRODUCTS, SANDBLASTING OR SHOTBLASTING, FELT & FELT PRODUCTS, AUDITORS, PUBLIC ACCOUNTANTS, INSULATION MATERIALS, GRINDING & POLISHING MATERIALS, PARTITIONS, SOLENOIDS, GRINDING WHEELS, SOUND PROOFING, LAPIDARY SUPPLIES, SANDBLASTING EQUIPMENT, ACCOUNTANTS/COST & WORKS, ACRYLIC SHEETS, DIAMOND TOOLS, BUILDING MATERIALS, SANDPAPER MANUFACTURERS, ACCOUNTING & BOOKKEEPING, MACHINES & SUPPLIES, ACTIVATED CARBON, ABSEILING, ADVENTURE SPORTS, ACCOUNTING & BOOKKEEPING SYSTEMS, CALCULATING & ADDING MACHINES, ACTUARIAL CONSULTANTS, ACADEMIC COLLEGES, CASH REGISTERS, COMPUTER EQUIPMENT & PERIPHERALS, ACTUATORS, OFFICE APPLIANCES & EQUIPMENT, ACCEPTING BANKS, STATIONERS, ACUPUNCTURE, BANKS/MERCHANT, TYPEWRITERS, BOOKKEEPING MACHINES, ACCESS CONTROL EQUIPMENT, ADDING & CHECKING SERVICES, ART DEALERS, LABELS/PLASTIC, METAL, ETC, MACHINES & SUPPLIES, ADDING MACHINE ROLLS, CARD CONTROL SYSTEMS, ACCOUNTING OFFICERS, BUSINESS FORMS & SYSTEMS, IDENTIFICATION CARDS, COMPUTER DATA PROCESSING, IDENTIFICATION EQUIPMENT & SERVICES, ARMATURE WINDERS, KARDEX VISIBLE RECORD SYSTEMS, IDENTITY DISCS, ACCOMMODATION/FLATS, ELECTRIC COIL WINDING, ACID PROOFING, ART GALLERIES, SCULPTORS, ACCESS FLOORING, ELECTRIC COILS, GRAPHIC DESIGN ARTISTS, ELECTRIC MOTOR REWINDING, ART NEEDLEWORK, ADVERTISING STUDIOS & AGENCIES, ELECTRIC MOTOR REPAIRS, CALLIGRAPHY, GENERATORS ALTERNATORS, LIGHTING, NEEDLEWORK, GRAPHIC ART, TRANSFORMER REPAIRS, ART PUBLISHERS, ARTISTS' MATERIALS & SUPPLIES, WELDING EQUIPMENT REPAIRS, REWINDERS, ART REPRODUCTION, CERAMIC EQUIPMENT, ARMED RESPONSE, CLAY, SECURITY SERVICES & SYSTEMS, ART RESTORATION, CRAYONS, EASELS, ARMOURED BANKING SERVICE, INK/WRITING & MARKING, ART SCHOOLS, PHOTOGRAPHIC SUPPLIES, GUARDS, PIGMENTS & COLOURS, ADULT EDUCATION, POTTERY MAKING INSTRUCTION, SCREEN PRINTING EQUIPMENT, POTTERS' SUPPLIES, ARMOURED VEHICLES, INDIVIDUAL TUITION, STENCIL & STENCIL SUPPLIES, ARMS & AMMUNITION, ART TUITION, CAMPING EQUIPMENT, FISHING TACKLE & EQUIPMENT, ARTIFICIAL EYES, HANDICRAFT MATERIALS, GUNSMITHS, OPTICAL GOODS, MANUFACTURING, HOME CRAFTS, AMMUNITION, LEATHERCRAFT SUPPLIES, CARTRIDGES (FIREARMS), ARTIFICIAL FLOWERS & WREATHS, GUNS, TAPESTRIES, RIFLES, SELF-PROTECTION DEVICES, ARTIFICIAL GRASS, ARMS & AMMUNITION INSTRUCTION, ASBESTOS, SHOOTING RANGES/INSTRUCTION, ARTIFICIAL INSEMINATION, ASBESTOS MINES, ARMS & AMMUNITION RELOADING, ARTIFICIAL LEATHER, ASBESTOS PRODUCTS, AMMUNITION RELOADING EQUIPMENT, ARTIFICIAL LIMBS, CEILING MATERIALS, ARMY & NAVY SURPLUS, ORTHOPAEDIC APPLIANCES, ORTHOPAEDIC SHOES, FILTERING MATERIALS & SUPPLIES, GARDEN REQUISITES, TOOLS, AROMATHERAPY, ARTIFICIAL ROCKS & LANDSCAPING, GASKETS, GARDEN SERVICES & LAYOUT, INSULATION MATERIALS (COLD & HOT), ARRESTORS LIGHTNING, ARTISANS FOR HIRE, REFRACTORY MATERIALS, LIGHTNING PROTECTION, ROOFING MATERIALS, LABOUR COMPONENT MANUFACTURERS, WASHERS, ART AUCTIONEERS, ASBESTOS REMOVAL, AUCTIONEERS, ASPHALT & ASPHALT PRODUCTS, CATALOGUE COMPILERS, DRAUGHTING & DESIGN SERVICES, MURALS, INSULATION MATERIALS, ANTIQUE DEALERS, PACKAGE DESIGN & DEVELOPMENT, ART GALLERIES, COMMERCIAL ARTISTS, PAVING BRICKS & SLABS, RARE BOOKS & PRINTS, ILLUSTRATORS, ROOFING MATERIALS, PERSIAN & ORIENTAL CARPETS, TAR & TAR PRODUCTS, BAKING POWDER MANUFACTURERS, BINS, BAKKIE HIRE, TRUCK &/OR BAKKIE HIRE, BASKETWARE, EGG MANUFACTURERS, BLINDS, BAKKIE LINERS, FOIL & FOIL PRODUCTS, GARDEN FURNITURE, LIGHT DELIVERY VEHICLE, HANDICRAFT MATERIALS, PARTS & ACCESSORIES, HOME CRAFTS, FOOD MANUFACTURERS, SCREEN DOORS & WINDOWS, GELATINE, GLUCOSE & STARCH MANUFACTURERS, BALANCED RATIONS, HONEY, ICE CREAM & ICE LOLLY, ANIMAL FEEDS, BAND SAWS, ICE CREAM CONES, DYNAMIC BALANCING, MAIZE PRODUCTS, CONDENSED, POWDERED & EVAPORATED MILK, BANDS, EDIBLE OILS & FATS, BALING EQUIPMENT & SUPPLIES, OILS/VEGETABLE, DANCE BANDS & ORCHESTRAS, PAPER & PLASTIC CUPS, CONTAINERS, AGRICULTURAL IMPLEMENTS, PAPER PRODUCTS, SPICE MERCHANTS, STAINLESS STEEL PRODUCTS, SWEET & CHOCOLATE MANUFACTURERS, ROLLARS, SYRUPS/FLAVOURED, BEARINGS, YEAST, CAKE DECORATIONS, BALL JOINTS/RESTORING, BAKERS' MACHINERY & EQUIPMENT, MORTGAGE BONDS, PEN & PENCIL MANUFACTURERS, CONVEYORS &/OR COMPONENTS, INVESTMENT CONSULTANTS, BALLET SCHOOLS, DANCING SCHOOLS/STUDIOS, FILLING MACHINERY, GAS APPLIANCES, BALLET SUPPLIES, FINANCING COMPANIES, LEASING COMPANIES, KITCHENWARE, LIQUID & POWDER MIXERS, BALLET TIGHTS, REFRIGERATION EQUIPMENT, HOSIERY, MANUFACTURERS, RESTAURANT EQUIPMENT & SUPPLIES, SCALES & MASS-MEASURING MACHINES, BALLOONS, STOVES & RANGES, ADVERTISING AIDS/CORPORATE, GIFTWARE, SWEET & CONFECTIONERY, NOVELTIES, TRUST COMPANIES, RUBBER PRODUCTS, BANNERS, BAKERS' OVENS, BAR CODING EQUIPMENT, FIRE ESCAPES, LABELLING EQUIPMENT, HANDRAIL COMPONENT MANUFACTURERS, PACKAGING MACHINERY, BAKING POWDER MANUFACTURERS, RAILINGS, PRICE MARKING EQUIPMENT, WALKWAYS & STAIRTREADS, WROUGHT IRON WORK, SUPERMARKET EQUIPMENT, HAND RAILS, BATHROOM FITTINGS & ACCESSORIES, BROOMS, BRICK MANUFACTURERS & SUPPLIERS, ENGINEERS SUPPLIES, HORSEMEAT BUTCHERS, SELF-LUBRICATING BUSHES, CABINETS/FILING, BUTCHERS/KOSHER, OFFICE APPLIANCES & EQUIPMENT, CARDBOARD, VIDEO, CARPETS/AFRICAN, RECYCLERS, WASTE PAPER, CAST IRON, CARTON ERECTING & CLOSING, FOUNDRIES, METAL DISTRIBUTORS, ANTIQUE DEALERS, PATTERNMAKERS, CARPET DEALERS, STEEL BROKERS, ORIENTAL CARPETS, PACKAGING MACHINERY, STEEL DISTRIBUTORS, PERSIAN CARPETS, STRAPPING & STRAPPING EQUIPMENT, CASTING AGENTS, CARPORTS/SHADEPORTS, WRAPPING & PACKAGING MACHINERY, THEATRICAL AGENTS, AWNINGS & CANOPIES, CARTON MANUFACTURERS, CABARET AGENTS, BUILDING ADDITIONS & ALTERATIONS, STAGE AGENTS, BOX MANUFACTURERS (CARDBOARD), FIBREGLASS PRODUCTS, TELEVISION CASTING, PREFABRICATED BUILDINGS, CARTOONISTS, CARRIAGE RESTORATION, CARTRIDGES (FIREARMS), CASTINGS/COLD REPAIR, HORSE CARRIAGES, ENGINEERS/MOTOR, PAPER & PLASTIC CARRIERS, CARTRIDGES (SOUND & VIDEO), METAL STITCHING, PAPER BAG MANUFACTURERS, RECORDS & TAPES, CARTAGE & TRANSPORT CONTRACTORS, ALUMINIUM CASES, CASTORS & WHEELS, AIR CARGO SERVICES, ALUMINIUM PRODUCTS, BUSES/HIRE, CONTAINERISED FREIGHT, CASH REGISTERS, CONVEYORS &/OR COMPONENTS, TRANSPORT SERVICE, CUSTOMS CLEARING, SHIPPING, WHEELS, FORWARDING, DELIVERY SERVICE, FURNITURE REMOVALS & PACKING, AIR CASTORS , HOUSEHOLD & OFFICE STORAGE, COMPUTER EQUIPMENT & PERIPHERALS, HAULAGE HEAVY, MOVING & ERECTING MACHINERY, MOTOR VEHICLE/CAR FERRY, CAT BREEDERS, PACKING & CRATING SERVICE, TYPEWRITERS, TRANSPORT/REFRIGERATED TRUCK, BULK TRANSPORT CONTRACTORS, POINT OF SALE MACHINES, CAT PARLOURS, TRANSPORT BROKERS & CONSULTANTS, CASINO &/OR GAMBLING EQUIPMENT, DOG &/OR CAT GROOMING SERVICES, WAREHOUSING & STORAGE, AMUSEMENT MACHINES, CATALOGUE COMPILERS, TRANSPORT CONTRACTORS, CASINOS, BROCHURE PRODUCERS, TRANSPORT CONTRACTORS/HEAVY, PRINTERS, HAULAGE, AMUSEMENT PLACES & PARKS, PUBLISHERS & PUBLICATIONS, TECHNICAL MANUAL PREPARATION, AGRICULTURAL IMPLEMENTS, CONCRETE TECHNOLOGISTS, CATALOGUE SERVICES, ENGINEERS/CONCRETE, ANIMAL FEEDS, CATALOGUE COVERS, CEREAL MANUFACTURERS, CEMENT MANUFACTURERS & SUPPLIERS, GRAIN MERCHANTS, BOOK COVERS, CATALOGUE ETC, MOLASSES, PRODUCE MERCHANTS, LIME MANUFACTURERS, CATTLE PENS, REFRACTORY MATERIALS, FENCES & FENCING, CATERERS, CD JUKE BOXES, CEMENT WATERPROOFERS & HARDENERS, CD ROM, CONCRETE ADMIXTURES, CHRISTMAS DECORATIONS, BOXES & CRATES/PLASTIC, COIN & NOTE COUNTING & WRAPPING, NOVELTIES, BOXES & CRATES (WOOD), COIN CHANGING MACHINES, CRACKERS & FIREWORKS, CONTROL SYSTEMS, CRAYONS, REGULATORS, FLEXTIME SUPPLIES, FRANKING MACHINES, CRANES, CHALK MANUFACTURERS, DRAWING OFFICE SUPPLIES, SPEEDOMETERS, HYDRAULIC AERIAL PLATFORMS, TACHOMETERS, MOTOR BREAKDOWN EQUIPMENT, SCHOOL EQUIPMENT & SUPPLIES, TAXIMETERS, TIME RECORDERS, CRECHES, EDUCARE & PRE-PRIMARY, TIMERS & TIMING DEVICES, CONTAINER HANDLING EQUIPMENT, TURNSTILES, NURSERY SCHOOLS, COUPLINGS, CRANE ACCESSORIES & PARTS, CHILDREN'S NURSERIES, CRANE REPAIRS, DAY CARE CENTRES, CLUTCHES, SECONDHAND CRANES, PLAY GROUPS, GEARBOXES/INDUSTRIAL & RECONDITIONED, AGRICULTURAL, CREDIT CARDS, PIPE FITTINGS, EARTHMOVING EQUIPMENT, TRANSMISSION & TORQUE CONVERTERS, HOISTS, LIFTING EQUIPMENT, COUPON & SAMPLING, LOADERS, MATERIALS HANDLING EQUIPMENT, BUSINESS SERVICES, CREDIT INFORMATION, MOBILE CRANES, DEBT ADJUSTERS, COURIER SERVICE, DEBT COLLECTORS, DELIVERY SERVICE, CROP PROTECTION, INSECTICIDES, RODENTICIDES, FUNGICIDES & WEEDKILLERS, CREDIT INSURANCE, BUILT-IN UNITS, CROP SPRAYING & DUSTING, INSURANCE COMPANIES, DO-IT-YOURSELF KITS, PLANT OR HARVEST PROTECTION, KITCHEN UNITS, CREMATION SERVICES, AGRICULTURAL SPRAYING, BUILT-IN CUPBOARDS (INTERIORS), UNDERTAKERS & FUNERAL DIRECTORS, JOINERY MANUFACTURERS, INDOOR CRICKET, MASS PRODUCED CUPBOARDS, INDOOR SPORTS, AGRICULTURAL IMPLEMENTS, PAPER CUPS, SPRAYING EQUIPMENT, CRICKET NETS, WEED CONTROL EQUIPMENT SUPPLIES, NET MANUFACTURERS/SPORTS, CURIO &/OR AFRICAN ART DEALERS, CRISIS CENTRES, CROWN CORK MANUFACTURERS, BEER & WINE MAKING EQUIPMENT, CRISPS, BEADS & BEADWORK, DENTAL PRACTITIONERS/ORAL, DESKS & CHAIRS, MEDICINE & PERIODONTICS, OFFICE FURNITURE, LABORATORIES, DESKTOP PUBLISHING & COMPUTER TESTING, GRAPHICS, MEDICAL &/OR REMEDIAL EQUIPMENT, PATHOLOGY, PHARMACEUTICALS, IMAGE BUREAU SERVICES, ORTHODONTICS, RADIO COMPONENTS & EQUIPMENT, DIAMOND & SHOT DRILLING, DETECTIVE AGENCIES, CONTRACTORS, DRILLING CONTRACTORS, PRIVATE INVESTIGATORS, MISSING PERSONS BUREAUX, DIAMOND BROKERS, DEBUGGING, PROSTHODONTICS, POLYGRAPHS, DIAMOND BUYERS, PRIVATE DETECTIVES, DIAMONDS/WHOLESALE, TRACING AGENTS, JEWELLERY BUYERS, DENTAL REQUISITES, DETERGENTS, FIRST AID SUPPLIES, ADHESIVES, DIAMOND BROKERS, INDUSTRIAL & MEDICAL GASES, BOILER DESLAGGING & DESCALING, COMPOUNDS, LABORATORY & SCIENTIFIC EQUIPMENT, CHEMICALS/CLEANING, DIAMOND CROWNS, CLEANING & POLISHING MATERIALS, INDUSTRIAL DIAMONDS, SURGICAL & HOSPITAL SUPPLIES, DRILLING EQUIPMENT, SURGICAL APPLIANCES & EQUIPMENT, DISINFECTANT MANUFACTURERS, SURGICAL INSTRUMENTS, X-RAY APPARATUS & SUPPLIES, DYES & DYESTUFFS, DIAMOND CUTTERS, FLOOR CLEANING EQUIPMENT, DEODORISERS, SETTERS & DEALERS, HAND CLEANERS, JEWELLERS/MANUFACTURING, PAINT MANUFACTURING MATERIALS, DEPARTMENT STORES, SOAP MANUFACTURERS & SUPPLIERS, SOLVENTS, BEAUTY SALONS, LAUNDRY DETERGENTS, COSMETICS/RETAIL, DEWATERING CONTRACTORS, CURTAINS & PELMETS, DIAMOND MINES, COVERS, MINING ENGINEERS, GROUTING CONTRACTORS, DIAMOND SETTERS, FORGINGS, DIESEL SUPPLIERS, GEM CUTTERS, SETTERS & DEALERS, MACHINE SHOPS, PATTERNMAKERS, SMELTERS & REFINERS, DIETITIANS, DIAMOND TESTING EQUIPMENT, DIE CUTTING MACHINERY, NUTRITIONISTS, DIFFERENTIALS, JIGS & FIXTURES, KNIVES/MACHINE, AUTOMOTIVE GEARBOXES, PUNCHES & DIES, DIMMER CONTROLS, TUNGSTEN CARBIDE TOOLS & DIES, SYNTHETIC DIAMONDS, DIE CUTTING SERVICE, DIRECT MAIL, PRECISION ENGINEERS, LITHOGRAPHIC PLATE MAKERS, ADVERTISING, PRINTERS' ENGINEERS, DIRECT SALES, DIE CASTING ENGINEERS, DIRECTIONAL BOARDS, NOTICE BOARDS, METAL PRESSINGS &/OR EQUIPMENT, DIAPER SERVICES, DIRECTORY BOARDS, NAPKIN SERVICE, PROCESS BLOCK MAKERS, DIRECTORY PUBLISHERS, TOOL & DIE MAKERS, DIARIES, DIESEL ELECTRIC GENERATING SETS, ADVERTISING AIDS/CORPORATE, DISCOTHEQUE EQUIPMENT, CALENDAR MANUFACTURERS, AMPLIFIERS, BATTERY CHARGING EQUIPMENT, HIGH FIDELITY SYSTEMS, PRINTERS, STATIONERS, PETROL ENGINES, PUBLIC ADDRESS SYSTEMS, STATIONERY WHOLESALERS, GENERATORS ALTERNATORS LIGHTING, LASER SHOWS, EMERGENCY LIGHTING EQUIPMENT, DISCOTHEQUE EQUIPMENT REPAIRS, DIATHERMY, TURBINES, PHYSIOTHERAPISTS, DIESEL ENGINE REPAIRS, DICTATING MACHINES, FUEL INJECTION REPAIRS, DISCOTHEQUES, TAPE RECORDERS, DIESEL ENGINE SPARES, WORD PROCESSING EQUIPMENT, MOBILE DISCOTHEQUES, DIE CASTING MACHINERY, DISCOUNT CLUBS, FOUNDRY EQUIPMENT & SUPPLIES, MILLING MACHINERY, STEEL PROCESSING & FABRICATING, DISCOUNT STORES, DIESEL INJECTION, DISH WASHING MACHINES, DIESEL/PETROL, ELECTRIC APPLIANCES (HOUSEHOLD), LIQUOR PRODUCERS & DISTILLERS, DOCUMENT COPYING, WINERIES, HOSPITAL EQUIPMENT, COPYING SERVICE, TYPING & SHORTHAND SERVICES, DOCUMENT IMAGE PROCESSING, DISHED & FLANGED ENDS, OPTICAL DISC SYSTEMS, METAL PRESSINGS &/OR EQUIPMENT, PAMPHLET & SAMPLE DISTRIBUTORS, PRESSURE VESSELS, DOCUMENTATION STORAGE, STAINLESS STEEL FABRICATORS, DISTRIBUTOR/IGNITION, FLANGED ENDS, FILING EQUIPMENT & SUPPLIES, WAREHOUSING & STORAGE, DISINFECTANTS MANUFACTURERS, ARCHIVES, MOTOR CAR PARTS & ACCESSORIES, PAPER STORAGE, RECORD STORAGE, IGNITION COMPONENTS, CLEANING CHEMICALS, DIVING BOARDS, KENNELS & CATTERIES, DIVING CONTRACTORS, DOG BREEDERS, VETERINARY SUPPLIES, DREDGING, TOILET SANITISERS, MARINE SERVICES, MARINE SALVAGE, DOG TRAINERS, DISPENSING OPTICIANS, SHIP REPAIRERS, OPTOMETRISTS, CARS, MARINE SURVEYORS & ASSESSORS, PET SHOPS & PET REQUISITES, MARINE SURVEYS, UNDERWATER CONSTRUCTION, DOG FOODS, DISPLAY ARTISTS, UNDERWATER SERVICES, PET FOOD, CONDUITS & CONDUIT FITTINGS, ELECTRIC LIGHT FITTINGS, DOG KENNELS, ELECTRIC STOVE REPAIRS, ELECTRIC SUPPLIES & EQUIPMENT, STOVE REPAIRS, ELECTRIC LIGHTING PLANT, ELECTRIC GEYSER MANUFACTURERS, DIVING EQUIPMENT, ELECTRICAL PLUGS & SOCKETS, ELECTRIC METERS, ELECTRICAL ACCESSORIES, WATER HEATERS & HOT WATER, ELECTRIC GLOBES, CYLINDERS, ELECTRIC MOTOR CONTROL GEAR, ELECTRIC LAMPS (BULBS OR GLOBES), MOTOR CONTROL GEAR, CARBON BRUSHES, ELECTRIC HAMMERS, ELECTRIC CONNECTORS, POWER TOOLS, ELECTRICAL WHOLESALERS, ARMATURE WINDERS, ELECTRIC COIL WINDING, ELECTRIC SWITCHES, ELECTRIC MOTOR REPAIRS, TRANSFORMER REPAIRS, ELECTRIC HEATING ELEMENTS, ELECTRIC TESTING INSTRUMENTS, RESISTANCE MANUFACTURERS, ELECTRIC MOTORS, ELECTRICAL INSTRUMENTS, RECONDITIONED ELECTRIC MOTORS, ELECTRONIC COMPONENTS, SWITCHGEAR MANUFACTURERS, TRANSFORMER MANUFACTURERS, ELECTRIC INSULATION MATERIALS, VARIABLE SPEED DRIVERS, RECORDING INSTRUMENTS, ELECTRIC LAMINATION & STAMPING, ELECTRIC TOOLS, LAMINATION & STAMPING, ELECTRIC VEHICLES, PALLET TRUCKS, ELECTRIC RELAYS, FLOOD LIGHTS & SEARCH LIGHTS, FLUORESCENT LIGHTING EQUIPMENT, ELECTRIC CONTACTS, INFRA-RED EQUIPMENT, LIGHT FITTINGS, LIGHTING SYSTEMS & EQUIPMENT, MOTION PICTURE EQUIPMENT, SWITCHGEAR COMPONENTS, ELECTRIC BULBS, ELECTRIC SHAVER SALES, CHEMICAL MANUFACTURERS, ELECTRONIC MEDIA CONSULTANTS, ELECTRODES, ELECTRONIC MUSICAL EQUIPMENT, SOFTWARE, GRAPHITE & GRAPHITE PRODUCTS, ELECTROLYSIS, BEAUTY SALONS, HAIR REMOVING, CALCULATORS, ANODISERS, ENAMELLING, ELECTRICAL MAINTENANCE, ELECTRONIC COMPONENTS ASSEMBLY, GALVANISING, HARDCHROME PLATING, CHROMEPLATERS, ELECTRICAL SPARES/MOTOR CAR, ELECTRONIC DEVELOPMENT, ELECTROPOLISHING, PLASTIC PLATING, VACUUM METALLISINGS, ELECTRICAL SWITCHBOARDS, INDUSTRIAL DESIGNERS, SWITCHBOARD MANUFACTURERS, ELECTRONIC DOOR OPENERS, DOOR & GATE OPERATING DEVICES, GALVANISING COMPOUNDS (COLD), LEAD, RUST REMOVING EQUIPMENT, SANDBLASTING EQUIPMENT, TANKS & CONTAINERS, CAPACITORS, ANODES FOR ELECTROPLATING, ELECTRICITY DISTRIBUTION, ELECTRIC FUSES, PRINTED CIRCUITS, SEMI-CONDUCTORS, ELEVATORS, ELECTRICITY SAVINGS, VARIABLE SPEED DRIVES, CONDENSER MANUFACTURERS, ENERGY CONSULTANTS, CRYSTAL/PIEZO/ELECTRIC, EMBASSIES, OSCILLATING, ELECTRIFIED FENCING, QUARTZ CRYSTAL, RADIO ELECTRONICS, EMBOSSING, ENGRAVERS, ELECTRO-MEDICAL EQUIPMENT, LABEL PRINTING, PLASTIC & METAL LABELS, NAMEPLATES, DIAGNOSTIC AIDS, SIGNS, EMBOSSING SUPPLIES & EQUIPMENT, PHYSIOTHERAPY EQUIPMENT, RADIATION SHIELDING, ULTRA-VIOLET LAMPS & APPARATUS, JEWELLERS' & WATCHMAKERS, LEATHERCRAFT SUPPLIES, PRINTERS' SUPPLIES, EMBROIDERING MACHINES, TEMPORARY STAFF, MOTOR CAR PARTS & ACCESSORIES, STAFF APPOINTMENTS, INDUSTRIAL KNITTING MACHINES, ENGINEERING INSURANCE, PRIVATE EMPLOYMENT OFFICES, EMBROIDERY, INSURANCE COMPANIES, ARTS & CRAFTS, PERSONNEL CONSULTANTS, ENGINEERING SURVEYORS, HANDICRAFT MATERIALS, KNITTING PATTERNS, ENAMELLED WIRE MANUFACTURERS, ENGINEERING SURVEYORS, KNITTING WOOL, NEEDLEWORK, WIRE, SEWING THREADS, ENGINEERS & CONTRACTORS, TAPESTRIES, ENAMELLERS SUPPLIES, WOOL SHOPS, PAINTING CONTRACTORS & EQUIPMENT, EMBROIDERY MANUFACTURERS & SUPPLIES, AIR FILTRATION ENGINEERS, ENAMELLING, AIR POLLUTION CONTROL, HEATING ENGINEERS, CURTAIN MANUFACTURERS, ANODISERS, VENTILATION, POWDER COATINGS, DRESSMAKERS SUPPLIES, PROTECTIVE COATINGS, ARCHITECTURAL ENGINEERS, FACSIMILE MACHINE REPAIRS, WELLPOINT MAINTENANCE & SERVICE, WHOLESALE GIFT MERCHANTS, WOOL SCOURERS & CARBONISERS, FACSIMILE COMMUNICATION, PLOUGHING, WOODEN FANCYWARE, FACSIMILE SERVICES, WOODENWARE, BLACKSMITHS, FAN MANUFACTURERS, FASCIA BOARDS, CONSTRUCTION, ROOFING MATERIALS, AIR CLEANING & PURIFYING, FASHION ACCESSORIES, FACTORING, AIR CONDITIONING EQUIPMENT, CLOTHING ACCESSORIES, FINANCIAL CONSULTANTS, BLOWERS & BLOWER SUPPLIES, FINANCING COMPANIES, VENTILATION EQUIPMENT, CENTRIFUGAL FANS, FASHION AGENTS, FACTORY CLEANERS, P V C PLASTIC FANS, MODELLING SCHOOLS, CLEANING SERVICES, FARM AGENTS, FASHION CONSULTANTS, FACTORY LOCKERS, FASHION AGENTS, LOCKERS, FARM EQUIPMENT, FASHION DESIGNING SCHOOLS, FACTORY REMOVALS, AGRICULTURAL IMPLEMENTS, MACHINERY & SUPPLIES, DRESSMAKING INSTRUCTION, MACHINERY MOVING & ERECTING, RIGGERS, FARM ESTATES, MILLINERY INSTRUCTION, DRESS DESIGNING INSTRUCTION, FACTORY SHOPS, ESTATE AGENTS, FASHION DESIGN SCHOOLS, FARM GATES, FASHION SHOW PRODUCERS, FAIRS, MODEL AGENCIES, MODELLING SCHOOLS, MILLING MACHINERY, BARBED WIRE, STOKERS, BARRICADES, FASHIONWEAR BOUTIQUES, CATTLE PENS, FEEDING TROUGHS, DECORATIVE FENCING, CLOTHING BOUTIQUES, ELECTRIC FENCING, ELECTRIFIED FENCING, FASHIONWEAR DESIGNERS, FELT & FELT PRODUCTS, CATTLE PENS, SPLIT POLES, DRESS MANUFACTURERS, ACOUSTIC MATERIALS & TREATMENT, SECURITY FENCING, DRESSMAKERS, GASKETS, SPLIT POLE FENCING CONTRACTORS, FASHION DESIGNING SCHOOLS, HAT MANUFACTURERS, NON-WOVEN FABRICS, SWIMMING POOL FENCING, OIL SEALS, FASTENERS & FASTENING SYSTEMS, MECHANICAL & HYDRAULIC SEALS, WALLS, RING SEALS, CONCRETE WALLS, BOLTS, NUTS & RIVETS, SHOE ACCESSORIES & TRIMMINGS, NAILS & TACKS, SHOE FINDINGS & SUPPLIES, FENCING MATERIALS & EQUIPMENT, RIVETS & RIVETTING GUNS, SHOE MATERIALS & COMPONENTS, SCREWS, SNOOKER/POOL/BILLIARD TABLES, STAPLES & STAPLING MACHINES, STRAPPING & STRAPPING EQUIPMENT, UPHOLSTERERS' SUPPLIES, FENCING POLES & FITTINGS, PNEUMATIC TOOLS, WASHERS, POWER TOOLS, WIRE ROPES & FITTINGS, ANCHOR BOLTS, FELT OIL SEAL MANUFACTURERS, CORRUGATED FASTENERS, CONCRETE WALLS & PRODUCTS, FASTENING SYSTEMS, FIXING & FASTENING EQUIPMENT, INDUSTRIAL FENCING, ZIP FASTENERS, HARDWARE, PIPES & PIPING, RAILINGS, TIMBER MERCHANTS, WIRE, SWIMMING POOL EQUIPMENT & SUPPLIES, FERRO ALLOYS, BRICK WALLS, BARBED WIRE & TAPE, FEATHER GOODS, DUVETS & DUVET COVERS, MATTRESS MANUFACTURERS, ELECTRIC FENCING, COMPOST SUPPLIERS, MANURE, FEATHER DUSTERS, PEAT MOSS, FEATHER TRIMMINGS, PHOSPHATING PRODUCTS, SECURITY SPIKES, AGRICULTURAL, TRACE ELEMENT FERTILISERS, FIBRE OPTIC INSTALLATION, FLORISTS' SUPPLIES, FEATHER TRIMMINGS, FEED SUPPLEMENTS, FIBREGLASS DOORS, ANIMAL FEEDS, FIBREGLASS MANUFACTURERS, INDUSTRIAL FEEDERS, CONVEYORS & COMPONENTS, ADHESIVES, CRUSHING & SCREENING EQUIPMENT, SWIMMING POOL EQUIPMENT, BODY FILLERS, FOUNDRY EQUIPMENT & SUPPLIES, FIBREGLASS MOULDING, MATERIALS HANDLING EQUIPMENT, TRELLIS MANUFACTURERS, LATEX PRODUCTS, FRUIT & VEGETABLE SUPPLIERS, PLASTIC FOAM, BAKERS' & CONFECTIONERS, POLYURETHANE PRODUCTS, FRUIT JUICES & SQUASHES, RUBBER PRODUCTS, FRUIT PACKERS & DISTRIBUTORS, FLAVOURING EXTRACTS, GROCERS & PROVISION MERCHANTS, RUBBER FOAM DISTRIBUTORS, HEALTH FOODS & SHOPS, FLEXIBLE FOAM POLYURETHANE, YEAST, MACARONI & NOODLE MANUFACTURERS, FOOD INGREDIENTS, MARGARINE, MEAT EXPORTERS, FOOD COLOURS, MEAT PRODUCTS, PLASTIC FOAM, FLAVOURING EXTRACTS, OLIVES & OLIVE OIL, FOIL & FOIL PRODUCTS, FOOD CHEMICALS, PEANUT PRODUCTS, PERFUMERY COMPOUNDS, PICKLES, PIGMENTS & COLOURS, POTATO MERCHANTS, POULTRY & EGG MERCHANTS, CONTAINERS, LOCKSMITHS, FOOD EMULSIFIERS & STABILISERS, POULTRY FARMS, METAL CONTAINERS, POULTRY PRODUCTS, PACKAGING MATERIALS, RICE, ALUMINIUM FOIL FOOD CONTAINERS, SALT, FOOD EXTRACTS, SOUP POWDERS, FOLDING DOORS, SWEET & CHOCOLATE MANUFACTURERS, FISH PASTE MANUFACTURERS, FLAVOURED SYRUPS, VINEGAR MANUFACTURERS, PAPER FOLDING MACHINES, EGG & POULTRY MERCHANTS, GELATINE, HIGH PROTEIN FOODS, MALT EXTRACT, POTATO CHIPS, FOOD BROKERS, CONDENSED & EVAPORATED MILK, FOOD PACKAGING MATERIALS, FISH & SEAFOOD MERCHANTS, FISH EXPORTERS & IMPORTERS, SOUP POWDERS, FOOD CANNERS & PACKERS, FOOD PROCESSING MACHINERY, GRAIN BROKERS, FOOD FACILITIES CONSULTANTS, GROCERS & PROVISION MERCHANTS, BOTTLING EQUIPMENT, CANNING MACHINERY MANUFACTURERS, MANUFACTURERS' REPRESENTATIVES, CATERING CONSULTANTS, CATERERS' EQUIPMENT & SUPPLIES, KITCHEN CONSULTANTS, DAIRY UTENSILS, SHIP CHANDLERS, FOOD INGREDIENTS, SUGAR DISTRIBUTORS, FILLING MACHINERY, REFINERS, FOOD CHEMICALS, AIR, GAS & LIQUID FILTERS, FOOD CANNERS & PACKERS, FOOD PROCESSING MACHINERY, HOTEL EQUIPMENT & SUPPLIES, AEROSOL PACKERS, MEAT PROCESSING & ABATTOIR EQUIPMENT, BABY FOOD MANUFACTURERS, DRIED FRUIT PROCESSORS & PACKERS, MILKING MACHINES, FISH CURERS & CANNERS, LIQUID & POWDER MIXERS, BILTONG MANUFACTURERS, REFRIGERATION EQUIPMENT, BISCUIT MANUFACTURERS, SLICING MACHINES, FROZEN FOODS, WHOLESALE BUTCHERS, BUTTER, DOMESTIC FOOD PROCESSORS, CEREAL MANUFACTURERS, CHEESE, ELECTRIC APPLIANCES, DAIRIES & CREAMERIES, HOUSEHOLD ELECTRIC APPLIANCES, INFANTS FOOD PROCESSORS, FISH PASTE MANUFACTURERS, MEAT CANNERS, IMPORT & EXPORT AGENTS, TRUCK TAIL LIFTS, WINCHES, STACKERS, FISH & DELICACIES, TRUCK MOUNTED FORKLIFTS, FORESTERS, FORK LIFT TRUCK HIRE, TREE FELLING & STUMP REMOVAL, TREE SERVICE, CRANE HIRE, TIMBER GROWERS, EARTHMOVING EQUIPMENT HIRE, FORK LIFT TRUCKS, GARDEN REQUISITES, HAIRCLOTH, BUILDING ADDITIONS, ALTERATIONS, LEATHER GOODS MANUFACTURERS, LUGGAGE MANUFACTURERS, BUILDING MAINTENANCE, CARPENTRY, LADIES HAIRDRESSERS, FLOOR SANDING, HANDBAG REPAIRS, HOME IMPROVEMENTS, KITCHEN UNITS, LEATHER GOODS REPAIRS, SHOE REPAIRS, HANG-GLIDERS, MEN'S HAIRDRESSERS, BAG REPAIRS, LUGGAGE REPAIRS, PARACHUTING & SKYDIVING, BARBERS, TRAVEL GOODS REPAIRS, PARAGLIDER MANUFACTURERS, HAIRDRESSERS' SUPPLIES, SPORTS GOODS & EQUIPMENT, BEAUTY SALON EQUIPMENT, CLOTHING BOUTIQUES, LEATHER FASHIONWEAR, HANGERS, HAIR ACCESSORIES, LEATHER GOODS, HAIRPIECES, LADIES' OUTFITTERS, COATHANGERS, OVERALLS, SCISSORS, SHEARS & TRIMMERS, WHOLESALE HANDBAGS, HANGGLIDING, TOILET PREPARATIONS, MANUFACTURERS & WHOLESALERS, LEATHER GOODS MANUFACTURERS, ADVENTURE SPORTS, TOWEL SERVICES, WIGS, WIGLETS & MANUFACTURERS, HANDICRAFT MATERIALS, HARDBOARD, HAIRBRUSHES, ARTISTS' MATERIALS & SUPPLIES, BOARD PRODUCTS, ARTS & CRAFTS, BAMBOO & BAMBOO PRODUCTS, HARDCHROME PLATING, GENERAL BOOKSELLERS, HARD CHROMING, TECHNICAL BOOKSELLERS, HAIR CARE CONSULTANTS, DO-IT-YOURSELF KITS, HOBBY & MODEL SHOPS, PROTECTIVE COATINGS, TRANSPORT SERVICE, HEARING AIDS, CORROSION CONTROL, MACHINERY MOVING & ERECTING, ELECTROPLATERS & POLISHERS, ROAD TANKER SERVICE, DEAF APPLIANCES, ENAMELLING, HEAVY HAULAGE, GALVANISING, HEARING CONSERVATION, METAL FINISHERS, HAWKERS, RUST-PROOFERS, SMOUSE, HEARING PROTECTION, RETAIL HARDWARE, HAY MERCHANTS, SAFETY EQUIPMENT & CLOTHING, BUILDING MATERIALS, PRODUCE MERCHANTS, EAR MUFFS, GARDEN REQUISITES & TOOLS, EARDRUM PROTECTORS, EQUIPMENT, HAZARD LIGHTS, PROTECTIVE EAR MUFFS, LAWNMOWERS & SPARES, RETAIL PAINT, WARNING LIGHTS & SIGNALS, HEARSES & COACHBUILDERS, TOOLS, HEADSTONES, HARDWARE WHOLESALE, TOMBSTONES, HEAT EXCHANGER REPAIRS, MANUFACTURERS, HEALTH APPLIANCES, BOILER INSTALLATION & REPAIRS, MAINTENANCE, ABRASIVES, HEALTH STUDIOS & GYMNASIUMS, HEAT EXCHANGERS, BOLTS, NUTS & RIVETS, EQUIPMENT & SUPPLIES, BUILDERS, HARDWARE MERCHANTS, LADDERS, LAWNMOWERS & SPARES, HEALTH CLINICS, CALORIFIERS, PLUMBERS SUPPLIES, COOLING TOWERS, WHOLESALERS, BEAUTY & HEALTH SCHOOLS, THERMAL ENGINEERS, TOOL AGENTS, HEALTH RESORTS, AFTERCOOLERS, LOCKS, PADLOCK DISTRIBUTORS, REFLEXOLOGY, HEAT PUMPS, STRESS CONSULTANTS, HARNESS MAKERS, HEATING EQUIPMENT & SYSTEMS, HEALTH FOODS & SHOPS, SADDLERY & HARNESS, HEAT SEALING MACHINES, NUTRITIONAL PRODUCTS, WIRING HARNESSES, CATERERS' EQUIPMENT & SUPPLIES, HEALTH MANAGEMENT INFORMATION, ELECTRIC LAMINATION & STAMPING, ELECTRICAL WIRE HARNESSES, PACKAGING MACHINERY, PLASTICS MACHINERY & EQUIPMENT, HARVESTING CONTRACTORS, PLASTIC HEAT SEALERS, SEALING EQUIPMENT, HEALTH CLINICS, SHRINK WRAPPING, HAT CLEANING & RENOVATING BID, HEALTH SCHOOLS, HEAT TREATMENT, BEAUTY & HEALTH SCHOOLS, PROTECTIVE COATINGS, FOUNDRIES, STRAW HAT MANUFACTURERS, METAL FINISHERS, GYMNASIUMS, HEATED TOWEL RAILS, YOGA INSTRUCTION, BEAUTY SALONS, PHYSICAL CULTURE, SLIMMING SALONS & CLUBS, HEATERS, SAUNA BATHS & MASSAGE, LADIES FASHIONWEAR, AIR HEATERS, MILLINERS, EQUIPMENT & SUPPLIES, ELECTRIC HEATERS, HATTERS, GYMNASIUM EQUIPMENT & SUPPLIES, GYMNASTIC MATS, HEAVY HAULAGE, HEARING TESTING & THERAPY, ELECTRIC WATER HEATERS, CARTOGRAPHERS, SPEECH THERAPISTS & AUDIOLOGISTS, WATER HEATERS & HOT WATER, CONTAINERISED FREIGHT & DEPOTS, CYLINDERS, GAS WATER HEATERS, AIR CHARTER, HIGH FIDELITY SYSTEMS, EQUIPMENT, GAS APPLIANCES, HELICOPTER MAINTENANCE & REPAIRS, RADIO REPAIRS, TELEVISION REPAIRS & HIRE, HEATING & VENTILATION ENGINEERS, SPEAKER REPAIRS, HELICOPTER SERVICES, HEATING ENGINEERS, IMAGE PROCESSING EQUIPMENT, ICE CREAM PARLOURS, EXPORT CONSULTANTS, OPTICAL DISC SYSTEMS, EXPORTERS, IMPORT & EXPORT AGENTS, ICE CREAM STABILIZERS, IMITATION JEWELLERY, TRADERS, ICE CREAM MACHINERY & SUPPLIES, MANUFACTURING JEWELLERS, ICE DISTRIBUTORS, WHOLESALE JEWELLERS, VISIBLE RECORD SYSTEMS, COLD STORAGE, INDOOR PLANTS, FLORISTS, ACCESSORIES, INDUSTRIAL CLEANING SERVICES, OFFICE PLANTS, MARINE, INDUSTRIAL FLOOR SWEEPING, INDOOR PLANTS, MACHINES, INDUSTRIAL COKE, INDUCTION HEATING, INDUSTRIAL SWEEPING MACHINES, COAL, COKE & WOOD, INDUSTRIAL FLOORING, INDUSTRIAL COUNCILS, INDUSTRIAL & COMMERCIAL, FLOORING CONTRACTORS, CONSULTANTS, INDUSTRIAL CURTAIN, INDUSTRIAL GASES, BUSINESS BROKERS, MANAGEMENT CONSULTANTS, MINING EQUIPMENT & SUPPLIES, INDUSTRIAL & MEDICAL GASES, MARKETING CONSULTANTS, BLASTING MATS, SALES PROMOTION CONSULTANTS, INDUSTRIAL CURTAINS, COMMERCIAL & INDUSTRIAL, STRIPS CURTAIN, CONSULTANTS, CANVAS, COTTON, HESSIAN SACKS, ADHESIVES, INDUSTRIAL & MOTOR LACQUERS, INDUSTRIAL DESIGNERS, RECONDITIONED MACHINERY, PAINT MANUFACTURERS, WHOLESALERS, DRAUGHTING & DESIGN SERVICES, INDUSTRIAL OVENS, PRODUCT DESIGNERS, INDUSTRIAL & SCIENTIFIC INSTRUMENTS, INDUSTRIAL DISPLAYS, INDUSTRIAL PAINTING, DISPLAY DESIGNERS & PRODUCERS, PAINTING CONTRACTORS & EQUIPMENT, INDUSTRIAL DRYING EQUIPMENT, INDUSTRIAL PREMISES, INDUSTRIAL ELECTRONICS, INDUSTRIAL PROPERTIES, SCIENTIFIC REPAIRS, ELECTRONIC EQUIPMENT MAINTENANCE, INDUSTRIAL BELTING, INDUSTRIAL PUMPS, INDUSTRIAL BROKERS, INDUSTRIAL REFRIGERATION, BUSINESS BROKERS, CONCRETE MIXERS FOR HIRE, OIL BURNERS, INDUSTRIAL CARS, LIGHTING & POWER PLANT HIRE, INDUSTRIAL RESEARCH, UTILITY MOTOR VEHICLES, PUMPS & PUMPING APPLIANCES, MALT MANUFACTURERS, YEAST, MICROSCOPES, INDENT AGENTS, MALT EXTRACT, TEXTILE MANUFACTURERS, TELESCOPES, MANAGEMENT INFRASTRUCTURE, MAIL COLLECTION SERVICES, MANAGEMENT CONSULTANTS, MANUFACTURING CHEMISTS, MANAGEMENT CONSULTANTS, MAIL ORDER HOUSES, MANURE, IT'S EASIER TO FIND IF YOU THINK YELLOW

36

**M**ODELS SO BEAUTIFUL, YOU'LL HATE THEM FOR IT.

For bookings call (021) 418 7540 or (011) 447 8963/4.

37

WEAR IT FOR YOURSELF. She{}Bear

38

37. **STORM MODELS**
JOE PUBLIC TAKE-AWAY
AGENCY, JOHANNESBURG,
1998
The agency defaced its own ad
to convey that this modeling
agency didn't take itself too
seriously.

38. **SHE BEAR LINGERIE**
TBWA HUNT LASCARIS,
JOHANNESBURG, 1999
South African ads have a
mischievous streak; this
campaign featured men in
drag and nuns in underwear.

advertisers; it was a smart business decision. After decades of apartheid, market researchers found that blacks were suspicious of products that seemed targeted just to them, assuming they might be of lesser quality; to overcome that, ads had to show the products being used by both blacks and whites.

South African ads don't necessarily try to sugarcoat the discussion of race; they can, in fact, be quite blunt. When an ad by J. Walter Thompson in Johannesburg wanted to make the point that a local newspaper had enjoyed huge readership gains among blacks, the headline read, "Circulation up 94%. An explosion you can categorically blame on the Blacks."

Perhaps that level of candor should not be surprising, considering that South African advertisers tend to be a bit cheeky. There's a penchant for troublemaking that sometimes takes the form of ads joking about sex, cross-dressing, and bodily functions. Hunt Lascaris

uses its brassiere clients (it has two, Wonderbra and She Bear) to show men in drag and nuns in their underwear. Meanwhile, Net#work's ads for Virgin Atlantic tease the viewer with pornographic scenes in which visibility is obscured by the back of someone's head (in an ad promoting personal-ized TV screens on Virgin flights). Advertisers have even been known to play juvenile pranks on their own ads—as in one that features a beautiful fashion model whose face has been marked up by a hand-drawn pen mustache.

If all of that mischief suggests an Australian influence, it's because the development of the local ad community involved a number of Australian expatriats. But as Hunt points out, there's also a British and American flavor. As Hunt says, "It's a home brew borrowed from all over the world." What's been missing up to now, Hunt acknowledges, is the voice of black Africa. "The ad industry in South Africa is still too white—that's a given. But it is changing pretty

rapidly. And I believe our next phase is bringing a lot of Africanness and finding the African voice in our advertising. A lot of people of color are coming into the industry, and I suspect within the next couple of years, you will see a voice of Africa appearing more and more in our ads, which is very exciting."

Part of that is flourishing in an indigenous ad community that has sprung up in recent years, led by small, black-run agencies that specialize in communicating to blacks. This has already brought a fresh new flavor to the mix of African advertising. But Hunt believes the future lies in moving away from separatism in advertising. "Rather than indigenous agencies doing indigenous work," he said, "the real progress is in seeing more people of color coming into the established agencies and making their mark on the industry overall. And proving they can do a great ad not just for indigenous food but for a BMW, too."

# 13. GUE
# ADVERTISI
# IT TO THE

f you happened to visit a certain dark and trendy nightclub in New York City on a given evening several years ago, you might have noticed a handsome couple at the bar engaged in a spirited conversation about a new cocktail. Gradually, others surrounding them might have joined in the conversation about this so-called Hennessy martini. Meanwhile, as you inched toward the bartender to place your order, you might have found yourself drawn into the discussion and asked for your views: Had you heard of this hot new drink everyone was talking about? Eventually, the attractive couple perhaps would have decided to settle this whole matter once and for all, telling the bartender: "Let me try one of these Hennessy martinis—and while you're at it, how about a round for my friends here at the bar." As you walked away, sipping your strange new drink and trying to decide if you liked it, it still might not have occurred to you that you had just participated in a living advertisement.

The Hennessy martini stunt was a classic bit of "guerrilla advertising" staged in the mid-1990s by the New York ad agency Kirshenbaum Bond & Partners, which was, at the time, trying to stir up interest in Hennessy cognac among young people who don't usually drink cognac. The first thing agency chief Richard Kirshenbaum did was to concoct a cocktail and name it; thus was born the Hennessy martini. Next, the agency wanted to create a "buzz" around town, so attractive actors and models were hired and planted in fashionable bars, with orders to initiate fake conversations about this "popular" drink that no one had ever heard of. According to Kirshenbaum, the tactic worked quite well; the Hennessy martini actually did become somewhat popular and helped boost sales of the cognac. Would ordinary advertising have worked as well? Kirshenbaum doesn't think so; he believes that increasingly, advertisers must sneak "under the radar" of consumers who are adept at tuning out conventional sales messages.

And the best way to do that, Kirshenbaum and many other advertisers believe, is via some form of unconventional guerrilla-style advertising— which lurks all around, hits us where we live, and invariably takes us by surprise.

Increasingly, around the world, ads are breaking the boundaries that once kept them contained on the printed page or in thirty-second slots on broadcast media. They are now materializing on sidewalks, in bathroom stalls, on the covers of schoolbooks, at the bottom of a drinking glass, on pieces of fruit—or, as with Hennessy, in the midst of a conversation. It is a trend that has already triggered alarms among those who see this as a form of environmental pollution that shows no sign of letting up until every surface—and perhaps the atmosphere, too—has been claimed. Writing in *Time* magazine in 1998, the journalist Jeffrey Kluger lamented the spread of ads everywhere, noting, "In the past few years, it seems, the endgame, the D-day, the final storming of the last

3

4

3 AND 4. **WRANGLER JEANS**
THE MARTIN AGENCY,
CHARLOTTE, NORTH
CAROLINA, 1998
A transparent salespitch: The
advertiser used cut-out billboards
to promote camouflage jeans.

# Cream good enough for Colombian Coffee isn't exactly easy to find.

100% Colombian Coffee

The richest coffee in the world.™

5

6

untrademarked beaches has begun." (What Kluger perhaps didn't know at the time was that the beaches had already been taken: On the shores of New Jersey, Skippy Peanut Butter and an entrepreneur with a customized tractor were imprinting the Skippy logo in the sand.)

In Kluger's military analogy, advertisers are cast as the ruthless invaders, continuing to advance upon new borders until the entire free world has been commercialized. But from the perspective of advertisers, the guerrilla movement is not so much an advance as a reaction—to a changing media landscape and an increasingly elusive consumer. "It used to be that with the three basic media of TV, radio, and print, you had enough reach to get your message out to just about everybody," said Rick Boyko, the creative chief of Ogilvy & Mather in New York. "But that's not true anymore. Everything has become so fragmented in terms of the way people use media today—they're no longer all watching the same

TV programs and reading the same publications." In addition, Boyko noted, lifestyles have become more varied and more mobile. "So you have to try to find all kinds of new points of contact with people," he said. Mary Warlick, director of The One Club for Art & Copy, a New York–based ad-industry group that promotes creativity, predicts, "Guerrilla advertising will continue to grow. It can be extremely effective because it is unexpected."

This new world of ubiquitous ads is not necessarily a utopia for advertisers. In fact, their lives were simpler (and it was more profitable for ad agencies) when all that was required was a handful of commercials that could be run and rerun and rerun on three major broadcast networks. The new guerrilla landscape requires advertisers to be more innovative not only in crafting the message but also in choosing—if not actually creating—the medium for that message. Or, to return to the military analogy, marketers who once plowed straight ahead with that

Sherman tank of advertising known as the TV commercial now must engage in small-arms sharpshooting from up on the rooftops and down in the toilet stalls.

Interestingly, as advertisers have tried to chase after the newly elusive consumer, it has become clear that one of the more effective tools also happens to be one of the oldest forms of advertising: the outdoor billboard. The big boards had become almost passé as TV commercials grew in popularity; they were reduced to carrying the ads that TV wouldn't accept, for liquor and tobacco. Many top ad creators thought billboard work was beneath them; in fact, one of the industry's foremost executives, Howard Gossage, suggested in the 1960s that billboards be abolished altogether on grounds that they were unsightly and intruded on the natural landscape. But by the mid-1990s, billboards were suddenly back in vogue as ad sales in this medium grew sharply. Times Square and its electronic billboards

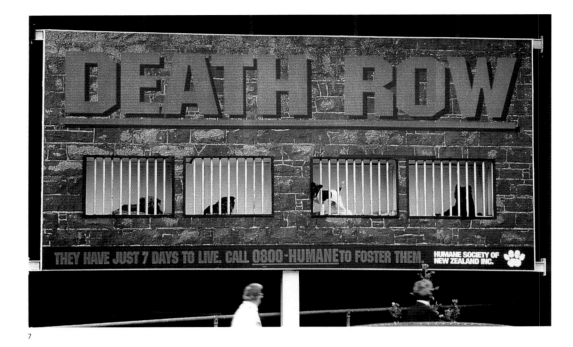

7

7. **HUMANE SOCIETY OF
NEW ZEALAND**
OGILVY & MATHER,
AUCKLAND, 1995
In New Zealand, billboards
included built-in cages with live
dogs; passersby could see
animals that were slated to be
killed unless someone adopted
them soon.

8. **KODAK**
OGILVY & MATHER,
NEW YORK, 1996
In the 1990s, the exteriors of
buses became another canvas
for advertisers; Kodak used it
to good effect in advertising
specialized imaging services.

9. **THE ECONOMIST**
ABBOTT MEAD VICKERS,
LONDON, 1990
*The Economist* put this message
on the rooftops of London buses
in the early 1990s; later, a U.S.
job search firm created bus
rooftop ads aimed at people
unhappy with their jobs (the
copy read "Don't jump!").

once again became an epicenter of the ad world.
And on the other side of America, in Silicon
Valley, billboards became a medium of choice for
the new dot-com entrepreneurs.

The reason for the revival was that billboards
addressed some of the critical issues in an
increasingly fragmented media marketplace.
With TV viewers armed with remote controls
enabling them to surf through a sea of channels,
it had become easier than ever to dodge TV spots.
A billboard, on the other hand, was immovable,
"unzappable," and therefore unavoidable. It was
also an ideal medium for reaching particular
demographic groups that advertisers were lusting
after: busy two-income couples, travelers, weekend outdoorsmen, young party animals—the
kind of active people who tend to watch less TV.
In the case of dot-com advertisers, billboards in
strategic locations were sometimes targeted to
small groups of venture capitalists in an effort to
raise investment money. Whoever the target

groups might be, and however little media they
consumed, they all had to travel a certain route to
work or play—and advertisers could use billboards to stalk them on that path.

It also helped that billboard technology took
several leaps forward in recent years. The use of
computer graphics and digital printing on new
surfaces, such as vinyl, yielded images that were
not only sharper but more dynamic; they could
move and change. The old flashing neon of
Times Square was augmented by huge video
screens, electronic strips, and vinyl ads that
transformed themselves every few seconds. And
throughout New York and other major cities,
huge "wallscapes" began to appear, digitally
printed on vinyl and draped over the entire sides
of buildings hundreds of feet tall; the images just
grew larger and larger. Advertisers also began to
take advantage of the three-dimensionality of
billboards, sometimes incorporating lifelike
objects into the ad, with startling effects. For

example, the Canadian agency Palmer Jarvis DDB
created a billboard promoting a roller-coaster
ride that featured what looked like a man's
body draped over the top of the board. And in
Auckland, New Zealand, billboards for the
Humane Society actually had built-in cages with
live dogs in them, beneath headlines like "Every
dog has its day. His is Monday." (The board
included a number to call in order to adopt the
dog before it was euthanized.)

But even as advertisers were embracing
improved billboards, they were also looking
beyond these roadside signs toward other, newer
forms of street-level communication. They began
to, in effect, hijack trains and buses (which had
always carried small, assorted promotional
messages) and turn them into singularly focused
moving ads; it's now common in New York to
find oneself aboard a "brand train" in which all
the ads are bought by one advertiser, enveloping
the rider in a wall-to-wall sales pitch. Even

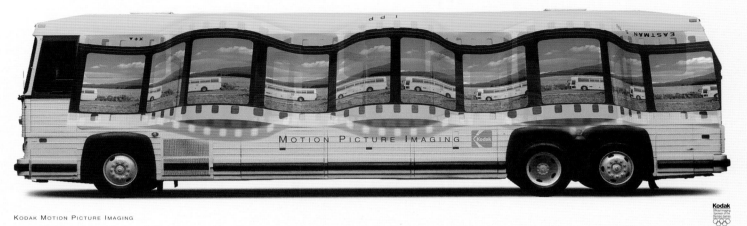

Kodak Motion Picture Imaging

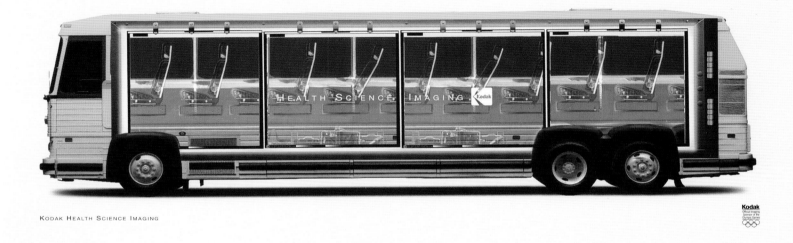

Kodak Health Science Imaging

8

9

GUERRILLA ADVERTISING: TAKING IT TO THE STREETS.

10

11

**10. NASHUA COPIERS**
TBWA HUNT LASCARIS,
JOHANNESBURG, 1999
South Africa has been a big
market for guerrilla-style ads.
This one touted the lifelike
reproduction capabilities of
Nashua photocopiers by creating
fake ATM machines.

**11. SOUTH AFRICAN
GUN CONTROL/ KFM
BROADCASTING**
JUPITER DRAWING ROOM,
JOHANNESBURG, 1998
Another South African ad, for
gun control, was designed to
look like a vending machine
filled with pistols.

12

12 AND 13. **MIAMI RESCUE MISSION**
CRISPIN PORTER +
BOGUSKY, MIAMI, 1996
The campaign turned dumpsters
and benches into ad vehicles;
the message (that a homeless
person views domestic features
differently) was tailored to the
media.

When you're homeless the world looks different. To help, call 571-2273. THE MIAMI RESCUE MISSION

13

more striking are the relatively new painted buses, which use the whole exterior of the vehicle (including windows) as a canvas for laying down an ad image. Recently, Apple Computer used this type of painted-bus advertising to recreate the famous 1955 civil rights incident in which the African-American Rosa Parks refused to sit at the back of a bus, thereby galvanizing the Civil Rights Movement in the U.S.

By the mid-1990s, street-level ads were being posted on just about anything with an available surface—bus shelters, benches, construction walls, kiosks, wastebaskets. In Miami, the ad agency Crispin Porter + Bogusky provided a textbook example of how to use these kinds of surfaces to infiltrate the local environment. The agency was assigned to raise support for a local shelter for the homeless but didn't have a large ad budget. So it printed mini-posters asking for support for the homeless and affixed these signs to park benches, shopping carts, and trash

Dumpsters. But the beauty of the campaign was that the message was tailored to the media: The idea had occurred to agency creative director Alex Bogusky that homeless people "live in a separate culture, where things take on new meanings— a bench becomes your bed; a shopping cart becomes your clothes closet." So Bogusky used the large headline "Bed" for the ads pasted on benches, while a "House" sign was placed on bus shelters, and so forth. (He admits he was a bit unnerved when he saw a homeless person sleeping on a bench that had one of the "Bed" signs— a stark reminder that the campaign's message was grounded in reality.)

This kind of street-level, ground-up approach has been called "viral marketing" because it tends to gradually, insidiously spread the word about a product or service—which can make it seem as if the "buzz" is coming from people on the streets, instead of from advertisers. (This trick of planting and orchestrating buzz isn't

new—in 1929 the legendary publicity man Edward Bernays recruited women to pose as feminists marching with cigarettes in their hands, on behalf of his client the American Tobacco Company.) When the ad agency TBWA/Chiat/Day took on the Levi's account recently, the ad team carefully studied the ways that underground party promoters drew crowds with flyers, wild postings, sidewalk ads, and the like. The agency set up a "viral" ad program that would do likewise for Levi's, using, for example, pirate radio stations that would broadcast "secret information" on where to find a new line of jeans. Rather than focus on ads, the agency wanted to sneak the Levi's name into the hottest clubs, street scenes, and Web sites.

When deciding where to plant street messages, ad agencies often look for busy, high-traffic areas— but they also favor locations that have a captive audience. In the U.S. and Europe, advertisers have already invaded bank automatic-teller

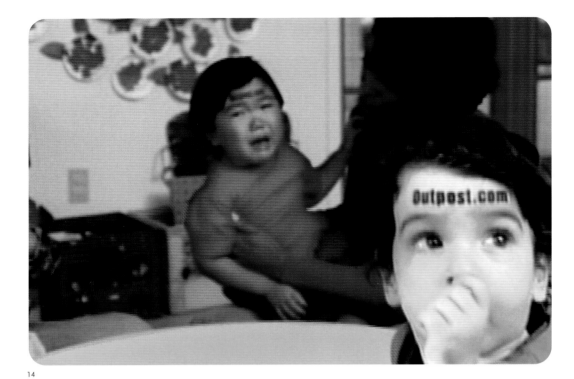

14

machines (who better to advertise to than someone with a fresh fistful of cash?) and gasoline pumps; in both venues, ads have been flashing messages for some time but are now becoming more advanced to include talking sales pitches. In South Africa, airports have become a testing ground for all kinds of unusual guerrilla tactics. For example, in Johannesburg, Virgin Atlantic airlines placed cartons of eggs on the baggage-claim carousel; as the eggs went round and round, so did the accompanying message to passengers that Virgin treats baggage with care. At the same airport, the agency TBWA Hunt Lascaris came up with a unique way to promote a chicken restaurant—on the runway, as planes were guided in, the guider's batons were replaced with chicken drumsticks. (Guerrilla advertising is widely practiced in South Africa, where many companies have limited ad budgets. "We use it because it's inexpensive, and it works big-time," says local ad executive John Hunt.)

The bathroom used to be a place of refuge, but no longer—it has become a favorite advertising venue because it is not only a captive environment but also gender-specific, making it ideal for targeted ads. Messages have been showing up directly above urinals (where it's almost impossible not to look), inside toilet stalls, on walls opposite the mirror (printed backwards of course). Ads are even being printed on toilet paper. Who would advertise on toilet paper? A company as reputable as SmithKline Beecham, for one. Or the young ad student who recently tried to get a job at the agency Kirshenbaum Bond & Partners by going into the agency bathroom and hand-printing a self-promotional message on the toilet paper, announcing, "I'm willing to start at the bottom." (The agency liked his cheeky approach, and hired him.)

One might suppose advertising couldn't get any lower than the toilet, but there's always the floor—of shopping malls, supermarkets, stores of all kinds, as well as outside on the sidewalk. The guerrilla masters at Kirshenbaum Bond were stenciling messages on the sidewalks of New York as far back as the early 1990s. One of the agency's more infamous sidewalk ads was for a lingerie company, and the message to pedestrians was "From here, it looks like you could use some new underwear." Not all sidewalk ads are played for laughs, however: In Australia, Young & Rubicam placed small round stickers on the ground that adhered to the shoes of people who stepped on them; when you tried to peel the ad off your foot and noticed the copy, it explained that, assuming the sticker were a land mine, "there's a 50% chance you will die within minutes." (The ad was asking for support to ban land mines around the world.) Meanwhile, in Amsterdam, pedestrians had to be particularly careful about stepping on ads for the Hans Brinker Budget Hotel. The hotel's agency, KesselsKramer, had placed tiny flags in dog

DOES THIS HURT?

Chiropractic Association of South Africa (058) 303 4571

15

GUERRILLA ADVERTISING: TAKING IT TO THE STREETS.

16

17

18

excrement outside the central train station, directing backpackers to the hotel. The down-and-dirty ads were in keeping with the spirit of the self-mocking ad campaign for this hotel, which makes fun of its poor amenities while heralding its rock-bottom rates.

In contrast to these minimalist attempts at sidewalk communication, in Stockholm the advertising for Gevalia coffee actually rises up from the ground with three-dimensional objects that resemble installation art. Created with molded plastic, one ad is designed to look like a roller-coaster car bursting up through the sidewalk; in another installation piece, a submarine is breaking through the street. The theme of the campaign is surprise intrusions—tying in with Gevalia coffee's tag line "What to serve the unexpected guest."

If Gevalia was taking a larger-than-life approach, many guerrilla advertisers were going the other way—looking for smaller and smaller

venues in which to squeeze a product plug. One South African ad agency placed its message in the bottom of drinking glasses in bars, where it printed the phone number of its client, a taxi service. "When you've seen this number three times," the glass-bottom message advised drinkers, "use it." And tiny ad stickers have been appearing on fruit for the past several years; one of the first to do this was, again, Kirshenbaum, who arranged to have a sticker featuring the logo of his client, the beverage Snapple, stamped onto 13 million mangos to promote Snapple's introduction of a new mango-flavored drink.

If ads can be stamped on fruit, why not on people? Perhaps the final frontier for guerrilla advertisers is the human body—as good a place as any to put an ad. To some extent, people wearing logo hats and T-shirts have been walking billboards for some time, and covering athletes in logos is nothing new. But even here, advertisers

keep finding quirky new places to squeeze ads. When the boxer Julius Francis squared off against Mike Tyson in a January 2000 match held in London, Francis decided beforehand to sell ad space to London's *Daily Mirror* on the soles of his shoes; he also boastfully predicted, just prior to the fight, that the ads would never be seen because he intended to remain standing throughout the fight. But alas, Tyson knocked Francis down a total of five times in two rounds—giving the newspaper plenty of ad exposure.

You don't have to be professional jock to become a walking ad. In South Africa, an airline hired a contortionist and had him position himself in the middle of the airport, twist his body up like a pretzel, and pose there for passersby; a sign on his briefcase read, "Give me time to unwind. I didn't fly Sun Air's Exec Economy." And British Airways hired an actress to go into movie theaters, sit in the audience, and

19

20

then interact with the company's advertising when it appeared on the screen (the woman would rise from her seat and shout at the characters on-screen; in turn, their lines had been scripted so that it seemed as if they were responding to what she was saying).

It's interesting to note that some kinds of guerrilla invasions irritate the public much more than others do. For example, turning people into ads doesn't seem to have bothered anyone, but stickers on fruit has. "I didn't want my apple defiled with advertisements," a Dallas woman complained to *The New York Times*, after noticing that the fruit in her supermarket was being used to promote a new movie. Invading the home is also risky: In the summer of 2000, the American Broadcasting Company was criticized for a plan to insert prerecorded messages on home telephone-answering machines; the messages were in the voices of TV stars, asking viewers to watch their new shows (ABC backed

off the plan, but this new technology, voice-mail broadcasting, is drawing interest among many marketers who believe that ads left on answering machines may be more effective than "live" sales pitches from telemarketers).

One of the most volatile areas has been advertising's ongoing attempts to infiltrate schools and schoolbooks. The textbook publisher McGraw-Hill was criticized for publishing a sixth-grade math book peppered with references to Nike, Gatorade, and other brands. The book publisher insisted that no sponsors had paid their way into the book; the writers had simply decided the math problems would seem more relevant if they involved products the kids used. (A typical entry: "Will is saving his allowance to buy a pair of Nike shoes that cost $68.25. If Will earns $3.25 per week, how many weeks will Will need to save?") Nike is not only inside the books but covering them, too—the company has distributed logo-drenched book covers free at

schools. Some schools, faced with budgetary pressures, have also begun to accept corporate sponsorships that can turn the school building itself into an ad. In Colorado Springs, for example, school hallways are plastered with billboards for soft drinks and other products (and to get to school, the kids ride in schoolbuses covered in corporate logos).

While ads in schools have sparked much debate, in most other instances, the advancement of guerrilla ads has been largely accepted by the public, which seems to be of two minds about it. There is certainly a keen awareness and some concern that ads are taking over more and more public spaces, but many people have also grown accustomed to this proliferation; in particular, younger people tend to be least likely to object to the trend because "their life is completely subsumed in commercial advertising," the advertising professor James Twitchell has observed. Trend analyst Tom Julian of the ad

How do you plan on providing for your family after you pass away?

Conseco's life insurance policies can give your loved ones a regular monthly paycheck. Make sure they're covered tomorrow, plan today. Call 1-877-CONSECO or visit CONSECO.COM.

CONSECO®
Step up.℠

INSURANCE INVESTMENTS LENDING

21

**19. SUN AIR**
FCB BOSMAN JOHNSON,
JOHANNESBURG, 1998
The use of people as "living
ads" is becoming more
popular; this advertiser hired
a contortionist and stationed
him at the airport.

**20. ECAMPUS.COM**
DEVITO VERDI, NEW YORK,
1999
In street advertising, the idea is
to not look too professional;
homemade-looking fliers and
posters can be effective. (This
ad appeared, as photographed,
in magazines.)

**21. CONSECO INSURANCE**
FALLON WORLDWIDE,
MINNEAPOLIS, MINNESOTA,
2000
This ad addresses one of the
driving forces behind the spread
of guerrilla marketing: Every space
is for sale these days, including
those once considered off-limits.

22. **ALTERED CAMEL
BILLBOARD**
BILLBOARD LIBERATION
FRONT, SAN FRANCISCO, 1995
The "culture jammers" have
been waging a counteroffensive
against the spread of ads. This
San Francisco anti-advertising
group rewired an electronic
Camel billboard to read "Am
I dead yet? "

23

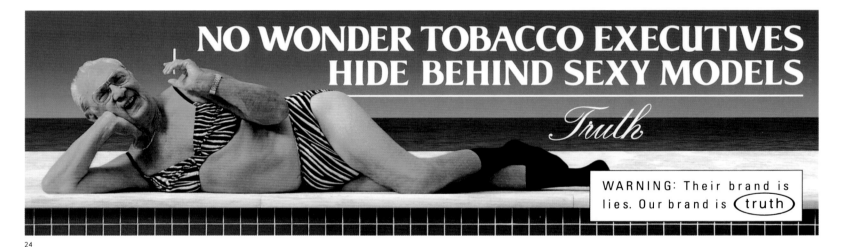

24

**23. CALIFORNIA
DEPARTMENT OF HEALTH**
ASHER & PARTNERS,
LOS ANGELES, 1997
In recent years, ad agencies have
mimicked the style of culture
jammers. An anti-smoking
campaign put a new headline
on a classic Marlboro image.

**24. FLORIDA ANTI-SMOKING
CAMPAIGN**
CRISPIN PORTER + BOGUSKY,
MIAMI, 1999
Here again, an anti-smoking
campaign created a billboard
that looked like a defaced
cigarette company billboard.

**25. FAKE MCDONALD'S
BILLBOARD**
RON ENGLISH, NEW JERSEY,
1990
Some artists have begun to use
billboards both to display their
work and to make anti-commercial
statements; here, Ron English
takes on McDonald's.

25

agency Fallon McElligott says that while today's consumers sometimes feel that ads in the surrounding environment are invasive, they also tend to appreciate the uniqueness and the appropriate placement of such ads. And many don't particularly mind being ambushed by guerrilla ads if they are done with a certain level of wit and style.

However, there is also a growing minority faction that has taken an active role in resisting the creeping commercialism in the environment; in a sense, these are the authentic "guerrillas" in the battle to control street-level mass communication. Sometimes calling themselves "culture jammers," they can be found around the world, waging war against advertising by creating their own strain of communication—which often consists of altering and subverting existing ads. Culture jamming burst on the scene in the U.S., Europe, and Australia in the 1980s, when underground groups with names like Guerilla [sic]

Girls and Negativland began altering and ridiculing messages from advertisers via pirate TV and radio broadcasting, public posters, elaborate media hoaxes, and various other stunts. But most often, culture jammers target what they consider the most intrusive form of advertising— the billboard. The often colorful and clever alterations on billboards have evolved into an engaging form of protest art.

A pioneer in this underground movement was San Francisco's Billboard Liberation Front (BLF), which first began altering billboards back in 1977. Members of the group were known for scaling billboards by rope and ladder in the dead of night and pasting "new and improved" headlines over the old ones. On a Camel cigarettes electronic billboard, the BLF rewired the neon lettering in 1995, so that the glowing message became "Am I Dead Yet?" In the late 1990s, the BLF targeted some of the most prevalent new outdoor campaigns, including

Apple's "Think different" boards. The headline of a "Think different" billboard featuring mogul Ted Turner was changed to "Think dividends." For the tragic aviator Amelia Earhart, the headline became "Think doomed."

Culture jamming became so popular by the early 1990s that the movement had its own ad-spoofing magazine, *AdBusters* (which is still published from its base in Canada). American magazines like the *Utne Reader* and *Wired* portrayed the BLF and other groups as "media heroes," while academic scholars wrote weighty theses on culture jamming, with some likening it to the Russian samizdat movement that defied government censorship by printing and circulating defiant messages among the public.

But advertising gradually became very aware of the enemy in its midst, and soon began to do what it has done to the pop and street culture for the past two decades—copy, co-opt, and absorb. By the late-1990s, the rough-hewn look and

# INTERVIEW: "JACK NAPIER"

For the past 25 years, the San Francisco–based Billboard Liberation Front has pioneered the art of "culture jamming." The group, which has remained underground through the years, specializes in altering billboards in creative ways, subverting the ad message in order to make a statement (whether political or just humorous). The BLF has been called "the Monkey Wrench Gang of outdoor advertising" by *Wired* magazine, and was named "one of the top 10 media heroes" by the *Utne Reader*. One of the founders and the current spokesman of the group goes by the nom de guerre of "Jack Napier" (pictured opposite in cosmetic disguise).

**AT THE TIME THE BLF WAS GETTING STARTED IN THE LATE 1970S, WAS ANYONE ELSE DOING THIS KIND OF THING?**

Apparently, there was a group in Michigan in the late 1960s, and an Australian group, called Bugger Up, in the late 1970s. In our own San Francisco area, another group started in 1979 called Truth in Advertising. But it goes way back—if you go back as far as World War II, there were advertisements and political posters being jammed.

**WHAT'S YOUR PHILOSOPHY ABOUT ADVERTISING?**

I have nothing against advertising, per se. I actually like a lot of ads, anything that's clever. But I have to admit I'm pretty irate that a handful of [outdoor advertising] corporations control all the public spaces. I find that to be completely un-democratic. I think all of us should be able to have a say in what appears on these billboards in public spaces. Whenever I see a billboard, I find myself thinking, Wouldn't it be funnier if it said this? So I change it.

**WHAT SEPARATES GOOD BILLBOARD ALTERATION FROM ORDINARY GRAFFITI?**

The first thing is coming up with a good idea. Something that works as a concept and something that'll work graphically. I think that if the messages are blatantly and stodgily political, that's just not going to get through to anyone except those who already agree. My favorite billboards are ones that are enigmatic, that people might have a hard time figuring out at first—but that stick in their minds.

**WHAT ABOUT THE TECHNICAL ASPECTS OF ALTERING A BILLBOARD?**

Well, the idea is to make it look as though the message came from the billboard company. If you're going to add an image, you want it to look like it's part of the background image. You've got to take your measurements. We often do layouts and sketches in advance to see what it looks like. We use computer-aided design, PhotoShop, and laser-cut vinyl for paste-overs. And we go to great pains to make sure everything we add to the billboard is removable.

**WHY IS THAT IMPORTANT?**

Because we're not anti-property, and we don't want to damage private property. We look at what we're doing as just borrowing the space. So all someone has to do is go up on a ladder to remove our work in order to restore the original billboard—sometimes we even leave a six-pack of beer up there for the guy who has to do that. We're also protecting ourselves. If there are no damages to the billboard, it's harder for us to be prosecuted.

**IT SEEMS THAT SOME PEOPLE WHO ALTER BILLBOARDS HAVE A POLITICAL AGENDA, WHILE OTHERS ARE MORE INTERESTED IN CREATING ARTWORK, RIGHT?**

Yes, you have someone like Ron English, who was just a good painter who couldn't get a gallery show, and he wanted people to see his work. So he went out and started putting up these giant paintings on billboards. He got a lot of attention for it, and it helped him establish his art career. The Cicada group on the East Coast would be an example of a more political group, going after cigarette billboards—but they do it with a sense of humor. I don't mind being hit with a blatant political message as long as it's funny.

**WHAT KINDS OF REACTIONS DO YOU GET FROM ADVERTISERS AFTER THEIR BILLBOARDS HAVE BEEN HIT?**

The billboard companies have responded in the press several times to our activities, and a number of times they've acknowledged that we don't damage the billboards. There was a controversy over our Apple [alterations]. An internal E-mail barrage went on at the company for some time; they were definitely aware of what we were doing. Some people thought it was funny; others didn't get it. Some even thought we were shills for Microsoft.

**WHAT ARE YOUR THOUGHTS ON THE WAY THAT ADVERTISERS HAVE CO-OPTED THE LOOK OF THE ANTI-ADVERTISING MOVEMENT?**

It was inevitable. I knew it was going to happen years ago. I was a little surprised and angry when I first saw ads crossing out their own headlines and writing in something self-mocking—my first reaction was "They should be paying residuals to the BLF!" But after the initial shock wore off, it made perfect sense. That's what I would do if I were one of those guys. They're continually mining what's hip. It seems like now you can't have any kind of subculture pop up that has originality or meaning to kids without it being co-opted immediately. They won't leave these poor kids alone to have their own culture. I have thought about this question of whether it's even possible anymore to question or ridicule advertising, given that it has become so accepted as the language of the culture. All I can say is, you have to at least try. If there isn't some kind of insurgent spirit popping up between the cracks, you might as well give it up as a society. We're not at that point yet—not even close.

OUTDOOR SYSTEMS

# Think disillusioned

## STOP The MADNESS!!!
### Potato on pizza is unnatural, subversive AND
# WRONG!

**ATTENTION! ATTENTION! ATTENTION!** LET THE SHOCKING TRUTH BE KNOWN: A RADICAL GROUP OF NONCONFORMISTS COMMONLY KNOWN AS **CPK** (CALIFORNIA PIZZA KITCHEN) IS RIGHT NOW SERVING POTATO ON PIZZA IN THIS COMMUNITY! **THIS GOES AGAINST EVERYTHING OUR FOREFATHERS INTENDED PIZZA TO BE!** Whatever happened to COMMON DECENCY?? Who died and gave CPK the RIGHT to CROSS THE INVISIBLE LINE between the *Four Food Groups??* Potatoes should NOT be integrated with Rosemary Chicken, let alone PIZZA! If people start adopting a permissive attitude towards potato on pizza. Next thing you know, it's the COLLAPSE OF CIVILIZATION IN THE FREE WORLD!!! Right now, MILLIONS OF CPK PIZZA-CRAZED "ZOMBIES" walk our streets. And the scourge is spreading!

Rosemary Chicken-Potato Pizza = Radical propaganda thinly veiled in a thin, flaky crust. Don't be fooled by its pizza-like appearance. IT IS THE ENEMY.

## WE MUST TAKE ACTION NOW!!
Consider the cold, hard, irrefutable FACTS!
Fact: "Savory" Rosemary Chicken-Potato Pizza is cooked with fire.
Fact: Fire is a destructive element.
Conclusion: "Savory" Rosemary Chicken-Potato Pizza is destructive!!!

We must STAND UP to protect pizza from being transformed into a tool of "COUNTERCULTURE" factions. Let's go back to a simpler time when pizza was a place for pepperoni. Not Tandoori Chicken, Shrimp Pesto, Peking Duck, Goat Cheese (Blasphemy!) or Rosemary Chicken-Potato. If we were intended to taste two different "exotic" foods at the same time, we would have been BORN WITH TWO TONGUES!! **WAKE UP AND SMELL THE GARLIC!!!** Every one of CPK's 27 highly addictive, unholy combinations must be ELIMINATED. TOGETHER, we can stop the crispy, wood-fired menace! A return to traditional pizza MORALS is OUR BEST SECURITY FOR OUR FUTURE!!!

*Support our grassroots action group, C.R.U.S.T. (Crusaders Resisting Unnatural Subversive Toppings).*

BOYCOTT ANTI-ESTABLISHMENT PIZZAMONGERS! Whatever you do, don't go to any of these CPK locations:
- 437 S. Highway 101, Solana Beach, (619) 793-0999.
- 3363 Nobel Dr., La Jolla, (619) 457-4222.
- 11602 Carmel Mountain Rd., San Diego, (619) 675-4424.
And, by all means, don't call for take-out orders.

## Potatoes Belong on a PLATE!! Not a PIZZA!!!

27

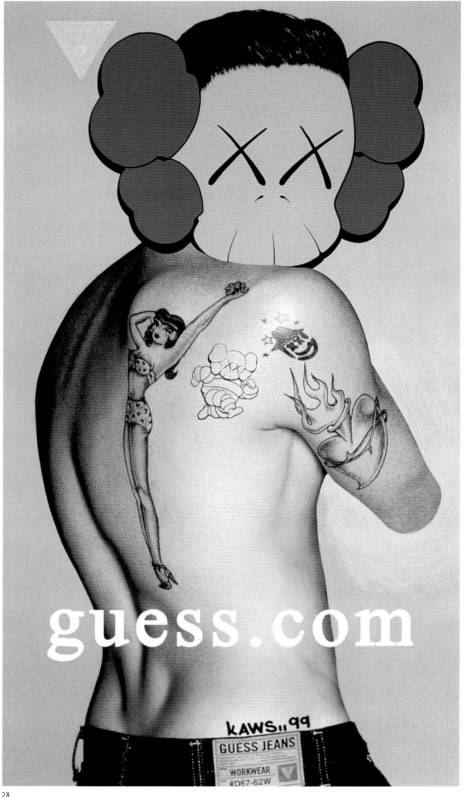

guess.com

28

**26. (PREVIOUS SPREAD)**
**ALTERED APPLE BILLBOARD**
BILLBOARD LIBERATION
FRONT, SAN FRANCISCO, 1998
The BLF targeted the popular
Apple "Think different"
billboards, changing one
word in the headline each
time. (For mogul Ted Turner,
the headline was changed to
"Think dividends"; for Amelia
Earhart, "Think doomed.")

**27. CALIFORNIA PIZZA
KITCHEN**
RUBIN POSTAER &
ASSOCIATES, LOS ANGELES,
1996
Another advertiser imitating
a culture jammer: this ad for
a pizza chain was designed
to look like a rant from an
underground radical.

**28. ALTERED GUESS JEANS AD**
KAWS, NEW YORK, 1999
The graffiti artist known as
"Kaws" uses outdoor ads as his
canvas, typically painting a new
head or one of his signature characters on the model in the ad.

**29. FAKE CALVIN KLEIN AD**
ADBUSTERS MAGAZINE,
VANCOUVER, 1995
The Canadian magazine
*AdBusters* emerged as the
journal of the culture jamming
movement. The magazine
created its own fake ads, like
this one for Calvin Klein.

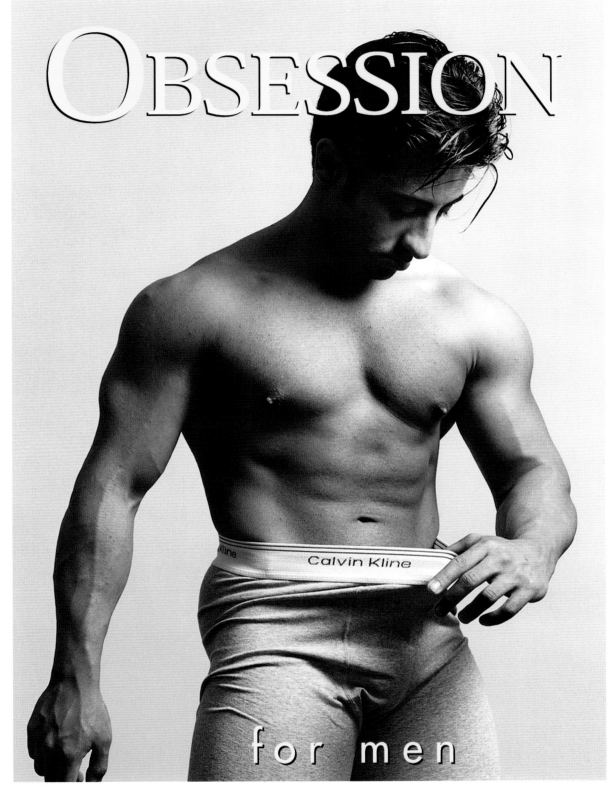

29

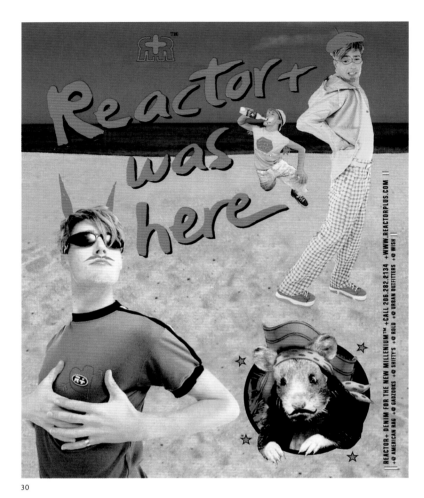

30

subversive attitude of altered billboards and street posters was being imitated in ads for jeans and beer. Some advertisers, such as the Captain Morgan rum brand, even took to "jamming" or altering their own billboards, by crossing out headlines or putting fake graffiti on the ads. Why would advertisers deface their own ads? To strike an anti-establishment pose, thereby making the brand seem more irreverent, hip, and self-aware. One of the more extreme examples was seen in a billboard campaign featuring ad copy that seemed to have been written by an anarchist urging the public to avoid Amstel Lite "at all costs," and warning of "impending doom"—the posters were, of course, created by Amstel Lite.

The look and language of anti-advertising has even found its way into million-dollar TV commercials—which have increasingly adopted a rough cinema-verité style and a self-mocking tone. As Sprite commercials began to point out that ad slogans were bogus and spokespersons

were bought and paid for, the advertiser was, in effect, doing the culture jammers' job for them.

It wasn't hard for advertising's creative Young Turks to adopt the style of culture jammers, considering how much the two groups have in common: the same irreverent attitude, absurd sense of humor, and compulsion to put one's cleverness on public display. Annie Finnegan, an ad executive who has taught a guerrilla-advertising course at the ad school Creative Circus in Atlanta, pointed out that the culture jammers and some of today's cutting-edge ad creators "both are products of the same culture, with the same sensibilities—they just went in opposite directions." Consider, for example, the Philadelphia ad executive Steve Grasse, founder of the hot agency Gyro: A specialist in targeting disaffected young audiences, Grasse claims to hate conventional advertising, and enjoys playfully defacing ad imagery in much the same way that culture

jammers do. But Grasse does it for mercenary purposes: His self-mocking, intentionally amateurish-looking ads are financed by huge client companies that sell liquor and cigarettes to the "twentysomething" market.

While it can be increasingly difficult to distinguish between real protest communications and advertising's ersatz version, culture jamming is continuing to survive and even flourish—not only in altered headlines on billboards but also in other forms that include painted outdoor signs and wall murals that reinterpret advertising images. The American culture jammer Ron English is known for impressionistic anti-advertising art on billboards around the East Coast of the U.S. Another American artist, Dick Detzner, creates Renaissance-style frescoes—but in place of religious figures are ad characters like Snuggles the Fabric Softener Bear. In a few instances, anti-advertising artists have jumped to the other side; one team of New York

32

33

graffiti artists signed on to produce street murals for Coca-Cola and others. Even those jammers who steadfastly refuse to "sell out" are well aware that they have no chance of winning the street-level communication war against the ever-growing, co-opting ad machine. But they persist anyway: The longtime leader of the BLF, who goes by the nom de guerre of Jack Napier, said that even though ads have copied the style and language of culture jammers, the movement still provides an alternative viewpoint on the street.

Meanwhile, ad agencies continue to expand their own arsenal of tricks, pranks, and stunts. One Swedish agency produced an ad for travel insurance that was placed in a wallet and glued to the sidewalk of a busy street—this was one advertiser who knew how to get people's attention. The Los Angeles office of the agency Deutsch Inc. recently fooled large numbers of people in Los Angeles with a series of fake billboards for "topless traffic school" and other

nonexistent businesses; when curious people called the number they were connected to the advertiser that sponsored the campaign. One of the more recent forms of ad pranksterism has targeted the much-sought-after venture-capitalist investors in Silicon Valley. The adman Michael Dweck has made an art of stalking and tricking these financiers on behalf of his dot-com clients, who will try anything to draw the attention (and money) of investors. Dweck has infiltrated delicatessens in order to slip client advertising messages into some of the lunch delivery bags bound for bankers' offices. Staking out bars frequented by the venture capitalists, he has planted actors there and instructed them to pretend to talk on cell phones and to repeatedly mention the name of the company that Dweck was slyly promoting. Knowing the investors tended to take certain taxi routes, Dweck left printed messages, touting his clients, in the backseats of cabs. And just in case these

subtleties were missed, he also turned loose a bunch of trained chimps, wearing promotional T-shirts, in the offices of one investor.

The trend of advertisers resorting to pranksterism to draw attention is perhaps the most extreme form of guerrilla marketing, and although it can be amusing and creative, it can also backfire. "Sometimes people become angry when they discover they've been tricked by an advertiser," Finnegan points out. But those who are troubled by the kind of "stalker advertising" practiced by the likes of Dweck had better brace themselves, because advertising that snoops on us and invades our space will very likely be part of the next wave. In fact, new technology will enable advertisers to know exactly where you are at any given time . . . what you're doing . . . and maybe even what you're thinking. So say goodbye to your privacy, and hello to the advertising of the future.

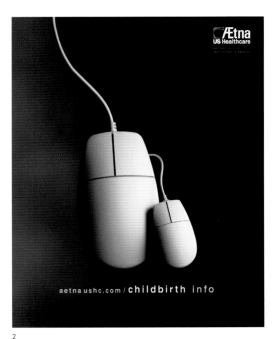

To the question "Where does advertising go from here?" the answer would seem to be obvious: everywhere. As noted in the preceding chapter, ads have already permeated the environment to such a degree that sanctuary can be found (for the moment at least) only in houses of worship. And if the major advertising agencies have their way—as they usually have before—the ad cocooning effect should continue. Consider that the agency Ogilvy & Mather, for example, has rooted much of its future in a strategy called "360-degree branding," whose primary purpose is to ensure that ads shadow us wherever we go.

Technology will continue to make it easier to do that. Dave Westreich, a futurist at Ogilvy & Mather, points out that through the use of satellite technology, it will be possible to track someone's movement and send him messages through devices he wears or carries—advanced Palm Pilots, for example, or "augmented reality"

eyeglasses. (Unlike the more familiar "virtual reality" helmets that envelop you in an artificial world, augmented reality might use translucent eyewear that would allow you to continue to see the real world around you—but with an overlay of images and messages.) "This means you would be able to stream advertising content to people based on where they're standing," says Westreich. "If I happen to be a few steps away from the delicatessen, today's menu might pop up in my eyewear." This kind of "stalking advertising" might follow you anywhere. For example, Westreich envisions the beach towel of the future as having a built-in receiver that will play the kind of music you happen to like—while also trying to sell you concert tickets for your favorite musicians.

While it may become increasingly difficult to get away from ads, we will have more control over their content, experts believe. Watts Wacker, whose firm FirstMatter helps companies plan

for the future, predicts: "Ads will be stratified, based on your needs at a given time. So if you're looking to buy a washing machine, you'll turn on 'the advertising channel' on your TV and it will show you continuous ads for washing machines—until you indicate that you want something else."

Even the faces we see in those ads may be customized for each of us. The high-tech guru Jaron Lanier (who coined the phrase "virtual reality") envisions next-generation advertising that will make us all stars of our own commercials. Internet test labs are already hooking up digital cameras to computers and refining the process of photographing the computer user's face, then recreating that image and inserting it into the midst of Web content—such as online movies or commercials. In effect, your face would replace that of an actor in a commercial, and you would even speak his or her lines. So, instead of seeing the rock star

We can live without guns.

3

Sting behind the wheel in a Jaguar ad, you'll see yourself. And that could prove to be a very compelling sales presentation because, as Lanier notes, "we may find that vanity trumps celebrity."

Such changes are still to come, but to some extent the future has already arrived in the form of interactive marketing on the Internet—which is allowing companies to track customers on the Web, engage in a dialogue with them, and, in effect, "read their minds" better than conventional advertisers ever could. In the past, advertising was mostly a one-way street, with all the messages going from the advertiser to the audience. But the Internet, and eventually interactive TV, is transforming it into a two-way thoroughfare, with information constantly flowing back and forth between the advertiser and the customer.

In some ways, this represents "the end of advertising as we know it" (a phrase that is constantly on the lips of new-media executives these days). Even within some of Madison Avenue's oldest ad agencies, many are bracing for a world without thirty-second commercials. Bob Jeffrey, the president of J. Walter Thompson's flagship New York office, has already declared the conventional TV commercial to be obsolete. Jeffrey and many others believe that the convergence of television and computer will form a multifaceted, interactive medium wherein old-fashioned sales pitches simply won't work. The viewer will be in control, dictating what appears onscreen—and who in his right mind will request commercials? Instead, viewers may use digital personal video recorders, known as PVRs, to fetch, assemble, and present the kind of shows they want to watch, with commercials edited out; or they may simply download programming right off the Internet.

This scenario doesn't mean that companies will stop pitching to us—only that the pitching will take a very different form. In the new model, marketers will still be disseminating information about their products, but they will need to be much craftier about it: weaving product plugs into programs, or creating "infotainment" that somehow promotes a brand, or offering us incentives to click a button on the TV screen that transports us to the company Web site—whereupon they will attempt to lavish us with information, advice, and coupons as they "build relationships" with us.

To some degree, all of this should be welcome news to anyone who has ever lamented that "the ads never tell me what I need to know before I buy." In the new advertising environment, detailed information about products will be readily available and tailored to the customer's questions and needs. The advertising of the future, says Clement Mok of the high-tech design and consulting company Sapient, will "no longer rely on clever sound bites" that try to "blast out a sales pitch to people." Rather, Mok says, it will provide detailed editorial-style information, will

4

respond to questions, and will tend to reward you for your interest by offering something of substance and value (a coupon, say, or free expert advice, or a piece of entertainment). Bob Herbold, a top executive at Microsoft, concurs that "you're going to see more brands do good things for people in terms of providing a service, as opposed to running a traditional message that pounds the attributes of a brand." The public, armed with the power to point-and-click not just on its computers but on its TV screens, will have more control over when and how ad messages are received; the marketers, meanwhile, will benefit by being able to communicate more directly with us, finding out what we really want and need from them. It certainly sounds like an "Everybody wins" scenario.

Of course, marketers *would* tend to make it sound that way. The reality of the new advertising environment will have its downside, and it may be a big one. The most explosive issue will be—

and in fact, already is—privacy. As advertisers use technology to get closer and closer to their customers, trying to discern details about our tastes and habits and peccadilloes that we might not be anxious to share, backlashes are inevitable. Already, a few opening shots have been fired across the Internet. One of the first skirmishes involved DoubleClick, America's biggest on-line advertising company, which has been amassing detailed information on consumers—including tracking people as they surf the Internet. Whenever a Web surfer visits any one of hundreds of sites in the DoubleClick network and clicks on certain ads, a bug, or "cookie," is immediately planted on that person's hard drive, without his knowledge. The cookies contain an identifying number that enables DoubleClick to watch where you surf and what you do on the Web long after you leave its site. DoubleClick is just one of many companies planting cookies on unsuspecting Web surfers'

computers, but in early 2000, the company tried to go a step further; it announced plans to combine the tracking information gathered from cookies with other personal data collected separately—to assemble complete "on-line profiles," which would then be shared with various advertisers (conceivably, this could have included revealing to advertisers everything from one's taste in ice cream to one's predilection for kinky Web sites). A storm of protest followed, causing DoubleClick to back off the plan. And in the summer of 2000, the U.S. Federal Trade Commission reached a voluntary agreement with advertisers promising that in the future, Web surfers would be informed of on-line advertisers attempts to "profile" them.

But it was clear that the DoubleClick controversy was just the tip of the iceberg. To think that marketers will exhibit self-restraint when it comes to gathering and disseminating information about customers is naive; the very

**THE NEXT WAVE.**

**No brain, no pain.**

100% GUILT-FREE MEAT

Another deliciously humane creation from the genetic engineers at the
**SWINE BREEDERS of AMERICA.** SBA

5

**5. "SWINE BREEDERS OF AMERICA"**
TBWA/CHIAT/DAY,
LOS ANGELES, 1999
This mock ad, created for
*Advertising Age*'s "Next Century"
issue, promotes genetic engineering. In the future, advertising
will probably be called upon to
make radical technology seem
less scary.

**6. AMERICAN STANDARD**
CARMICHAEL LYNCH,
MINNEAPOLIS, MINNESOTA,
1999
In the Internet age, even old
products must be given a new
spin; here, a toilet becomes
"interactive sculpture."

**7. TOASTMASTERS**
TBWA HUNT LASCARIS,
JOHANNESBURG, 1998
The less said, the better: The
new global advertising will
have little use for words.

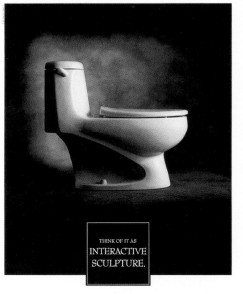

THINK OF IT AS
INTERACTIVE
SCULPTURE.

Behold the *Savona* toilet, the product of a unique artistic collaboration. We asked people what their ideal toilet would look like. Then we sculpted this. Call 1-800-524-9797 ext. 484 for a guidebook full of similarly inspired creations. *American Standard*

6

7

reason they are rushing to the Internet is to be "closer" to customers—by talking to us on-line, building databases on us, tracking our on-line movements and purchases, and getting inside our heads in a way that the old focus-group research never could. And, of course, this is not limited to adults; already marketers have been using the Internet to build marketing profiles on children, offering kids rewards for giving up personal information. Herbold of Microsoft is right that marketers "will be doing more things for people" on the Web—but what they'll want in return is more and more access to our thoughts, habits, and lives.

Whether the convenience of being provided with more customized information and more free "perks" from marketers will outweigh the attendant loss of privacy is a question that can't be answered here. But what can be examined is the impact of the current changes on the style and the craft of advertising. Because as technology

promises (or threatens, depending on one's view) to usher in "the end of advertising as we know it," the questions arise: What form of communication will be offered in its place? Will the new incarnations of advertising be more aesthetically pleasing and emotionally satisfying, or less? Will there still be room for creative expression by writers and designers, or will engineers and technologists rule the day?

For those who value creativity in ads, the early stages of the revolution have not been particularly encouraging. The beauty of interactivity is that it makes advertising more measurable, more controllable—on the Web, advertisers can immediately see how you respond to every offer, every image, every word. Naturally, this tilts the balance that advertising has maintained between art and science much more in the direction of science. And it begins to shift the power from the ad creators to the researchers and technicians.

This is seen as good news to many advertisers who never truly bought into the value of creativity, because they couldn't properly measure it. True, an ad might be highly pleasing to the audience, it might be recognized and honored for its style and creativity, but to what extent was it actually moving product off the shelf? That's always been a difficult question to answer with precision— until now. As Grey Advertising's Norman Lehoullier told *The New York Times*, the precise measurement provided by interactive advertising is a kind of "Holy Grail" for advertisers, allowing them to "figure out what works and what doesn't" as they track the responses and actions of someone interacting with ads on a Web site. In this new environment, Lehoullier said, "increasingly money will be spent not on lore or art—but on science."

But the problem for the audience on the receiving end of the communication is that science has rarely produced interesting or

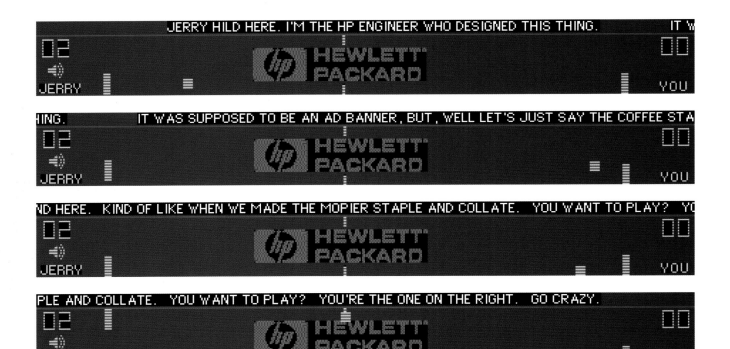

02 / JERRY / YOU / 00

ING. IT WAS SUPPOSED TO BE AN AD BANNER, BUT, WELL LET'S JUST SAY THE COFFEE STA

02 / JERRY / YOU / 00

ND HERE. KIND OF LIKE WHEN WE MADE THE MOPIER STAPLE AND COLLATE. YOU WANT TO PLAY? YO

02 / JERRY / YOU / 00

PLE AND COLLATE. YOU WANT TO PLAY? YOU'RE THE ONE ON THE RIGHT. GO CRAZY.

02 / JERRY / YOU / 00

8

**8. HEWLETT PACKARD**
GOODBY SILVERSTEIN &
PARTNERS, SAN FRANCISCO,
LATE 1990s
This banner ad introduced a
fictional HP employee named
Jerry, who challenged the public
to play him at the computer
game Pong, right there in the ad.

**9. IBM**
OGILVY & MATHER,
NEW YORK, 1999
Advertising, and in particular
the IBM campaign, is creating
a new language, wherein every
word begins with "e".

creative advertising. As the top creators of ads frequently attest, there is practically an inverse relationship between research and creativity in the ad world; generally speaking, the more that an advertising idea is tested, prodded, and manipulated on the basis of customer research, the more watered down it becomes. It is the reason larger, more bureaucratic, and research-driven companies have invariably produced more bland ads than small, entrepreneurial, risk-taking companies. As Tim Delaney of the agency Leagas Delaney noted, the best advertising more often results from intuition and leaps into the creative unknown—not from parroting back what the customer wants to hear. Of course, this truism extends beyond advertising to other creative fields such as filmmaking, where it's widely accepted that formulaic approaches often result in the worst movies. However, this is something of an alien concept so far in the Internet-marketing realm—which, as the

journalist Randall Rothenberg has pointed out, tends to follow the philosophies and principles of "direct" marketing, a field that slavishly adheres to research and formula. The producers of direct-mail promotions generally have no interest in winning style points or generating good feelings about a brand; rather, they strive to elicit an immediate response from consumers, by any means necessary—including resorting to empty promises on envelopes ("You may already be a winner!"). In its early stages, Internet advertising bears a much closer resemblance to the direct-mail business and is quite different from the commercials and print advertising that often attempt to build positive feelings about a brand through soft-sell emotional storytelling. According to *The Economist,* "on the Internet, brand-building is out and straight selling is in," because, as the magazine noted, "the combination of interactivity and precision makes the Internet ideally suited to the hard sell."

That may explain why, so far, advertising on the Internet has failed to stoke the imagination of the public. There's certainly no shortage of it out there: In 1999, advertisers spent more than $4 billion on Internet ads, and that figure is expected to climb to $30 billion by 2004, according to Forrester Research, a high-tech consultancy. All of those on-line pop-up windows, banners, and buttons are trying to do the same job that TV commercials try to do—but they don't seem to be doing it nearly as well. "We have abominable creative [advertising] on-line, the worst of the worst," a leading Internet advertising-industry spokesman, Rich LeFurgy, acknowledged. Another industry executive complained of "cheesy banners that obnoxiously scream out a free offer." Most Web banner ads are like old-fashioned billboards, and not very good ones at that; they seem to lack the capacity for charm or wit, and many simply flash a teaser message, often with the word *free* in it.

11

Not surprisingly, travelers on the information highway have been speeding past them and not bothering to click; most banners are experiencing minuscule click-through rates of less than half of one percent.

Banner ads have tried various means of engaging the audience, often by utilizing the ace in the hole of interactivity. Some have used the available technology to incorporate game-playing, which can be effective and amusing. Among the first to draw attention with this approach was a series of banner ads for Hewlett-Packard that introduced a fictional HP employee named Jerry, who challenged the public to play him in a game of Pong (played right there on the banner). Similarly, an IBM banner promoting its E-business partnership with the Professional Golf Association turned the banner into a tiny putting green, with the user's cursor serving as the putter. While some have played games, others have resorted to trickery—designing banners

that, for example, resembled a computer-error warning prompt on the user's screen (if you tried to respond to the warning by clicking an "OK" button, you were immediately hijacked to the advertiser's Web site). Even more bothersome than trick banners are "interstitials"—ad screens that pop up to interrupt Web surfing, and which must be removed from the screen before you can proceed. Some Internet advertisers argue that this form of advertising is no more intrusive than a TV commercial or roadside billboard, but in truth, the interstitial is like a roadside billboard that has been dragged to the middle of the road and left there, forcing drivers to stop and maneuver around it.

In fairness, the relatively poor quality of on-line ads is partly a function of the newness of the medium. The banner ads appearing now are only the first-generation versions of Internet marketing, and will rapidly evolve and improve. Andy Berlin of the agency Berlin Cameron &

Partners draws comparisons to the early days of television advertising, which tended to yield clumsy efforts. Part of the problem, Berlin notes, is that "technical revolutions tend to be led by the people that understand the technology and the people that finance it. And that's the sensibility early on. And then eventually they recognize that artistic people have to get involved or they won't get the full benefit of it." So far, the art crowd of the ad world—the award-winning creators of the best advertising in recent years— have been largely detached from advertising's Internet revolution, often by their own choice. According to Bob Schmetterer, who heads the Euro RSCG international advertising-agency network, a schism has developed in the ad business in which the Internet advertising arena is perceived to be a kind of ghetto, shunned by top creative stars who prefer to work in TV and print. "There is a very big and very prevalent belief that the Internet is the province of

# INTERVIEW: ESTHER DYSON

Esther Dyson has emerged as one of the preeminent thinkers and leaders of the new digital culture. Dyson's highly influential newsletter, "Release 1.0," and her book, *Release 2.1: A Design for Living in the Digital Age,* have provided a road map to what's unfolding and what is yet to come as the high-tech revolution reshapes the world. Today Dyson serves as chairman of the New York–based company EDventure Holdings, Inc., while also advising the WPP Group advertising conglomerate. She also oversees the governmental body dealing with registration of Internet domain names.

**IS THE THIRTY-SECOND COMMERCIAL GOING TO BE EXTINCT SOON?**
Like everything else, the changes being brought about by the Internet are cumulative, rather than things being suddenly replaced. I don't think mass-market commercials will go away. But I think people are using the Net wrong by putting mass-market commercials onto it. The Net is for one-to-one communication and customer support. It's not a place for making promises about the brand—it's the place to deliver on those promises.

**SO FAR, A LOT OF MARKETERS HAVE TRIED TO USE BANNER ADS, AND THEY HAVEN'T BEEN THAT EFFECTIVE.**
Yes, because it's not interactive. So it's sort of like going to a store where you expect to talk to a salesperson—and all you see is billboards surrounding you.

**WHAT WILL ADVERTISERS HAVE TO DO TO BRING MORE INTERACTIVITY TO THEIR COMMUNICATION ON THE WEB?**
You do it by paying attention to the consumer, rather than just clamoring for his attention. You can use the Net to listen to people and to help them talk to one another. And in that sense, maybe what we're talking about is not really advertising at all. It may be more a matter of providing information—maybe about someone's air-miles account or about using the product or creating a sense of community among users. There are lots of good things you can do, but simply saying, "Wow, I'm great" isn't one of them.

**IT SOUNDS LIKE YOU'RE SAYING THERE'S NO PLACE ON THE INTERNET FOR MAKING CLAIMS ABOUT A PRODUCT OR USING SOUND BITES TO GET ATTENTION.**
No, the Internet will still be a medium for delivering that. But that kind of message won't be considered native to the Internet format. What will be native is interactive communication. That can include storytelling ads, though they might be presented in a different way—probably more like serials or continuing cartoons. Or letting viewers vote on what they see. Right now, advertisers try to guess what the consumer wants to see. But why not just let consumers select from a list of what kinds of ads they want to see? Presumably they'll pay more attention to ads they've chosen, and they'll change the list when they change their mood. Seems like a very sensible idea—and it's something that interactivity allows you to do.

**AS ADVERTISING INCREASINGLY DRIVES PEOPLE TO WEB SITES, WHAT DO THE WEB SITES HAVE TO DO TO ENGAGE PEOPLE ONCE THEY ARRIVE?**
When you walk into a restaurant, usually you can tell whether it's the kind of fast-food place where you have to stand in line with a tray, or a fancier restaurant where you sit down and get waited on. But sometimes you walk into a restaurant and you can't tell—and that's annoying. With a Web site, people should know what to do and what to expect when they get there. Fundamentally, a Web site is not a window that people look through; it's a door, and when people walk through it they expect to interact with what they find inside.

**AS ADVERTISING BECOMES MORE OF A TWO-WAY DIALOGUE INSTEAD OF THE OLD ONE-WAY SALES PITCH, IS THIS A POSITIVE DEVELOPMENT FOR EVERYONE INVOLVED?**
Well, I think it's positive for consumers. But it's tough for marketers, because it's very expensive, people-intensive, and it's hard to do well. You can't simply produce a message at headquarters and slap it out to millions of people. And what's also disconcerting in this new communication is that people are uppity— they talk back. And they don't necessarily believe what you tell them. So I think it will be good for the world, but it's kind of tough for traditional advertising agencies.

**DO YOU THINK THOSE TRADITIONAL AD AGENCIES— THE MADISON AVENUE ESTABLISHMENT—WILL CONTINUE TO CONTROL ADVERTISING AND MARKETING AS IT SHIFTS MORE TOWARD THE WEB?**
Some agencies will and some won't. It's a matter of who understands how to use the new medium, and who is smart and open-minded. It's not a matter of big or small. In fact, being small usually correlates to being open-minded because you have less to protect. So that favors the newer companies.

**IN TERMS OF THE TWO-WAY DIALOGUE BETWEEN ADVERTISER AND CONSUMER, ONE AREA OF CONCERN IS PRIVACY AND THE SENSE THAT WE SHOULD BE WORRIED ABOUT HOW THE INFORMATION WE GIVE TO MARKETERS ENDS UP BEING USED. WILL THIS BE A PROBLEM IN INTERNET MARKETING FOR A LONG TIME TO COME?**
Not if people handle it right. I don't see it as a plague; I see it as a misunderstanding right now. When I give my money to a bank, it's still my money—and the same is true with the data I give to companies. But I think companies don't understand that; they think it's their data. What people can do about this is to make a contract with marketers about how they can and can't use those personal data. Companies need to begin to understand this, and consumers need to understand it. A lot of consumers are very happy to share the information if it means they'll get better offers in return—but you've got to ask them first. And people should be able to make different choices; we don't have to find one way that suits everyone. It's like choosing a credit card that has an expensive rate: People choose those for a reason, because it gives them credit they couldn't get otherwise. The challenge marketers will face is managing their data effectively and tagging them for what they can and can't do with them, based on the choices consumers have made. But the consumer should set the guidelines about which information can be used and where. In that regard, the balance of power is changing, and most companies don't get that yet.

NICO uit Amsterdam

SHOEBALOO

Amsterdam–Rotterdam

12

13

technocrats," Schmetterer wrote recently, "while TV, print, and other traditional media remain the province of *real* creative people. This is a huge problem for our industry."

One reason advertising's best storytellers and creators have ignored new media is that so far it's still difficult to bring emotion and story to life on the Internet, partly because of technical limitations. But as Internet access and data transmission improve via the growth of broad-band information-delivery systems, advertisers on the Web will be able to make better use of "rich media," combining high-grade graphics with audio and interactive capabilities. They will, in effect, be able to bring video storytelling qualities to more and more on-line ads (some advertisers already use rich media, but it's costly and can't be viewed by computer users with inadequate equipment).

While there's little doubt that technology will gradually provide the capability to bring more

emotional advertising to the Internet, some Internet experts maintain that emotional appeals have no real place in cyberspace—a world where speed and functionality are the top priorities. "Today, brands on the Web are all about how quick and easy it is for a consumer to find what he's looking for," according to Web analyst Jim Nail of Forrester Research. Nail argues that emotional appeals are needed by only those marketers who must draw people to a store with a promise; "but on-line, the delivery of that promise is one click away," he says. Sapient's Mok believes that in place of emotional sales pitches, Internet marketers will "craft and create real content and editorial," perhaps taking a form more similar to on-line magazines. But other advertisers still see a critical role for emotional appeals, storytelling, and entertainment. In fact, some believe that in the new media environment, emotional advertising will blend and blur with entertainment programming offered on the Web

and on TV—to the extent that it may be difficult to tell where the programming ends and the ad starts.

Ad agencies are already gearing up for this new form of "stealth advertising." A number of them have been creating in-house entertainment divisions or forging alliances with television and film producers; for example, in January 2000, J. Walter Thompson formed a creative alliance with Hollywood's Basic Entertainment, producers of the hit HBO television series "The Sopranos." The plan is for the ad agency to become more involved in the development of TV programs. This could go well beyond the kind of standard product placement that has been a part of moviemaking for years—it may involve coming up with concepts for shows in which the client's product is an integral part of the entertainment. J. Walter Thompson's Marina Hahn, who is overseeing the alliance, offers the following example: Listerine, a JWT client, might sponsor a comedy show in which some of the jokes and

**14. MOËT & CHANDON**
FRIERSON MEE & KRAFT,
NEW YORK, 1997
Web site marketing has the
advantage of being interactive,
unlike conventional ads. But so
far, most sites and on-line ads
have not been particularly
compelling.

**15. J&B SCOTCH**
J. WALTER THOMPSON,
NEW YORK, 1999
New ad characters, like the "J&B
Liquor Fairy," have been created
for the Web. They can engage
in banter with customers,
making them seem more like
trusted friends.

14

sketches revolve around a Listerine product. The program could be aired as a trailer in movie theaters, or shown on the Web as a piece of "advertainment." The thinking is that if consumers have the ability to bypass ads in selecting their shows, then advertising must be seamlessly woven into the shows themselves. To this end, new technology can help in planting ads in a television scene, even when the scene is a "live" event such as a ball game; already advertisers have used digital "virtual ads" to plant logos that look like they're painted on a stadium wall—though in fact, the ads don't exist in real space and are visible only to the TV viewer.

To some observers, the merging of ads and entertainment does not seem like progress. Reacting to the announcement of JWT's plan to align with TV producers, the television writer Marshall Herskovitz noted in a press interview that "the networks spent a lot of years trying to get out from under the control of sponsors in

terms of content," and Herskovitz said he was worried that the new alliance signaled a possible retreat by entertainment producers in giving advertisers control over programming. And it's reasonable to assume that as advertising becomes more involved in the creation of entertainment programs, quality will be compromised. Past attempts to turn ads into full-length programs resulted in the much-maligned "infomercial"— that strange hybrid of commercial and TV talk show that was supposed to revolutionize advertising when it first came along a decade ago. In fact, infomercials have served mostly as laughably bad, late-night filler programming in those desolate time slots that cannot attract real ads.

In one sense, attempts to fully merge ads and entertainment actually run counter to post-modern advertising's endeavor to be more candid with the audience and to say, "Yes, we all know this is an ad, but let's just try to enjoy it." Andy Berlin points out that commercials tend to

be more palatable when "there's a dumb honesty to them. It's sort of like young people and sex— they're there, they want what they want, we know what they want. And if they're sufficiently charming, we give them our attention." But when ads try to disguise themselves through product placement, the ploy is usually recognized quickly by today's media-savvy audience, and "it's a turnoff," Berlin says. "I find myself saying, 'What the hell does this have to do with the movie?' It's trying to work subliminally, but I don't think it persuades anyone."

While the "advertising is dead" school scrambles to come up with alternative and futuristic ways to plug products, a separate faction insists that commercials won't die but will coexist with new media—and may even flourish. Rick Boyko, creative chief of Ogilvy & Mather, says the predictions of the demise of commercials are based partly on the widely held assumption that the public *wants* commercials to die—which is not

"LIQUOR FAIRY," I

"..... ANY WISH YOU WANT, AS LONG AS IT'S J&B + COLA."
— J&B + COLA

DON'T EVER, *EVER* DRINK n DRIVE.

15

## It's ugly, but it gets you there.

**The new Volkswagen Time Machine.**

17

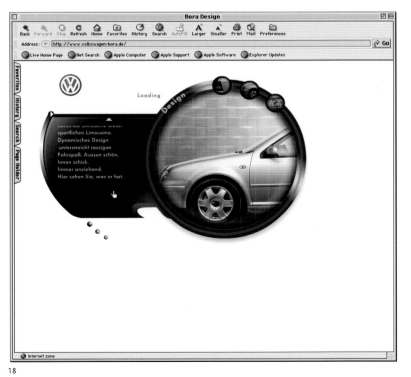

18

### 16. VOLKSWAGEN "TIME MACHINE"
DM9 DDB PUBLICIDADE, SÃO PAULO, 1999
This mock ad was originally created for *Advertising Age's* "Next Century" issue in Fall 1999. This time, DM9 took a crack at promoting a VW time machine.

### 17. VOLKSWAGEN
ARNOLD COMMUNICATIONS, BOSTON, 1999
VW's current TV commercials have begun to feature more "visual narratives," like this wordless tale of a flirtatious encounter between two parents driving a VW Passat.

### 18. VOLKSWAGEN WEB SITE (GERMANY)
BBDO INTERACTIVE GMBH, DUSSELDORF, 2000
The new, uncluttered ads are now designed to drive consumers to the Web site—which then uses detailed information to close the sale.

20

21

THE NEXT WAVE.

22. **REFLECT.COM**
DEUTSCH INC., NEW YORK,
2000
This ad plays up the positive
side of interactive marketing—
that you now have the opportunity to tell the advertiser what
you want and need (if you are
willing to share that private
information).

23 **MONSTER.COM**
MULLEN, BOSTON, 1999
This commercial for a job-search
Web site debuted during the
Super Bowl football champ-
ionship and showed children
fantasizing about dreary careers
as middle-managers.

23

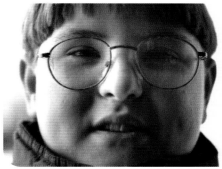

true, Boyko insists. "People had the means to zap commercials a long time ago," he points out, referring to remote controls, mute buttons, and VCRs. "The fact that they haven't done it suggests that commercials have become a part of our life that we've accepted and sometimes enjoy. Look at the Super Bowl, and the way some people pay more attention to the ads than to the game itself."

Moreover, even as customized Web marketing becomes more prevalent, there will still be a need for something to drive people to the Web site—a task for which today's entertainment-heavy, info-light commercials are actually well suited. Already, most commercials list Web-site addresses, though some recent ads have tried to create a more compelling link to the Internet. One series of Nike commercials featured scenes in which a character is being chased; in mid-chase, the commercial stops and directs viewers to visit a Web site in order to find out how the story ends (once there, the viewer

could see several different endings to the com-mercial). It was a clever idea, but might have been ahead of its time; in the pre-convergence world, this required someone to actually get up and move from TV to computer, which is a lot to ask of the average couch potato. (There was another problem with the ads: A couple of TV networks declined to run them, fearing they might end up pulling viewers away from the TV and the show they were watching.)

Similarly, Ford and its agency J. Walter Thompson produced a series of live commercials in the spring of 2000 that tried to entice viewers to the Web site by offering to turn over creative control of the advertising to the audience. Once at the Web site, viewers could actually dictate the content of the next commercial in the series—by voting on which characters would appear, what they would wear and say, etc. Not surprisingly, the Frankenstein's monster of a commercial that resulted from this experiment was a bit awkward;

the lesson there may be that even in the brave new "viewer controlled" media world, perhaps we'd best leave admaking to the professionals.

Evidence suggests that even without resorting to such gimmickry, commercials can do a good job of funneling people to Web sites. During the 1999 Super Bowl, a new employment Web site named Monster.com gambled a large portion of its start-up funds on a striking commercial that featured children fantasizing about dreary, dead-end careers ("I want to work my way up to middle management!" dreamed one boy). In the twenty-four hours after the commercial ran, traffic to the Web site jumped from 600,000 searches a day to over 2 million—and it spiked particularly high in the moments right after the ad ran, indicating that people had actually risen from the couch, turned away from the game, and gone to their computers. Monster.com's enormous success prompted a host of other dot-com companies to snap up ad time (at a

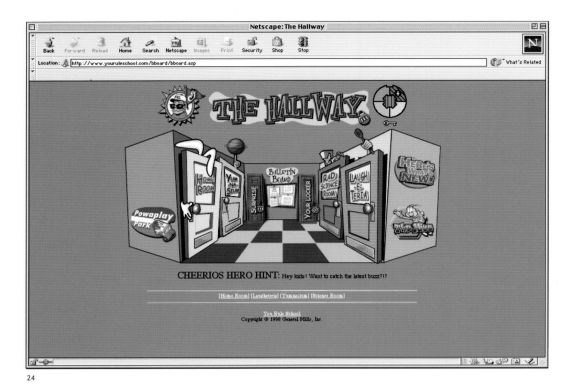

CHEERIOS HERO HINT: Hey kids! Want to catch the latest buzz?!?

[Home Room] [Laugheteria] [Yumnasium] [Science Room]

You Rule School
Copyright © 1998 General Mills, Inc.

24

**24. GENERAL MILLS**
RARE MEDIUM, NEW YORK,
1997
Interactive Web sites often
market to children by providing
games to play and prizes to win,
such as in this site for Cheerios
cereal. In return, kids may be
asked to key in personal
information.

**25. NIKE**
WIEDEN + KENNEDY,
PORTLAND, 2000
One series of Nike TV
commercials featuring snowboarder Rob Kingwell began
telling dramatic stories, then
stopped in the middle—to see
how the commercial ended,
you had to visit the Web site.

**26. ADIDAS INTERNATIONAL**
SAATCHI & SAATCHI NEW
ZEALAND, WELLINGTON, 1999
Ads in the future will target
"small, highly ethnocentric
tribal societies," says one
futurist. Advertisers may
create hundreds of versions
of the same ad, targeting
different groups.

whopping cost of more than $2 million for thirty seconds) on the Super Bowl the following year, and most reported similarly impressive jumps in site traffic resulting from their commercials.

One of the interesting aspects of commercials by Monster.com and the other dot-com advertisers in America and Europe is that much of this new advertising doesn't engage in the straightforward "direct sell" associated with Internet-style marketing. On the contrary, while the dot-coms are part of the Internet culture, many have been following the advertising model of sneaker, jeans, and cola marketers by opting for highly entertaining, sometimes outrageous ads. Not all the dot-com advertising has been a joy to watch—young and desperate for attention, the players in this category have often resorted to stunts, shock appeal, and bathroom humor in ads. But the fact that dot-coms have opted to entertain in their ads rather than hammer home a sales pitch suggests that the soft sell (albeit

with a hard edge) may yet survive in the new media world. In fact, some advertisers believe that in this new landscape, commercials should be freer than ever to entertain and be creative—because all the dreary facts and detailed information can now be provided on the Web site instead of in the ad. Hence, the commercial of the future need not compel you to buy as much as to browse the site—at which point the rich editorial-style content envisioned by Mok will be expected to close the sale.

It has been observed that the tremendous influx of money into TV commercials by dot-com entrepreneurs is something of an ironic turn of events—after all, the Internet was supposed to pull money away from old-fashioned advertising. Instead it has been a gold mine for ad agencies, and also "has provided shock treatment for the advertising industry" by encouraging more daring, risk-taking advertising, said David Wecal, a creative director at Hill Holliday. "It's giving

us the opportunity to prove that advertising can be powerful for a brand again." Bob Bowman, president of the Web site Outpost.com, explained that for dot-coms trying to introduce themselves to the world, there was little choice but to invest heavily in TV commercials.

But the dot-coms have also learned some hard lessons about the limitations of commercials. As many of these young companies flooded the airwaves with entertaining thirty-second spots, it had a numbing effect on the audience, noted Roy Grace, now of the agency Grace & Rothschild. "I know it's happened to me—listening to the radio, one company after another: Dot-com, dot-com, and you just start to turn it all off," Grace said. Another problem was that some dot-coms were so desperate to be entertaining that they practically neglected to tell the audience anything relevant about the Web site. Ellis Verdi of the ad agency DeVito Verdi noted that "with half of the dot-com ads, I don't even

25

26

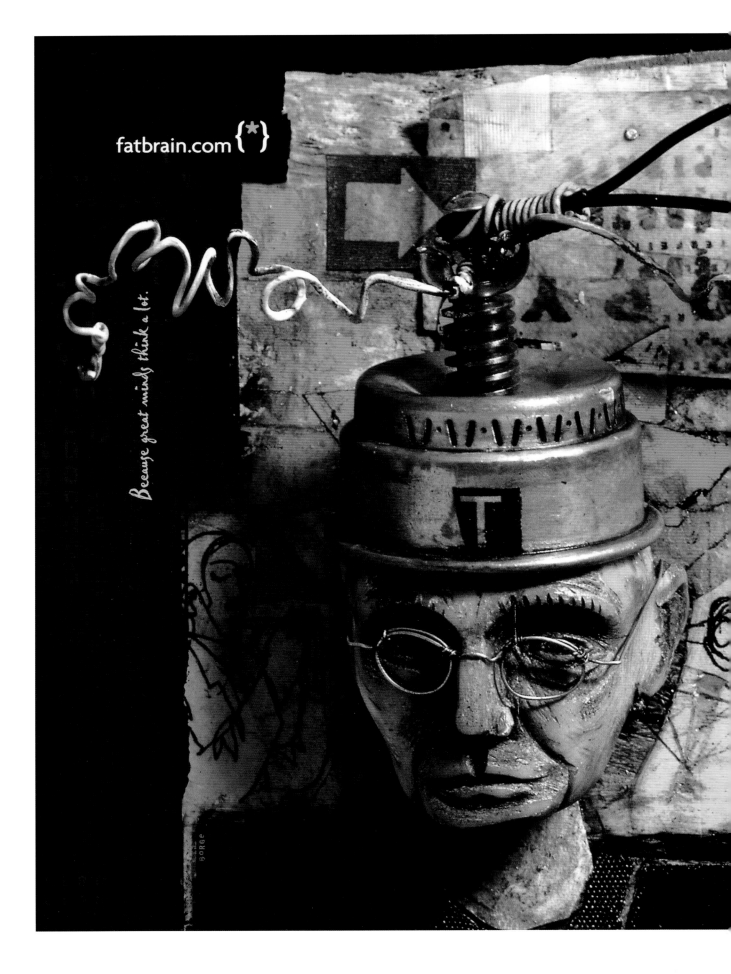

fatbrain.com {*}

*Because great minds think a lot.*

You're **100%** technology.

Why go to a bookstore that's **99.3%** everything else **?**

**27. FATBRAIN.COM**
GOLDBERG MOSER O'NEILL,
SAN FRANCISCO, 1999
Traditional print advertising
was a huge beneficiary of the
technology boom. Magazines
such as *Wired* overflowed with
wild ads like this one for a Web-
based business information
manager.

28. **AMERICAN LEGACY FOUNDATION**
ALLIANCE (CRISPIN PORTER +
BOGUSKY, MIAMI / ARNOLD
COMMUNICATIONS,
BOSTON), 2000
The "Truth" anti-smoking ads
are like short documentary films,
following rebellious teenagers
who challenge tobacco marketers.
In this commercial, "Body Bags,"
kids piled body bags outside the
offices of a cigarette company.

29. **BRODERBUND SOFTWARE**
SAATCHI & SAATCHI,
SAN FRANCISCO, 1997
This series of ads promoting
the Riven CD-ROM turned
the print ad itself into a kind of
game (can you find the Web site
address in this picture?)

28

29

know what they're selling; I don't know what the benefits are to them." Many dot-coms, including Outpost.com and its flying gerbils, failed at this. In the new millennium, some forty years after DDB's Bill Bernbach laid down the law that advertising had to balance art and commerce, and that it needed to entertain yet never lose sight of the product and the message, the problem was still the same—many advertisers just couldn't seem to figure out how to achieve that very delicate balance.

The balancing act won't get easier in days ahead, and may in fact become more difficult. Among the new challenges facing ads in the future: The need to connect with an audience that is, itself, divided into many distinct and very separate groups. According to the futurist Jim Taylor, coauthor of the book *The 500-Year Delta*, the coming years will bring "the deconstruction of the concept of collective, so-called mass society. We will see the growth of small, highly

ethnocentric 'tribal' societies." Reaching a more culturally diverse society of consumers, new ads will travel by way of a more fragmented and splintered delivery system. How splintered? One major marketer recently experimented with an advertising delivery system that would send customized versions of its commercials to different rooms within the same house—so that children upstairs might see one version of the commercial, while one parent in the den would see another version, and the other parent, in the kitchen, would see yet another version of that ad. O&M's Westreich foresees the possibility of software that could take a single ad and "create two-hundred versions of it automatically," so that the ad is seen differently by each ethnic or demographic group; the perception and interpretation of such advertising will truly be in the eye of the beholder. Meanwhile, the targeting of ads is expected to zero in on ever-narrower and quirkier audience segments. (Already, one

pet-food advertiser has created and run a TV commercial targeted to cats; it features a montage of scenes involving a fish swimming, a ball of yarn, and a mouse, with a sound track of actual catcalls.)

But for advertisers to be able to connect with the various tribes in an increasingly global and multicultural world, the business itself must diversify. As the new millennium began, advertising in America and Europe was still a predominantly white male bastion, particularly in creative departments of top agencies. Executives throughout the ad industry are attuned to the problem, but many seem at a loss as to how to resolve it. Training programs and scholarships have been tried, but the cycle has been difficult to break; for members of minority groups, there are "no heroes to emulate in advertising," says Ron Seichrist of the Miami Ad School. And while advertising must learn to speak the language of ethnic groups, it must avoid the

**THE NEXT WAVE.**

Where can I find my uncle? Search ALTAVISTA

alta<sup>vista</sup>: smart is beautiful

30

kind of pandering that has, so far, caused ads targeted to minority groups to be among the least creative of all advertising. "An idea whose primary purpose is to convey ethnicity is likely to be weak," noted Jo Muse, who runs the agency Muse Cordero Chen, a specialist in ads to the African-American, Asian, and Hispanic communities. "The fact is, a compelling idea has no color; it has its own truth and texture."

As advertising of the future struggles to become more diverse and to do a better job of reflecting a changing world, it may also increasingly have to confront matters of ethics. While some may think of "ethics in advertising" as an oxymoron, younger practitioners of advertising seem to be more socially conscious now than in years past. In the U.S., Jelly Helm, a former creative star at Wieden + Kennedy, has become the leader of a homegrown movement advocating ethical advertising—wherein advertisers question the kinds of products they

promote, whether it's proper to advertise to children, and so forth. Helm says that just as advertising has in recent years weeded out most of the old sexist and racist imagery, it must now go to the next level—"applying the same standards to work that advocates reckless and irresponsible consumption." Helm's views have sparked lively debate in the industry and have particularly drawn interest at ad schools around the U.S. A similar attitude can be found in Europe, where agencies like St. Luke's in London and KesselsKramer in Amsterdam have adopted socially responsible stances. "We think that just as the engine of twentieth-century economic growth has been marketing, the engine of the twenty-first century economic future will be ethics," said Johan Kramer, co-founder of KesselsKramer. "We try to work for clients and products that benefit human and social development. And we try to make ads that avoid promoting reckless consumption." For advertis-

ing's own ethical watchdogs, the challenges ahead will involve not just certain products but also questionable practices—such as high-tech trickery that alters images and engages in sly product placement, or the use of psychological profiling information gathered on the Internet.

With all of these swirling issues and turbulent changes in the air, advertising in the early part of the twenty-first century could be said to be in the midst of a revolution more jarring and profound than the one led by Bernbach forty years ago. That particular insurrection brought forth advertising that was more sophisticated and stylish than what had come before; indeed, it established that advertising could be, at least in the view of some, a vital and interesting form of communication and might even, on rare occasions, aspire to the level of art. If the current revolution advances that cause and yields similar progress, it will be worth watching. For now all that can be said is, stay tuned.

# SOMETHING TO KEEP
## IN MIND AS WE CONTINUE
## — TO SCREW UP —
## THE EARTH'S ENVIRONMENT:
### THE SPACE SHUTTLE ONLY SEATS FIVE.

The last 200 years of human activity have left our planet with a wicked hangover. So what will the next 200 bring? Will we balance the demands of civilization and nature? Or turn the earth into a giant polluted strip mall? During March and April, Project Millennium invites you to ask these questions by presenting 100 events focusing on the Environment. Check out *Our Letter to the World*, a multimedia performance of music, poetry and visual arts that pays tribute to the natural world. Presented by Mostly Music at Northeastern Illinois University, March 13 at 11 am, $10 for admission. And on April 22, bring your family to *Earth Day* at the Lincoln Park Zoo, a free event running from 10 am to 1 pm. Enjoy fun activities while learning about endangered species and what you can do to make a difference for wildlife and the environment.

---

### SAY "THANK YOU" TO A TREE FOR PROVIDING SHADE AND OXYGEN. WE SUGGEST DOING IT WHEN NO ONE'S LOOKING.

Make a tree happy by visiting the Morton Arboretum for their *Arbor Day Celebration*, April 30–May 1. Program includes tree plantings, nature art activities, tours and more. Admission $7 per vehicle. Free on Arbor Day, April 30, 10 am–4 pm. Asian Longhorn Beetles are not welcome. Or take a *Treekeepers Class* to learn basic tree care skills, including insect and disease recognition, planting, pruning techniques and tree identification. Presented by Openlands Project at the North Park Village Administration Bldg., call 312.427.4256 to register; course fee $65. Classes are held on seven consecutive Saturday mornings, March 14–April 25, 9:30 am–12:30 pm.

When you consider that water covers three-fourths of the earth, maybe our appreciation of the sea should extend beyond a Long John Silver's Value Platter. Marine biologist and deep sea explorer Dr. Sylvia Earle would agree, having spent 6,000 hours of her life diving underwater. A 1998 recipient of the United Nations Environment Prize, she has helped bring attention to

how pollution and overfishing threaten our oceans and, ultimately, our own existence. In the second installment of *Future Perfect: Conversations for the New Millennium*, Earle and author/naturalist Diane Ackerman discuss

---

Throughout 1999, more than 190 organizations will present nearly 1,000 exhibits, performances, film series, tours, lectures and kid's events. To learn more, visit **www.ProjectMillennium.org** or contact us at 312.322.8889.

### AN EXHIBITION OF WORMS, BEETLES AND EARWIGS. NO WONDER BUSINESS AT THE MUSEUM CAFÉ IS SLOW.

Get a "bug's-eye" view of the soil beneath your feet at The Field Museum's newest permanent exhibit, *Underground Adventure*. This 15,000-square-foot total immersion environment lets you walk through a soil ecosystem recreated at 100 times life-size and visit a mud room chock full of live dirt-dwelling creatures. Opening on March 27. Those of you seeking a special admission fee. different kind of beauty should visit the Terra Museum of American Art for *From Forests to Farms*, a lecture/tour on 19th-century American landscape paintings that illustrates how farming and development have changed the physical appearance of our country. March 16 at 6 pm, free, reservations required.

*Earwig, Latin for "gross"*

### WILL THE MOST DANGEROUS THING IN OUR OCEANS SOON BE THE WATER?

how we can begin to reconcile the effects of human enterprise with the natural world. Ackerman's works include "The Rarest of the Rare," about the plight of endangered animals and the best-selling "A Natural History of the Senses." Moderated by Bill Kurtis, *Conversations for the New Millennium* takes place March 3 from 7–8 pm and will be broadcast live on Channel 11, WTTW. And be sure to visit the Shedd Aquarium for a behind-the-scenes look at their amazing *Coral Construction* program. March 9, 6:30 pm, admission is $20. Just call 312.692.3324 to register.

---

### SEE WHAT HAPPENS WHEN A TOXIC WASTE SITE CHECKS INTO REHAB.

Sometimes, a polluted piece of land gets a second chance. Like the Wisconsin Steel Works, the subject of *Cleaning Up 101*, a free lecture by EnvironCom Inc. that describes the environmental cleanup at the site of an old steel mill. March 24, 6:30 pm at the Chicago Public Library, Vodak/East Side Branch, call 312.747.5500 for info. The theme of transformation is also explored in *Footprints on the Land* at the Spring Valley Nature Sanctuary in Schaumburg. This workshop uses a new trail to show changes that have taken place in both human and natural landscapes. April 18, 1–4 pm, free admission.

31

# NOTES

Excerpts are listed in italics, by page number, followed by their source or attribution.

## CHAPTER 1

p. 10: *More than $400 billion a year is spent on advertising worldwide.* Projections from universal McCann forecasting director Robert J. Coen, announced Dec. 4, 2000.

p. 10: *A recent survey by the Starch Roper research firm found people today actually like watching commercials more than ever before, no doubt because ads have evolved to become far more watchable in recent years.* Survey published in **AMERICAN DEMOGRAPHICS**, Nov. 1997. Other studies conducted by **ADVERTISING AGE** for its special issue "The Next Century," Fall 1999, found that people are more likely to "view advertising as an entertainment medium in its own right."

p. 10: *"Art is something that reinterprets for people the life they're leading, it allows you to experience what you know about life,"* Fenske says. *"And because advertising deals with the minutiae of everyday life, any art that comes out of it is going to be particularly relevant and powerful."* Fenske's comments originally appeared in **ONE. A MAGAZINE**, Vol. 1, Issue 2, 1997.

p. 16: *(In the U.S. last year, companies spent more than $100 million researching and testing their own ads).* **THE NEW YORK TIMES**, April 13, 2000.

p. 16: *"They have a talent they're born with, and they happen to wander into advertising, where that particular talent begins to grow and flower,"* says the celebrated British advertising writer Tim Delaney. From my interview with Delaney for the newsletter **ONE-TO-ONE**, Nov./Dec. 1994.

p. 16: *George Lois . . . believes Pablo Picasso's observation that "art is the lie that tells the truth" can be applied to great advertising. "Almost all products are comparable in quality,"* Lois has noted, *"but when advertising is great advertising—when it's inventive, irreverent, audacious and loaded with chutzpah—it literally becomes a benefit for the product, and Picasso's 'lie' becomes the truth."* From **WHAT'S THE BIG IDEA?** by George Lois, 1991.

p. 17: *"There used to be a lot of pride taken in the creation of very utilitarian things,"* observes Dan Wieden of Wieden + Kennedy. *"In fact we dig them up all over the world now, we look at vases and bowls and forks and spoons from different eras and cultures. At the time, they were basically commodities—but the person making them cared enough about them to put something special into them, and that made them art."* From my interview with Wieden, originally published in **ONE. A MAGAZINE**, Vol. 2, Issue 3, 1999.

pp. 17–18: *"Advertising has become so entrenched in the Brazilian culture that it is one of the preferred topics of conversation in bars, along with soccer and politics,"* says Sergio Caruso of the Brazilian agency Carillo Pastore Euro RSCG. Caruso adds that *"the names of some of Brazil's advertising people have become part of the layman's repertoire,"* and *"more Brazilians now want to become advertising people than doctors, engineers, or journalists."* **STAR MAGAZINE**, published by Euro RSCG, Spring 1999.

p. 20: *As one industry pundit commented recently, "the creatives have taken over the asylum."* Rance Crain, **ADVERTISING AGE**, special issue, "The Advertising Century," Spring 1999.

p. 28: *The author Marshall McLuhan called advertisements "the richest and most faithful daily reflections that any society ever made of its entire range of activities."* Marshall McLuhan, **UNDERSTANDING MEDIA: THE EXTENSIONS OF MAN**, 1964.

p. 39: *The Salk Institute . . . once said of him, "He could explain us to ourselves."* From **BILL BERNBACH'S BOOK**, by Bob Levenson, 1967.

## CHAPTER 2

p. 46: *The idea was to identify a compelling reason people should buy a product—Reeves called this the "Unique Selling Proposition"—and then harp on that point, over and over. Reeves's mission, and that of advertising as a whole, was simply to "get a message into the heads of as many people as possible at the lowest possible cost."* Rosser Reeves introduced and explained the USP theory in his book **REALITY IN ADVERTISING**, 1961.

p. 46: *The impact of an ad, [Bernbach] reasoned, "is a direct result of how fresh and original it is, because you react strongly to something you've never seen or heard before."* Interview between Richard Coyne and Bill Bernback, 1971. Republished in **COMMUNICATION ARTS**, March/April 1999.

pp. 46–49: *Bernbach felt that "if two good people get together, an art director and a copywriter, sometimes you don't know who's writing the copy and who's doing the art because you get excited about the thought—which is the important thing."* Ibid.

p. 49: *"Listen to the ideas percolating up from your unconscious,"* Bernbach advised his creative troops. From **THE MIRROR MAKERS**, by Stephen Fox, 1984.

p. 50: *[The Levy's ads] "helped people feel comfortable with America's ethnic diversity in a way that any number of human relations commissions could not,"* wrote the journalist Michael Kinsley. **HARPER'S**, Jan. 1983.

p. 50: *"Bernbach took the exclamation point out of advertising,"* Krone would later remark, *"and I put in the period."* From my interview with Marty Cooke, biographer of Helmut Krone.

p. 59: *"You would have to look to Toulouse Lautrec's posters to find another artist with as wide an influence on the printed advertising message,"* she says. Phyllis Robinson tribute to Bob Gage, in **ONE. A MAGAZINE**, Vol. 4, Issue 1, 2000.

p. 59: *At the time, says Roy Grace, "A funeral was the worst thing you could have in a commercial—and that's why it was so right."* **ENTERTAINMENT WEEKLY**, special issue, "Fab 400 TV," 1999.

p. 67: *"My attitude,"* he later explained to a journalist, *"was that I could wait for Ford."* From Craig Reiss's profile of Ed McCabe in **SMART** magazine, Oct. 1990.

p. 73: *The author Thomas Frank has noted that the writers and artists driving the Creative Revolution were truly part of the 1960s spirit of the counterculture; they may have worked within the "establishment" of Madison Avenue, but they were also trying their best to overthrow that old bureaucracy and its conservative ways.* From **THE CONQUEST OF COOL**, by Thomas Frank, 1997.

p. 73: *According to McCabe, "We wanted to be able to tell our family and friends that we were in advertising, and when we told them [which ads] we were doing, watch the disdain on their faces melt into something almost like admiration."* **ONE. A MAGAZINE**, Vol. 1, Issue 2, 1997.

p. 73: *"The cocktail circuit buzz found television commercials, for the first time, more compelling than the programs,"* observed one publication, *and advertising's creative stars "were favored guests of talk show hosts . . . and their entrances at the rococo photographer's parties of the 1960s set off a stir the way hot young fashion designers do in trendy nightclubs today."* Ron Gales, "Where have the ad giants gone?," **ACROSS THE BOARD**, June 1993.

p. 81: *Harper's magazine was one of the few to observe this at the time, noting that Bernbach "probably had a greater impact on American culture than any of the distinguished writers and artists who have appeared in the pages of Harper's during the past 133 years."* **HARPER'S**, Jan. 1983.

## CHAPTER 3

p. 87: *As TBWA/Chiat/Day executive Bob Kuperman noted, "With more product parity, the differences and unique benefits became increasingly slight, and more easily copied by competitors that didn't have one of their own."* **ONE. A MAGAZINE**, Vol. 1, Issue 3, 1998.

p. 93: *The co-creator Geoff Hayes came up with the idea at home one evening, while watching an episode of the television show The Honeymooners.* **ADWEEK**, "20th Anniversary Issue," Nov. 9, 1998.

p. 115: *Hegarty says the language-driven advertising that has been popular in the UK "obviously becomes a problem if you're going to talk to lots of people in different countries. Consequently, we now have to think of advertising as being more driven by the image. This doesn't mean you can't use words—only that you have to think about the words you're using in a different way."* **ONE. A MAGAZINE**, Vol. 3, Issue 2, 1999.

## CHAPTER 4

p. 124: *"Most of my stuff wouldn't be funny on the page,"* Sedelmaier acknowledged. **BACK STAGE**, Sept. 15, 1989.

p. 125: *"There is no time to build character in a commercial,"* the director told Adweek, *"so you have to find characters."* **ADWEEK**, "20th Anniversary Issue," Nov. 9, 1998.

p. 125: *(Esquire magazine dubbed Steve Horn "The Thirty Second David Lean").* **ESQUIRE**, August 1983.

p. 132: *("I use fear and intimidation," said Pytka of his approach to dealing with clients. "It works for the Catholic Church, and it works for me.")* **ONE. A MAGAZINE**, Vol. 3, Issue 1, 1999.

p. 132: *Dektor would ask actors to improvise, and, as Adweek magazine noted, he relied on non-intrusive film techniques, such as long-lensed cameras.* **ADWEEK**, Nov. 9, 1998.

p. 132: *"I watch them and I feel like I'm in a nuthouse or something,"* Sedelmaier commented. *"It's like the guy running the camera is on something."* **THE LOS ANGELES TIMES**, Dec. 20, 1987.

pp. 132–37: *Tarsem had been influenced by the visual extravagance, vibrant colors, and spiritualism of Hindi films, as well as by the surrealism of Salvador Dalí and David Lynch.*
**SHOOT** magazine, March 26, 1999.

pp. 137–40: *In Advertising Age, Vagnoni called the commercial "arguably the most surreal, abstract bit of impressionism ever produced by a major agency for a major brand."*
**ADVERTISING AGE**, special issue, "The Advertising Century," Spring 1999.

p. 140: *[At] the prestigious Design & Art Directors president's lecture in London, Kaye stunned the audience by appearing onstage dressed as a Hasidic Jew and singing "My Way."*
**THE GUARDIAN**, May 13, 1996.

p. 140: *"The problem is that in commercials, you're trained to tell a story visually in thirty seconds," commented film director Barry Sonnenfeld. "So these guys are very good at creating a visual style, and using special effects, and quick-cut editing. But there's not much room in commercials for emotion, or character development, or plot."*
From my interview with Sonnenfeld for **THE LOS ANGELES TIMES**, July 25, 1999.

p. 140: *Pytka, who once compiled his own reel of obscure commercials shot by Martin Scorsese, Jean-Luc Godard, and Federico Fellini, noted that the ads were "were uniformly dreadful." Why? According to Pytka, film directors often underestimate how difficult it is to make a good commercial. "They don't take it seriously," he says. "They treat the ad like a jokey scene in a movie."*
From my interview with Pytka for **PREMIERE** magazine, Oct. 2000.

## CHAPTER 5

p. 148: *"I never liked advertising," Wieden acknowledged years later. He had no taste for the glad-handing ways of the business, nor for the inanity of much of the work the industry produced.*
From my interview with Wieden for **THE NEW YORK TIMES MAGAZINE**, Nov. 11, 1990.

p. 151: *These new complex commercials were dubbed "postmodern advertising" by some journalists and academics, because they seemed to share many of the identifying characteristics of postmodern art and architecture—they mixed old and new styles, borrowed from other forms of communication, blended high and low culture, deconstructed themselves, were filled with inside references, and often adopted an ironic and self-aware tone.*
The application of the term "postmodern" to advertising cannot be attributed to any one source; but among the first to publish writings on this subject was Robert Goldman, author of **READING ADS SOCIALLY**, 1992. Postmodern advertising was also analyzed and explained in Randall Rothenberg's book **WHERE THE SUCKERS MOON**, 1994.

pp. 151–54: *Wieden recalls that when his producer Larry Bridges finished editing the spot and showed him the rough cut, "'We just looked at each other and said, 'Jiminy Christmas, what the hell is that?' We knew we'd stumbled on a different way of communicating in sixty seconds."*
From my interview with Wieden for **ONE. A MAGAZINE**, Vol. 2, Issue 3, 1999.

p. 154: *The author Randall Rothenberg has described the Lou Reed spot as a seminal work that may have been the first postmodern ad.*
The Reed commercial is discussed at length in chapter 12 of Rothenberg's book **WHERE THE SUCKERS MOON**.

p. 154: *The American journalist John Leo suspected that Nike's message might contain some dark agenda, commanding urban kids to go wild and wreak havoc—an interpretation that astounded and mildly offended Wieden when he was told of it.*
From my interviews with Leo and Wieden for **THE NEW YORK TIMES MAGAZINE**, Nov. 11, 1990.

p. 155: *The American filmmaker Spike Lee observed at the time that, along with the much-hyped release of the movie Batman, the commercial had taken the American culture by storm in 1989.*
**CREATIVITY** magazine, Fall 1989.

p. 155: *As Wieden said, such ads were "like pulling back the curtain and showing the little man behind Oz."*
From my interview with Wieden for **ONE. A MAGAZINE**, Vol. 2, Issue 3, 1999.

p. 155: *Rothenberg suggests, in effect, that some of the creative people at W+K may have sold out their own countercultural values when they placed rebel heroes like Reed in ads.*
Chapter 12 of **WHERE THE SUCKERS MOON**.

p. 161: *[As] Mark Crispin Miller pointed out, the modus operandi of ironic advertisers like Wieden + Kennedy was to wink at the audience, and flatter their intelligence with clever inside jokes—all for the single purpose of closing the sale.*
From my interview with Miller in Feb. 1999.

p. 161: *"My sense is that we were just having fun," Wieden says. "I think our best work has never been trying to appropriate pop culture and turn it into advertising. It was simply a reflection of people who have contemporary brains and taste, just exploring things that they liked, things that turned them on."*
From my interview with Wieden for **ONE. A MAGAZINE**, Vol. 2, Issue 3, 1999.

pp. 161–64: *As the Adweek columnist Barbara Lippert noted, just about every advertiser developed a case of "Nike envy."*
From an article by Lippert in **NEW YORK** magazine, Aug. 18, 1997.

p. 164: *The partners Jeff Goodby and Rich Silverstein—one a veteran of Harvard Lampoon magazine, the other from Rolling Stone—seemed to share Wieden's "outsider" mentality and his general distaste for most advertising.*
From my article about Goodby Silverstein in **THE LOS ANGELES TIMES MAGAZINE**, May 5, 1996.

p. 178: *Eric Tilford argued that the raw style of his ads was more than an affected look—it was an attempt to make the ads feel as real and weathered as the outdoorsy brands that CORE represented.*
From my profile of CORE in **GRAPHIS**, Nov. 1999.

p. 181: *Michiko Kakutani, a New York Times book reviewer and culture critic, wrote, "Advertising implacably forges ahead like one of those indestructible sci-fi monsters, nonchalantly co-opting the very techniques used against it. Just as it has co-opted rock-and-roll alienation . . . and Dadaist jokes, so it has now co-opted irony, parody and satire."*
From Kakutani's column in **THE NEW YORK TIMES MAGAZINE**, summer 1998.

p. 181: *"Advertising is a reflection of our shared experience as human beings," says Bob Kuperman of TBWA/Chiat/ Day. "I see no problem with using anything that makes up that shared experience."*
**ONE. A MAGAZINE**, Vol. 2, Issue 2, 1998.

## CHAPTER 6

p. 185: *"People have a real yearning for the unexpected now," observes the New York ad executive Cliff Freeman.*
**THE NEW YORK TIMES**, May 2, 2000.

p. 193: *An extremely popular ad campaign in Japan recently, for Sega, was not just peculiar but almost masochistic: Acknowledging that Sega's past products were inferior to competitors, the commercials featured a real-life senior executive at the company who was repeatedly humiliated onscreen as punishment for Sega's past mistakes.*
**CREATIVITY** magazine, Oct. 1999.

pp. 200–03: *"Even the big clients are loosening up," Freeman notes. Engulfed by more competition, greater product parity, and a fragmented media, "they're realizing that nobody can play it safe anymore," he says.*
From my interview with Freeman in **ONE. A MAGAZINE**, Vol. 1, Issue 4, 1998.

p. 203: *The result, as The New York Times noted in mid-1999, was often not a pretty sight: "Dot-com advertising seems to be the place where practically no bodily function is too private and no rude behavior is too coarse to be featured in a spot."*
**THE NEW YORK TIMES**, Sept. 30, 1999 (The wild dot-com ads were also described in **ENTERTAINMENT WEEKLY**, Nov. 5, 1999).

pp. 203–04: *The noted Massachusetts Institute of Technology economist Paul Krugman also observed a link between economics and wild ads. "When TV commercials get funny, that's a sign of excessive optimism," Krugman noted. Advertisers loosen up because, Krugman says, "when the market is very bubbly, they think they can get away with that. The point is to get the attention of people who have plenty of money to spend."*
**THE NEW YORK TIMES MAGAZINE**, 1999

p. 212: *Freeman observed in 1998 that "the opportunities to try something different or unusual are probably greater now than they've ever been."*
**ONE. A MAGAZINE**, Vol. 1, Issue 4, 1998.

p. 212: *And the veteran New York ad executive Jerry Della Femina described the new wild advertising's relationship to consumers as follows: "We don't sell them anymore, we stun them."*
**FORBES**, Oct. 1, 1990.

p. 212: *Advertising Age publisher Rance Crain, who continually argued that ads were losing all touch with reason and strategy. "The technique most in vogue today is sheer unabashed outrageousness," Crain wrote, adding that "the creative people have taken over the asylum and we're all being held captive."*
First quote from **ADVERTISING AGE**, Dec. 14, 1998; second from **ADVERTISING AGE**, "The Advertising Century," Spring 1999.

p. 215: *"When the strategy clearly shows through in an ad," Fenske observed, "that's about as effective as fishing with a hook that has no worm on it."*
**ONE. A MAGAZINE**, Vol. 1, Issue 2, 1997.

## CHAPTER 7

p. 221: *"We're not consciously trying to stir controversy," Clow said. "But somehow, we touch nerves."*
From my interview with Clow for **CREATIVITY** magazine, Dec. 1998.

pp. 221–24: *Kirshenbaum would subsequently describe this phenomenon as "the multiplier effect"—meaning that as ads attracted heavy news coverage, their exposure level was multiplied without additional expense.*
From my interviews with Kirshenbaum for articles in **CREATIVITY** magazine, Fall 1989, and **COMMUNICATION ARTS**, March 1993.

p. 224: *Advertising Age critic Bob Garfield called Klein "the pioneer of 'shockvertising,'" noting that the designer's modus operandi was to "inflame the many in order to impress the few."*
From my interview with Garfield for this book.

p. 224: *Mary Stow of London's Howell Henry Chaldecott Lury & Partners, that "the biggest risk is to be safe—because if you're safe you're invisible and you waste your money."*
From Chapter 2 of **CUTTING EDGE ADVERTISING**, by Jim Aitchison, 1999.

p. 224: *One of Stow's agency partners, Steve Henry, advised fellow ad creators: "Get your work banned."*
**ONE. A MAGAZINE**, Vol. 4, Issue 1, 2000.

p. 227: As a French advertising executive from the agency Leo Burnett recently said, when it comes to French advertising, "You can use a breast in anything, provided you can think of a vaguely plausible reason for doing so." **CREATIVITY** magazine, July 1999.

p. 232: Klein later insisted that the imagery was misinterpreted, but he came under heavy fire before pulling the ads. In the aftermath, the longtime provocateur began to tone down much of his advertising and remarked, "The country has moved to the right, and creatively I don't think this is a moment where people should take too many chances." Klein's quote originally appeared in **W** magazine, Jan. 1996.

p. 235: A recent ad for the Adam Sandler movie Big Daddy featured an image of Sandler and his young co-star urinating against a wall; as The New York Times noted at the time, the ad drew surprisingly few complaints from anyone, which led a number of ad executives to conclude that the culture had grown so coarse it was now actually becoming difficult for ads to offend. **THE NEW YORK TIMES**, July 17, 1999.

p. 235: "There's increasingly a nasty undertone detectable in some of the commercials," observed the renowned British ad executive Adrian Holmes. **THE WALL STREET JOURNAL**, April 10, 1995.

p. 238: "I think when you look at the success of a movie like There's Something About Mary, that was a big moment in defining how far you can stretch popular culture in a commercially successful piece of entertainment," observed Neal Tiles, a top advertising executive with the Fox television network. From my interview with Tiles for **ONE. A MAGAZINE**, Vol. 4, Issue 1, 2000.

p. 238: Rich Silverstein, co-founder of Goodby Silverstein & Partners, observed that at his own agency, the standards seemed to change overnight. "I'm getting scripts every day," Silverstein noted, "where I say, 'We can't do that stuff! It's advertising, you can't swear, can't have a butt joke, can't say penis!'" From my interview with Silverstein for **ONE. A MAGAZINE**, Vol. 3, Issue 2, 1999.

p. 238: According to the American journalist John Leo, today's corporations "understand that in-your-face messages that shred social norms can move the merchandise by playing to the current sour, antisocial mood. Thus, the rapid spread of ads urging us to break all the rules or just make up our own." **U.S. NEWS & WORLD REPORT**, April 22, 1996.

p. 243: "Our main concern when we consider our ads is whether they're right for [our] target audience," says Fox's Tiles. "Because if we try to be appropriate for everybody, then we become relevant to nobody." **ONE. A MAGAZINE**, Vol. 4, Issue 1, 2000.

p. 243: A noteworthy recent example appeared during the 1999 Super Bowl and promoted a footwear chain by showing a barefoot black Kenyan runner being hunted down by whites, then drugged and forced to wear sneakers. **THE NEW YORK TIMES**, Feb. 2, 1999.

p. 248: "Political correctness inhibits good advertising," says Rogier van Bakel, the editor of the magazine Creativity. He notes that because advertisers are paralyzed by fear of offending members of minority groups, the ads aimed at these groups end up being particularly bland and patronizing. **CREATIVITY** magazine, May 2000.

p. 248: While the campaign's creators took pains to point out that the ads were intended to be tongue-in-cheek, critics weren't buying that line; as one skeptic noted, it seemed clear that Stroh's was trying to "have it both ways." **TIME**, Jan. 6, 1992.

p. 250: In France, a recent Volkswagen ad created an uproar by mimicking The Last Supper; the ad featured people in modern dress posed in exactly the same positions as the figures in Leonardo da Vinci's famous fresco, with the headline, "My Friends, let us rejoice because a new Golf is born." French Catholic bishops sued Volkswagen and its agency. **THE NEW YORK TIMES**, Feb. 7, 1998.

p. 250: To some critics, Toscani's advertising seemed exploitive and manipulative; in effect, they argued that he was using the suffering of the world to sell clothes. Toscani's critics are many, but among them are Bob Garfield of **ADVERTISING AGE** and Timothy Noah of **SLATE**.

p. 253: In the ensuing weeks, the American media swarmed all over the ABC campaign, which was accused of being overly cynical and of promoting illiteracy. Somehow, the campaign seemed to touch on strong opinions people had about two separate issues—the effects of watching TV, and the use of cynical irony in ads. All of which stunned ad-agency president Bob Kuperman, who says, "We never thought the ads would cause so much intellectual masturbation." Critics of this campaign included columnist Maureen Dowd of **THE NEW YORK TIMES**; Bill Maher, host of U.S. television's "Politically Incorrect"; and others. Kuperman's quote appeared in my article in **CREATIVITY** magazine, Fall 1998.

p. 253: "The confusion may have been that it was thought to be Nike's voice saying these words, rather than the voice of the athlete," said Wieden. "The whole idea of the campaign was that the Olympics is war minus the killing—for an athlete, just before that gun goes off, it's a very uncompromising moment." From my interview with Wieden for **ONE. A MAGAZINE**, Vol. 3, Issue 2, 1999.

## CHAPTER 8

p. 261: The Advertising Age columnist Bob Garfield once called Thomas "a steer in a half-sleeve shirt." **USA TODAY**, Feb. 19, 1992.

p. 261: Thomas became legendary in the ad industry for his ineptitude as a performer (one commercial script requiring him to say "Muchas gracias" necessitated four hours of retakes before Thomas got the line right). And yet it spite of all that, or more likely because of it, he was a huge hit with the television audience. Ibid.

p. 261: Jim McKennan, who wrote the original commercials starring Thomas, noted that he had "an Everyman quality" that "appeals to people on all kinds of levels." **THE CHICAGO SUN-TIMES**, Feb. 21, 1992.

p. 262: Influential research studies in the late 1990s by the firm Lubin Lawrence revealed that women had simply had enough of ads projecting standards of beauty that were seen as unreal and unattainable. . . . At the same time, ads for Elizabeth Arden cosmetics started portraying women who, while physically attractive, looked less like fashion models and more like fully functioning human beings; the copy in the ads downplayed beauty with lines like "My best feature is my big beautiful sexy brain." **THE NEW YORK TIMES**, July 16, 1999.

p. 262: In 1999, the cosmetics company Lancôme actually made news when one of its fragrance ads featured a woman with freckles on her face. **THE NEW YORK TIMES**, Dec. 17, 1999.

p. 262: The British ad executive Frank Lowe, founder of the Lowe group of agencies, has noted that stars "are a short cut to getting attention." Quoted in **FUTURE TALK: CONVERSATIONS ABOUT TOMORROW WITH TODAY'S MOST PROVOCATIVE PERSONALITIES**, by Larry King, 1998.

p. 262: According to the Journal of Consumer Research, as consumers process information from an ad, they often "use information about the celebrity to make inferences about the product. This transfer of information from celebrity to product is, in part, what makes the endorsement effective." **JOURNAL OF CONSUMER MARKETING**, Nov./Dec. 1996.

p. 262: Star-worshipping in ads is not strictly American or even Western: In recent years, Chinese companies have begun to associate their products with celebrities and mythic figures. **CHINA BUSINESS REVIEW**, July/Aug. 1997.

p. 267: A recent ad campaign for American Express featured the Hollywood film-studio executive David Geffen . . . as well as the architect Frank Gehry . . . and a leading advertising executive, Lee Clow of TBWA/Chiat/Day. The ads didn't bother to identify the subjects, leaving the audience guessing. "We wanted interest and intrigue," said an American Express spokesperson, Emily Porter. **THE LOS ANGELES TIMES**, Feb. 24, 1999.

p. 267: Nicholas Leeson, the rogue stock trader who was infamous for causing the financial collapse of the British bank Barings, was recently featured in the advertising for a Swedish on-line stock trading company. **THE NEW YORK TIMES**, March 28, 2000.

p. 268: A few years back, the Philadelphia ad agency, Gyro, featured the mass murderers Charles Manson and Jeffrey Dahmer in its ads for a clothing merchant, Zipper Head . . . The ads drew an avalanche of complaints, but it also turned a spotlight on both the brand and the agency. From my profile of Gyro in **GRAPHIS**, March/April 2000.

p. 268: And the basketball star Magic Johnson, who announced in 1991 that he had contracted the AIDS virus, seemed to lose some of his luster as an ad star thereafter. One of Johnson's sponsors, Converse sneakers, publicly voiced its support—but also backed off from producing new ads with Johnson after the news broke. **THE LOS ANGELES TIMES**, Nov. 7, 1993.

p. 268: At the time, even the notoriously daring advertising man George Lois said of Jackson: "I'm supposed to be outrageous, and I'd be too chicken to touch him." **USA TODAY**, June 16, 1995.

p. 273: As the raucous musician Kid Rock told a newspaper reporter: "I'm about to start hitting everyone up for money. I want to be like NASCAR, where people are going to pay me to wear stuff. . . . I've never seen too many hippies make a difference—no one listened to them because they didn't have any money." **SAN DIEGO UNION-TRIBUNE**, Oct. 24, 1999 (Source: **CHICAGO TRIBUNE**).

p. 273: Appearing in ads "doesn't have the stigma it once had," Liz Rosenberg, Madonna's spokeswoman, recently observed. As Rosenberg noted, "It's a way of [gaining] exposure without having to tell your life story to a reporter all over again." Plus, she added, unlike an interview with the press, "you can have control over an ad shoot— and that's what artists want." **WOMEN'S WEAR DAILY**, April 26, 1996.

p. 274: The singer Pat Boone once came under fire from the U.S. Federal Trade Commission just for reading aloud lines from a script that contained unsubstantiated claims about an acne medicine. **FORTUNE**, Aug. 19, 1985.

p. 274: When Jordan entered professional basketball, he announced that he wanted to be the best-marketed player in the game. **WASHINGTON POST MAGAZINE,** Feb. 9, 1992.

p. 279: *While all celebrities can, as research has shown, "transfer" positive feelings to the product, star athletes are a particularly rich source of transferable good feelings; when they appear in ads, one advertising creator told USA Today, viewers associate the products with the joy of watching sports—hence, "what you're getting is the borrowed interest of the excitement."*
Quote from BBDO executive Jeff Mordos appeared in **USA TODAY**, Dec. 4, 1995.

p. 280: *The creators of the ads, TBWA/Chiat/Day's Chuck Bennett and Clay Williams, had been struggling to come up with ideas when, during an outdoor lunch break, they observed a passing Chihuahua "who looked like he was on a mission," said Bennett.*
**CREATIVITY** magazine, Dec. 1998.

p. 280: *Vada Hill, chief marketing officer of Taco Bell, theorized that it was because the Chihuahua was "a perfect personification of a quirky, iconoclastic, quasi-Mexican brand."*
Ibid.

p. 289: *The fact is, "many dead celebrities have more earning potential now than when they were alive."*
**THE CHICAGO SUN-TIMES**, Feb. 17, 1998.

p. 289: *"The people that we're using in our ads are never used to sell the product," explained Allen Olivo, the company's former ad director. Instead, Olivo maintained, the ads "celebrate who they are, and we try to recognize them for their accomplishments."*
From my interview with Olivo for **ONE. A MAGAZINE**, Vol. 2, Issue 1, 1998.

# CHAPTER 9

p. 292: *Sackman was so eager to do a good job in the ads that she took up smoking (following the suggestion of her employers, she said) so that she'd look more natural when holding a cigarette.*
Sackman explained this at a press conference in London organized by the British Medical Association; her comments appeared in **THE GUARDIAN**, Sept. 22, 1992. Information about the Sackman campaign also came from my interviews with Dr. Gregory Connelly at the Massachussetts Department of Health.

p. 292: *The ads . . . were a centerpiece in a larger ad campaign that helped drive down smoking in Massachusetts by a remarkable 30 percent in the late 1990s.*
From statistics provided by the Massachusetts Department of Health.

pp. 292–95: *In the United Kingdom, an ongoing major ad campaign on the issue of child abuse has been so widely and thoroughly disseminated that it has reached the attention of some 90 percent of the population. The campaign's ambitious goal: To actually wipe out child abuse.*
This campaign and the controversy surrounding it were covered in **THE GUARDIAN**, March 15, 1999; and **THE DAILY TELEGRAPH** of London, March 16, 1999 and Oct. 19, 1999.

p. 295: *Addressing the problem of men neglecting their families to focus on work, one ad campaign showed well-known and respected Japanese men engaged in fathering, with the headline: "You cannot call a man who doesn't care for his child a man." (The ads have stirred controversy among some Japanese men, drawing complaints about meddling in private family affairs).*
**THE CHRISTIAN SCIENCE MONITOR**, June 16, 1999.

pp. 295–96: *James Webb Young, a consultant to the ad agency J. Walter Thompson, suggested that advertisers could offset mounting public criticism of their business by creating ads for good causes. Young challenged his colleagues to use their persuasion skills "to confound the critics of advertising with the greatest demonstration of [advertising's] power they have ever seen."*
**ADVERTISING AGE**, special section on the Ad Council, Nov. 11, 1991.

p. 296: *(In 1990, in America alone, roughly $2 billion worth of advertising time was devoted to public service announcements, or PSAs).*
Based on combined figures provided by The Ad Council and The Partnership for a Drug-Free America.

p. 302: *(On the other hand, the Dutch tend to use ads for social engineering—preaching tolerance for people of other races, those with disabilities, etc.)*
From my interview with the advertising journalist Rogier van Bakel.

p. 302: *The campaign brought scores of complaints from viewers across the UK who were upset by it—including victims of child abuse who said that it caused them to relive painful experiences.*
**THE GUARDIAN**, March 15, 1999; and **THE DAILY TELEGRAPH** of London, March 16, 1999 and Oct. 19, 1999.

p. 307: *Rather than showing what happened to the drunk driver, "our attitude became 'Screw the drunks—let's focus on the real victims,'"* said Steve Landsberg, one of the creators of the campaign from the agency Wells Rich Greene.
From a presentation by Landsberg at The One Club in New York; also published in **ONE-TO-ONE NEWSLETTER**, June 1995.

p. 307: *Bob Garfield . . . recently wrote of PSAs, "Let's face it, the damn things are depressing. You're watching TV and at the commercial break, just when you think that you're going to see talking cars or adorable kittens or slow-motion images of women tossing their hair, on comes some gritty black-and-white film about spousal abuse."*
**ADVERTISING AGE**, Aug. 1996.

pp. 307–08: *One subway rider wrote to The New York Times, "Can't something be done to change the unrelentingly downbeat messages on display? Sure, people have problems, but one gets the impression that most of our fellow passengers are addicted, abused, diseased wretches living in roach-infested apartments."*
**THE LOS ANGELES TIMES**, July 22, 1991.

p. 308: *The Italian ad executive Marco Mignani, of Euro RSCG MCM, works on public-service ads himself but nevertheless recently observed: "On (TV) screens all over the world, anti-drug, anti-alcohol, anti-AIDS commercials follow one after the other; they raise social awareness, but they are powerless to offer an alternative."*
**STAR** magazine, published by Euro RSCG, 1999.

p. 308: *Garfield echoes that view, saying that such ads, for all of their noble intentions and attention-getting tactics, often leave the audience feeling overwhelmed by so many social problems and "powerless to help."*
**ADVERTISING AGE**, Aug. 1996.

p. 308: *Since the American public was introduced to Vince and Larry— a couple of crash-test dummies that starred in a long-running "buckle up" ad campaign that debuted in the mid-1980s—American safety belt usage tripled.*
Figures provided by The Ad Council.

p. 308: *One study by the Harvard School of Public Health found that melodramatic scenes in PSAs did not have a lasting impact on young people who viewed them.*
From the report **RECOMMENDATIONS FOR FUTURE MASS MEDIA CAMPAIGNS TO PREVENT PRETEEN AND ADOLESCENT SUBSTANCE ABUSE**, Harvard School of Public Health, 1990.

p. 313: *Dr. Gregory Connolly, who oversees the Massachussetts Department of Health anti-smoking campaign, acknowledges that the 30 percent declines in smoking achieved by the campaign were the result of a number of combined factors. "One thirty-second ad is not going to affect anybody's behavior. . . . We view advertising as the air cover for our ground troops. It frames the debate."*
From my interview with Connolly for **ONE. A MAGAZINE**, Vol. 1, Issue 3, 1998.

p. 313: *When ads in America first targeted the issue of child abuse twenty-five years ago, the subject was still practically taboo. "People didn't understand it and the media didn't want to get involved with it," according to Anne Cohn, who served as president of the National Committee for the Prevention of Child Abuse.*
**ADVERTISING AGE**, Nov. 11, 1991.

p. 313: *At one point, 92 percent of American teenagers reported that they had seen the "Fried Egg" spot (some drug users even took to joking, "Let's go fry an egg").*
**FORBES**, Feb. 4, 1991.

p. 314: *That was a tough claim for the Partnership to prove; even in instances where some types of drug usage declined after the ads ran, as with cocaine in the early 1990s, there were various other factors aside from ads that could be credited. At the time, high-profile cocaine deaths among celebrities and other real-life horror stories in the news media may have had a larger impact than all of those make-believe ads.*
**BACK STAGE**, Feb. 12, 1988.

p. 314: *"I am constantly amazed," Cohen said, "by how many stories of good will and good deeds I still hear of that were generated by the 'New York, New York' ad we did years ago."*
From an on-line debate conducted by and published in **ONE. A MAGAZINE**, Vol. 1, Issue 3, 1998.

p. 314: *Dave Buonaguidi of the British agency St. Luke's believes that "probably less than 10 percent of the people who get involved in the production of [public service] ads give a damn about the end result."*
Ibid.

p. 317: *The American ad copywriter Richard Yelland, who has worked on anti-drug ads, said, "A couple of friends of mine had died because of heroin problems, and my partner and I felt desperate to do what we could to help."*
Ibid.

p. 317: *As noted by columnist Frank Rich of The New York Times, the woman in the ad doesn't look like an addict but more like "Winona Ryder; she's wearing a tight tank top; there are no visible track marks on her arms; and the kitchen representing her drug-induced hell is right out of the Pottery Barn, if not Williams-Sonoma."*
**THE NEW YORK TIMES**, July 29, 1998.

p. 322: *Or they can offend large segments of the population, as with recent South African rape-prevention ads, which alienated males who felt the ads seemed to be suggesting that all men are rapists.*
**THE ATLANTA JOURNAL AND CONSTITUTION**, Oct. 4, 1999.

p. 322: *The result, said issue-advertising specialist Victor Kamber, is that "TV has become a battleground of disparate voices, because groups realize the need to appeal to the public to effect change."*
**THE NEW YORK TIMES**, Dec. 16, 1999.

p. 322: *The Brazilian agency DM9 DDB recently unveiled an anti-gun campaign, asking Brazilians to declare "Sou da paz" or "I am for peace," which borrowed the basic ingredients of product advertising—star endorsers, a slogan, a jingle (actually a peace song) and even a logo designed for the cause.*
**THE NEW YORK TIMES**, Dec. 24, 1997.

# CHAPTER 10

p. 330: *Contemporary advertisers in the 1980s and particularly in the 1990s gradually realized they were dealing with a much more self-assured consumer, and "so it made more sense to sell through positive empowerment, rather than through fear and insecurity."*
These and other comments attributed to Iconoculture are from my interviews with co-founder Larry Samuel and his partner Mary Meehan.

p. 337: The author Thomas Frank points to Apple's anti-establishment "1984" commercial as a leader in spreading the message that products could set us free, and help us all to be the mavericks we really want to be. From that point forward, Thomas believes, the nature of business theory itself was transformed, so that it became "about revolution, not status or hierarchy . . . about liberation, not order."
From **CONGLOMERATES AND THE MEDIA**, by Erik Barnouw, Todd Gitlin, and Thomas C. Frank, 1997. A discussion of Frank's theory also appeared in **BRANDWEEK**, March 9, 1998.

p. 337: "People now believe, 'I have to think out-of-the-box in order to be successful, and I must live my whole life that way.'"
These and other comments by Tom Julian in this chapter are from my interviews and e-mail exchanges with Julian, trend analyst with the agency Fallon Worldwide.

p. 343: Champ and her partner on the campaign, Charlotte Moore, sensed that women were ready for a new kind of individualistic, empowering advertising—and they were right. The Nike women's campaign was heralded as revolutionary within the ad industry, and was embraced by women Nike was swamped with 100,000 letters, the most ever received for any of its ads.
From my interviews with Moore and Champ for various publications, including **THE NEW YORK TIMES, CREATIVITY** magazine, and **ONE. A MAGAZINE**.

p. 347: "This is . . . the first commandment of advertising and always has been—the notion that you can change your life by way of a particular purchase."
From my interviews for this book with Robert Thompson, director of Syracuse University's Center for the Study of Popular Television.

p. 347: "Will I really feel like being naked more on Norwegian Cruise Lines," Supple wondered, "or will I be fighting an old couple from Missouri for a deck chair?"
This statement by Jack Supple of Carmichael Lynch is from an on-line debate published in **ONE. A MAGAZINE**, Vol. 3, Issue 3, 2000.

p. 348: "Sometimes members of minority groups appreciate it if an advertiser speaks to them in their own vernacular, but other times they may feel that it's pandering."
These and other comments in this chapter by Stuart Elliott of **THE NEW YORK TIMES** are from my interviews with Elliott for this book.

p. 356: Rogier van Bakel . . . describes this approach as "advertising biting itself in the tail and chomping down hard. No one knows where it will end."
Excerpted from an e-mail "interview" with Rogier van Bakel, editor of **CREATIVITY** magazine.

p. 358: "The message is 'Your life will be empty and meaningless unless you get on board the technology train.'"
From my e-mail exchanges with Jelly Helm, currently professor at the Ad Center at Virginia Commonwealth University .

## CHAPTER 11

p. 367: "What can you say about milk? It's white and comes in gallons."
From my interview with Jeffrey Manning for my article in **THE LOS ANGELES TIMES MAGAZINE**, May 5, 1996.

p. 367: Milk consumption in the state was plummeting, and had been for twenty years straight.
Data provided by the California Milk Processors Board.

p. 367: Goodby slipped Manning a piece of paper with two words on it: "Got Milk?" That question—a minimalist slogan, if ever there was one—summed up an entire strategy that Goodby had concocted before coming to the meeting.
From my interviews with Goodby for **THE LOS ANGELES TIMES MAGAZINE**, May 5, 1996.

p. 370: Steel spied on the ad agency's own employees by slyly planting a video camera in the back of the office refrigerator, to tape the distressed reactions of agency employees as they discovered there was no milk for their coffee.
From my interviews with Steel for **THE LOS ANGELES TIMES MAGAZINE**, May 5, 1996.

p. 375: Garfield pointed out that the "Got Milk?" refrain serves not only as a punchline to the ads' jokes, but also as a nagging question that follows consumers all the way to the supermarket. "The agency does all of this so smoothly it's almost sublime," he said.
From my interviews with Garfield for **THE LOS ANGELES TIMES MAGAZINE**, May 5, 1996.

p. 375: "Goodby's reaction was warm but not overly positive. Kind of like when your kid proudly shows you his first poop in the toilet."
Quote from Sean Ehringer IN **ONE. A MAGAZINE**, Vol. 3, Issue 2, 1999.

p. 376: (Goodby even got a call from filmmaker Steven Spielberg, asking for a videotape of "Heaven").
**ADWEEK**, Nov. 9, 1998.

p. 376: Lee Clow . . . called it "a bastardization."
From **ONE. A MAGAZINE**, Vol. 3, Issue 2, 1999.

pp. 376–77: Only 19 percent of Brazilian households were using the brand. Women, in particular, seemed to feel no connection to it.
From **ADVERTISING AGE**, Oct. 5, 1998, and my interviews with Parmalat's Vania Machado.

p. 379: "People sang the mammals song, kids wanted to be mammals, at birthday parties the theme was . . . mammals! It was 'mammalsmania' everywhere."
These and other comments from my e-mail exchanges with DM9's Erh Ray.

p. 379: Each day, some 60,000 Brazilians were lining up to exchange $7 plus twenty Parmalat bar codes for a mammal toy.
**ADVERTISING AGE**, Oct. 5, 1998.

p. 383: "We had to deal with the assumption that the takeover might ruin this local beer, too."
These and other comments from my interviews with Martin Smith of Bartle Bogle Hegarty.

p. 383: The other brewers had "forgotten about the product," focusing their advertising on "male bonding, talking about sex or football."
Quote from Steve Kershaw originally appeared in **SHOTS** magazine, March 1998.

p. 389: ("Traditionally, beer advertising in the UK has almost always featured three men in a pub because . . . "Four or more was a potential riot . . . two could only be a gay couple . . . and one was just sad!"
Quote from Trevor Beattie originally appeared in **SHOTS** magazine, March 1998.

## CHAPTER 12

p. 393: By the mid-1990s, the party in Cannes was being stormed by outsiders.
From my profile of DM9 DDB in **GRAPHIS**, May 2000.

pp. 393–94: "International advertising was a creative graveyard," said John Hegarty of the British agency Bartle Bogle Hegarty. "Nobody wanted to work on it, and most of the advertising produced was dull and creatively dead." Hegarty says that such ads "tended to overemphasize cultural differences."
From my interview with Hegarty for **ONE. A MAGAZINE**, Vol. 3, Issue 2, 1999.

p. 394: By the mid-1990s British ad executive Tim Delaney of Leagas Delaney observed, "one culture is sweeping across the entire planet. It is the only game in town. Whether you go to India, Australia, or South America, agencies with a global perspective are selling American culture. It's going to be the only 'kids culture' in the future."
These and other comments by Tim Delaney in this chapter are from my interview with Delaney for **ONE. A MAGAZINE**, Vol. 2, Issue 2, 1998.

p. 394: This one-world approach has been labeled "global consumer culture positioning" by the Journal of Marketing, and is based on the idea of "associating a brand with a widely understood and recognized set of symbols."
**JOURNAL OF MARKETING,** Jan. 1999.

p. 397: The public got its first taste of real consumerism in the early 1990s: Branded consumer products flooded in from the West, credit cards became available, the Asian media expanded—all of which helped fuel a burgeoning Asian consumer class.
**CHINA BUSINESS REVIEW**, Sept. 1998.

p. 403: According to Rutaiwan Wongsirasawad, creative director at JWT in Bangkok, "You can make fun of the product, of yourself—nothing is out of bounds."
**ADWEEK**, Oct. 20, 1997.

p. 403: The wild humor in ads "is based on the comic book and slapstick comedy style we grew up with. You can see this kind of entertainment everywhere, in the coffee shops across the country, on the TV game shows."
These and other comments by Bhanu Inkawat of Leo Burnett Thailand are from my e-mail exchanges with him.

p. 403–04: In recent years, Japanese ads have lost some of their stylishness, and have come to rely more on celebrities and on quick salespitches packed into the now-popular fifteen-second commercial format.
From a written interview with Jun Yoshitake, a top executive at the Dentsu agency in Tokyo.

p. 404: Copywriting stars, . . . "have beaten a path to Hong Kong and Singapore," Aitchison notes, "because they can earn much more money there than back in India.
From Jim Aitchison's essay in **ONE. A MAGAZINE**, Vol. 3, Issue 4, 2000.

p. 409: "Why is Australian advertising so hilariously obnoxious? How do they get away with it?"
These and other comments by Paul Bernasconi in this chapter are from his guest column in **ADVERTISING AGE INTERNATIONAL**, 1998.

p. 410: The advertiser said that local teens "do not necessarily relate to the cover girl and supermodel look. . . . the images they find most powerful are those closer to their own individual reality."
Quoted from Catriona Stewart, general manager for Bendon, in **ADVERTISING AGE INTERNATIONAL**, 1998.

p. 411: Yet the [Meds tampons] campaign was pulled from the air after a barrage of complaints, mostly from women. And the Australian Standards Council called the ads "a bit gauche."
**ADVERTISING AGE**, March 27, 1989.

p. 414: Says Saatchi New Zealand art director John Fisher, "A strong idea becomes even more important here, because it can get the job done even if the production values aren't quite where you'd want them to be in an ideal world."
From my interview with Fisher for **ONE. A MAGAZINE**, Vol. 3, Issue 4, 2000.

p. 414: Award-winning ad men became local celebrities, "granted the status of pop stars," observed the veteran Brazilian ad man Washington Olivetto.
Olivetto's observation and subsequent comments about "ghost advertising" originally appeared in **ONE. A MAGAZINE**, Vol. 3, Issue 4, 2000.

p. 415: *Guanaes was already experimenting with a postmodern style of advertising that seemed light-years ahead of the kinds of ads previously seen in South America.*
From my profile of DM9 in **GRAPHIS**, May 2000.

p. 415: *By the mid-1990s, Advertising Age noted, "global marketers rushed in to win the hearts and wallets of Brazilian consumers."*
**ADVERTISING AGE**, Sept. 28, 1998.

p. 421: *In Peru . . . a late-1990s controversy erupted over an overtly racist commercial that showed Africans preparing to eat white tourists— then opting for Nabisco pudding instead.*
This controversy was covered in **THE WALL STREET JOURNAL**, April 1, 1998.

p. 421: *"We lived in a very strict Calvinist society and we knew all about barriers, and how to confine things, how to split things into black and white."*
These and other comments by John Hunt are from my interview with Hunt for **ONE. A MAGAZINE**, Vol. 3, Issue 4, 2000.

p. 422: *And finally, after Nelson Mandela came to power, advertising helped white-owned companies overcome some of the ill will felt by black consumers. For example, one government-owned oil company that had been linked to the apartheid regime was advised by Hunt Lascaris to start addressing blacks in its ads.*
**THE SAN FRANCISCO CHRONICLE**, Nov. 10, 1991.

pp. 422–27: *As one local ad executive explained in the press, ads used to cut from showing blacks to showing whites, but "now we can show a more extended interaction," he said . . . After decades of apartheid, market researchers found that blacks were suspicious of products that seemed targeted just to them, assuming they might of lesser quality; to overcome that, ads had to show the product being used by both blacks and whites.*
Ibid.

## CHAPTER 13

pp. 430–35: *The journalist Jeffrey Kluger lamented the spread of ads everywhere, noting, "In the past few years, it seems, the endgame, the D-day, the final storming of the last untrademarked beaches has begun."*
**TIME**, Nov. 23, 1998.

p. 441: *(He admits he was a bit unnerved when he saw a homeless person sleeping on a bench that had one of the "Bed" signs—a stark reminder that the campaign's message was grounded in reality.)*
**THE ONE-TO-ONE NEWSLETTER**, Summer 1996.

p. 441: *(This trick of planting and orchestrating buzz isn't new—in 1929 the legendary publicity man Edward Bernays recruited women to pose as feminists marching with cigarettes in their hands, on behalf of his client the American Tobacco Company.)*
Bernays' tactics are examined in **PR! A HISTORY OF SPIN**, by Stuart Ewen, 1996.

p. 445: *When the boxer Julius Francis squared off against Mike Tyson in a January 2000 match held in London, Francis decided beforehand to sell ad space to London's Daily Mirror on the soles of his shoes. . . . Tyson knocked Francis down a total of five times in two rounds—giving the newspaper plenty of ad exposure.*
**THE NEW YORK TIMES**, Jan. 29, 2000.

p. 446: *"I didn't want my apple defiled with advertisements," a Dallas woman complained to The New York Times, after noticing that the fruit in her supermarket was being used to promote a new movie.*
**THE NEW YORK TIMES**, Feb 26, 1998.

p. 446: *The book publisher insisted that no sponsors had paid their way into the book; the writers had simply decided the math problems would seem more relevant if they involved products the kids used. (A typical entry: "Will is saving his allowance to buy a pair of Nike shoes that cost $68.25. If Will earns $3.25 per week, how many weeks will Will need to save?")*
**THE NEW YORK TIMES**, March 21, 1999.

p. 446: *Younger people tend to be least likely to object to the trend because "their life is completely subsumed in commercial advertising," the advertising professor James Twitchell has observed.*
**THE NEW YORK TIMES**, Feb. 26, 1998.

p. 451: *Members of the group were known for scaling billboards by rope and ladder in dead of night, and pasting "new and improved" headlines over the old ones.*
From my profile of the BLF in **CREATIVITY** magazine, July 2000.

p. 451: *American magazines like the Utne Reader and Wired portrayed the BLF and other groups as "media heroes," while scholars wrote weighty theses on culture jamming, with some likening it to the Russian samizdat movement that defied government censorship.*
The **UTNE READER** named BLF one of its "top 10 media heroes" of 1991; **WIRED** was similarly praiseworthy of the group in its April 1996 issue; one of the leading scholars on culture jamming is Mark Dery.

p. 458: *By the late-1990s, the rough-hewn look and subversive attitude of altered billboards and street posters was being imitated in ads for jeans and beer.*
The co-opting of culture jammers by advertisers was reported at length in **ADWEEK**, Aug. 18, 1997.

p. 461: *The adman Michael Dweck has made an art of stalking and tricking these financiers on behalf of his dot-com clients, who will try anything to draw the attention (and money) of investors.*
From my profile of Dweck in **WIRED**, May 2000.

## CHAPTER 14

p. 465: *Jaron Lanier . . . envisions next-generation advertising that will make us all stars of our own commercials.*
Lanier's predictions about technology that replaces an actor's face with the viewer's are from my interview with him for **ONE. A MAGAZINE**, Dec. 2000, and from Lanier's speech during the international ad festival in Cannes, summer 2000.

p. 466: *The advertising of the future, says Clement Mok of the high-tech design and consulting company Sapient, will "no longer rely on clever soundbites" that try to "blast out a sales pitch to people."*
From my interview with Mok for **ONE. A MAGAZINE**, Vol. 3, Issue 3, 2000.

p. 467: *Bob Herbold, a top executive at Microsoft, concurs that "You're going to see more brands do good things for people in terms of providing a service, as opposed to running a traditional message that pounds the attribute of a brand."*
From **ADVERTISING AGE**, special issue, "The Next Century," Fall 1999.

p. 469: *One of the first skirmishes involved DoubleClick, America's biggest on-line advertising company, which has been amassing detailed information on consumers—including tracking people as they surf the Internet.*
**THE NEW YORK TIMES**, March 3, 2000.

p. 469: *As Grey Advertising's Norman Lehoullier told The New York Times, the precise measurement provided by interactive advertising is a kind of "Holy Grail" for advertisers, allowing them to "figure out what works and what doesn't" as they track the responses and actions of someone interacting with ads on a Web site. In this new environment, Lehoullier said, "increasingly money will be spent not on lore or art—but on science."*
**THE NEW YORK TIMES**, Sept. 22, 1999.

p. 470: *However, this is something of an alien concept so far in the Internet-marketing realm—which, as the journalist Randall Rothenberg has pointed out, tends to follow the philosophies and principles of "direct" marketing, a field that slavishly adheres to research and formula.*
From Rothenberg's column in **ADVERTISING AGE**, Sept. 27, 1999.

p. 470: *According to The Economist, "on the Internet, brand-building is out and straight selling is in," because, as the magazine noted, "the combination of interactivity and precision makes the Internet ideally suited to the hard sell."*
**THE ECONOMIST**, Oct. 9, 1999.

p. 470: *"We have abominable creative [advertising] online, the worst of the worst," a leading Internet advertising industry spokesman, Rich LeFurgy, acknowledged recently. Another industry executive complained of "cheesy banners that obnoxiously scream out a free offer."*
First quote from Randall Rothenberg's column in **ADVERTISING AGE**, Sept. 27, 1999; second from Susan Bratton of Excite@home, in **THE ECONOMIST**, Oct. 9, 1999.

pp. 473–77: *"There is a very big and very prevalent belief that the Internet is the province of technocrats," Schmetterer wrote recently, "while TV, print and other traditional media remain the province of real creative people. This is a huge problem for our industry."*
From Bob Schmetterer's essay in **ONE. A MAGAZINE**, Vol. 3. Issue 3, 2000.

p. 477: *"Today, brands on the Web are all about how quick and easy it is for a consumer to find what he's looking for," according to Web analyst Jim Nail of Forrester Research.*
**THE NEW YORK TIMES**, March 22, 2000.

p. 477: *J. Walter Thompson formed a creative alliance with Hollywood's Basic Entertainment, producers of the hit HBO television series, "The Sopranos." The plan is for the ad agency to become more involved in the development of TV programs.*
From my profile of JWT in **WIRED**, March 2000.

p. 478: *Reacting to the announcement of JWT's plan to align with TV producers, the television writer Marshall Herskovitz noted in a press interview that "the networks spent a lot of years trying to get out from under the control of sponsors in terms of content."*
**THE NEW YORK OBSERVER**, Jan. 2000.

p. 485: *In the twenty-four hours after the commercial ran, traffic to the Web site jumped from 600,000 searches a day to over 2 million—and it spiked particularly high in the moments right after the ad ran, indicating that people had actually risen from the couch, turned away from the game, and gone to their computers.*
From my article on dot-com Super Bowl ads in **WIRED**, Feb. 2000.

p. 486: *Bob Bowman, president of the Web site Outpost.com explained that for dot-coms trying to introduce themselves to the world, there was little choice but to invest heavily in TV commercials.*
Bowman's comments, and those by David Wecal, Roy Grace, and Ellis Verdi in this chapter are from a roundtable discussion hosted by the author, which appeared in **THE NEW YORK TIMES**, March 2000.

p. 491: *According to Jim Taylor, co-author of the book The 500-Year Delta, the coming years will bring "the deconstruction of the concept of collective, so-called mass society. We will see the growth of small, highly ethnocentric 'tribal' societies."*
**ADVERTISING AGE**, special issue, "The Next Century," Fall 1999

p. 492: *"An idea whose primary purpose is to convey ethnicity is likely to be weak," noted Jo Muse, who runs the agency Muse Cordero Chen, a specialist in ads to the African-American, Asian, and Hispanic communities. "The fact is, a compelling idea has no color; it has its own truth and texture."*
From my interview with Muse for **ONE-TO-ONE**, March 1995.

# ADVERTISING AGENCIES

p. 492: *Jelly Helm, a former creative star at Wieden + Kennedy, has become the leader of a kind of homegrown movement advocating ethical advertising—wherein advertisers question the kinds of products they promote, whether it's proper to advertise to children, and so forth. Helm's writing on ethics in advertising appeared in a number of publications, including* **ONE. A MAGAZINE**, *Vol. 3, Issue 3, 2000.*

**ABBOTT MEAD VICKERS** Founded 1977, London
British agency led by the award-winning copywriter David Abbott, a veteran of Collett Dickenson Pearce and the early British creative movement. AMV, which was eventually acquired by BBDO, is perhaps best known for its long-running print campaign for *The Economist* magazine.

**AD COUNCIL** Founded 1942, New York
Non-profit American group formed by top executives in the ad industry during World War II to create public-service advertising. Part of the original purpose of the council was to offset growing criticism of product advertising, and it quickly became an important player in the war effort, creating memorable ads with lines like "A slip of your lip will sink a ship." The council has gone on to produce famous ads addressing many social concerns, ranging from forest fires (the "Smokey the Bear" campaign) to pollution (the "Crying Indian" commercial).

**ALLY & GARGANO** Founded 1962, New York
Originally named Carl Ally Inc., this groundbreaking agency was started by Ally, who left Papert Koenig Lois and opened shop with art director Amil Gargano and writer Jim Durfee. The agency quickly made a mark with its work for Volvo and Hertz, and emerged as a rival to Doyle Dane Bernbach (which handled Volkswagen and Avis). Ally & Gargano, which closed in 1995, also created one of the most successful and well-known American ad campaigns ever, for Federal Express.
**KEY FIGURES:** Ed McCabe, Dick Raboy, Mike Tesch, Patrick Kelly.

**AMSTER YARD** Founded 1995, New York
A small, creative-based offshoot of McCann-Erickson, specializing in stylish work for both the European and American markets. Led by creative director Jeff Weiss, with Bacardi rum serving as a key client.

**ARNOLD COMMUNICATIONS** Founded 1996, Boston
Powerhouse Boston agency that came together during the 1990s through a series of mergers by leading Boston agencies Arnold, Fortuna, Lawner & Cabot; and Houston Effler Herstek Favat. Arnold is best known for its advertising for Volkswagen in the late 1990s (including the launch of the new Beetle), which helped that storied brand return to prominence in the ad world.
**KEY FIGURES:** Creative directors Ron Lawner, Pete Favat.

**N. W. AYER** Founded 1868, Philadelphia
A pioneer of American advertising opened by Francis Wayland Ayer, whose early clients included John Wanamaker department stores, Singer sewing machines, Pond's Beauty Cream, and later, Morton salt ("When it rains, it pours"). It remained a leading New York agency through the 1980s and was responsible for memorable campaigns for Chrysler, AT&T ("Reach out and touch someone"), and the U.S. Army ("Be all that you can be"). The agency fell on hard times in the 1990s, losing accounts and much of its prestige, but Ayer is still in operation today.

**BALL PARTNERSHIP** Founded 1985, Singapore
An agency launched when ad executive Michael Ball bought a Singapore regional office from Ogilvy & Mather and brought in the talented copywriter Neil French to head the creative department. French's sassy ads for clients like Kaminomoto hair-growth treatment helped establish Singapore as a top ad market. The agency was eventually acquired by the Euro RSCG network.

**BARTLE BOGLE HEGARTY** Founded 1982, London
One of the most influential British ad agencies of the past twenty years, BBH launched with three founding clients—Whitbread beer, Audi, and Levi Strauss—and has continued to produce breakthrough ad campaigns for all three, as well as for clients like Häagen-Dazs. Under the creative leadership of John Hegarty (interviewed in Chapter 6), the agency has been responsible for several of the most popular British ad campaigns in recent memory, including the "Cream of Manchester" campaign for Boddingtons beer (featured in Chapter 11) and the "Flat Eric" campaign for Levi's.

**TED BATES & CO.** Founded 1940, New York
Launched when founder Ted Bates left Benton & Bowles, taking the Wonder bread and Colgate accounts. Under the creative leadership of Rosser Reeves—who held that every product contained a "Unique Selling Proposition"—the agency developed a formulaic yet effective approach to advertising that tended to rely more on research and repetitiveness than on originality. One of Bates's most oft-repeated slogans was "Melts in your mouth, not in your hands," for M&M candy. The Creative Revolution of the 1960s was, to some extent, a backlash against the Reeves approach. The agency exists today as part of a global network known as Bates Worldwide, which produced the well-known campaign for Wendy's hamburger chain, featuring founder Dave Thomas.

**BATEY ADS** Founded 1972, Singapore
A pioneer in Asian advertising, the agency was opened by Australian native Ian Batey to service his first client, Singapore Airlines. Batey created one of Asia's most enduring ad icons, the "Singapore girl," but also produced stylish award-winning work for clients like Visa and Mercedes-Benz.
**KEY FIGURE:** Writer and creative director Jim Aitchison.

**BBDO** Founded 1928, New York
Originally known by its full name of Batten, Barton, Durstine & Osborn, the agency emerged as a powerhouse of Madison Avenue. As the longtime agency for Pepsi, BBDO in the 1990s was associated with big-budget, blockbuster commercials, featuring stars like Madonna and Michael Jackson and shot by top ad directors like Joe Pytka. Its stellar work for this brand and other clients, including Gillette and HBO, has earned BBDO a reputation in advertising as one of the more creative of the large Madison Avenue agencies.
**KEY FIGURES:** Pioneering copywriter John Caples ("They laughed when I sat down at the piano—but when I started to play!"); creative directors Phil Dusenberry, Ted Sann.

**BILLBOARD LIBERATION FRONT** Founded 1977, San Francisco
One of the leading practitioners of the underground communication form known as "culture jamming." The BLF is perhaps the best-known member of an international creative movement that alters advertising billboards and subverts commercial messages, for either political or artistic reasons. Co-founder "Jack Napier" (interviewed in Chapter 13) has been spokesman for the group since 1989.

**BOASE MASSIMI POLLITT** Founded 1968, London
A pioneer of the British ad revolution in the 1960s, along with Collett Dickenson Pearce. Led by co-founder Stanley Pollitt, BMP produced famous ads for clients such as John Smiths Yorkshire Bitter. But the agency is also widely credited with helping to develop "account planning," a more qualitative, less numbers-driven approach to advertising research that encourages agencies to try to gain a deeper understanding of consumer lifestyles and attitudes before developing ads. The agency now exists as BMP DDB and produced award-winning advertising for Volkswagen in the late 1990s.
**KEY FIGURE:** John Webster.

**LEO BURNETT** Founded 1935, Chicago
Famous for its character-based commercials, Burnett's agency created "Marlboro Country," Charlie the Tuna, Tony the Tiger, and other immortal icons of advertising. Burnett, who died in 1971, was named advertising executive of the century by *Time* magazine. More recently, the agency has modernized its style on campaigns like the award-winning one for Altoids mints.
**KEY FIGURES:** Creative director Rick Fizdale; Leo Burnett's Bangkok-based creative director Bhanu Inkawat, a leader of Thailand's creative ad movement.

**BUTLER SHINE & STERN** Founded 1993, Sausalito, California
Small creative agency started by veterans of Chiat/Day, known for stylish print advertising on behalf of clients such as Specialized bicycles, Millers Outpost retail stores, and various public-service causes such as The Hemlock Society.
KEY FIGURES: Creative directors John Butler and Mike Shine.

**CAMPAIGN PALACE** Founded 1972, Melbourne
A pioneer of the Australian creative advertising movement, this agency was led by creative director Lionel Hunt, who emigrated from England and brought a cheeky British style that initially manifested itself in controversial ads for Ansett Airlines. The agency has also been known for its work for Target stores and Stella Artois beer.

**CARMICHAEL LYNCH** Founded 1964, Minneapolis, Minnesota
Regarded as one of American advertising's "classic" creative agencies, with a particular emphasis on smart, elegantly designed print ads. For its longtime client Harley-Davidson and various other makers of outdoor products (bicycles, boats, fishing lines), the agency has consistently delivered award-winning campaigns.
KEY FIGURES: Creative directors Jack Supple, Kerry Casey.

**CHIAT/DAY** Founded 1968, Los Angeles
A daring agency led by the maverick ad executive Jay Chiat and the agency's longtime creative director Lee Clow. In the somewhat tame 1970s, Chiat/Day stood out as a rebel with a flair for stirring controversy in its ads for Yamaha motorcycles and others. But it was the agency's collaboration with an equally brash young client, Apple Computer, that made ad history with work such as the memorable Orwellian commercial "1984." In the late 1980s, Chiat/Day created another breakthrough campaign promoting Energizer batteries with ads starring a wind-up toy bunny. The agency was acquired by Omnicom conglomerate in 1995, and became TBWA/Chiat/Day, at which time Jay Chiat departed. Clow remained and has overseen stellar recent work, including Apple's "Think different" campaign and the popular Taco Bell Chihuahua commercials.
KEY FIGURES: Former planner Jane Newman; former creative directors Steve Hayden, Marty Cooke, Rob Siltanen.

**CLEMENGER** Founded 1946, Melbourne
Along with Campaign Palace and the Sydney outpost of Saatchi & Saatchi, this agency has emerged as one of the creative leaders of Australian advertising. Its print campaign for the Yellow Pages has been a consistent award-winner, and in the late 1990s, the agency shook the local culture with its risqué television commercials for milk.
KEY FIGURE: Longtime creative director David Blackley.

**COLLETT DICKENSON PEARCE** Founded 1961, London
Considered by many to be the leader of the Creative Revolution in London, which followed close on the heels of the New York creative movement. Agency co-founder John Pearce was heavily influenced by Doyle Dane Bernbach and instilled the same creative principles in his new agency, which became a breeding ground for talent—producing not just top ad executives but leading film directors as well. Clients have included Whitbread Pale, Harvey's Bristol Cream, Hovis, Bird's Eye, Fiat Strada, and Benson & Hedges.
KEY FIGURES: Colin Millward, Charles Saatchi, Alan Parker.

**CORE** Founded 1994, St. Louis, Missouri
Known for a gritty, postmodern design style that sometimes features unusual type treatments and dark or blurred images, the agency adheres to the philosophy that ads can be particularly effective if they seem rough, raw, and "authentic." The small Midwestern agency, run by the Tilford brothers (Eric, Keith, and sometime contributor Todd), has attracted national attention with its work for clients in the hunting, fishing, and farming sectors.

**CRISPIN PORTER + BOGUSKY** Founded 1988, Miami
One of the hottest agencies in America in the late 1990s, in spite of its location in a city not known for advertising. The agency made its mark initially with smaller clients like Sunglass Hut and Shimano bicycle parts, but its breakthrough came in a late-1990s public-service campaign attacking the tobacco industry. The so-called "Truth" campaign applied sophisticated branding techniques and guerrilla marketing tactics that included pulling live pranks on unsuspecting tobacco marketers.
KEY FIGURES: Founder Chuck Porter, creative director Alex Bogusky.

**DENTSU** Founded 1901, Tokyo
This giant of advertising in Japan helped launch that country's creative ad movement in the mid-1960s. Dentsu continues to dominate Japanese advertising from both a business and creative standpoint. Among its many clients around the world are Panasonic, Mercedes-Benz, and Tokyo Gas.

**DEUTSCH** Founded 1969, New York
An agency named after its irrepressible leader, the New York ad executive Donny Deutsch, who took over the business from his father, David. Remarkable growth in the late 1990s made this the largest independent ad agency in the world until it was acquired by the Interpublic agency network in fall 2000. Known for its groundbreaking ad campaigns for Ikea furniture stores; Deutsch also helped produce ads that led to the 1992 election of Bill Clinton as U.S. president.

**DEVITO/VERDI** Founded 1991, New York
With its sassy New York attitude, this agency run by partners Ellis Verdi and Sal DeVito has been at the center of several small controversies involving ads for Daffy's clothing stores, *New York* magazine, and *Time Out New York* magazine (for which the agency once posted an outdoor ad that read, "Welcome to New York. Now get out."). DeVito/Verdi has also been involved in public-service advertising for PETA, abortion rights, and other hot-button issues and causes.

**DM9 DDB PUBLICIDADE** Founded 1989, São Paulo
Undoubtedly the most creative ad agency in South America, DM9 is known for simple, visually arresting ads that cross language and cultural barriers. Under creative director Nizan Guanaes (who left the agency in 2000), DM9 began to dominate local award festivals in the early 1990s and eventually earned recognition at the Cannes ad festival as "best agency in the world" in 1998. The agency's work for Parmalat milk (featured in Chapter 11) achieved phenomenal results for that brand.
KEY FIGURES: Creative directors Erh Ray, Camilla Franco, Sergio Valente.

**DOYLE DANE BERNBACH** Founded 1949, New York
Considered by many to be the agency that launched advertising's Creative Revolution in the 1960s. Headed by creative director Bill Bernbach, who practically invented the modern advertising creative process by teaming writers and art directors for the first time and by emphasizing conceptual thinking and risk-taking. DDB broke new ground with candid advertising for the Volkswagen Beetle headlined "Think small." and with the "We Try Harder" campaign for Avis, which acknowledged and celebrated the rental-car company's runner-up status. Other important ad campaigns included Cracker Jack, Levy's Jewish Rye bread, and Alka-Seltzer (all featured in Chapter 2). Eventually merged with Needham Harper to become DDB Needham, now known as DDB Worldwide.
KEY FIGURES: Art directors Helmut Krone, Bob Gage, Roy Grace; copywriters Phyllis Robinson, Bob Levenson; director Howard Zieff.

**EURO RSCG** Founded 1991, Paris/New York
An international network of agencies owned by the Paris–based Havas Advertising parent company. It includes a number of highly regarded creative units, including the Euro RSCG BETC agency in Paris, which creates Evian ads; Wnek Gosper in London, creator of noteworthy campaigns for Peugeot; and the network's flagship agency, Messner Vetere Berger McNamee Schmetterer in New York, the agency for Volvo, Intel, and other major brands.
KEY FIGURES: Ron Berger in New York, Mercedes Erra in Paris.

**FALLON MCELLIGOTT** Founded 1981, Minneapolis, Minnesota
A pioneer in the regional ad movement in the U.S., this agency was originally known as Fallon McElligott Rice. The agency broke through in the early 1980s with startling print work for small accounts like a local barbershop and the Episcopal Church. It produced one of the most influential print ad campaigns, the long-running "Perception/Reality" series for *Rolling Stone* magazine (see Chapter 3). After the departures of founding art director Nancy Rice and the famously talented and temperamental writer Tom McElligott, remaining partner Pat Fallon guided the agency (now known as Fallon Worldwide) to huge growth in the 1990s, while keeping the creative bar high. Work for clients Lee jeans, BMW, Purina, and *Time* magazine has consistently earned praise, while the agency's "oddvertising" for Miller Lite touched off controversy in the late 1990s.
KEY FIGURES: Pat Burnham, Luke Sullivan; creative leaders David Lubars, Bob Barrie, Bruce Bildsten.

**FOOTE CONE & BELDING** Founded 1943, New York
An outgrowth of the legendary agency Lord & Thomas, run by industry pioneer Albert Lasker. Lasker sold the agency to three of his lieutenants, the name was changed, and FCB grew into one of the most powerful names in advertising. Perhaps best known for its groundbreaking work for Clairol (whose ads asked, "Does she or doesn't she?") and for Levi's jeans, whose relationship with FCB—which ended in the late 1990s—was one of the longest and most fruitful client/agency relationships ever.
KEY FIGURES: Writer Shirley Polykoff, creator of the Clairol campaign.

**CLIFF FREEMAN & PARTNERS** Founded 1987, New York
A leader of the trend toward outrageous, absurd humor in advertising. Founder Cliff Freeman created some of the funniest commercials ever made, including the "Where's the Beef?" commercial for Wendy's (made while Freeman worked at the agency Dancer Fitzgerald Sample). After opening his own shop, Freeman produced a series of slapstick-style ads for Little Caesars pizza, and brought the same wild streak to his later work for Outpost.com (for whom Freeman's agency produced an infamous ad in which gerbils were seemingly shot from a cannon; see chapter 6), and Budget car rental.
KEY FIGURES: Creative directors Arthur Bijur, Eric Silver.

**FREEMAN MANDLER & GOSSAGE** Founded 1957, San Francisco
One of a number of agencies run by Howard Gossage, the influential California copywriter. Gossage, author of the much-admired "Book of Gossage," stressed that advertising could and should take on good causes; he championed the Sierra Club and others. He was also a pioneer in guerrilla-style marketing, creating promotional events and plastering promotional logos and images on sweatshirts, and also in parodying ads with his own ads. Clients included Land Rover and Quantas Airways.

**GOLDSMITH/JEFFREY** Founded 1987, New York
A small agency known for bringing a minimalist design style to advertising. Led by creative director Gary Goldsmith, the agency's startlingly simple and provocative ads for Everlast active wear are considered classics. The agency was acquired in the mid-1990s by Lowe & Partners, which eventually became Lowe Lintas.

**GOODBY SILVERSTEIN & PARTNERS** Founded 1982, San Francisco
Regarded by some as the most creative ad agency of the 1990s. Original partners Jeff Goodby, Rich Silverstein, and Andy Berlin (who left in 1991) first made their mark in the business with a postmodern, mock-documentary commercial for the local Mill Valley Film Festival, which became a cult-favorite ad in the early 1980s. But the agency gradually proved it could work in any style, from classic to contemporary, and for clients large and small, as it produced award-winning campaigns for the *San Francisco Examiner*, Norwegian Cruise Line, Polaroid cameras, Isuzu cars, and Budweiser. It is perhaps best known for its series of storytelling commercials ending with the line, "Got Milk?" (featured in Chapter 11).
KEY FIGURES: Former agency creatives Steve Stone, Harry Cocciolo, Sean Ehringer, Tracy Wong; creative director Steve Simpson.

**GYRO** Founded 1990, Philadelphia
Small agency known for being on the cutting edge of underground-style "anti-advertising," an approach used to pitch products to young-adult consumers. Under the leadership of founder Steve Grasse, Gyro has used shocking images (including a clothing ad campaign featuring mass murderer Charles Manson; see Chapter 8), self-mocking cynical humor, and unusual typography and layouts to appeal to a target audience that is believed to be less receptive to conventional ad styles and messages.

**HILL HOLLIDAY** Founded 1968, Boston
The agency launched by art director Stavros Cosmopulos, copywriter Jay Hill, and account executive Jack Connors helped bring a national spotlight to Boston advertising in the 1970s and 1980s, particularly with its work for John Hancock insurance, which featured dramatic realism and used the tagline "Real Life, Real Answers." Hill Holliday also created an infamous early 1990s campaign for Nissan Infiniti that featured rocks, trees, philosophical musings—but no car. Most recently, the agency has been known for its campy Priceline.com commercials starring a singing William Shatner.

**HOWELL HENRY CHALDECOTT LURY** Founded 1987, London
The bad boys of the London ad scene in the 1990s, HHCL became known for experimental ad approaches and for stirring up controversy. For clients such as Tango soft drinks, Pot Noodle soup, and Molson beer, the agency produced campaigns that starred outrageous antisocial characters, were often built around stunts and pranks, and sometimes playfully insulted the audience and warned it against using the products being advertised. HHCL was named Agency of the 1990s in the UK by *Campaign* magazine.
**KEY FIGURES:** Founder/writer Steve Henry, founder/art director Axel Chaldecott.

**HUNT ADKINS** Founded 1991, Minneapolis, Minnesota
A small regional agency known for biting humor in its advertising. Its campaign for the local Native American–run Mystic Lake Casino (including the noteworthy headline, "Walk in a Democrat. Walk out a Republican."), along with subsequent award-winning ads for Domtar paper and Dublin Productions, helped establish Hunt Adkins as one of the top creative American start-up agencies of the 1990s.
**KEY FIGURES:** Founder Patrick Hunt, creative director Doug Adkins.

**HUNT LASCARIS** Founded 1983, Johannesburg
A leader of the current surge in creative advertising in South Africa. Partners John Hunt and Reg Lascaris were prominent voices in the social movement to end apartheid, producing some of the advertising that helped usher Nelson Mandela into power. In the post-apartheid economy, Hunt Lascaris (which is partnered with the TBWA international ad network), has produced clever and at times risqué advertising for BMW, South African Airways, Land Rover, and Wonderbra.

**JUPITER DRAWING ROOM** Founded 1989, Johannesburg
South Africa's largest independent ad agency has emerged as a challenger to Hunt Lascaris for the title of most creative South African agency. Under the leadership of founder and co–creative director Graham Warsop, Jupiter's work is known for striking design, particularly on its Yellow Pages campaign. The agency also has occasionally taken a provocative stance on racial issues, mixing black and white characters in ads and even showing interracial couples in sexual situations.

**KESSELSKRAMER** Founded 1995, Amsterdam
A Dutch agency known for its social-activist philosophy and its startlingly candid, no-frills sales pitches. The agency's work has featured physically handicapped people in ads (including one-legged people in shoe ads) and has used overweight housewives as models. In its breakthrough campaign for The Hans Brinker Hotel, Kessels-Kramer focused on various shortcomings of the hotel, taking great pains to point out the lack of amenities. In keeping with this theme, the agency placed tiny flags promoting the hotel in dog excrement on sidewalks in Amsterdam.
**KEY FIGURES:** Co-founders Johan Kramer and Erik Kessels.

**KIRSHENBAUM & BOND** Founded 1987, New York
K&B burst on the New York ad scene in the late 1980s with a series of controversial ad campaigns that some considered to be mere publicity stunts. Following the principle that controversy provided a "multiplier effect" that dramatically increased ads' visibility, founder and creative director Richard Kirshenbaum's early ads featured ethnic jokes in the headlines, scandalous figures as spokespersons, and naughty ad messages stenciled on sidewalks. But the agency proved to be more than a mischief-maker; K&B pioneered the kind of "guerrilla marketing" tactics now widely accepted and used, and the agency (now Kirshenbaum Bond & Partners) has grown into a New York powerhouse.
**KEY FIGURES:** Co-founder Jonathan Bond, creative director Bill Oberlander.

**LEAGAS DELANEY** Founded 1980, London
One of the top British agencies, led by the maverick creative director Tim Delaney. It is known for its clever and stylish ads for the BBC, Harrods department store, Timberland apparel, Adidas, and British Airways' travel shops (for which Leagas Delaney once urged travelers to "kiss your wife in places she's never been kissed before"). In the ad world, Delaney is a well-known philosophical disciple of Bill Bernbach and has emerged as one of industry's most vocal champions of the power of creative intuition; he is an equally vocal critic of advertising that relies too heavily on research or formulaic approaches.
**KEY FIGURES:** Longtime art director Steve Dunn, San Francisco–based creative directors Harry Cocciolo and Sean Ehringer.

**LOWE LINTAS** Founded 1999, New York
This agency was formed by the merger of Ammirati Puris Lintas and Lowe & Partners SMS. Though Lowe Lintas has a relatively short history, the various agencies that helped to form it have produced memorable advertising in recent years. Ammirati & Puris, a highly regarded creative shop in the 1970s and 1980s led by art director Ralph Ammirati, was responsible for BMW advertising and the phrase "The Ultimate Driving Machine." Lowe & Partners was a hot 1990s agency that produced the popular postmodern campaign for Sprite as well as a stylish series of ads for Mercedes-Benz featuring Marilyn Monroe, rubber ducks, and other icons. Lowe Lintas also includes the remnants of Scali McCabe Sloves and Goldsmith/Jeffrey.
**KEY FIGURES:** Creative directors Lee Garfinkel and Gary Goldsmith.

**MAD DOGS & ENGLISHMEN** Founded 1991, New York
A small New York agency specializing in witty, occasionally outrageous ad campaigns for clients such as *The Village Voice* newspaper, Thom McAn shoes, and others. Founder and creative director Nick Cohen's postmodern approach sometimes pokes fun at the company or product being advertised, as in a series of Thom McAn ads that apologized for the company's formerly unstylish shoes.

**THE MARTIN AGENCY** Founded 1965, Richmond, Virginia
Long considered the premier creative agency of the Southern United States, Martin was started by David Martin and creative director Harry Jacobs, a veteran of another pioneering Southern agency, Cargill Wilson & Acree. In the 1980s and particularly in the 1990s, The Martin Agency grew rapidly as it attracted major national clients such as Wrangler jeans, Mercedes-Benz, Saab, and Healthtex children's clothing. But it has also been known for its attention-getting print campaigns for small regional clients like Bernie's Tattooing (for whom the agency produced a memorable poster; see Chapter 3), as well as its moving and evocative work for various museums and historical groups such as the Virginia Holocaust Museum.
**KEY FIGURES:** Former creative director Bill Westbrook, creative director Mike Hughes.

**McCANN-ERICKSON** Founded 1911, New York
One of the original Madison Avenue powerhouses and still one of the biggest agencies in the world today. Best known through the years for its advertising for Coca-Cola. McCann-Erickson's memorable creations for that brand included the slogan "It's the real thing," as well as classic commercials such as "I'd Like to Teach the World to Sing," and "Mean

Joe Greene." The agency was shaken when, after decades of working with Coke, it lost a portion of the account to Hollywood's Creative Artists Agency in the early 1990s. But M-E recovered from that setback, continued to grow, and produced stellar creative work for MasterCard in the late 1990s, with the acclaimed "Priceless" campaign.

**MOTHER** Founded 1997, London
Mother emerged in the late 1990s as one of the most talked-about London agencies, owing largely to its penchant for cheeky ads and stunts. One of the agency's most popular campaigns follows the humorous exploits of beautiful Swedish women who also happen to be cold-blooded murderers; another well-known Mother ad featured a close-up picture of a dead cat.

**MULLEN** Founded 1969, Boston
One of the top creative agencies in the New England market, Mullen made its mark in the 1980s with a print campaign for Timberland footwear that featured stunning nature scenes and compelling copy. More recently, the agency has garnered praise with a print campaign for Swiss Army knives, and with a memorable Super Bowl commercial for the job Web site Monster.com, which featured children talking optimistically about dead-end futures in the workplace.
**KEY FIGURES:** Former art director John Doyle, longtime writer and creative director Paul Silverman, creative director Ed Boches.

**OGILVY & MATHER** Founded 1948, New York
Originally known as Hewitt, Ogilvy, Benson & Mather, this agency was led by the erudite and witty copywriter David Ogilvy. His famous creations included the eye-patched Hathaway man; the character known as Commander Whitehead, who coined the term "Schweppervescence" in ads for Schweppes soda; and one of the most well-known ad headlines, for Rolls-Royce: "At 60 miles an hour, the loudest noise in this new Rolls-Royce comes from the electric clock." Ogilvy was also known for his rules-based approach to advertising ("On average, long headlines sell more merchandise than short ones," etc.), some of which were set down in books, including his most famous, *Confessions of an Advertising Man.* Today Ogilvy & Mather remains one of the most creative of the large agencies, particularly in its work for IBM and its American Express campaign starring comedian Jerry Seinfeld (interviewed in Chapter 8).
**KEY FIGURE:** Creative director Rick Boyko.

**PAGANO SCHENCK & KAY** Founded 1986, Providence, Rhode Island
An offshoot of the groundbreaking agency Leonard Monahan Saabye, which helped establish tiny Providence as a hotbed of creative advertising during the 1980s. Creative partners Woody Kay and Ernie Schenk left LMS to form their own agency and went on to produce award-winning campaigns for Dexter shoes and others. Schenk has since departed, and PS&K is now based in Boston.

**PALMER JARVIS DDB** Founded 1969, Vancouver
One of the most creative agencies in Canada, known for its lighthearted ad campaigns for McDonald's and Playland amusement parks. The agency often relies on striking imagery, with minimal copy. Launched by Frank Palmer, in the 1990s it was led creatively by Chris Staples, who later formed his own startup agency, called Rethink, in Vancouver.

**PAPERT KOENIG LOIS** Founded 1961, New York
Renegade ad executive George Lois (interviewed in Chapter 2) formed this agency when he left Doyle Dane Bernbach along with writer Julian Koenig. PKL became one of the leaders of the New York creative movement in the 1960s, and its ads for Smirnoff vodka and Coty cosmetics had a hard-edged humor that differentiated PKL from the more urbane DDB.

**PARADISET DDB** Founded 1990, Stockholm
The agency that helped turn Diesel jeans into an international phenomenon in the 1990s by way of surreal and absurd advertising. With highly stylized images of politicians in diapers, evil dentists, and sun-worshipping senior citizens, the ads promised to dispense life lessons—how to get rich, how to get a suntan, how to control wild

nimals—but the copy dripped with irony and seemed to be satirizing dvertising, fashion, and American values. One of the more puzzling ad ampaigns ever, it helped trigger a wave of "oddvertising" from other ainstream brands, including Miller Brewing Co. Paradiset creative irector Joakim Jonason created similar absurdist campaigns for ther clients, including Bjorn Borg's line of underwear.

**ARTNERSHIP FOR A DRUG-FREE AMERICA** Founded 1987, New York
coalition of advertising agencies and executives that was the brainchild f California adman Phillip Joanou. The group solicits ideas for anti-drug ds from top copywriters and art directors who volunteer their creative ervices; then the Partnership runs those ads in TV and print-media lots that are donated, or purchased with government funds. One of he Partnership's first ads remains its most famous: an image of an gg being fried, with the line "This is your brain on drugs." While the artnership has produced many harrowing and dramatic anti-drug ads hrough the years, it has sometimes come under criticism by those ho believe there is insufficient evidence that the advertising works.
**EY FIGURE:** Vice-chairman Doria Steedman, longtime director of reative development (interviewed in Chapter 9).

**YTKA PRODUCTIONS** Founded 1984, Los Angeles
he film company of Joe Pytka, one of advertising's most sought-after irectors (featured in Chapter 4). Pytka blends stylistic film technique ith heartwarming storytelling. He directed the renowned "Fried Egg" pot for the Partnership for a Drug-Free America, as well as the eadpan Bartles & Jaymes commercials, lush vineyard scenes for Gallo ines, slice-of-life vignettes for the John Hancock insurance company, nd countless big-budget bonanzas for Pepsi and Nike, including the emorable commercial "Bo Knows." The director demands complete ontrol over commercials and has been known to intimidate meddling lients and agency executives.

**ADICAL MEDIA** Founded 1993, New York
ommercial production house that represents some of the hottest ommercial directors, including Tarsem Singh (interviewed in Chapter ), Errol Morris, and others. Headed by Jon Kamen.

**AL RINEY & PARTNERS** Founded 1986, San Francisco
gency opened by the highly influential creative director of Ogilvy & lather's San Francisco office. Riney emerged as one of the most mportant figures in the ad business in the 1980s. His most memorable ork may be the series of commercials for Bartles & Jaymes wine coolers, eaturing the wry, plainspoken spokesman named Frank and his silent artner Ed. But Riney is also credited, in his work for Gallo wines and errier, with producing commercials that brought a warm, emotional, nd richly cinematic quality to ads. Among Riney's other triumphs was he launch of the Saturn car and the 1984 reelection of Ronald Reagan s U.S. president (Riney led the "Tuesday Team" of ad executives who orked on the campaign). Riney also provided the warm-and-folksy oiceovers in many commercials.

**OCHE MACAULAY & PARTNERS** Founded 1991, Toronto
creative leader in the Canadian ad community, Roche Macaulay has avored offbeat humor in its work for Ikea, Petro Canada, the Canadian gg Marketing Board, the Toronto Argonauts football team, and thers. A much-talked-about RM&P commercial that ran in Canadian novie theaters featured a mailman being chased by a dog onscreen; the gency brought the spot to life by having an actor in a postal uniform ace through theaters as the ad was showing.

**AATCHI & SAATCHI** Founded 1970, London
One of the most influential ad agencies of the past thirty years. aunched by the brothers Maurice and Charles Saatchi, the agency mmediately became known for its dramatic creative work in the early 970s, including an ad for the British Health Education Council that eatured an image of a pregnant man, with the headline "Would you be nore careful if it was you that got pregnant?" By the 1980s, Saatchi & aatchi was an international force in advertising as a result of an ggressive mergers and acquisitions strategy, and it continued to

produce outstanding commercials for clients like British Airways. After various business alliances ended in acrimonious disagreement, the brothers extricated themselves from Saatchi & Saatchi (though they still have an interest in the spinoff M&C Saatchi agencies); these days, Charles is known more for his involvement with the London art scene than with advertising. But Saatchi & Saatchi still has a number of highly creative regional offices around the world, most notably the agencies in New Zealand, Sydney, and Singapore (all featured in Chapter 12).

**SCALI MCCABE SLOVES** Founded 1967, New York
A copywriting star at Carl Ally's agency, Ed McCabe joined with Sam Scali and Marvin Sloves to open an agency in New York's Gotham Hotel. Throughout the 1970s and early 1980s, SMS produced some of advertising's classic campaigns for Volvo, Maxell cassette tape, Hebrew National hot dogs ("We answer to a higher authority") and Perdue chicken, featuring the spokesman Frank Perdue. The agency was eventually acquired by Lowe & Partners/SMS (now Lowe Lintas).

**RIDLEY SCOTT ASSOCIATES** Founded 1968, London
Commercial production house opened by the director Ridley Scott, known for his films and for the landmark Apple Computer commercial "1984." The company represents not only Scott but many other top film directors in their commercial-making endeavors, including Woody Allen, Spike Lee, Tony Scott, and Doug Liman.

**J. WALTER THOMPSON** Founded 1878, New York
One of the oldest and best-known American ad agencies, it flourished under the leadership of Stanley Resor, who turned it into the largest agency in the world by the 1950s. Resor was a fervent believer in research and conferred great power on the agency's account executives. Yet J. Walter Thompson was also known as a creative pioneer and helped develop various forms of advertising: It was the first to produce a radio ad, the first to sponsor a TV soap opera, and it was long considered a master at the craft of creating TV commercials. In the 1990s, JWT's creative reputation slipped somewhat, but it has rebounded with recent award-winning work for Kellogg's cereals and Qwest telecommunications.
**KEY FIGURE:** Copywriter Helen Resor (Stanley's wife).

**W/BRASIL** Founded 1986, São Paulo
A leading South American ad agency headed by Washington Olivetto, "the Bernbach of Brazil." Olivetto had helped introduce creative advertising to the region in the 1970s at his previous agency, DPZ. He served as a mentor to some of Brazil's new creative leaders, including DM9's Nizan Guanaes. W/Brasil's clients include Mercedes-Benz.

**WEISS STAGLIANO & PARTNERS** Founded 1990, New York
Small creative agency known for the clean-and-classic design sensibility of its founding partner, Marty Weiss. The agency's print campaigns for clients such as Guinness Stout, Bass Ale, Apriori clothing, and Giorgio Armani are driven by strong visuals and clever ideas. Weiss was a vet-eran of Chiat/Day, where he helped create the memorably minimalist "Human Cartoons" campaign for NYNEX Yellow Pages, in which characters' strange actions (e.g., soldiers playing air guitar) would be explained at the end by showing a Yellow Pages listing ("Rock drills").
**KEY FIGURE:** Former co–creative director Nat Whitten.

**WELLS RICH GREENE** Founded 1967, New York
Headed by Mary Wells, first woman to run a major ad agency, WRG produced such memorable advertising as "I can't believe I ate the whole thing," and "Plop, plop, fizz, fizz" for Alka-Seltzer, while also developing a colorful identity for Braniff Airlines. The agency's Benson & Hedges ads broke new ground by pointing out the disadvantages of the longer cigarette. Wells eventually left the agency (and advertising), and WRG shut down in 1998.
**KEY FIGURES:** Stan Dragoti, Charlie Moss, Bob Kuperman.

**WIEDEN + KENNEDY** Founded 1982, Portland
Launched by then-unknown partners Dan Wieden and David Kennedy, this agency emerged as one of the most influential creative forces in

advertising of the 1980s and 1990s. Best known for its work for Nike, W+K imbued that company's ads with a postmodern style that featured arch, self-aware humor and of-the-moment pop-cultural references (see Chapter 5). Nike and Wieden + Kennedy helped make it "cool" for anyone—poets, rock stars, independent filmmakers—to become involved with ads. The agency's ads also had a knack for turning athletes into heroes of mythic dimension—including the multitalented Bo Jackson (who starred in the "Bo Knows" commercials), basketball star Michael Jordan, and golfer Tiger Woods. For another client, ESPN sports network, W+K produced a much-imitated "mockumentary" style series of commercials that has been hailed as one of the best ad campaigns of the 1990s. Other clients have included Miller Brewing Co., Microsoft, and Coca-Cola.
**KEY FIGURES:** Veteran creative director Jim Riswold (interviewed in Chapter 5); Janet Champ and Charlotte Moore (creators of lauded Nike ads to women); Jelly Helm, Stacy Wall.

**YOUNG & RUBICAM** Founded 1923, Philadelphia
(moved to New York in 1926)
One of the pillars of the American ad industry, Y&R was started by copywriter Raymond Rubicam, who focused on creative excellence. He also produced popular radio shows and was one of the first to utilize research in advertising, hiring George Gallup to study ad readership. The agency's early ads for Steinway pianos are considered classics, as is its later work for Eastern Airlines and Jell-O, featuring American comedian Bill Cosby.
**KEY FIGURE:** Art director Steve Frankfurt.

# CHRONOLOGY

## 1960S

### 1960
Doyle Dane Bernbach's "Think small." ad for Volkswagen, created at end of 1959, begins to attract attention as a new kind of advertisement.

### 1961
Rosser Reeves of Ted Bates Agency publishes *Reality in Advertising*, promulgating the Unique Selling Proposition approach.
George Lois and Julian Koenig leave DDB to form Papert Koenig Lois in New York.
Collett Dickenson Pearce opens in London.

### 1962
Carl Ally leaves PKL to open Carl Ally Inc. in New York.
David Ogilvy publishes *Confessions of an Advertising Man*.

### 1963
Avis's "No. 2" campaign, a breakthrough in "candid" advertising, is a success.
Volkswagen "Snowplow" commercial shows "how the man who drives the snowplow drives to the snowplow."
Ronald McDonald is born.

### 1964
Dentsu's "Yeah-yeah" commercial, featuring pop music and colorful animation, helps launch the Japanese creative ad revolution.
"Daisy" commercial for U.S. President Lyndon Baines Johnson features an atomic blast.
"Please don't squeeze the Charmin" bathroom-tissue campaign begins in the U.S.

### 1965
Leo Burnett creates the Pillsbury Doughboy.

### 1966
Wells Rich Greene opens in New York, with Mary Wells becoming the first woman to run a major ad agency.

### 1967
Wells Rich Greene introduces a campaign for Benson & Hedges that plays off the disadvantages of a long cigarette.
Ed McCabe and partners open Scali McCabe Sloves in New York.

### 1968
Jay Chiat joins forces with Guy Day to open Chiat/Day in Los Angeles.
The phrase "Ring around the collar" is popularized by ads for Wisk detergent.

### 1969
To promote racial harmony in the United States, the National Urban Coalition brings together celebrities in a commercial to sing "Let the Sunshine In."
Volkswagen's "Funeral" commercial shows that death can be funny.

## 1970S

### 1970
Alka-Seltzer's "Spicy Meatball" commercial is a hit in the U.S.
The brothers Maurice and Charles Saatchi open Saatchi & Saatchi in London.

### 1971
Leo Burnett dies.

Frank Perdue stars in commercials for Perdue chicken, with the line "It takes a tough man to make a tender chicken."
The American ad industry forms the National Advertising Review Board, a self-policing group.
"Crying Indian" ad urges viewers to "Keep America beautiful."
U.S. Congress bans TV commercials for cigarettes in the U.S.
Nike "Swoosh" symbol is designed by an art student and sold to the company for $35.
Saatchi & Saatchi birth-control ad features shocking image of a pregnant man.

### 1972
Gordon Tremblath and Lionel Hunt open Campaign Palace in Australia, a pioneer in creative advertising Down Under.
Batey Ads opens in Singapore, creating the "Singapore girl" airline campaign.
Life cereal scores big with the "Hey, Mikey" commercial.
Jerry Della Femina creates a singing cat for Meow Mix cat food.

### 1973
Washington Olivetto launches the Brazilian creative-ad movement at DPZ agency.

### 1974
Ally & Gargano teams with Federal Express to begin a long and groundbreaking campaign.
Hebrew National ad campaign from Scali McCabe Sloves claims, "We answer to a higher authority."

### 1975
American comedian Bill Cosby becomes a ubiquitous ad spokesman, starring in Jell-O commercials.
American Express campaign features semi-celebrities asking, "Do you know me?"

### 1976
The One Club for Art & Copy is formed in New York.

### 1977
Abbott Mead Vickers opens in London.

### 1978
Saatchi & Saatchi promotes conservative Prime Minister Margaret Thatcher with ad showing a long line outside an unemployment office, and the headline "Labour's Not Working."

### 1979
"Mean Joe Greene" ad for Coca-Cola debuts as one of the first "blockbuster" commercials.
British director Ridley Scott introduces art-cinema style with his "Share the Fantasy" commercial for Chanel.

## 1980S

### 1980
Leagas Delaney opens in London.
In a Calvin Klein jeans commercial, fifteen-year-old Brooke Shields declares, "Nothing comes between me and my Calvins."
Absolut bottle print campaign debuts with "halo" ad.

### 1981
Fallon McElligott opens in Minneapolis, Minnesota, launching the regional ad movement in the U.S.

### 1982
Wieden + Kennedy opens in Portland with one account—a small athletic-shoe company named Nike.
Goodby Berlin & Silverstein opens in San Francisco.
Federal Express's "fast-talking man" commercials are the talk of the ad world.

Bartle Bogle Hegarty opens in London.
Bill Bernbach dies.

### 1984
The commercial "1984," for the Apple Macintosh computer, runs just once in the U.S., during the Super Bowl, but has a lasting impact on advertising.
"Where's the Beef?" commercial for Wendy's hamburger chain makes a star out of Clara Peller.

### 1985
Apple returns to the Super Bowl with less successful "Lemmings" commercial.
Bartles & Jaymes wine coolers campaign introduces the characters "Frank" and "Ed."
Rolling Stone's "Perception/Reality" campaign begins a fifteen-year run.
Pop singer Michael Jackson stars in blockbuster advertising for Pepsi.

### 1986
Ed McCabe leaves advertising to race sportscars.
Saatchi & Saatchi buys Ted Bates's agency.
Needham Harper Worldwide merges with Doyle Dane Bernbach.
Hal Riney takes charge of the San Francisco office of Ogilvy & Mather, naming it Hal Riney & Partners.

### 1987
Partnership for a Drug-Free America fries an egg to demonstrate the effects of drug use on the brain.
Nike's "Revolution" commercial co-opts the Beatles and launches advertising's postmodern era.
Howell Henry Chaldecott Lury opens in London.
Kirshenbaum & Bond opens in New York.

### 1988
"Just do it" becomes the tagline to Nike ads and one of the most famous slogans ever.
"Human Cartoons" campaign from Chiat/Day for Yellow Pages asserts: "If it's out there, it's in here."

### 1989
Nike's "Bo Knows" commercial raises the bar for star-studded, cinematic ads.
The Energizer Bunny begins his long march.

## 1990S

### 1990
Abbott Mead Vickers's print campaign for *The Economist* magazine shows that a few choice words on a red background can be powerful.
Basketball star Michael Jordan and filmmaker Spike Lee team up in a series of self-mocking Nike commercials.

### 1991
Ernie Schenck and John Doyle team up for an award-winning series of print ads for Dunham boots.
Saatchi & Saatchi plants an actress in audiences at movie theaters in London; she interacts with an onscreen commercial for British Airways.
Controversy erupts over Stroh's beer's "Swedish Bikini Team" campaign, which attempts to parody sexist advertising but ends up being sexist itself.

### 1992
Oliviero Toscani features a dying AIDS victim in an advertisement for Benetton; the ad is banned in some markets.
Nike women's print campaign debuts, starting a trend toward "empowering" ads directed at women.
Kirshenbaum & Bond sidewalk ad in New York reads, "From here, it looks like you could use some new underwear."

A Dutch production company exports to the United States a series of clumsy, amateurish ads for Mentos; they become a cult hit.

**1993**
California Milk Board's "Got Milk?" campaign is introduced with the "Aaron Burr" commercial.
Philadelphia agency Gyro features mass murderer Charles Manson in a clothing ad.

**1994**
Advertising from the Hunt Lascaris agency urges South African whites to end apartheid and support Nelson Mandela.
TBWA/Simons Palmer in London stops traffic with the Wonderbra billboard "Hello Boys."
*Time* magazine's "Red Box" campaign from Fallon McElligott debuts.
Ikea ad from Deutsch features two male companions shopping together for furniture.

**1995**
Goodby Silverstein's seductive campaign for Norwegian Cruise Line ("It's different out here") sweeps advertising's One Show awards.
KesselsKramer agency opens in an old church in Amsterdam.
Ally & Gargano closes.
Calvin Klein ads feature young models appearing in what seem to be scenes from pornographic film shoots.

**1996**
Quirky outdoor ads start popping up across the United States promoting an obscure British mint called Altoids.
Nissan "Toys" commercial, featuring GI Joe– and Barbie–like dolls, is a hit.
ESPN's "This Is SportsCenter" campaign debuts and starts the "mockumentary" trend.

**1997**
The Brazilian agency DM9 DDB wins Agency of the Year honors at the Cannes ad festival, breaking a British/American stranglehold.
ABC television network hires TBWA/Chiat/Day, whose tongue-in-cheek ads extolling the virtues of TV spark a controversy.

**1998**
Taco Bell Chihuahua makes its first appearance.
New Volkswagen Beetle is introduced with an ad campaign from Arnold Communications.
Gap's "Khakis Swing" commercial debuts.
The Dalai Lama joins Gandhi as a star of Apple's "Think different" campaign.
Cliff Freeman & Partners shoots a gerbil from a cannon on behalf of a dot-com client.
Wells Rich Greene closes.

**1999**
Carl Ally dies.
Nike runs a series of commercials that begin on TV and conclude on the Internet.
Levi's "Flat Eric" becomes a phenomenon throughout Europe.
Australia is enthralled by a Toyota commercial featuring one word—"Bugger!"

**2000**
America's Super Bowl is dominated by small dot-com advertisers, who spend $2 million per spot.
Taco Bell Chihuahua (along with TBWA/Chiat/Day) is replaced.
Letters forming the word "RATS" appear briefly on screen in a commercial attacking U.S. presidential candidate Al Gore.
New Benetton controversy as ads feature death-row inmates.
Golfer Tiger Woods signs an $85 million endorsement contract with Nike.
Budweiser's "Wassup?" ad campaign wins top international honors at Cannes ad festival.

# SELECT BIBLIOGRAPHY

## BOOKS

Aitchison, Jim. **CUTTING EDGE ADVERTISING** (Singapore: Prentice Hall, 1999).

Bernbach, Bill. **BILL BERNBACH SAID...** (New York, 1995).

Bond, Jonathan, and Kirshenbaum, Richard. **UNDER THE RADAR: TALKING TO TODAY'S CYNICAL CONSUMER** (New York: John Wiley & Sons, 1998).

Designers and Art Directors Association of the UK (D&AD). **THE COPY BOOK** (London: Rotovision, 1995).

———. **THE ART DIRECTOR BOOK** (London, 1997).

Della Femina, Jerry. **FROM THOSE WONDERFUL FOLKS WHO GAVE YOU PEARL HARBOR** (New York: Simon & Schuster, 1970).

Dobrow, Larry. **WHEN ADVERTISING TRIED HARDER: THE SIXTIES** (New York: Friendly Press, 1984).

Ewen, Stuart. **PR! A SOCIAL HISTORY OF SPIN** (New York: Basic Books, 1996).

Fox, Stephen. **THE MIRROR MAKERS: A HISTORY OF AMERICAN ADVERTISING AND ITS CREATORS** (New York: University of Illinois Press [trade], 1984).

Frank, Thomas. **THE CONQUEST OF COOL** (Chicago: University of Chicago Press, 1997).

Goldman, Robert. **READING ADS SOCIALLY** (New York: Routledge, 1992).

Goodrum, Charles, and Dalrymple, Helen. **ADVERTISING IN AMERICA** (New York: Abrams, 1990).

Gossage, Howard Luck. **THE BOOK OF GOSSAGE** (Chicago: Copy Workshop, 1995).

Halberstam, David. **PLAYING FOR KEEPS: MICHAEL JORDAN AND THE WORLD HE MADE** (New York: Broadway Books, 1999).

Heller, Steven. **PAUL RAND** (London: Phaidon Press Ltd., 1999).

Heller, Steven, and Lasky, Julie. **BORROWED DESIGN: USE AND ABUSE OF HISTORICAL FORM** (New York: Van Nostrand Reinhold, 1992).

Kanner, Bernice. **THE 100 BEST TV COMMERCIALS** (Chicago: Times Books, 1999).

Levenson, Bob. **BILL BERNBACH'S BOOK: A HISTORY OF THE ADVERTISING THAT CHANGED THE HISTORY OF ADVERTISING** (New York: Villard Books, 1987).

Lois, George, with Pitts, Bill. **GEORGE, BE CAREFUL** (New York: Saturday Review, 1972).

Lois, George. **WHAT'S THE BIG IDEA?** (New York: Plume, 1991).

Mayer, Martin. **MADISON AVENUE, USA** (New York: National Tradebook Co., 1958).

———. **WHATEVER HAPPENED TO MADISON AVENUE** (New York: Little Brown & Co., 1991).

McLuhan, Marshall. **UNDERSTANDING MEDIA: THE EXTENSIONS OF MAN** (New York: Signet Paperback, 1964).

Miller, Mark Crispin. **BOXED IN: THE CULTURE OF TV** (Chicago: Northwestern University Press, 1988).

Ogilvy, David. **CONFESSIONS OF AN ADVERTISING MAN** (New York: Atheneum, 1962).

———. **OGILVY ON ADVERTISING** (New York: Random House, 1983).

Reeves, Rosser. **REALITY IN ADVERTISING** (New York: Knopf, 1961).

Reis, Al, and Trout, Jack. **POSITIONING: THE BATTLE FOR YOUR MIND** (New York: Warner Books, 1981).

Rothenberg, Randall. **WHERE THE SUCKERS MOON: AN ADVERTISING STORY** (New York: Vintage Books, 1994).

Savan, Leslie. **THE SPONSORED LIFE** (Philadelphia: Temple University Press, 1994).

Stabiner, Karen. **INVENTING DESIRE: INSIDE CHIAT/DAY** (New York: Simon & Schuster, 1993).

Steel, Jon. **TRUTH, LIES AND ADVERTISING: THE ART OF ACCOUNT PLANNING** (New York: John Wiley & Sons, 1998).

Sullivan, Luke. **HEY WHIPPLE, SQUEEZE THIS: A GUIDE TO CREATING GREAT ADS** (New York: John Wiley & Sons, 1998).

Twitchell, James B. **ADCULT USA: THE TRIUMPH OF ADVERTISING IN AMERICAN CULTURE** (New York: Columbia University Press, 1996).

Wacker, Watts, and Taylor, Jim. **THE 500 YEAR DELTA: WHAT HAPPENS AFTER WHAT COMES NEXT** (New York: HarperCollins, 1997)

Wolf, Michael J. **THE ENTERTAINMENT ECONOMY** (New York: Times Books, 1999).

Wolf, Naomi. **THE BEAUTY MYTH: HOW IMAGES OF BEAUTY ARE USED AGAINST WOMEN** (New York: Anchor Press, 1991).

## PERIODICALS: SPECIAL ISSUES

**ADVERTISING AGE** (Chicago). "The Advertising Century," Spring 1999.

**ADVERTISING AGE** (Chicago). "The Next Century," Fall 1999.

**ADWEEK** (New York). "20th Anniversary Issue," November 9, 1998.

**CAMPAIGN MAGAZINE** (London). "30th Anniversary Issue," September 18, 1998.

**COMMUNICATION ARTS** (Palo Alto, California). "40th Anniversary Issue," March/April 1999.

**ONE. A MAGAZINE** (New York). "Best of Decade Issue," Vol. 3, Issue. 2, Fall 1999.

# INDEX

Figures in italics refer to captions as well as their corresponding illustrations.

# ILLUSTRATION CREDITS

Unless otherwise noted below, the advertisements reprinted herein were generously provided by the advertising agencies listed in the corresponding captions. Additional illustration credits are listed below. Numbers indicate page numbers.

COURTESY ARNOLD COMMUNICATIONS: 295

COURTESY WARREN BERGER: 10, 21, 34, 69 TOP AND BOTTOM RIGHT, 89, 96, 99, 101 TOP, 112, 117, 119, 123, 126, 127, 128, 130–31, 137, 139, 171, 174, 177, 184, 186, 187, 240, 251, 257 LEFT, 311, 319, 345, 406–07, 410, 418 BOTTOM, 423 LEFT, 438, 442, 448–49, 450 TOP, 454–55, 472, 484

COURTESY BEACH 'N BILLBOARD, LEONA, NEW JERSEY: 431

REPRODUCED WITH PERMISSION FROM BILL BERNBACH'S BOOK, BY BOB LEVENSON (NEW YORK: VILLARD BOOKS, 1987), COURTESY DDB WORLDWIDE, NEW YORK: 45, 49, 56, 58, 59

COURTESY BETTER VISION INSTITUTE: 55

PHOTO BY STEVEN BLOCH: 156

COURTESY BMP/DDB, LONDON: 80 TOP

© 2001 BMW OF NORTH AMERICA. USED WITH PERMISSION. THE BMW NAME AND LOGO ARE REGISTERED TRADEMARKS.: 483 BOTTOM

PHOTO BY EDWARD CALDWELL: 372

COURTESY CHURCH AD PROJECT, ROSEMOUNT, MINNESOTA: 91

THE COCA-COLA COMPANY/MCCANN-ERICKSON: 124

COURTESY PETER COHEN, NEW YORK: 306, 307

COURTESY COMMUNICATION ARTS MAGAZINE: 52–53

COURTESY CREATIVE ARTIST AGENCY, LOS ANGELES: 134

© DEMOCRATIC NATIONAL COMMITTEE; COURTESY LYNDON BAINES JOHNSON LIBRARY, AUSTIN, TEXAS: 219

COURTESY JOHN DOYLE: 318

BY FALLON MCELLIGOTT/ROLLING STONE; BY STRAIGHT ARROW PUBLISHERS, INC. ALL RIGHTS RESERVED. REPRINTED BY PERMISSION: 94–95

GASLIGHT ADVERTISING ARCHIVES, INC.: 44, 47, 48, 50, 57, 66, 69 BOTTOM LEFT, 70–71, 72, 74, 75, 223

COURTESY GOODBY, SILVERSTEIN & PARTNERS: 372

COURTESY NIZAN GUANAES: 102

© BRIAN KAWS: 456

COURTESY KEEP AMERICA BEAUTIFUL, INC.: 312 BOTTOM

PHOTO BY MARTIN LIDDELL: 196

COURTESY LITTLE CAESARS: 17, 162–63, 202

COURTESY GEORGE LOIS: 60

COURTESY KITTY LUN: 400

PHOTO BY MARK LUTTRELL (ADS IN MAGAZINES): 8, 51, 62, 64–65, 97, 114, 180, 230–31, 263,

MASTERCARD INTERNATIONAL/MCCANN-ERICKSON: 354

© 2000 PETER MCARTHUR: 464

© MILL VALLEY FILM FESTIVAL: 138

TOMAS MUSCIONICO/CONTACT PRESS IMAGES: 244

PHOTO BY A. LEO NASH: 452

COURTESY BILL OBERLANDER, KIRSHENBAUM BOND & PARTNERS, NEW YORK: 266

COURTESY OGILVY & MATHER, NEW YORK: 264

COURTESY THE ONE CLUB FOR ART AND COPY, NEW YORK: 12, 22, 37, 46, 63, 68, 78, 85, 100, 106, 109, 118, 122, 140, 198–99, 258, 287, 288 LEFT, 293, 366, 371 BOTTOM, 375, 392, 418 TOP, 420 BOTTOM, 436, 459, 467, 468, 478, 480, 486

COURTESY PARTNERSHIP FOR A DRUG-FREE AMERICA: 297, 304

COURTESY RED SKY, NEW YORK: 470–71

© REEBOK INTERNATIONAL, LTD.: 154

COURTESY ANITA SANTIAGO: 352

COURTESY MATT STEIN: 466

LUKE SULLIVAN: 36

O. TOSCANI (CONCEPT); COURTESY OF UNITED COLORS OF BENETTON AND GREGORIETTI ASSOCIATI, MILAN: 246–249

U.S. DEPARTMENT OF TRANSPORTATION AND THE AD COUNCIL: 298

COURTESY WENDY'S RESTAURANTS: 125

REPRODUCED FROM WHEN ADVERTISING TRIED HARDER, BY LARRY DOBROW (NEW YORK: FRIENDLY PRESS, INC., 1984): 67, 73, 81

COURTESY YOUNG & RUBICAM, NEW YORK: 399, 444, 445

FRONTISPIECE:

APPLE COMPUTER
TBWA/CHIAT/DAY, LOS ANGELES, 1997

JACKET ILLUSTRATION:

COLGATE PLAX (DETAIL OF PRINT AD)
YOUNG & RUBICAM, SÃO PAULO, 1997
CREATIVE DIRECTOR: ALEXANDRE GAMA
ART DIRECTOR: FABIO MENEGHINI
PHOTOGRAPHED BY FELIPE HELLMEISTER

# AUTHOR'S ACKNOWLEDG-MENTS

In writing this book, I was helped enormously by many people, especially the following:

The editors at Phaidon Press, specifically Karen Stein and Megan McFarland. They provided strong and clear guidance, with a light touch (which is what any writer wants from an editor). Also thanks to photo editor David Brown, who tracked down hundreds of ads, from all corners of the globe.

The designers at Pentagram, in particular Woody Pirtle and his assistant, Daisuke Endo, who melded the words and images seamlessly.

Adrian Fogel and Dana Fogel, advertising students at Virginia Commonwealth University, who served as my research assistants. Without their tireless digging, this book would not have been possible.

The One Club for Art & Copy, whose quarterly magazine, ONE, was an important source for this book. In particular, thanks go to Mary Warlick, the Club's executive director and a champion of creativity in advertising, and to Todd Gaffney and Tiffany Meyers, who helped obtain numerous hard-to-find ads.

Randall Rothenberg, who introduced me to Phaidon Press, and whose own writings on advertising have been a rich resource.

Stuart Elliott and the other ad columnists at The New York Times; their insightful daily reporting has provided important documentation of advertising today.

Anthony Vagnoni, Rogier van Bakel, and Bob Garfield from Advertising Age and Creativity magazines; their insider's expertise has been invaluable.

Laura Kelly, my wife, my most enthusiastic editor, and my inspiration in all things I do.

I also want to thank the many people who agreed to be interviewed for this book, including: Jerry Seinfeld and his creative partner David Apicella; Oliviero Toscani; "Jack Napier" of the Billboard Liberation Front, who gave me a peek into the underground world of culture jamming; the immortal George Lois; Phyllis Robinson, Bob Levenson, and Roy Grace, all of whom helped me understand the magic and the importance of Doyle Dane Bernbach; Joe Pytka and Tarsem, who shared the director's perspective; Jim Aitchison, Kitty Lun, and Kash Sree, who explained the mysteries of Asian advertising; John Hunt, who did likewise with South African ads; Syracuse University's eminently quotable Robert Thompson; Jelly Helm, the advertising ethicist (no, that's not an oxymoron); the futurists Esther Dyson, Watts Wacker, and Dave Westreich, along with the trendspotting firm Iconoculture, all of whom helped me to look ahead; Myrna Davis of The Art Directors Club of New York; and the talented ad creators Bob Barrie, Andy Berlin, Alex Bogusky, Rick Boyko, Marty Cooke, Greg DiNoto, John Doyle, Michael Dweck, Mark Fenske, Gary Goldsmith, Mike Hughes, Bob Jeffrey, Woody Kay, Johan Kramer, Bill Oberlander, Anita Santiago, Ernie Schenck, Paul Spencer, Gerard Stamp, Luke Sullivan, Jack Supple, Mark Waites, and Jeff Weiss.

And lastly, I pay tribute to ten people who have shaped creative advertising over the past two decades: Jeff Goodby, Rich Silverstein, Dan Wieden, Jim Riswold, Lee Clow, Pat Fallon, Nizan Guanaes, John Hegarty, Tim Delaney, and Cliff Freeman. Thanks to all of you for creating something worth writing about.

PHAIDON PRESS LIMITED
REGENT'S WHARF
ALL SAINTS STREET
LONDON N1 9PA

PHAIDON PRESS INC.
180 VARICK STREET
NEW YORK, NY 10014

WWW.PHAIDON.COM

FIRST PUBLISHED 2001
REPRINTED 2003
© 2001 PHAIDON PRESS
LIMITED

TEXT © 2001
WARREN BERGER

ISBN 0 7148 3923 X

A CIP CATALOGUE RECORD OF
THIS BOOK IS AVAILABLE
FROM THE BRITISH LIBRARY.

DESIGNED BY PENTAGRAM
PRINTED IN HONG KONG

PUBLISHER'S NOTE:

ADVERTISING AGENCIES
ARE CITED IN THE CAPTIONS
BY THE AGENCY NAME IN
EFFECT AT THE TIME THE
ADVERTISEMENT WAS
PRODUCED.

ALL REASONABLE EFFORTS
HAVE BEEN MADE TO
CONFIRM THE DATES OF THE
ADVERTISEMENTS WITH THE
ADVERTISING AGENCIES OR
ORGANIZATIONS THAT
PRODUCED THEM. WHERE A
PRECISE DATE COULD NOT
BE CONFIRMED, THE DATE
THAT APPEARS IN THE
CAPTION IS BASED ON
SECONDARY SOURCES.